**Samuel Langhorne Clemens** (November 30, 1835 – April 21, 1910), known by his pen name Mark Twain, was an American writer, humorist, entrepreneur, publisher, and lecturer. He was lauded as the "greatest humorist this country has produced", and William Faulkner called him "the father of American literature". His novels include The Adventures of Tom Sawyer (1876) and its sequel, the Adventures of Huckleberry Finn (1884), the latter often called "The Great American Novel".

Twain was raised in Hannibal, Missouri, which later provided the setting for Tom Sawyer and Huckleberry Finn. He served an apprenticeship with a printer and then worked as a typesetter, contributing articles to the newspaper of his older brother Orion Clemens. He later became a riverboat pilot on the Mississippi River before heading west to join Orion in Nevada. (Source: Wikipedia)

**Literary works:**

The Gilded Age: A Tale of Today (1873)
The Prince and the Pauper (1881)
A Connecticut Yankee in
King Arthur's Court (1889)
The American Claimant (1892)
Pudd'nhead Wilson (1894)
Personal Recollections of Joan of Arc (1896)
A Horse's Tale (1907)
The Mysterious Stranger (1916, posthumous)
The Adventures of Tom Sawyer (1876)
Adventures of Huckleberry Finn (1884)
Tom Sawyer Abroad (1894)
Tom Sawyer, Detective (1896)
"Eve's Diary"(1906)

THRONE CLASSICS

# MARK TWAIN'S LETTERS

## VOLUME 3 & 4

Mark Twain

THRONE CLASSICS

This is a work of fiction. Names, characters, places, and incidents either are the product of the author's imagination or are used fictitiously. Any resemblance to actual persons, living or dead, events, or locales is entirely coincidental.



First Printing: 2020

ISBN 978-93-5383-906-2 (paperback)

ISBN 978-93-5383-907-9 (Hardcover)

Published by Throne Classics

www.throneclassics.com

# Contents

# MARK TWAIN'S LETTERS
## VOLUME 3 & 4

# MARK TWAIN'S LETTERS—1853-1866

## VOLUME 3

## XVI. LETTERS, 1876, CHIEFLY TO W. D. HOWELLS. LITERATURE AND POLITICS. PLANNING A PLAY WITH BRET HARTE.

*The Monday Evening Club of Hartford was an association of most of the literary talent of that city, and it included a number of very distinguished members. The writers, the editors, the lawyers, and the ministers of the gospel who composed it were more often than not men of national or international distinction. There was but one paper at each meeting, and it was likely to be a paper that would later find its way into some magazine.*

*Naturally Mark Twain was one of its favorite members, and his contributions never failed to arouse interest and discussion. A "Mark Twain night" brought out every member. In the next letter we find the first mention of one of his most memorable contributions—a story of one of life's moral aspects. The tale, now included in his collected works, is, for some reason, little read to-day; yet the curious allegory, so vivid in its seeming reality, is well worth consideration.*

To W. D. Howells, in Boston:

*HARTFORD, Jan. 11, '76.*

MY DEAR HOWELLS,—Indeed we haven't forgotten the Howellses, nor scored up a grudge of any kind against them; but the fact is I was under the doctor's hands for four weeks on a stretch and have been disabled from working for a week or so beside. I thought I was well, about ten days ago, so I sent for a short-hand writer and dictated answers to a bushel or so of letters that had been accumulating during my illness. Getting everything shipshape and cleared up, I went to work next day upon an Atlantic article, which ought to be worth $20 per page (which is the price they usually pay for my work, I believe) for although it is only 70 pages MS (less than two days work, counting by bulk,) I have spent 3 more days trimming, altering and working at it. I shall put in one more day's polishing on it, and then read it before our Club, which is to meet at our house Monday evening, the 24th inst. I think it will bring out considerable discussion among the gentlemen of the Club—though the title of the article will not give them much notion of what is to follow,—this title being "The Facts Concerning the Recent Carnival of Crime in Connecticut"—which reminds me that today's Tribune says there will be a startling article in the current Atlantic, in which a being which is tangible bud invisible will figure-exactly the case with the sketch of mine which I am talking about! However, mine can lie unpublished a year or two as well as not—though I wish that contributor of yours had not interfered with his coincidence of heroes.

But what I am coming at, is this: won't you and Mrs. Howells come down Saturday the 22nd and remain to the Club on Monday night? We always have a rattling good time at the Club and we do want you to come, ever so much. Will you? Now say you will. Mrs. Clemens and I are persuading ourselves that you twain will come.

My volume of sketches is doing very well, considering the times; received my quarterly statement today from Bliss, by which I perceive that 20,000 copies have been sold—or rather, 20,000 had been sold 3 weeks ago; a lot more, by this time, no doubt.

I am on the sick list again—and was, day before yesterday—but on the whole I am getting along.

*Yrs ever*

*MARK*

*Howells wrote that he could not come down to the club meeting, adding that sickness was "quite out of character" for Mark Twain, and hardly fair on a man who had made so many other people feel well. He closed by urging that Bliss "hurry out" 'Tom Sawyer.' "That boy is going to make a prodigious hit." Clemens answered:*

To W. D. Howells, in Boston.

*HARTFORD, Jan. 18, '76.*

MY DEAR HOWELLS,—Thanks, and ever so many, for the good opinion of 'Tom Sawyer.' Williams has made about 300 rattling pictures for it—some of them very dainty. Poor devil, what a genius he has and how he does murder it with rum. He takes a book of mine, and without suggestion from anybody builds no end of pictures just from his reading of it.

There was never a man in the world so grateful to another as I was to you day before yesterday, when I sat down (in still rather wretched health) to set myself to the dreary and hateful task of making final revision of Tom Sawyer, and discovered, upon opening the package of MS that your pencil marks were scattered all along. This was splendid, and swept away all labor. Instead of reading the MS, I simply hunted out the pencil marks and made the emendations which they suggested. I reduced the boy battle to a curt paragraph; I finally concluded to cut the Sunday school speech down to the first two sentences, leaving no suggestion of satire, since the book is to be for boys and girls; I tamed the various obscenities until I judged that they no longer carried offense. So, at a single sitting I began and finished a revision which I had supposed would occupy 3 or 4. days and leave me mentally and physically fagged out at the end. I was careful not to inflict the MS upon you until I had thoroughly and painstakingly revised it. Therefore, the only faults left were those that would discover themselves to others, not me—and these you had pointed out.

There was one expression which perhaps you overlooked. When Huck is complaining to Tom of the rigorous system in vogue at the widow's, he says the servants harass him with all manner of compulsory decencies, and he winds up by saying: "and they comb me all to hell." (No exclamation point.) Long ago, when I read that to Mrs. Clemens, she made no comment; another time I created occasion to read that chapter to her aunt and her mother (both sensitive and loyal subjects of the kingdom of heaven, so to speak) and they let it pass. I was glad, for it was the most natural remark in the world for that boy to make (and he had been allowed few privileges of speech in the book;) when I saw that you, too, had let it go without protest, I was glad, and afraid; too—afraid you hadn't observed it. Did you? And did you question the propriety of it? Since the book is now professedly and confessedly a boy's and girl's hook, that darn word bothers me some, nights, but it never did until I had ceased to regard the volume as being for adults.

Don't bother to answer now, (for you've writing enough to do without allowing me to add to the burden,) but tell me when you see me again!

Which we do hope will be next Saturday or Sunday or Monday. Couldn't you come now and mull over the alterations which you are going to make in your MS, and make them after you go back? Wouldn't it assist the work if you dropped out of harness and routine for a day or two and have that sort of revivification which comes of a holiday-forgetfulness of the work-shop? I can always work after I've been to your house; and if you will come to mine, now, and hear the club toot their various horns over the exasperating metaphysical question which I mean to lay before them in the disguise of a literary extravaganza, it would just brace you up like a cordial.

(I feel sort of mean trying to persuade a man to put down a critical piece of work at a critical time, but yet I am honest in thinking it would not hurt the work nor impair your interest in it to come under the circumstances.) Mrs. Clemens says, "Maybe the Howellses could come Monday if they cannot come Saturday; ask them; it is worth trying." Well, how's that? Could you? It would be splendid if you could. Drop me a postal card—I should have a twinge of conscience if I forced you to write a letter, (I am honest about that,)—and if you find you can't make out to come, tell me that you bodies will come the next Saturday if the thing is possible, and stay over Sunday.

*Yrs ever*

*MARK.*

*Howells, however, did not come to the club meeting, but promised to come soon when they could have a quiet time to themselves together. As to Huck's language, he declared:*

*"I'd have that swearing out in an instant. I suppose I didn't notice it because the locution was so familiar to my Western sense, and so exactly the thing that Huck would say." Clemens changed the phrase to, "They comb me all to thunder," and so it stands to-day.*

*The "Carnival of Crime," having served its purpose at the club, found quick acceptance by Howells for the Atlantic. He was so pleased with it, in fact, that somewhat later he wrote, urging that its author allow it to be printed in a dainty book, by Osgood, who made a specialty of fine publishing. Meantime Howells had written his Atlantic notice of Tom Sawyer, and now inclosed Clemens a proof of it. We may judge from the reply that it was satisfactory.*

To W. D. Howells, in Boston:

*Apl 3, '76.*

MY DEAR HOWELLS,—It is a splendid notice and will embolden weak-kneed journalistic admirers to speak out, and will modify or shut up the unfriendly. To "fear God and dread the Sunday school" exactly described that old feeling which I used to have, but I couldn't have formulated it. I want to enclose one of the illustrations in this letter, if I do not forget it. Of course the book is to be elaborately illustrated, and I think that many of the pictures are considerably above the American average, in conception if not in execution.

I do not re-enclose your review to you, for you have evidently read and corrected it, and so I judge you do not need it. About two days after the Atlantic issues I mean to begin to send books to principal journals and magazines.

I read the "Carnival of Crime" proof in New York when worn and witless and so left some things unamended which I might possibly have altered had I been at home. For instance, "I shall always address you in your own S-n-i-v-e-l-i-n-g d-r-a-w-l, baby." I saw that you objected to something there, but I did not understand what! Was it that it was too personal? Should the language be altered?—or the hyphens taken out? Won't you please fix it the way it ought to be, altering the language as you choose, only making it bitter and contemptuous?

"Deuced" was not strong enough; so I met you halfway with "devilish."

Mrs. Clemens has returned from New York with dreadful sore throat, and bones racked with rheumatism. She keeps her bed. "Aloha nui!" as the Kanakas say. MARK.

*Henry Irving once said to Mark Twain: "You made a mistake by not adopting the stage as a profession. You would have made even a greater actor than a writer."*

*Mark Twain would have made an actor, certainly, but not a very tractable one. His appearance in Hartford in "The Loan of a Lover" was a distinguished event, and his success complete, though he made so many extemporaneous improvements on the lines of thick-headed Peter Spuyk, that he kept the other actors guessing as to their cues, and nearly broke up the performance. It was, of course, an amateur benefit, though Augustin Daly promptly wrote, offering to put it on for a long run.*

*The "skeleton novelette" mentioned in the next letter refers to a plan concocted by Howells and Clemens, by which each of twelve authors was to write a story, using the same plot, "blindfolded" as to what the others had written. It was a regular "Mark Twain" notion, and it is hard to-day to imagine Howells's continued enthusiasm in it. Neither he nor Clemens gave up the idea for a long time. It appears in their letters again and again, though perhaps it was just as well for literature that it was never carried out.*

To W. D. Howells, in Boston:

*Apl. 22, 1876.*

MY DEAR HOWELLS, You'll see per enclosed slip that I appear for the first time on the stage next Wednesday. You and Mrs. H. come down and you shall skip in free.

I wrote my skeleton novelette yesterday and today. It will make a little under 12 pages.

Please tell Aldrich I've got a photographer engaged, and tri-weekly issue is about to begin. Show him the canvassing specimens and beseech him to subscribe.

*Ever yours,*

*S. L. C.*

*In his next letter Mark Twain explains why Tom Sawyer is not to appear as soon as planned. The reference to "The Literary Nightmare" refers to the "Punch, Conductor, Punch with Care" sketch, which had recently appeared in the Atlantic. Many other versifiers had had their turn at horse-car poetry, and now a publisher was anxious to collect it in a book, provided he could use the Atlantic sketch. Clemens does not tell us here the nature of Carlton's insult, forgiveness of which he was not yet qualified to grant, but there are at least two stories about it, or two halves of the same incident, as related afterward by Clemens and Canton. Clemens said that when he took the Jumping Frog book to Carlton, in 1867, the latter, pointing to his stock, said, rather scornfully: "Books? I don't want your book; my shelves are full of books now," though the reader may remember that it was Carlton himself who had given the frog story to the Saturday Press and had seen it become famous. Carlton's half of the story was that he did not accept Mark Twain's book because the author looked so disreputable. Long afterward, when the two men met in Europe, the publisher said to the now rich and famous author: "Mr. Clemens, my one claim on immortality is that*

*I declined your first book."*

To W. D. Howells, in Boston:

*HARTFORD, Apl. 25, 1876*

MY DEAR HOWELLS,—Thanks for giving me the place of honor.

Bliss made a failure in the matter of getting Tom Sawyer ready on time—the engravers assisting, as usual. I went down to see how much of a delay there was going to be, and found that the man had not even put a canvasser on, or issued an advertisement yet—in fact, that the electrotypes would not all be done for a month! But of course the main fact was that no canvassing had been done—because a subscription harvest is before publication, (not after, when people have discovered how bad one's book is.)

Well, yesterday I put in the Courant an editorial paragraph stating that Tam Sawyer is "ready to issue, but publication is put off in order to secure English copyright by simultaneous publication there and here. The English edition is unavoidably delayed."

You see, part of that is true. Very well. When I observed that my "Sketches" had dropped from a sale of 6 or 7000 a month down to 1200 a month, I said "this ain't no time to be publishing books; therefore, let Tom lie still till Autumn, Mr. Bliss, and make a holiday book of him to beguile the young people withal."

I shall print items occasionally, still further delaying Tom, till I ease him down to Autumn without shock to the waiting world.

As to that "Literary Nightmare" proposition. I'm obliged to withhold consent, for what seems a good reason—to wit: A single page of horse-car poetry is all that the average reader can stand, without nausea; now, to stack together all of it that has been written, and then add it to my article would be to enrage and disgust each and every reader and win the deathless enmity of the lot.

Even if that reason were insufficient, there would still be a sufficient reason left, in the fact that Mr. Carlton seems to be the publisher of the magazine in which it is proposed to publish this horse-car matter. Carlton insulted me in Feb. 1867, and so when the day arrives that sees me doing him a civility I shall feel that I am ready for Paradise, since my list of possible and impossible forgivenesses will then be complete.

Mrs. Clemens says my version of the blindfold novelette "A Murder and A Marriage" is "good." Pretty strong language—for her.

The Fieldses are coming down to the play tomorrow, and they promise to get you and Mrs. Howells to come too, but I hope you'll do nothing of the kind if it will inconvenience you, for I'm not going to play either strikingly bad enough or well enough to make the journey pay you.

My wife and I think of going to Boston May 7th to see Anna Dickinson's debut on the 8th. If I find we can go, I'll try to get a stage box and then you and Mrs. Howells must come to Parker's and go with us to the crucifixion.

(Is that spelt right?—somehow it doesn't look right.)

With our very kindest regards to the whole family.

*Yrs ever,*

*MARK.*

*The mention of Anna Dickinson, at the end of this letter, recalls a prominent reformer and lecturer of the Civil War period. She had begun her crusades against temperance and slavery in 1857, when she was but fifteen years old, when her success as a speaker had been immediate and extraordinary. Now, in this later period, at the age of thirty-four, she aspired to the stage—unfortunately for her, as her gifts lay elsewhere. Clemens and Howells knew Miss Dickinson, and were anxious for the success which they hardly dared hope for.*

*Clemens arranged a box party.*

To W. D. Howells, in Boston:

*May 4, '76.*

MY DEAR HOWELLS,—I shall reach Boston on Monday the 8th, either at 4:30 p.m. or 6 p.m. (Which is best?) and go straight to Parker's. If you and Mrs. Howells cannot be there by half past 4, I'll not plan to arrive till the later train-time (6,) because I don't want to be there alone—even a minute. Still, Joe Twichell will doubtless go with me (forgot that,) he is going to try hard to. Mrs. Clemens has given up going, because Susy is just recovering from about the savagest assault of diphtheria a child ever did recover from, and therefore will not be entirely her healthy self again by the 8th.

Would you and Mrs. Howells like to invite Mr. and Mrs. Aldrich? I have a large proscenium box—plenty of room. Use your own pleasure about it—I mainly (that is honest,) suggest it because I am seeking to make matters pleasant for you and Mrs. Howells. I invited Twichell because I thought I knew you'd like that. I want you to fix it so that you and the Madam can remain in Boston all night; for I leave next day and we can't have a talk, otherwise. I am going to get two rooms and a parlor; and would like to know what you decide about the Aldriches, so as to know whether to apply for an additional bedroom or not.

Don't dine that evening, for I shall arrive dinnerless and need your help.

I'll bring my Blindfold Novelette, but shan't exhibit it unless you exhibit yours. You would simply go to work and write a novelette that would make mine sick. Because you would know all about where my weak points lay. No, Sir, I'm one of these old wary birds!

*Don't bother to write a letter—3 lines on a postal card is all that I can permit from a busy man.*

*Yrs ever*

*MARK.*

P. S. Good! You'll not have to feel any call to mention that debut in the Atlantic—they've made me pay the grand cash for my box!—a thing which most managers would be too worldly-wise to do, with journalistic folks. But I'm most honestly glad, for I'd rather pay three prices, any time, than to have my tongue half paralyzed with a dead-head ticket.

Hang that Anna Dickinson, a body can never depend upon her debuts! She has made five or six false starts already. If she fails to debut this time, I will never bet on her again.

*In his book, My Mark Twain, Howells refers to the "tragedy" of Miss Dickinson's appearance. She was the author of numerous plays, some of which were successful, but her career as an actress was never brilliant.*

*At Elmira that summer the Clemenses heard from their good friend Doctor Brown, of Edinburgh, and sent eager replies.*

To Dr. John Brown, in Edinburgh:

*ELMIRA, NEW YORK, U. S. June 22, 1876.*

DEAR FRIEND THE DOCTOR,—It was a perfect delight to see the well-known handwriting again! But we so grieve to know that you are feeling miserable. It must not last—it cannot last. The regal summer is come and it will smile you into high good cheer; it will charm away your pains, it will banish your distresses. I wish you were here, to spend the summer with us. We are perched on a hill-top that overlooks a little world of green valleys, shining rivers, sumptuous forests and billowy uplands veiled in the haze of distance. We have no neighbors. It is the quietest of all quiet places, and we are hermits that eschew caves and live in the sun. Doctor, if you'd only come!

I will carry your letter to Mrs. C. now, and there will be a glad woman,

I tell you! And she shall find one of those pictures to put in this for Mrs. Barclays and if there isn't one here we'll send right away to Hartford and get one. Come over, Doctor John, and bring the Barclays, the Nicolsons and the Browns, one and all!

*Affectionately,*

*SAML. L. CLEMENS.*

*From May until August no letters appear to have passed between Clemens and Howells; the latter finally wrote, complaining of the lack of news. He was in the midst of campaign activities, he said, writing a life of Hayes, and gaily added: "You know I wrote the life of Lincoln, which elected him." He further reported a comedy he had completed, and gave Clemens a general stirring up as to his own work.*

*Mark Twain, in his hillside study, was busy enough. Summer was his time for work, and he had tried his hand in various directions. His mention of Huck Finn in his reply to Howells is interesting, in that it shows the measure of his enthusiasm, or lack of it, as a gauge of his ultimate achievement*

To W. D. Howells, in Boston:

*ELMIRA, Aug. 9, 1876.*

MY DEAR HOWELLS,—I was just about to write you when your letter came—and not one of those obscene postal cards, either, but reverently, upon paper.

I shall read that biography, though the letter of acceptance was amply sufficient to corral my vote without any further knowledge of the man. Which reminds me that a campaign club in Jersey City wrote a few days ago and invited me to be present at the raising of a Tilden and Hendricks flag there, and to take the stand and give them some "counsel." Well, I could not go, but gave them counsel and advice by letter, and in the kindliest terms as to the raising of the flag—advised them "not to raise it."

Get your book out quick, for this is a momentous time. If Tilden is elected I think the entire country will go pretty straight to—Mrs. Howells's bad place.

I am infringing on your patent—I started a record of our children's sayings, last night. Which reminds me that last week I sent down and got Susie a vast pair of shoes of a most villainous pattern, for I discovered that her feet were being twisted and cramped out of shape by a smaller and prettier article. She did not complain, but looked degraded and injured. At night her mamma gave her the usual admonition when she was about to say her prayers—to wit:

"Now, Susie—think about God."

"Mamma, I can't, with those shoes."

The farm is perfectly delightful this season. It is as quiet and peaceful as a South Sea Island. Some of the sunsets which we have witnessed from this commanding eminence were marvelous. One evening a rainbow spanned an entire range of hills with its mighty arch, and from a black hub resting upon the hill-top in the exact centre, black rays diverged upward in perfect regularity to the rainbow's arch and created a very strongly defined and altogether the most majestic, magnificent and startling half-sunk wagon wheel you can imagine. After that, a world of tumbling and prodigious clouds came drifting up out of the West and took to themselves a wonderfully rich and brilliant green color—the decided green of new spring foliage. Close by them we saw the intense blue of the skies, through rents in the cloud-rack, and away off in another quarter were drifting clouds of a delicate pink color. In one place hung a pall of dense black clouds, like compacted pitch-smoke. And the stupendous wagon wheel was still in the supremacy of its unspeakable grandeur. So you see, the colors present in the sky at once and the same time were blue, green, pink, black, and the vari-colored splendors of the rainbow. All strong and decided colors, too. I don't know whether this weird and astounding spectacle most suggested heaven, or hell. The wonder, with its constant, stately, and always surprising changes, lasted upwards of two hours, and we all stood on the top of the hill by my study till the final miracle was complete and the greatest day ended that we ever saw.

Our farmer, who is a grave man, watched that spectacle to the end, and then observed that it was "dam funny."

The double-barreled novel lies torpid. I found I could not go on with it. The chapters I had written were still too new and familiar to me. I may take it up next winter, but cannot tell yet; I waited and waited to see if my interest in it would not revive, but gave it up a month ago and began another boys' book—more to be at work than anything else. I have written 400 pages on it—therefore it is very nearly half done. It is Huck Finn's Autobiography. I like it only tolerably well, as far as I have got, and may possibly pigeonhole or burn the MS when it is done.

So the comedy is done, and with a "fair degree of satisfaction." That rejoices me, and makes me mad, too—for I can't plan a comedy, and what have you done that God should be so good to you? I have racked myself baldheaded trying to plan a comedy harness for some promising characters of mine to work in, and had to give it up. It is a noble lot of blooded stock and worth no end of money, but they must stand in the stable and be profitless. I want to be present when the comedy is produced and help enjoy the success.

Warner's book is mighty readable, I think.

*Love to yez.*

*Yrs ever*

*MARK*

*Howells promptly wrote again, urging him to enter the campaign for Hayes. "There is not another man in this country," he said, "who could help him so much as you." The "farce" which Clemens refers to in his reply, was "The Parlor Car," which seems to have been about the first venture of Howells in that field.*

To W. D. Howells, in Boston:

*ELMIRA, August 23, 1876.*

MY DEAR HOWELLS,—I am glad you think I could do Hayes any good, for I have been wanting to write a letter or make a speech to that end. I'll be careful not to do either, however, until the opportunity comes in a natural, justifiable and unlugged way; and shall not then do anything unless I've got it all digested and worded just right. In which case I might do some good—in any other I should do harm. When a humorist ventures upon the grave concerns of life he must do his job better than another man or he works harm to his cause.

The farce is wonderfully bright and delicious, and must make a hit. You read it to me, and it was mighty good; I read it last night and it was better; I read it aloud to the household this morning and it was better than ever. So it would be worth going a long way to see it well played; for without any question an actor of genius always adds a subtle something to any man's work that none but the writer knew was there before. Even if he knew it. I have heard of readers convulsing audiences with my "Aurelia's Unfortunate Young Man." If there is anything really funny in the piece, the author is not aware of it.

All right—advertise me for the new volume. I send you herewith a sketch which will make 3 pages of the Atlantic. If you like it and accept it, you should get it into the December No. because I shall read it in public in Boston the 13th and 14th of Nov. If it went in a month earlier it would be too old for me to read except as old matter; and if it went in a month later it would be too old for the Atlantic—do you see? And if you wish to use it, will you set it up now, and send me three proofs?—one to correct for Atlantic, one to send to Temple Bar (shall I tell them to use it not earlier than their

November No.) and one to use in practising for my Boston readings.

We must get up a less elaborate and a much better skeleton-plan for the Blindfold Novels and make a success of that idea. David Gray spent Sunday here and said we could but little comprehend what a rattling stir that thing would make in the country. He thought it would make a mighty strike. So do I. But with only 8 pages to tell the tale in, the plot must be less elaborate, doubtless. What do you think?

When we exchange visits I'll show you an unfinished sketch of Elizabeth's time which shook David Gray's system up pretty exhaustively.

*Yrs ever,*

*MARK.*

*The MS. sketch mentioned in the foregoing letter was "The Canvasser's Tale," later included in the volume, Tom Sawyer Abroad, and Other Stories. It is far from being Mark Twain's best work, but was accepted and printed in the Atlantic. David Gray was an able journalist and editor whom Mark Twain had known in Buffalo.*

*The "sketch of Elizabeth's time" is a brilliant piece of writing —an imaginary record of conversation and court manners in the good old days of free speech and performance, phrased in the language of the period. Gray, John Hay, Twichell, and others who had a chance to see it thought highly of it, and Hay had it set in type and a few proofs taken for private circulation. Some years afterward a West Point officer had a special font of antique type made for it, and printed a hundred copies. But the present-day reader would hardly be willing to include "Fireside Conversation in the Time of Queen*

*Elizabeth" in Mark Twain's collected works.*

*Clemens was a strong Republican in those days, as his letters of this period show. His mention of the "caves" in the next is another reference to "The Canvasser's Tale."*

To W. D. Howells, in Boston:

*Sept. 14, 1876.*

MY DEAR HOWELLS,—Yes, the collection of caves was the origin of it. I changed it to echoes because these being invisible and intangible, constituted a still more absurd species of property, and yet a man could really own an echo, and sell it, too, for a high figure—such an echo as that at the Villa Siminetti, two miles from Milan, for instance. My first purpose was to have the man make a collection of caves and afterwards of echoes; but perceived that the element of absurdity and impracticability was so nearly identical as to amount to a repetition of an idea.....

I will not, and do not, believe that there is a possibility of Hayes's defeat, but I want the victory to be sweeping.....

It seems odd to find myself interested in an election. I never was before. And I can't seem to get over my repugnance to reading or thinking about politics, yet. But in truth I care little about any party's politics—the man behind it is the important thing.

You may well know that Mrs. Clemens liked the Parlor Car—enjoyed it ever so much, and was indignant at you all through, and kept exploding into rages at you for pretending that such a woman ever existed—closing each and every explosion with "But it is just what such a woman would do."—"It is just what such a woman would say." They all voted the Parlor Car perfection—except me. I said they wouldn't have been allowed to court and quarrel there so long, uninterrupted; but at each critical moment the odious train-boy would come in and pile foul literature all over them four or five inches deep, and the lover would turn his head aside and curse—and presently that train-boy would be back again (as on all those Western roads) to take up the literature and leave prize candy.

Of course the thing is perfect, in the magazine, without the train-boy; but I was thinking of the stage and the groundlings. If the dainty touches went over their heads, the train-boy and other possible interruptions would fetch them every time. Would it mar the flow of the thing too much to insert that devil? I thought it over a couple of hours and concluded it wouldn't, and that he ought to be in for the sake of the groundlings (and to get new copyright on the piece.)

And it seemed to me that now that the fourth act is so successfully written, why not go ahead and write the 3 preceding acts? And then after it is finished, let me put into it a low-comedy character (the girl's or the lover's father or uncle) and gobble a big pecuniary interest in your work for myself. Do not let this generous proposition disturb your rest—but do write the other 3 acts, and then it will be valuable to managers. And don't go and sell it to anybody, like Harte, but keep it for yourself.

Harte's play can be doctored till it will be entirely acceptable and then it will clear a great sum every year. I am out of all patience with Harte for selling it. The play entertained me hugely, even in its present crude state.

*Love to you all.*

*Yrs ever,*

*MARK*

*Following the Sellers success, Clemens had made many attempts at dramatic writing. Such undertakings had uniformly failed, but he had always been willing to try again. In the next letter we get the beginning of what proved his first and last direct literary association, that is to say, collaboration, with Bret Harte.*

*Clemens had great admiration for Harte's ability and believed that between them they could turn out a successful play. Whether or not this belief was justified will appear later. Howells's biography of Hayes, meanwhile, had not gone well. He reported that only two thousand copies had been sold in what was now the height of the campaign. "There's success for you," he said; "it makes me despair of the Republic."*

*Clemens, on his part, had made a speech for Hayes that Howells declared had put civil-service reform in a nutshell; he added: "You are the only Republican orator, quoted without distinction of party by all the newspapers."*

To W. D. Howells, in Boston:

*HARTFORD, Oct. 11, 1876.*

MY DEAR HOWELLS, This is a secret, to be known to nobody but you (of course I comprehend that Mrs. Howells is part of you) that Bret Harte came up here the other day and asked me to help him write a play and divide the swag, and I agreed. I am to put in Scotty Briggs (See Buck Fanshaw's Funeral, in "Roughing It.") and he is to put in a Chinaman (a wonderfully funny creature, as Bret presents him—for 5 minutes—in his Sandy Bar play.) This Chinaman is to be the character of the play, and both of us will work on him and develop him. Bret is to draw a plot, and I am to do the same; we shall use the best of the two, or gouge from both and build a third. My plot is built—finished it yesterday—six days' work, 8 or 9 hours a day, and has nearly killed me.

Now the favor I ask of you is that you will have the words "Ah Sin, a Drama," printed in the middle of a note-paper page and send the same to me, with Bill. We don't want anybody to know that we are building this play. I can't get this title page printed here without having to lie so much that the thought of it is disagreeable to one reared as I have been. And yet the title of the play must be printed—the rest of the application for copyright is allowable in penmanship.

We have got the very best gang of servants in America, now. When George first came he was one of the most religious of men. He had but one fault—young George Washington's. But I have trained him; and now it fairly breaks Mrs. Clemens's heart to hear George stand at that front door and lie to the unwelcome visitor. But your time is valuable; I must not dwell upon these things.....I'll ask Warner and Harte if they'll do Blindfold Novelettes. Some time I'll simplify that plot. All it needs is that the hanging and the marriage shall not be appointed for the same day. I got over that difficulty, but it required too much MS to reconcile the thing—so the movement of the story was clogged.

*I came near agreeing to make political speeches with our candidate for Governor the 16th and 23 inst., but I had to give up the idea, for Harte and I will be here at work then.*

*Yrs ever,*

*MARK*

*Mark Twain was writing few letters these days to any one but Howells, yet in November he sent one to an old friend of his youth, Burrough, the literary chair-maker who had roomed with him in the days when he had been setting type for the St. Louis Evening News.*

To Mr. Burrough, of St. Louis:

*HARTFORD, Nov. 1, 1876.*

MY DEAR BURROUGHS,—As you describe me I can picture myself

as I was 20 years ago. The portrait is correct. You think I have grown some; upon my word there was room for it. You have described a callow fool, a self-sufficient ass, a mere human tumble-bug.... imagining that he is remodeling the world and is entirely capable of doing it right. Ignorance, intolerance, egotism, self-assertion, opaque perception, dense and pitiful chuckle-headedness—and an almost pathetic unconsciousness of it all. That is what I was at 19 and 20; and that is what the average Southerner is at 60 today. Northerners, too, of a certain grade. It is of children like this that voters are made. And such is the primal source of our government! A man hardly knows whether to swear or cry over it.

I think I comprehend the position there—perfect freedom to vote just as you choose, provided you choose to vote as other people think—social ostracism, otherwise. The same thing exists here, among the Irish. An Irish Republican is a pariah among his people. Yet that race find fault with the same spirit in Know-Nothingism.

Fortunately a good deal of experience of men enabled me to choose my residence wisely. I live in the freest corner of the country. There are no social disabilities between me and my Democratic personal friends. We break the bread and eat the salt of hospitality freely together and never dream of such a thing as offering impertinent interference in each other's political opinions.

Don't you ever come to New York again and not run up here to see me. I Suppose we were away for the summer when you were East; but no matter, you could have telegraphed and found out. We were at Elmira N. Y. and right on your road, and could have given you a good time if you had allowed us the chance.

Yes, Will Bowen and I have exchanged letters now and then for several years, but I suspect that I made him mad with my last—shortly after you saw him in St. Louis, I judge. There is one thing which I can't stand and won't stand, from many people. That is sham sentimentality—the kind a school-girl puts into her graduating composition; the sort that makes up the Original Poetry column of a country newspaper; the rot that deals in the "happy days of yore," the "sweet yet melancholy past," with its "blighted hopes" and its "vanished dreams" and all that sort of drivel. Will's were always of this stamp. I stood it years. When I get a letter like that from a grown man and he a widower with a family, it gives me the stomach ache. And I just told Will Bowen so, last summer. I told him to stop being 16 at 40; told him to stop drooling about the sweet yet melancholy past, and take a pill. I said there was but one solitary thing about the past worth remembering, and that was the fact that it is the past—can't be restored. Well, I exaggerated some of these truths a little—but only a little—but my idea was to kill his sham sentimentality once and forever, and so make a good fellow of him again. I went to the unheard-of trouble of re-writing the letter and saying the same harsh things softly, so as to sugarcoat the anguish and make it a little more endurable and I asked him to write and thank me honestly for doing him the best and kindliest favor that any friend ever had done him—but he hasn't done it yet. Maybe he will, sometime. I am grateful to God that I got that letter off before he was married (I get that news from you) else he would just have slobbered all over me and drowned me when that event happened.

I enclose photograph for the young ladies. I will remark that I do not wear seal-skin for grandeur, but because I found, when I used to lecture in the winter, that nothing else was able to keep a man warm sometimes, in these high latitudes. I wish you had sent pictures of yourself and family—I'll trade picture for picture with you, straight through, if you are commercially inclined.

*Your old friend,*

*SAML L. CLEMENS.*

## XVII. LETTERS, 1877. TO BERMUDA WITH TWICHELL. PROPOSITION TO TH. NAST. THE WHITTIER DINNER.

*Mark Twain must have been too busy to write letters that winter. Those that have survived are few and unimportant. As a matter of fact, he was writing the play, "Ah Sin," with Bret Harte, and getting it ready for production. Harte was a guest in the Clemens home while the play was being written, and not always a pleasant one. He was full of requirements, critical as to the 'menage,' to the point of sarcasm. The long friendship between Clemens and Harte weakened under the strain of collaboration and intimate daily intercourse, never to renew its old fiber. It was an unhappy outcome of an enterprise which in itself was to prove of little profit. The play, "Ah Sin," had many good features, and with Charles T. Parsloe in an amusing Chinese part might have been made a success, if the two authors could have harmoniously undertaken the needed repairs. It opened in Washington in May, and a letter from Parsloe, written at the moment, gives a hint of the situation.*

From Charles T. Parsloe to S. L. Clemens:

*WASHINGTON, D. C. May 11th, 1877.*

MR. CLEMENS,—I forgot whether I acknowledged receipt of check by telegram. Harte has been here since Monday last and done little or nothing yet, but promises to have something fixed by tomorrow morning. We have been making some improvements among ourselves. The last act is weak at the end, and I do hope Mr. Harte will have something for a good finish to the piece. The other acts I think are all right, now.

Hope you have entirely recovered. I am not very well myself, the excitement of a first night is bad enough, but to have the annoyance with Harte that I have is too much for a beginner. I ain't used to it. The houses have been picking up since Tuesday Mr. Ford has worked well and hard for us.

*Yours in, haste,*

*CHAS. THOS. PARSLOE.*

*The play drew some good houses in Washington, but it could not hold them for a run. Never mind what was the matter with it; perhaps a very small change at the right point would have turned it into a fine success. We have seen in a former letter the obligation which Mark Twain confessed to Harte—a debt he had tried in many ways to repay—obtaining for him a liberal book contract with Bliss; advancing him frequent and large sums of money which Harte could not, or did not, repay; seeking to advance his fortunes in many directions. The mistake came when he introduced another genius into the intricacies of his daily life. Clemens went down to Washington during the early rehearsals of "Ah Sin."*

*Meantime, Rutherford B. Hayes had been elected President, and Clemens one day called with a letter of introduction from Howells, thinking to meet the Chief Executive. His own letter to Howells, later, probably does not give the real reason of his failure, but it will be amusing to those who recall the erratic personality of George Francis Train. Train and Twain were sometimes confused by the very unlettered; or pretendedly, by Mark Twain's friends.*

To W. D. Howells, in Boston:

*BALTIMORE, May 1, '77.*

MY DEAR HOWELLS,—Found I was not absolutely needed in Washington so I only staid 24 hours, and am on my way home, now. I called at the White House, and got admission to Col. Rodgers, because I wanted to inquire what was the right hour to go and infest the President. It was my luck to strike the place in the dead waste and middle of the day, the very busiest time. I perceived that Mr. Rodgers took me for George Francis Train and had made up his mind not to let me get at the President; so at the end of half an hour I took my letter of introduction from the table and went away. It was a great pity all round, and a great loss to the nation, for I was brim full of the Eastern question. I didn't get to see the President or the Chief Magistrate either, though I had sort of a glimpse of a lady at a window who resembled her portraits.

*Yrs ever,*

*MARK.*

*Howells condoled with him on his failure to see the President, "but," he added, "if you and I had both been there, our combined skill would have no doubt procured us to be expelled from the White House by Fred Douglass. But the thing seems to be a complete failure as it was." Douglass at this time being the Marshal of Columbia, gives special point to Howells's suggestion.*

*Later, in May, Clemens took Twichell for an excursion to Bermuda.*

> *He had begged Howells to go with them, but Howells, as usual, was full of literary affairs. Twichell and Clemens spent four glorious days tramping the length and breadth of the beautiful island, and remembered it always as one of their happiest adventures. "Put it down as an Oasis!" wrote Twichell on his return, "I'm afraid I shall not see as green a spot again soon. And it was your invention and your gift. And your company was the best of it. Indeed, I never took more comfort in being with you than on this journey, which, my boy, is saying a great deal."*

*To Howells, Clemens triumphantly reported the success of the excursion.*

To W. D. Howells, in Boston:

*FARMINGTON AVENUE, HARTFORD, May 29, 1877.*

Confound you, Joe Twichell and I roamed about Bermuda day and night and never ceased to gabble and enjoy. About half the talk was—"It is a burning shame that Howells isn't here." "Nobody could get at the very meat and marrow of this pervading charm and deliciousness like Howells;" "How Howells would revel in the quaintness, and the simplicity of this people and the Sabbath repose of this land." "What an imperishable sketch Howells would make of Capt. West the whaler, and Capt. Hope with the patient, pathetic face, wanderer in all the oceans for 42 years, lucky in none; coming home defeated once more, now, minus his ship—resigned, uncomplaining, being used to this." "What a rattling chapter Howells would make out of the small boy Alfred, with his alert eye and military brevity and exactness of speech; and out of the old landlady; and her sacred onions; and her daughter; and the visiting clergyman; and the ancient pianos of Hamilton and the venerable music in vogue there—and forty other things which we shall leave untouched or touched but lightly upon, we not being worthy." "Dam Howells for not being here!" (this usually from me, not Twichell.)

O, your insufferable pride, which will have a fall some day! If you had gone with us and let me pay the $50 which the trip and the board and the various nicknacks and mementoes would cost, I would have picked up enough droppings from your conversation to pay me 500 per cent profit in the way of the several magazine articles which I could have written, whereas I can now write only one or two and am therefore largely out of pocket by your proud ways. Ponder these things. Lord, what a perfectly bewitching excursion it was! I traveled under an assumed name and was never molested with a polite attention from anybody.

*Love to you all.*

*Yrs ever*

*MARK*

*Aldrich, meantime, had invited the Clemenses to Ponkapog during the Bermuda absence, and Clemens hastened to send him a line expressing regrets. At the close he said:*

To T. B. Aldrich, in Ponkapog, Mass.:

*FARMINGTON AVENUE, HARTFORD, June 3, 1877.*

Day after tomorrow we leave for the hills beyond Elmira, N. Y. for the summer, when I shall hope to write a book of some sort or other to beat the people with. A work similar to your new one in the Atlantic is what I mean, though I have not heard what the nature of that one is. Immoral, I suppose. Well, you are right. Such books sell best, Howells says. Howells says he is going to make his next book indelicate. He says he thinks there is money in it. He says there is a large class of the young, in schools and seminaries who—But you let him tell you. He has ciphered it all down to a demonstration.

With the warmest remembrances to the pair of you

*Ever Yours*

*SAMUEL L. CLEMENS.*

*Clemens would naturally write something about Bermuda, and began at once, "Random Notes of an Idle Excursion," and presently completed four papers, which Howells eagerly accepted for the Atlantic. Then we find him plunging into another play, this time alone.*

To W. D. Howells, in Boston:

*ELMIRA, June 27, 1877.*

MY DEAR HOWELLS,—If you should not like the first 2 chapters, send them to me and begin with Chapter 3—or Part 3, I believe you call these things in the magazine. I have finished No. 4., which closes the series, and will mail it tomorrow if I think of it. I like this one, I liked the preceding one (already mailed to you some time ago) but I had my doubts about 1 and 2. Do not hesitate to squelch them, even with derision and insult.

Today I am deep in a comedy which I began this morning—principal character, that old detective—I skeletoned the first act and wrote the second, today; and am dog-tired, now. Fifty-four close pages of MS in 7 hours. Once I wrote 55 pages at a sitting—that was on the opening chapters of the "Gilded Age" novel. When I cool down, an hour from now, I shall go to zero, I judge.

*Yrs ever,*

*MARK.*

*Clemens had doubts as to the quality of the Bermuda papers, and with some reason. They did not represent him at his best. Nevertheless, they were pleasantly entertaining, and Howells expressed full approval of them for Atlantic use. The author remained troubled.*

To W. D. Howells, in Boston:

*ELMIRA, July 4, 1877.*

MY DEAR HOWELLS,—It is splendid of you to say those pleasant things. But I am still plagued with doubts about Parts 1 and 2. If you have any, don't print. If otherwise, please make some cold villain like Lathrop read and pass sentence on them. Mind, I thought they were good, at first—it was the second reading that accomplished its hellish purpose on me. Put them up for a new verdict. Part 4 has lain in my pigeon-hole a good while, and when I put it there I had a Christian's confidence in 4 aces in it; and you can be sure it will skip toward Connecticut tomorrow before any fatal fresh reading makes me draw my bet.

I've piled up 151 MS pages on my comedy. The first, second and fourth acts are done, and done to my satisfaction, too. Tomorrow and next day will finish the 3rd act and the play. I have not written less than 30 pages any day since I began. Never had so much fun over anything in my life-never such consuming interest and delight. (But Lord bless you the second reading will fetch it!) And just think!—I had Sol Smith Russell in my mind's eye for the old detective's part, and hang it he has gone off pottering with Oliver Optic, or else the papers lie.

I read everything about the President's doings there with exultation.

I wish that old ass of a private secretary hadn't taken me for George Francis Train. If ignorance were a means of grace I wouldn't trade that gorilla's chances for the Archbishop of Canterbury's.

I shall call on the President again, by and by. I shall go in my war paint; and if I am obstructed the nation will have the unusual spectacle of a private secretary with a pen over one ear a tomahawk over the other.

I read the entire Atlantic this time. Wonderful number. Mrs. Rose Terry Cooke's story was a ten-strike. I wish she would write 12 old-time New England tales a year.

Good times to you all! Mind if you don't run here for a few days you will go to hence without having had a fore-glimpse of heaven.

*MARK.*

*The play, "Ah Sin," that had done little enough in Washington, was that summer given another trial by Augustin Daly, at the Fifth Avenue Theater, New York, with a fine company. Clemens had undertaken to doctor the play, and it would seem to have had an enthusiastic reception on the opening night. But it was a summer audience, unspoiled by many attractions. "Ah Sin" was never a success in the New York season—never a money-maker on the road.*

*The reference in the first paragraph of the letter that follows is to the Bermuda chapters which Mark Twain was publishing simultaneously in England and America.*

*ELMIRA, Aug 3, 1877.*

MY DEAR HOWELLS,—I have mailed one set of the slips to London, and told Bentley you would print Sept. 15, in October Atlantic, and he must not print earlier in Temple Bar. Have I got the dates and things right?

I am powerful glad to see that No. 1 reads a nation sight better in print than it did in MS. I told Bentley we'd send him the slips, each time, 6 weeks before day of publication. We can do that can't we? Two months ahead would be still better I suppose, but I don't know.

"Ah Sin" went a-booming at the Fifth Avenue. The reception of Col. Sellers was calm compared to it.

The criticisms were just; the criticisms of the great New York dailies are always just, intelligent, and square and honest—notwithstanding, by a blunder which nobody was seriously to blame for, I was made to say exactly the opposite of this in a newspaper some time ago. Never said it at all, and moreover I never thought it. I could not publicly correct it before the play appeared in New York, because that would look as if I had really said that thing and then was moved by fears for my pocket and my reputation to take it back. But I can correct it now, and shall do it; for now my motives cannot be impugned. When I began this letter, it had not occurred to me to use you in this connection, but it occurs to me now. Your opinion and mine, uttered a year ago, and repeated more than once since, that the candor and ability of the New York critics were beyond question, is a matter which makes it proper enough that I should speak through you at this time. Therefore if you will print this paragraph somewhere, it may remove the impression that I say unjust things which I do not think, merely for the pleasure of talking.

There, now, Can't you say—

*"In a letter to Mr. Howells of the Atlantic Monthly, Mark*

*Twain describes the reception of the new comedy 'Ali Sin,'*

*and then goes on to say:" etc.*

Beginning at the star with the words, "The criticisms were just." Mrs. Clemens says, "Don't ask that of Mr. Howells—it will be disagreeable to him." I hadn't thought of it, but I will bet two to one on the correctness of her instinct. We shall see.

Will you cut that paragraph out of this letter and precede it with the remarks suggested (or with better ones,) and send it to the Globe or some other paper? You can't do me a bigger favor; and yet if it is in the least disagreeable, you mustn't think of it. But let me know, right away, for I want to correct this thing before it grows stale again. I explained myself to only one critic (the World)—the consequence was a noble notice of the play. This one called on me, else I shouldn't have explained myself to him.

I have been putting in a deal of hard work on that play in New York, but it is full of incurable defects.

My old Plunkett family seemed wonderfully coarse and vulgar on the stage, but it was because they were played in such an outrageously and inexcusably coarse way. The Chinaman is killingly funny. I don't know when I have enjoyed anything as much as I did him. The people say there isn't enough of him in the piece. That's a triumph—there'll never be any more of him in it.

John Brougham said, "Read the list of things which the critics have condemned in the piece, and you have unassailable proofs that the play contains all the requirements of success and a long life."

That is true. Nearly every time the audience roared I knew it was over something that would be condemned in the morning (justly, too) but must be left in—for low comedies are written for the drawing-room, the kitchen and the stable, and if you cut out the kitchen and the stable the drawing-room can't support the play by itself.

There was as much money in the house the first two nights as in the first ten of Sellers. Haven't heard from the third—I came away.

*Yrs ever,*

*MARK.*

*In a former letter we have seen how Mark Twain, working on a story that was to stand as an example of his best work, and become one of his surest claims to immortality (The Adventures of Huckleberry Finn), displayed little enthusiasm in his undertaking. In the following letter, which relates the conclusion of his detective comedy, we find him at the other extreme, on very tiptoe with enthusiasm over something wholly without literary value or dramatic possibility. One of the hall-marks of genius is the inability to discriminate as to the value of its output. "Simon Wheeler, Amateur Detective" was a dreary, absurd, impossible performance, as wild and unconvincing in incident and dialogue as anything out of an asylum could well be. The title which he first chose for it, "Balaam's Ass," was properly in keeping with the general scheme. Yet Mark Twain, still warm with the creative fever, had the fullest faith in it as a work of art and a winner of fortune. It would never see the light of production, of course. We shall see presently that the distinguished playwright, Dion Boucicault, good-naturedly complimented it as being better than "Ahi Sin." One must wonder what that skilled artist really thought, and how he could do even this violence to his conscience.*

To W. D. Howells, in Boston:

*ELMIRA, Wednesday P.M. (1877)*

MY DEAR HOWELLS,—It's finished. I was misled by hurried mis-paging. There were ten pages of notes, and over 300 pages of MS when the play was done. Did it in 42 hours, by the clock; 40 pages of the Atlantic—but then of course it's very "fat." Those are the figures, but I don't believe them myself, because the thing's impossible.

But let that pass. All day long, and every day, since I finished (in the rough) I have been diligently altering, amending, re-writing, cutting down. I finished finally today. Can't think of anything else in the way of an improvement. I thought I would stick to it while the interest was hot—and I am mighty glad I did. A week from now it will be frozen—then revising would be drudgery. (You see I learned something from the fatal blunder of putting "Ah Sin" aside before it was finished.)

She's all right, now. She reads in two hours and 20 minutes and will play not longer than 2 3/4 hours. Nineteen characters; 3 acts; (I bunched 2 into 1.)

Tomorrow I will draw up an exhaustive synopsis to insert in the printed title-page for copyrighting, and then on Friday or Saturday I go to New York to remain a week or ten days and lay for an actor. Wish you could run down there and have a holiday. 'Twould be fun.

My wife won't have "Balaam's Ass"; therefore I call the piece "Cap'n Simon Wheeler, The Amateur Detective."

*Yrs*

*MARK.*

To W. D. Howells, in Boston:

*ELMIRA, Aug. 29, 1877.*

MY DEAR HOWELLS,—Just got your letter last night. No, dern that article,—[One of the Bermuda chapters.]—it made me cry when I read it in proof, it was so oppressively and ostentatiously poor. Skim your eye over it again and you will think as I do. If Isaac and the prophets of Baal can be doctored gently and made permissible, it will redeem the thing: but if it can't, let's burn all of the articles except the tail-end of it and use that as an introduction to the next article—as I suggested in my letter to you of day before yesterday. (I had this proof from Cambridge before yours came.)

Boucicault says my new play is ever so much better than "Ah Sin;" says the Amateur detective is a bully character, too. An actor is chawing over the play in New York, to see if the old Detective is suited to his abilities. Haven't heard from him yet.

If you've got that paragraph by you yet, and if in your judgment it would be good to publish it, and if you absolutely would not mind doing it, then I think I'd like to have you do it—or else put some other words in my mouth that will be properer, and publish them. But mind, don't think of it for a moment if it is distasteful—and doubtless it is. I value your judgment more than my own, as to the wisdom of saying anything at all in this matter.

To say nothing leaves me in an injurious position—and yet maybe I might do better to speak to the men themselves when I go to New York. This was my latest idea, and it looked wise.

We expect to leave here for home Sept. 4, reaching there the 8th—but we may be delayed a week.

Curious thing. I read passages from my play, and a full synopsis, to Boucicault, who was re-writing a play, which he wrote and laid aside 3 or 4 years ago. (My detective is about that age, you know.) Then he read a passage from his play, where a real detective does some things that are as idiotic as some of my old Wheeler's performances. Showed me the passages, and behold, his man's name is Wheeler! However, his Wheeler is not a prominent character, so we'll not alter the names. My Wheeler's name is taken from the old jumping Frog sketch.

I am re-reading Ticknor's diary, and am charmed with it, though I still say he refers to too many good things when he could just as well have told them. Think of the man traveling 8 days in convoy and familiar intercourse with a band of outlaws through the mountain fastnesses of Spain—he the fourth stranger they had encountered in thirty years—and compressing this priceless experience into a single colorless paragraph of his diary! They spun yarns to this unworthy devil, too.

I wrote you a very long letter a day or two ago, but Susy Crane wanted to make a copy of it to keep, so it has not gone yet. It may go today, possibly.

We unite in warm regards to you and yours.

*Yrs ever,*

*MARK.*

*The Ticknor referred to in a former letter was Professor George Ticknor, of Harvard College, a history-writer of distinction. On the margin of the "Diary" Mark Twain once wrote, "Ticknor is a Millet, who makes all men fall in love with him." And adds: "Millet was the cause of lovable qualities in people, and then he admired and loved those persons for the very qualities which he (without knowing it) had created in them. Perhaps it would be strictly truer of these two men to say that they bore within them the divine something in whose presence the evil in people fled away and hid itself, while all that was good in them came spontaneously forward out of the forgotten walls and comers in their systems where it was accustomed to hide."*

*It is Frank Millet, the artist, he is speaking of—a knightly soul whom all the Clemens household loved, and who would one day meet his knightly end with those other brave men that found death together when the Titanic went down.*

*The Clemens family was still at Quarry Farm at the end of August, and one afternoon there occurred a startling incident which Mark Twain thought worth setting down in practically duplicate letters to Howells and to Dr. John Brown. It may be of interest to the reader to know that John T. Lewis, the colored man mentioned, lived to a good old age—a pensioner of the Clemens family and, in the course of time, of H. H. Rogers. Howells's letter follows. It is the "very long letter" referred to in the foregoing.*

To W. D. Howells and wife, in Boston:

*ELMIRA, Aug. 25 '77.*

MY DEAR HOWELLSES,—I thought I ought to make a sort of record of it for further reference; the pleasantest way to do that would be to write it to somebody; but that somebody would let it leak into print and that we wish to avoid. The Howellses would be safe—so let us tell the Howellses about it.

Day before yesterday was a fine summer day away up here on the summit. Aunt Marsh and Cousin May Marsh were here visiting Susie Crane and Livy at our farmhouse. By and by mother Langdon came up the hill in the "high carriage" with Nora the nurse and little Jervis (Charley Langdon's little boy)—Timothy the coachman driving. Behind these came Charley's wife and little girl in the buggy, with the new, young, spry, gray horse—a high-stepper. Theodore Crane arrived a little later.

The Bay and Susy were on hand with their nurse, Rosa. I was on hand, too. Susy Crane's trio of colored servants ditto—these being Josie, housemaid; Aunty Cord, cook, aged 62, turbaned, very tall, very broad, very fine every way (see her portrait in "A True Story just as I Heard It" in my Sketches;) Chocklate (the laundress) (as the Bay calls her—she can't say Charlotte,) still taller, still more majestic of proportions, turbaned, very black, straight as an Indian—age 24. Then there was the farmer's wife (colored) and her little girl, Susy.

Wasn't it a good audience to get up an excitement before? Good excitable, inflammable material?

Lewis was still down town, three miles away, with his two-horse wagon, to get a load of manure. Lewis is the farmer (colored). He is of mighty frame and muscle, stocky, stooping, ungainly, has a good manly face and a clear eye. Age about 45—and the most picturesque of men, when he sits in his fluttering work-day rags, humped forward into a bunch, with his aged slouch hat mashed down over his ears and neck. It is a spectacle to make the broken-hearted smile. Lewis has worked mighty hard and remained mighty poor. At the end of each whole year's toil he can't show a gain of fifty dollars. He had borrowed money of the Cranes till he owed them $700 and he being conscientious and honest, imagine what it was to him to have to carry this stubborn, helpless load year in and year out.

Well, sunset came, and Ida the young and comely (Charley Langdon's wife) and her little Julia and the nurse Nora, drove out at the gate behind the new gray horse and started down the long hill—the high carriage receiving its load under the porte cochere. Ida was seen to turn her face toward us across the fence and intervening lawn—Theodore waved good-bye to her, for he did not know that her sign was a speechless appeal for help.

The next moment Livy said, "Ida's driving too fast down hill!" She followed it with a sort of scream, "Her horse is running away!"

We could see two hundred yards down that descent. The buggy seemed to fly. It would strike obstructions and apparently spring the height of a man from the ground.

Theodore and I left the shrieking crowd behind and ran down the hill bare-headed and shouting. A neighbor appeared at his gate—a tenth of a second too late! the buggy vanished past him like a thought. My last glimpse showed it for one instant, far down the descent, springing high in the air out of a cloud of dust, and then it disappeared. As I flew down the road my impulse was to shut my eyes as I turned them to the right or left, and so delay for a moment the ghastly spectacle of mutilation and death I was expecting.

I ran on and on, still spared this spectacle, but saying to myself: "I shall see it at the turn of the road; they never can pass that turn alive." When I came in sight of that turn I saw two wagons there bunched together—one of them full of people. I said, "Just so—they are staring petrified at the remains."

But when I got amongst that bunch, there sat Ida in her buggy and nobody hurt, not even the horse or the vehicle. Ida was pale but serene. As I came tearing down, she smiled back over her shoulder at me and said, "Well, we're alive yet, aren't we?" A miracle had been performed—nothing else.

You see Lewis, the prodigious, humped upon his front seat, had been toiling up, on his load of manure; he saw the frantic horse plunging down the hill toward him, on a full gallop, throwing his heels as high as a man's head at every jump. So Lewis turned his team diagonally across the road just at the "turn," thus making a V with the fence—the running horse could not escape that, but must enter it. Then Lewis sprang to the ground and stood in this V. He gathered his vast strength, and with a perfect Creedmoor aim he seized the gray horse's bit as he plunged by and fetched him up standing!

It was down hill, mind you. Ten feet further down hill neither Lewis nor any other man could have saved them, for they would have been on the abrupt "turn," then. But how this miracle was ever accomplished at all, by human strength, generalship and accuracy, is clean beyond my comprehension—and grows more so the more I go and examine the ground and try to believe it was actually done. I know one thing, well; if Lewis had missed his aim he would have been killed on the spot in the trap he had made for himself, and we should have found the rest of the remains away down at the bottom of the steep ravine.

Ten minutes later Theodore and I arrived opposite the house, with the servants straggling after us, and shouted to the distracted group on the porch, "Everybody safe!"

Believe it? Why how could they? They knew the road perfectly. We might as well have said it to people who had seen their friends go over Niagara.

However, we convinced them; and then, instead of saying something, or going on crying, they grew very still—words could not express it, I suppose.

Nobody could do anything that night, or sleep, either; but there was a deal of moving talk, with long pauses between pictures of that flying carriage, these pauses represented—this picture intruded itself all the time and disjointed the talk.

But yesterday evening late, when Lewis arrived from down town he found his supper spread, and some presents of books there, with very complimentary writings on the fly-leaves, and certain very complimentary letters, and more or less greenbacks of dignified denomination pinned to these letters and fly-leaves,—and one said, among other things, (signed by the Cranes) "We cancel $400 of your indebtedness to us," &c. &c.

(The end thereof is not yet, of course, for Charley Langdon is West and will arrive ignorant of all these things, today.)

The supper-room had been kept locked and imposingly secret and mysterious until Lewis should arrive; but around that part of the house were gathered Lewis's wife and child, Chocklate, Josie, Aunty Cord and our Rosa, canvassing things and waiting impatiently. They were all on hand when the curtain rose.

Now, Aunty Cord is a violent Methodist and Lewis an implacable Dunker—Baptist. Those two are inveterate religious disputants. The revealments having been made Aunty Cord said with effusion—

"Now, let folks go on saying there ain't no God! Lewis, the Lord sent you there to stop that horse."

Says Lewis:

"Then who sent the horse there in sich a shape?"

But I want to call your attention to one thing. When Lewis arrived the other evening, after saving those lives by a feat which I think is the most marvelous of any I can call to mind—when he arrived, hunched up on his manure wagon and as grotesquely picturesque as usual, everybody wanted to go and see how he looked. They came back and said he was beautiful. It was so, too—and yet he would have photographed exactly as he would have done any day these past 7 years that he has occupied this farm.

*Aug. 27.*

P. S. Our little romance in real life is happily and satisfactorily completed. Charley has come, listened, acted—and now John T. Lewis has ceased to consider himself as belonging to that class called "the poor."

It has been known, during some years, that it was Lewis's purpose to buy a thirty dollar silver watch some day, if he ever got where he could afford it. Today Ida has given him a new, sumptuous gold Swiss stem-winding stop-watch; and if any scoffer shall say, "Behold this thing is out of character," there is an inscription within, which will silence him; for it will teach him that this wearer aggrandizes the watch, not the watch the wearer.

I was asked beforehand, if this would be a wise gift, and I said "Yes, the very wisest of all;" I know the colored race, and I know that in Lewis's eyes this fine toy will throw the other more valuable testimonials far away into the shade. If he lived in England the Humane Society would give him a gold medal as costly as this watch, and nobody would say: "It is out of character." If Lewis chose to wear a town clock, who would become it better?

Lewis has sound common sense, and is not going to be spoiled. The instant he found himself possessed of money, he forgot himself in a plan to make his old father comfortable, who is wretchedly poor and lives down in Maryland. His next act, on the spot, was the proffer to the Cranes of the $300 of his remaining indebtedness to them. This was put off by them to the indefinite future, for he is not going to be allowed to pay that at all, though he doesn't know it.

A letter of acknowledgment from Lewis contains a sentence which raises it to the dignity of literature:

"But I beg to say, humbly, that inasmuch as divine providence saw fit to use me as a instrument for the saving of those presshious lives, the honner conferd upon me was greater than the feat performed."

That is well said.

*Yrs ever*

*MARK.*

*Howells was moved to use the story in the "Contributors' Club," and warned Clemens against letting it get into the newspapers. He declared he thought it one of the most impressive things he had ever read. But Clemens seems never to have allowed it to be used in any form. In its entirety, therefore, it is quite new matter.*

To W. D. Howells, in Boston:

*HARTFORD, Sept. 19, 1877.*

MY DEAR HOWELLS,—I don't really see how the story of the runaway horse could read well with the little details of names and places and things left out. They are the true life of all narrative. It wouldn't quite do to print them at this time. We'll talk about it when you come. Delicacy—a sad, sad false delicacy—robs literature of the best two things among its belongings. Family-circle narrative and obscene stories. But no matter; in that better world which I trust we are all going to I have the hope and belief that they will not be denied us.

Say—Twichell and I had an adventure at sea, 4 months ago, which I did not put in my Bermuda articles, because there was not enough to it. But the press dispatches bring the sequel today, and now there's plenty to it. A sailless, wasteless, chartless, compassless, grubless old condemned tub that has been drifting helpless about the ocean for 4 months and a half, begging bread and water like any other tramp, flying a signal of distress permanently, and with 13 innocent, marveling chuckleheaded Bermuda niggers on board, taking a Pleasure Excursion! Our ship fed the poor devils on the 25th of last May, far out at sea and left them to bullyrag their way to New York—and now they ain't as near New York as they were then by 250 miles! They have drifted 750 miles and are still drifting in the relentless Gulf Stream! What a delicious magazine chapter it would make—but I had to deny myself. I had to come right out in the papers at once, with my details, so as to try to raise the government's sympathy sufficiently to have better succor sent them than the cutter Colfax, which went a little way in search of them the other day and then struck a fog and gave it up.

If the President were in Washington I would telegraph him.

When I hear that the "Jonas Smith" has been found again, I mean to send for one of those darkies, to come to Hartford and give me his adventures for an Atlantic article.

Likely you will see my today's article in the newspapers.

*Yrs ever,*

*MARK.*

The revenue cutter Colfax went after the Jonas Smith, thinking there was mutiny or other crime on board. It occurs to me now that, since there is only mere suffering and misery and nobody to punish, it ceases to be a matter which (a republican form of) government will feel authorized to interfere in further. Dam a republican form of government.

*Clemens thought he had given up lecturing for good; he was prosperous and he had no love for the platform. But one day an idea popped into his head: Thomas Nast, the "father of the American cartoon," had delivered a successful series of illustrated lectures —talks for which he made the drawings as he went along. Mark Twain's idea was to make a combination with Nast. His letter gives us the plan in full.*

To Thomas Nast, Morristown, N. J.:

*HARTFORD, CONN. 1877.*

MY DEAR NAST,—I did not think I should ever stand on a platform again until the time was come for me to say "I die innocent." But the same old offers keep arriving. I have declined them all, just as usual, though sorely tempted, as usual.

Now, I do not decline because I mind talking to an audience, but because (1) traveling alone is so heartbreakingly dreary, and (2) shouldering the whole show is such a cheer-killing responsibility.

Therefore, I now propose to you what you proposed to me in 1867, ten years ago (when I was unknown) viz., that you stand on the platform and make pictures, and I stand by you and blackguard the audience. I should enormously enjoy meandering around (to big towns—don't want to go to the little ones) with you for company.

My idea is not to fatten the lecture agents and lyceums on the spoils, but put all the ducats religiously into two equal piles, and say to the artist and lecturer, "Absorb these."

For instance—[Here follows a plan and a possible list of cities to be visited. The letter continues]

Call the gross receipts $100,000 for four months and a half, and the profit from $60,000 to $75,000 (I try to make the figures large enough, and leave it to the public to reduce them.)

I did not put in Philadelphia because Pugh owns that town, and last winter when I made a little reading-trip he only paid me $300 and pretended his concert (I read fifteen minutes in the midst of a concert) cost him a vast sum, and so he couldn't afford any more. I could get up a better concert with a barrel of cats.

I have imagined two or three pictures and concocted the accompanying remarks to see how the thing would go. I was charmed.

Well, you think it over, Nast, and drop me a line. We should have some fun.

*Yours truly,*

*SAMUEL L. CLEMENS.*

*The plan came to nothing. Nast, like Clemens, had no special taste for platforming, and while undoubtedly there would have been large profits in the combination, the promise of the venture did not compel his acceptance.*

*In spite of his distaste for the platform Mark Twain was always giving readings and lectures, without charge, for some worthy Hartford cause. He was ready to do what he could to help an entertainment along, if he could do it in his own way—an original way, sometimes, and not always gratifying to the committee, whose plans were likely to be prearranged.*

*For one thing, Clemens, supersensitive in the matter of putting himself forward in his own town, often objected to any special exploitation of his name. This always distressed the committee, who saw a large profit to their venture in the prestige of his fame. The following characteristic letter was written in self-defense when, on one such occasion, a committee had become sufficiently peevish to abandon a worthy enterprise.*

To an Entertainment Committee, in Hartford:

*Nov. 9.*

*E. S. SYKES, Esq:*

Dr. SIR,—Mr. Burton's note puts upon me all the blame of the destruction of an enterprise which had for its object the succor of the Hartford poor. That is to say, this enterprise has been dropped because of the "dissatisfaction with Mr. Clemens's stipulations." Therefore I must be allowed to say a word in my defense.

There were two "stipulations"—exactly two. I made one of them; if the other was made at all, it was a joint one, from the choir and me.

My individual stipulation was, that my name should be kept out of the newspapers. The joint one was that sufficient tickets to insure a good sum should be sold before the date of the performance should be set. (Understand, we wanted a good sum—I do not think any of us bothered about a good house; it was money we were after)

Now you perceive that my concern is simply with my individual stipulation. Did that break up the enterprise?

Eugene Burton said he would sell $300 worth of the tickets himself.—Mr. Smith said he would sell $200 or $300 worth himself. My plan for Asylum Hill Church would have ensured $150 from that quarter.—All this in the face of my "Stipulation." It was proposed to raise $1000; did my stipulation render the raising of $400 or $500 in a dozen churches impossible?

My stipulation is easily defensible. When a mere reader or lecturer has appeared 3 or 4 times in a town of Hartford's size, he is a good deal more than likely to get a very unpleasant snub if he shoves himself forward about once or twice more. Therefore I long ago made up my mind that whenever I again appeared here, it should be only in a minor capacity and not as a chief attraction.

Now, I placed that harmless and very justifiable stipulation before the committee the other day; they carried it to headquarters and it was accepted there. I am not informed that any objection was made to it, or that it was regarded as an offense. It seems late in the day, now, after a good deal of trouble has been taken and a good deal of thankless work done by the committees, to, suddenly tear up the contract and then turn and bowl me down from long range as being the destroyer of it.

If the enterprise has failed because of my individual stipulation, here you have my proper and reasonable reasons for making that stipulation.

If it has failed because of the joint stipulation, put the blame there, and let us share it collectively.

I think our plan was a good one. I do not doubt that Mr. Burton still approves of it, too. I believe the objections come from other quarters, and not from him. Mr. Twichell used the following words in last Sunday's sermon, (if I remember correctly):

"My hearers, the prophet Deuteronomy says this wise thing: 'Though ye plan a goodly house for the poor, and plan it with wisdom, and do take off your coats and set to to build it, with high courage, yet shall the croaker presently come, and lift up his voice, (having his coat on,) and say, Verily this plan is not well planned—and he will go his way; and the obstructionist will come, and lift up his voice, (having his coat on,) and say, Behold, this is but a sick plan—and he will go his way; and the man that knows it all will come, and lift up his voice, (having his coat on,) and say, Lo, call they this a plan? then will he go his way; and the places which knew him once shall know him no more forever, because he was not, for God took him. Now therefore I say unto you, Verily that house will not be budded. And I say this also: He that waiteth for all men to be satisfied with his plan, let him seek eternal life, for he shall need it.'"

This portion of Mr. Twichell's sermon made a great impression upon me, and I was grieved that some one had not wakened me earlier so that I might have heard what went before.

*S. L. CLEMENS.*

*Mr. Sykes (of the firm of Sykes & Newton, the Allen House Pharmacy) replied that he had read the letter to the committee and that it had set those gentlemen right who had not before understood the situation. "If others were as ready to do their part as yourself our poor would not want assistance," he said, in closing.*

*We come now to an incident which assumes the proportions of an episode-even of a catastrophe—in Mark Twain's career. The disaster was due to a condition noted a few pages earlier—the inability of genius to judge its own efforts. The story has now become history —printed history—it having been sympathetically told by Howells in My Mark Twain, and more exhaustively, with a report of the speech that invited the lightning, in a former work by the present writer.*

*The speech was made at John Greenleaf Whittier's seventieth birthday dinner, given by the Atlantic staff on the evening of December 17, 1877. It was intended as a huge joke—a joke that would shake the sides of these venerable Boston deities, Longfellow, Emerson, Holmes, and the rest of that venerated group. Clemens had been a favorite at the Atlantic lunches and dinners—a speech by him always an event. This time he decided to outdo himself.*

*He did that, but not in the way he had intended. To use one of his own metaphors, he stepped out to meet the rainbow and got struck by lightning. His joke was not of the Boston kind or size. When its full nature burst upon the company—when the ears of the assembled diners heard the sacred names of Longfellow, Emerson, and Holmes lightly associated with human aspects removed—oh, very far removed —from Cambridge and Concord, a chill fell upon the diners that presently became amazement, and then creeping paralysis. Nobody knew afterward whether the great speech that he had so gaily planned ever came to a natural end or not. Somebody—the next on the program—attempted to follow him, but presently the company melted out of the doors and crept away into the night.*

*It seemed to Mark Twain that his career had come to an end. Back in Hartford, sweating and suffering through sleepless nights, he wrote Howells his anguish.*

To W. D. Howells, in Boston:

*Sunday Night. 1877.*

MY DEAR HOWELLS,—My sense of disgrace does not abate. It grows. I see that it is going to add itself to my list of permanencies—a list of humiliations that extends back to when I was seven years old, and which keep on persecuting me regardless of my repentancies.

I feel that my misfortune has injured me all over the country; therefore it will be best that I retire from before the public at present. It will hurt the Atlantic for me to appear in its pages, now. So it is my opinion and my wife's that the telephone story had better be suppressed. Will you return those proofs or revises to me, so that I can use the same on some future occasion?

It seems as if I must have been insane when I wrote that speech and saw no harm in it, no disrespect toward those men whom I reverenced so much. And what shame I brought upon you, after what you said in introducing me! It burns me like fire to think of it.

The whole matter is a dreadful subject—let me drop it here—at least on paper.

*Penitently yrs,*

*MARK.*

*Howells sent back a comforting letter. "I have no idea of dropping you out of the Atlantic," he wrote; "and Mr. Houghton has still less, if possible. You are going to help and not hurt us many a year yet, if you will.... You are not going to be floored by it; there is more justice than that, even in this world."*

*Howells added that Charles Elliot Norton had expressed just the right feeling concerning the whole affair, and that many who had not heard the speech, but read the newspaper reports of it, had found it without offense.*

*Clemens wrote contrite letters to Holmes, Emerson, and Longfellow, and received most gracious acknowledgments. Emerson, indeed, had not heard the speech: His faculties were already blurred by the mental mists that would eventually shut him in. Clemens wrote again to Howells, this time with less anguish.*

To W. D. Howells, in Boston:

*HARTFORD, Friday, 1877.*

MY DEAR HOWELLS,—Your letter was a godsend; and perhaps the welcomest part of it was your consent that I write to those gentlemen; for you discouraged my hints in that direction that morning in Boston—rightly, too, for my offense was yet too new, then. Warner has tried to hold up our hands like the good fellow he is, but poor Twichell could not say a word, and confessed that he would rather take nearly any punishment than face Livy and me. He hasn't been here since.

It is curious, but I pitched early upon Mr. Norton as the very man who would think some generous thing about that matter, whether he said it or not. It is splendid to be a man like that—but it is given to few to be.

I wrote a letter yesterday, and sent a copy to each of the three. I wanted to send a copy to Mr. Whittier also, since the offense was done also against him, being committed in his presence and he the guest of the occasion, besides holding the well-nigh sacred place he does in his people's estimation; but I didn't know whether to venture or not, and so ended by doing nothing. It seemed an intrusion to approach him, and even Livy seemed to have her doubts as to the best and properest way to do in the case. I do not reverence Mr. Emerson less, but somehow I could approach him easier.

Send me those proofs, if you have got them handy; I want to submit them to Wylie; he won't show them to anybody.

Had a very pleasant and considerate letter from Mr. Houghton, today, and was very glad to receive it.

You can't imagine how brilliant and beautiful that new brass fender is, and how perfectly naturally it takes its place under the carved oak. How they did scour it up before they sent it! I lied a good deal about it when I came home—so for once I kept a secret and surprised Livy on a Christmas morning!

I haven't done a stroke of work since the Atlantic dinner; have only moped around. But I'm going to try tomorrow. How could I ever have.

Ah, well, I am a great and sublime fool. But then I am God's fool, and all His works must be contemplated with respect.

Livy and I join in the warmest regards to you and yours,

*Yrs ever,*

*MARK.*

*Longfellow, in his reply, said: "I do not believe anybody was much hurt. Certainly I was not, and Holmes tells me he was not. So I think you may dismiss the matter from your mind without further remorse."*

*Holmes wrote: "It never occurred to me for a moment to take offense, or feel wounded by your playful use of my name."*

*Miss Ellen Emerson replied for her father (in a letter to Mrs. Clemens) that the speech had made no impression upon him, giving at considerable length the impression it had made on herself and other members of the family.*

*Clearly, it was not the principals who were hurt, but only those who held them in awe, though one can realize that this would not make it much easier for Mark Twain.*

## XVIII. LETTERS FROM EUROPE, 1878-79. TRAMPING WITH TWICHELL. WRITING A NEW TRAVEL BOOK. LIFE IN MUNICH.

*Whether the unhappy occurrence at the Whittier dinner had anything to do with Mark Twain's resolve to spend a year or two in Europe cannot be known now. There were other good reasons for going, one in particular being a demand for another book of travel. It was also true, as he explains in a letter to his mother, that his days were full of annoyances, making it difficult for him to work. He had a tendency to invest money in almost any glittering enterprise that came along, and at this time he was involved in the promotion of a variety of patent rights that brought him no return other than assessment and vexation.*

*Clemens's mother was by this time living with her son Onion and his wife, in Iowa.*

To Mrs. Jane Clemens, in Keokuk, Iowa:

*HARTFORD, Feb. 17, 1878*

MY DEAR MOTHER,—I suppose I am the worst correspondent in the whole world; and yet I grow worse and worse all the time. My conscience blisters me for not writing you, but it has ceased to abuse me for not writing other folks.

Life has come to be a very serious matter with me. I have a badgered, harassed feeling, a good part of my time. It comes mainly of business responsibilities and annoyances, and the persecution of kindly letters from well meaning strangers—to whom I must be rudely silent or else put in the biggest half of my time bothering over answers. There are other things also that help to consume my time and defeat my projects. Well, the consequence is, I cannot write a book at home. This cuts my income down. Therefore, I have about made up my mind to take my tribe and fly to some little corner of Europe and budge no more until I shall have completed one of the half dozen books that lie begun, up stairs. Please say nothing about this at present.

We propose to sail the 11th of April. I shall go to Fredonia to meet you, but it will not be well for Livy to make that trip I am afraid. However, we shall see. I will hope she can go.

Mr. Twichell has just come in, so I must go to him. We are all well, and send love to you all.

*Affly,*

*SAM.*

*He was writing few letters at this time, and doing but little work. There were always many social events during the winter, and what with his European plans and a diligent study of the German language, which the entire family undertook, his days and evenings were full enough. Howells wrote protesting against the European travel and berating him for his silence:*

*"I never was in Berlin and don't know any family hotel there. I should be glad I didn't, if it would keep you from going. You deserve to put up at the Sign of the Savage in Vienna. Really, it's a great blow to me to hear of that prospected sojourn. It's a shame. I must see you, somehow, before you go. I'm in dreadfully*

*low spirits about it.*

*"I was afraid your silence meant something wicked."*

*Clemens replied promptly, urging a visit to Hartford, adding a postscript for Mrs. Howells, characteristic enough to warrant preservation.*

P. S. to Mrs. Howells, in Boston:

*Feb. '78.*

*DEAR MRS. HOWELLS. Mrs. Clemens wrote you a letter, and handed it to me half an hour ago, while I was folding mine to Mr. Howells. I laid that letter on this table before me while I added the paragraph about R,'s application. Since then I have been hunting and swearing, and swearing and hunting, but I can't find a sign of that letter. It is the most astonishing disappearance I ever heard of. Mrs. Clemens has gone off driving—so I will have to try and give you an idea of her communication from memory. Mainly it consisted of an urgent desire that you come to see us next week, if you can possibly manage it, for that will be a reposeful time, the turmoil of breaking up beginning the week after. She wants you to tell her about Italy, and advise her in that connection, if you will. Then she spoke of her plans—hers, mind you, for I never have anything quite so definite as a plan. She proposes to stop a fortnight in (confound the place, I've forgotten what it was,) then go and live in Dresden till sometime in the summer; then retire to Switzerland for the hottest season, then stay a while in Venice and put in the winter in Munich. This program subject to modifications according to circumstances. She said something about some little by-trips here and there, but they didn't stick in my memory because the idea didn't charm me.*

(They have just telephoned me from the Courant office that Bayard Taylor and family have taken rooms in our ship, the Holsatia, for the 11th April.)

Do come, if you possibly can!—and remember and don't forget to avoid letting Mrs. Clemens find out I lost her letter. Just answer her the same as if you had got it.

*Sincerely yours*

*S. L. CLEMENS.*

*The Howellses came, as invited, for a final reunion before the breaking up. This was in the early half of March; the Clemenses were to sail on the 11th of the following month.*

*Orion Clemens, meantime, had conceived a new literary idea and was piling in his MS. as fast as possible to get his brother's judgment on it before the sailing-date. It was not a very good time to send MS., but Mark Twain seems to have read it and given it some consideration. "The Journey in Heaven," of his own, which he mentions, was the story published so many years later under the title of "Captain Stormfield's Visit to Heaven." He had began it in 1868, on his voyage to San Francisco, it having been suggested by conversations with Capt. Ned Wakeman, of one of the Pacific steamers. Wakeman also appears in 'Roughing It,' Chap. L, as Capt. Ned Blakely, and again in one of the "Rambling Notes of an Idle Excursion," as "Captain Hurricane Jones."*

To Orion Clemens, in Keokuk:

*HARTFORD, Mch. 23, 1878.*

MY DEAR BRO.,—Every man must learn his trade—not pick it up. God requires that he learn it by slow and painful processes. The apprentice-hand, in black-smithing, in medicine, in literature, in everything, is a thing that can't be hidden. It always shows.

But happily there is a market for apprentice work, else the "Innocents Abroad" would have had no sale. Happily, too, there's a wider market for some sorts of apprentice literature than there is for the very best of journey-work. This work of yours is exceedingly crude, but I am free to say it is less crude than I expected it to be, and considerably better work than I believed you could do, it is too crude to offer to any prominent periodical, so I shall speak to the N. Y. Weekly people. To publish it there will be to bury it. Why could not same good genius have sent me to the N. Y. Weekly with my apprentice sketches?

You should not publish it in book form at all—for this reason: it is only an imitation of Verne—it is not a burlesque. But I think it may be regarded as proof that Verne cannot be burlesqued.

In accompanying notes I have suggested that you vastly modify the first visit to hell, and leave out the second visit altogether. Nobody would, or ought to print those things. You are not advanced enough in literature to venture upon a matter requiring so much practice. Let me show you what a man has got to go through:

Nine years ago I mapped out my "Journey in Heaven." I discussed it with literary friends whom I could trust to keep it to themselves.

I gave it a deal of thought, from time to time. After a year or more I wrote it up. It was not a success. Five years ago I wrote it again, altering the plan. That MS is at my elbow now. It was a considerable improvement on the first attempt, but still it wouldn't do—last year and year before I talked frequently with Howells about the subject, and he kept urging me to do it again.

So I thought and thought, at odd moments and at last I struck what I considered to be the right plan! Mind I have never altered the ideas, from the first—the plan was the difficulty. When Howells was here last, I laid before him the whole story without referring to my MS and he said: "You have got it sure this time. But drop the idea of making mere magazine stuff of it. Don't waste it. Print it by itself—publish it first in England—ask Dean Stanley to endorse it, which will draw some of the teeth of the religious press, and then reprint in America." I doubt my ability to get Dean Stanley to do anything of the sort, but I shall do the rest—and this is all a secret which you must not divulge.

Now look here—I have tried, all these years, to think of some way of "doing" hell too—and have always had to give it up. Hell, in my book, will not occupy five pages of MS I judge—it will be only covert hints, I suppose, and quickly dropped, I may end by not even referring to it.

And mind you, in my opinion you will find that you can't write up hell so it will stand printing. Neither Howells nor I believe in hell or the divinity of the Savior, but no matter, the Savior is none the less a sacred Personage, and a man should have no desire or disposition to refer to him lightly, profanely, or otherwise than with the profoundest reverence.

The only safe thing is not to introduce him, or refer to him at all, I suspect. I have entirely rewritten one book 3 (perhaps 4.) times, changing the plan every time—1200 pages of MS. wasted and burned—and shall tackle it again, one of these years and maybe succeed at last. Therefore you need not expect to get your book right the first time. Go to work and revamp or rewrite it. God only exhibits his thunder and lightning at intervals, and so they always command attention. These are God's adjectives. You thunder and lightning too much; the reader ceases to get under the bed, by and by.

Mr. Perkins will send you and Ma your checks when we are gone. But don't write him, ever, except a single line in case he forgets the checks—for the man is driven to death with work.

I see you are half promising yourself a monthly return for your book. In my experience, previously counted chickens never do hatch. How many of mine I have counted! and never a one of them but failed! It is much better to hedge disappointment by not counting.—Unexpected money is a delight. The same sum is a bitterness when you expected more.

My time in America is growing mighty short. Perhaps we can manage in this way: Imprimis, if the N. Y. Weekly people know that you are my brother, they will turn that fact into an advertisement—a thing of value to them, but not to you and me. This must be prevented. I will write them a note to say you have a friend near Keokuk, Charles S. Miller, who has a MS for sale which you think is a pretty clever travesty on Verne; and if they want it they might write to him in your care. Then if any correspondence ensues between you and them, let Mollie write for you and sign your name—your own hand writing representing Miller's. Keep yourself out of sight till you make a strike on your own merits there is no other way to get a fair verdict upon your merits.

Later-I've written the note to Smith, and with nothing in it which he can use as an advertisement. I'm called—Good bye-love to you both.

We leave here next Wednesday for Elmira: we leave there Apl. 9 or 10—and sail 11th

*Yr Bro.*

*SAM.*

*In the letter that follows the mention of Annie and Sam refers, of course, to the children of Mrs. Moffett, who had been, Pamela Clemens. They were grown now, and Annie Moffett was married to*

*Charles L. Webster, who later was to become Mark Twain's business partner. The Moffetts and Websters were living in Fredonia at this time, and Clemens had been to pay them a good-by visit. The Taylor dinner mentioned was a farewell banquet given to Bayard Taylor, who had been appointed Minister to Germany, and was to sail on the ship with Mark Twain. Mark Twain's mother was visiting in Fredonia when this letter was written.*

To Mrs. Jane Clemens, in Fredonia:

*Apr. 7, '78.*

MY DEAR MOTHER,—I have told Livy all about Annie's beautiful house, and about Sam and Charley, and about Charley's ingenious manufactures and his strong manhood and good promise, and how glad I am that he and Annie married. And I have told her about Annie's excellent house-keeping, also about the great Bacon conflict; (I told you it was a hundred to one that neither Livy nor the European powers had heard of that desolating struggle.)

And I have told her how beautiful you are in your age and how bright your mind is with its old-time brightness, and how she and the children would enjoy you. And I have told her how singularly young Pamela is looking, and what a fine large fellow Sam is, and how ill the lingering syllable "my" to his name fits his port and figure.

Well, Pamela, after thinking it over for a day or so, I came near inquiring about a state-room in our ship for Sam, to please you, but my wiser former resolution came back to me. It is not for his good that he have friends in the ship. His conduct in the Bacon business shows that he will develop rapidly into a manly man as soon as he is cast loose from your apron strings.

You don't teach him to push ahead and do and dare things for himself, but you do just the reverse. You are assisted in your damaging work by the tyrannous ways of a village—villagers watch each other and so make cowards of each other. After Sam shall have voyaged to Europe by himself, and rubbed against the world and taken and returned its cuffs, do you think he will hesitate to escort a guest into any whisky-mill in Fredonia when he himself has no sinful business to transact there? No, he will smile at the idea. If he avoids this courtesy now from principle, of course I find no fault with it at all—only if he thinks it is principle he may be mistaken; a close examination may show it is only a bowing to the tyranny of public opinion.

I only say it may—I cannot venture to say it will. Hartford is not a large place, but it is broader than to have ways of that sort. Three or four weeks ago, at a Moody and Sankey meeting, the preacher read a letter from somebody "exposing" the fact that a prominent clergyman had gone from one of those meetings, bought a bottle of lager beer and drank it on the premises (a drug store.)

A tempest of indignation swept the town. Our clergymen and everybody else said the "culprit" had not only done an innocent thing, but had done it in an open, manly way, and it was nobody's right or business to find fault with it. Perhaps this dangerous latitude comes of the fact that we never have any temperance "rot" going on in Hartford.

I find here a letter from Orion, submitting some new matter in his story for criticism. When you write him, please tell him to do the best he can and bang away. I can do nothing further in this matter, for I have but 3 days left in which to settle a deal of important business and answer a bushel and a half of letters. I am very nearly tired to death.

I was so jaded and worn, at the Taylor dinner, that I found I could not remember 3 sentences of the speech I had memorized, and therefore got up and said so and excused myself from speaking. I arrived here at 3 o'clock this morning. I think the next 3 days will finish me. The idea of sitting down to a job of literary criticism is simply ludicrous.

A young lady passenger in our ship has been placed under Livy's charge. Livy couldn't easily get out of it, and did not want to, on her own account, but fully expected I would make trouble when I heard of it. But I didn't. A girl can't well travel alone, so I offered no objection. She leaves us at Hamburg. So I've got 6 people in my care, now—which is just 6 too many for a man of my unexecutive capacity. I expect nothing else but to lose some of them overboard.

We send our loving good-byes to all the household and hope to see you again after a spell.

*Affly Yrs.*

*SAM.*

*There are no other American letters of this period. The Clemens party, which included Miss Clara Spaulding, of Elmira, sailed as planned, on the Holsatia, April 11, 1878. As before stated, Bayard Taylor was on the ship; also Murat Halstead and family. On the eve of departure, Clemens sent to Howells this farewell word:*

*"And that reminds me, ungrateful dog that I am, that I owe as much to your training as the rude country job-printer owes to the city boss who takes him in hand and teaches him the right way to handle his art. I was talking to Mrs. Clemens about this the other day, and grieving because I never mentioned it to you, thereby seeming to ignore it, or to be unaware of it. Nothing that has passed under your eye needs any revision before going into a volume, while all my other stuff does need so much."*

*A characteristic tribute, and from the heart.*

*The first European letter came from Frankfort, a rest on their way to Heidelberg.*

To W. D. Howells, in Boston:

*FRANKFORT ON THE MAIN, May 4, 1878.*

MY DEAR HOWELLS,—I only propose to write a single line to say we are still around. Ah, I have such a deep, grateful, unutterable sense of being "out of it all." I think I foretaste some of the advantages of being dead. Some of the joy of it. I don't read any newspapers or care for them. When people tell me England has declared war, I drop the subject, feeling that it is none of my business; when they tell me Mrs. Tilton has confessed and Mr. B. denied, I say both of them have done that before, therefore let the worn stub of the Plymouth white-wash brush be brought out once more, and let the faithful spit on their hands and get to work again regardless of me—for I am out of it all.

We had 2 almost devilish weeks at sea (and I tell you Bayard Taylor is a really lovable man—which you already knew) then we staid a week in the beautiful, the very beautiful city of Hamburg; and since then we have been fooling along, 4 hours per day by rail, with a courier, spending the other 20 in hotels whose enormous bedchambers and private parlors are an overpowering marvel to me: Day before yesterday, in Cassel, we had a love of a bedroom, 31 feet long, and a parlor with 2 sofas, 12 chairs, a writing desk and 4 tables scattered around, here and there in it. Made of red silk, too, by George.

The times and times I wish you were along! You could throw some fun into the journey; whereas I go on, day by day, in a smileless state of solemn admiration.

What a paradise this is! What clean clothes, what good faces, what tranquil contentment, what prosperity, what genuine freedom, what superb government. And I am so happy, for I am responsible for none of it. I am only here to enjoy. How charmed I am when I overhear a German word which I understand. With love from us 2 to you 2.

*MARK.*

P. S. We are not taking six days to go from Hamburg to Heidelberg because we prefer it. Quite on the contrary. Mrs. Clemens picked up a dreadful cold and sore throat on board ship and still keeps them in stock—so she could only travel 4 hours a day. She wanted to dive straight through, but I had different notions about the wisdom of it. I found that 4 hours a day was the best she could do. Before I forget it, our permanent address is Care Messrs. Koester & Co., Backers, Heidelberg. We go there tomorrow.

Poor Susy! From the day we reached German soil, we have required Rosa to speak German to the children—which they hate with all their souls. The other morning in Hanover, Susy came to us (from Rosa, in the nursery) and said, in halting syllables, "Papa, vie viel uhr ist es?"—then turned with pathos in her big eyes, and said, "Mamma, I wish Rosa was made in English."

(Unfinished)

*Frankfort was a brief halting-place, their destination being Heidelberg. They were presently located there in the beautiful Schloss hotel, which overlooks the old castle with its forest setting, the flowing Neckar, and the distant valley of the Rhine. Clemens, who had discovered the location, and loved it, toward the end of May reported to Howells his felicities.*

Fragment of a letter to W. D. Howells, in Boston:

*SCHLOSS-HOTEL HEIDELBERG,*

*Sunday, a. m., May 26, 1878.*

MY DEAR HOWELLS,—....divinely located. From this airy porch among the shining groves we look down upon Heidelberg Castle, and upon the swift Neckar, and the town, and out over the wide green level of the Rhine valley—a marvelous prospect. We are in a Cul-de-sac formed of hill-ranges and river; we are on the side of a steep mountain; the river at our feet is walled, on its other side, (yes, on both sides,) by a steep and wooded mountain-range which rises abruptly aloft from the water's edge; portions of these mountains are densely wooded; the plain of the Rhine, seen through the mouth of this pocket, has many and peculiar charms for the eye.

Our bedroom has two great glass bird-cages (enclosed balconies) one looking toward the Rhine valley and sunset, the other looking up the Neckar cul-de-sac, and naturally we spend nearly all our time in these—when one is sunny the other is shady. We have tables and chairs in them; we do our reading, writing, studying, smoking and suppering in them.

The view from these bird-cages is my despair. The pictures change from one enchanting aspect to another in ceaseless procession, never keeping one form half an hour, and never taking on an unlovely one.

And then Heidelberg on a dark night! It is massed, away down there, almost right under us, you know, and stretches off toward the valley. Its curved and interlacing streets are a cobweb, beaded thick with lights—a wonderful thing to see; then the rows of lights on the arched bridges, and their glinting reflections in the water; and away at the far end, the Eisenbahnhof, with its twenty solid acres of glittering gas-jets, a huge garden, as one may say, whose every plant is a flame.

These balconies are the darlingest things. I have spent all the morning in this north one. Counting big and little, it has 256 panes of glass in it; so one is in effect right out in the free sunshine, and yet sheltered from wind and rain—and likewise doored and curtained from whatever may be going on in the bedroom. It must have been a noble genius who devised this hotel. Lord, how blessed is the repose, the tranquillity of this place! Only two sounds; the happy clamor of the birds in the groves, and the muffled music of the Neckar, tumbling over the opposing dykes. It is no hardship to lie awake awhile, nights, for this subdued roar has exactly the sound of a steady rain beating upon a roof. It is so healing to the spirit; and it bears up the thread of one's imaginings as the accompaniment bears up a song.

While Livy and Miss Spaulding have been writing at this table, I have sat tilted back, near by, with a pipe and the last Atlantic, and read Charley Warner's article with prodigious enjoyment. I think it is exquisite. I think it must be the roundest and broadest and completest short essay he has ever written. It is clear, and compact, and charmingly done.

The hotel grounds join and communicate with the Castle grounds; so we and the children loaf in the winding paths of those leafy vastnesses a great deal, and drink beer and listen to excellent music.

When we first came to this hotel, a couple of weeks ago, I pointed to a house across the river, and said I meant to rent the centre room on the 3d floor for a work-room. Jokingly we got to speaking of it as my office; and amused ourselves with watching "my people" daily in their small grounds and trying to make out what we could of their dress, &c., without a glass. Well, I loafed along there one day and found on that house the only sign of the kind on that side of the river: "Moblirte Wohnung zu Vermiethen!" I went in and rented that very room which I had long ago selected. There was only one other room in the whole double-house unrented.

(It occurs to me that I made a great mistake in not thinking to deliver a very bad German speech, every other sentence pieced out with English, at the Bayard Taylor banquet in New York. I think I could have made it one of the features of the occasion.)—[He used this plan at a gathering of the American students in Heidelberg, on July 4th, with great effect; so his idea was not wasted.]

We left Hartford before the end of March, and I have been idle ever since. I have waited for a call to go to work—I knew it would come. Well, it began to come a week ago; my note-book comes out more and more frequently every day since; 3 days ago I concluded to move my manuscript over to my den. Now the call is loud and decided at last. So tomorrow I shall begin regular, steady work, and stick to it till middle of July or 1st August, when I look for Twichell; we will then walk about Germany 2 or 3 weeks, and then I'll go to work again—(perhaps in Munich.)

We both send a power of love to the Howellses, and we do wish you were here. Are you in the new house? Tell us about it.

*Yrs Ever*

*MARK.*

*There has been no former mention in the letters of the coming of Twichell; yet this had been a part of the European plan. Mark Twain had invited his walking companion to make a tramp with him through Europe, as his guest. Material for the new book would grow faster with Twichell as a companion; and these two in spite of their widely opposed views concerning Providence and the general scheme of creation, were wholly congenial comrades. Twichell, in Hartford, expecting to receive the final summons to start, wrote: "Oh, my! do you realize, Mark, what a symposium it is to be? I do. To begin with, I am thoroughly tired, and the rest will be worth everything. To walk with you and talk with you for weeks together—why, it's my dream of luxury."*

*August 1st brought Twichell, and the friends set out without delay on a tramp through the Black Forest, making short excursions at first, but presently extending them in the direction of Switzerland. Mrs. Clemens and the others remained in Heidelberg, to follow at their leisure. To Mrs. Clemens her husband sent frequent reports of their wanderings. It will be seen that their tramp did not confine itself to pedestrianism, though they did, in fact, walk a great deal, and Mark Twain in a note to his mother declared, "I loathe all travel, except on foot." The reports to Mrs. Clemens follow:*

Letters to Mrs. Clemens, in Heidelberg:

*ALLERHEILIGEN Aug. 5, 1878 8:30 p.m.*

Livy darling, we had a rattling good time to-day, but we came very near being left at Baden-Baden, for instead of waiting in the waiting-room, we sat down on the platform to wait where the trains come in from the other direction. We sat there full ten minutes—and then all of a sudden it occurred to me that that was not the right place.

On the train the principal of the big English school at Nauheim (of which Mr. Scheiding was a teacher), introduced himself to me, and then he mapped out our day for us (for today and tomorrow) and also drew a map and gave us directions how to proceed through Switzerland. He had his entire school with him, taking them on a prodigious trip through Switzerland—tickets for the round trip ten dollars apiece. He has done this annually for 10 years. We took a post carriage from Aachen to Otterhofen for 7 marks—stopped at the "Pflug" to drink beer, and saw that pretty girl again at a distance. Her father, mother, and two brothers received me like an ancient customer and sat down and talked as long as I had any German left. The big room was full of red-vested farmers (the Gemeindrath of the district, with the Burgermeister at the head,) drinking beer and talking public business. They had held an election and chosen a new member and had been drinking beer at his expense for several hours. (It was intensely Black-foresty.)

There was an Australian there (a student from Stuttgart or somewhere,) and Joe told him who I was and he laid himself out to make our course plain, for us—so I am certain we can't get lost between here and Heidelberg.

We walked the carriage road till we came to that place where one sees the foot path on the other side of the ravine, then we crossed over and took that. For a good while we were in a dense forest and judged we were lost, but met a native women who said we were all right. We fooled along and got there at 6 p.m.—ate supper, then followed down the ravine to the foot of the falls, then struck into a blind path to see where it would go, and just about dark we fetched up at the Devil's Pulpit on top of the hills. Then home. And now to bed, pretty sleepy. Joe sends love and I send a thousand times as much, my darling.

*S. L. C.*

*HOTEL GENNIN.*

Livy darling, we had a lovely day jogged right along, with a good horse and sensible driver—the last two hours right behind an open carriage filled with a pleasant German family—old gentleman and 3 pretty daughters. At table d'hote tonight, 3 dishes were enough for me, and then I bored along tediously through the bill of fare, with a back-ache, not daring to get up and bow to the German family and leave. I meant to sit it through and make them get up and do the bowing; but at last Joe took pity on me and said he would get up and drop them a curtsy and put me out of my misery. I was grateful. He got up and delivered a succession of frank and hearty bows, accompanying them with an atmosphere of good-fellowship which would have made even an English family surrender. Of course the Germans responded—then I got right up and they had to respond to my salaams, too. So "that was done."

We walked up a gorge and saw a tumbling waterfall which was nothing to Giessbach, but it made me resolve to drop you a line and urge you to go and see Giessbach illuminated. Don't fail—but take a long day's rest, first. I love you, sweetheart.

*SAML.*

*OVER THE GEMMI PASS.*

*4.30 p.m. Saturday, Aug. 24, 1878.*

Livy darling, Joe and I have had a most noble day. Started to climb (on foot) at 8.30 this morning among the grandest peaks! Every half hour carried us back a month in the season. We left them harvesting 2d crop of hay. At 9 we were in July and found ripe strawberries; at 9.30 we were in June and gathered flowers belonging to that month; at 10 we were in May and gathered a flower which appeared in Heidelberg the 17th of that month; also forget-me-nots, which disappeared from Heidelberg about mid-May; at 11.30 we were in April (by the flowers;) at noon we had rain and hail mixed, and wind and enveloping fogs, and considered it March; at 12.30 we had snowbanks above us and snowbanks below us, and considered it February. Not good

February, though, because in the midst of the wild desolation the forget-me-not still bloomed, lovely as ever.

What a flower garden the Gemmi Pass is! After I had got my hands full Joe made me a paper bag, which I pinned to my lapel and filled with choice specimens. I gathered no flowers which I had ever gathered before except 4 or 5 kinds. We took it leisurely and I picked all I wanted to. I mailed my harvest to you a while ago. Don't send it to Mrs. Brooks until you have looked it over, flower by flower. It will pay.

Among the clouds and everlasting snows I found a brave and bright little forget-me-not growing in the very midst of a smashed and tumbled stone-debris, just as cheerful as if the barren and awful domes and ramparts that towered around were the blessed walls of heaven. I thought how Lilly Warner would be touched by such a gracious surprise, if she, instead of I, had seen it. So I plucked it, and have mailed it to her with a note.

Our walk was 7 hours—the last 2 down a path as steep as a ladder, almost, cut in the face of a mighty precipice. People are not allowed to ride down it. This part of the day's work taxed our knees, I tell you. We have been loafing about this village (Leukerbad) for an hour, now we stay here over Sunday. Not tired at all. (Joe's hat fell over the precipice—so he came here bareheaded.) I love you, my darling.

*SAML.*

*ST. NICHOLAS, Aug. 26th, '78.*

Livy darling, we came through a-whooping today, 6 hours tramp up steep hills and down steep hills, in mud and water shoe-deep, and in a steady pouring rain which never moderated a moment. I was as chipper and fresh as a lark all the way and arrived without the slightest sense of fatigue. But we were soaked and my shoes full of water, so we ate at once, stripped and went to bed for 2 1/2 hours while our traps were thoroughly dried, and our boots greased in addition. Then we put our clothes on hot and went to table d'hote.

Made some nice English friends and shall see them at Zermatt tomorrow.

Gathered a small bouquet of new flowers, but they got spoiled. I sent you a safety-match box full of flowers last night from Leukerbad.

I have just telegraphed you to wire the family news to me at Riffel tomorrow. I do hope you are all well and having as jolly a time as we are, for I love you, sweetheart, and also, in a measure, the Bays.—[Little Susy's word for "babies."]—Give my love to Clara Spaulding and also to the cubs.

*SAML.*

*This, as far as it goes, is a truer and better account of the excursion than Mark Twain gave in the book that he wrote later. A Tramp Abroad has a quality of burlesque in it, which did not belong to the journey at all, but was invented to satisfy the craving for what the public conceived to be Mark Twain's humor. The serious portions of the book are much more pleasing—more like himself. The entire journey, as will be seen, lasted one week more than a month.*

*Twichell also made his reports home, some of which give us interesting pictures of his walking partner. In one place he wrote: "Mark is a queer fellow. There is nothing he so delights in as a swift, strong stream. You can hardly get him to leave one when once he is within the influence of its fascinations."*

*Twichell tells how at Kandersteg they were out together one evening where a brook comes plunging down from Gasternthal and how he pushed in a drift to see it go racing along the current. "When I got back to the path Mark was running down stream after it as hard as he could go, throwing up his hands and shouting in the wildest ecstasy, and when a piece went over a fall and emerged to view in the foam below he would jump up and down and yell. He said afterward that he had not been so excited in three months."*

*In other places Twichell refers to his companion's consideration for the feeling of others, and for animals. "When we are driving, his concern is all about the horse. He can't bear to see the whip used, or to see a horse pull hard."*

After the walk over Gemmi Pass he wrote: "Mark to-day was immensely absorbed in flowers. He scrambled around and gathered a great variety, and manifested the intensest pleasure in them. He crowded a pocket of his note-book with his specimens, and wanted more room."

Whereupon Twichell got out his needle and thread and some stiff paper he had and contrived the little paper bag to hang to the front of his vest.

The tramp really ended at Lausanne, where Clemens joined his party, but a short excursion to Chillon and Chamonix followed, the travelers finally separating at Geneva, Twichell to set out for home by way of England, Clemens to remain and try to write the story of their travels. He hurried a good-by letter after his comrade:

To Rev. J. H. Twichell:

*(No date)*

DEAR OLD JOE,—It is actually all over! I was so low-spirited at the station yesterday, and this morning, when I woke, I couldn't seem to accept the dismal truth that you were really gone, and the pleasant tramping and talking at an end. Ah, my boy! it has been such a rich holiday to me, and I feel under such deep and honest obligations to you for coming. I am putting out of my mind all memory of the times when I misbehaved toward you and hurt you: I am resolved to consider it forgiven, and to store up and remember only the charming hours of the journeys and the times when I was not unworthy to be with you and share a companionship which to me stands first after Livy's. It is justifiable to do this; for why should I let my small infirmities of disposition live and grovel among my mental pictures of the eternal sublimities of the Alps?

Livy can't accept or endure the fact that you are gone. But you are, and we cannot get around it. So take our love with you, and bear it also over the sea to Harmony, and God bless you both.

*MARK.*

*From Switzerland the Clemens party worked down into Italy, sight-seeing, a diversion in which Mark Twain found little enough of interest. He had seen most of the sights ten years before, when his mind was fresh. He unburdened himself to Twichell and to Howells, after a period of suffering.*

To J. H. Twichell, in Hartford:

*ROME, Nov. 3, '78.*

DEAR JOE,—.....I have received your several letters, and we have prodigiously enjoyed them. How I do admire a man who can sit down and whale away with a pen just the same as if it was fishing—or something else as full of pleasure and as void of labor. I can't do it; else, in common decency, I would when I write to you. Joe, if I can make a book out of the matter gathered in your company over here, the book is safe; but I don't think I have gathered any matter before or since your visit worth writing up. I do wish you were in Rome to do my sightseeing for me. Rome interests me as much as East Hartford could, and no more. That is, the Rome which the average tourist feels an interest in; but there are other things here which stir me enough to make life worth living. Livy and Clara Spaulding are having a royal time worshiping the old Masters, and I as good a time gritting my ineffectual teeth over them.

A friend waits for me. A power of love to you all.

*Amen.*

*MARK.*

*In his letter to Howells he said: "I wish I could give those sharp satires on European life which you mention, but of course a man can't write successful satire except he be in a calm, judicial good-humor; whereas I hate travel, and I hate hotels, and I hate the opera, and I hate the old masters. In truth, I don't ever seem to be in a good-enough humor with anything to satirize it. No, I want to stand up before it and curse it and foam at the mouth, or take a club and pound it to rags and pulp. I have got in two or three chapters about Wagner's operas, and managed to do it without showing temper, but the strain of another such effort would burst me!"*

*From Italy the Clemens party went to Munich, where they had arranged in advance for winter quarters. Clemens claims, in his report of the matter to Howells, that he took the party through without the aid of a courier, though thirty years later, in some comment which he set down on being shown the letter, he wrote concerning this paragraph: "Probably a lie." He wrote, also, that they acquired a great affection for Fraulein Dahlweiner: "Acquired it at once and it outlasted the winter we spent in her house."*

To W. D. Howells, in Boston:

*No 1a, Karlstrasse, 2e Stock.*

*Care Fraulein Dahlweiner.*

*MUNICH, Nov. 17, 1878.*

MY DEAR HOWELLS,—We arrived here night before last, pretty well fagged: an 8-hour pull from Rome to Florence; a rest there of a day and two nights; then 5 1/2 hours to Bologna; one night's rest; then from noon to 10:30 p.m. carried us to Trent, in the Austrian Tyrol, where the confounded hotel had not received our message, and so at that miserable hour, in that snowy region, the tribe had to shiver together in fireless rooms while beds were prepared and warmed, then up at 6 in the morning and a noble view of snow-peaks glittering in the rich light of a full moon while the hotel-devils lazily deranged a breakfast for us in the dreary gloom of blinking candles; then a solid 12 hours pull through the loveliest snow ranges and snow-draped forest—and at 7 p.m. we hauled up, in drizzle and fog, at the domicile which had been engaged for us ten months before. Munich did seem the horriblest place, the most desolate place, the most unendurable place!—and the rooms were so small, the conveniences so meagre, and the porcelain stoves so grim, ghastly, dismal, intolerable! So Livy and Clara (Spaulding) sat down forlorn, and cried, and I retired to a private, place to pray. By and by we all retired to our narrow German beds; and when Livy and I finished talking across the room, it was all decided that we would rest 24 hours then pay whatever damages were required, and straightway fly to the south of France.

But you see, that was simply fatigue. Next morning the tribe fell in love with the rooms, with the weather, with Munich, and head over heels in love with Fraulein Dahlweiner. We got a larger parlor—an ample one—threw two communicating bedrooms into one, for the children, and now we are entirely comfortable. The only apprehension, at present, is that the climate may not be just right for the children, in which case we shall have to go to France, but it will be with the sincerest regret.

Now I brought the tribe through from Rome, myself. We never had so little trouble before. The next time anybody has a courier to put out to nurse, I shall not be in the market.

Last night the forlornities had all disappeared; so we gathered around the lamp, after supper, with our beer and my pipe, and in a condition of grateful snugness tackled the new magazines. I read your new story aloud, amid thunders of applause, and we all agreed that Captain Jenness and the old man with the accordion-hat are lovely people and most skillfully drawn—and that cabin-boy, too, we like. Of course we are all glad the girl is gone to Venice—for there is no place like Venice. Now I easily understand that the old man couldn't go, because you have a purpose in sending Lyddy by herself: but you could send the old man over in another ship, and we particularly want him along. Suppose you don't need him there? What of that? Can't you let him feed the doves? Can't you let him fall in the canal occasionally? Can't you let his good-natured purse be a daily prey to guides and beggar-boys? Can't you let him find peace and rest and fellowship under Pere Jacopo's kindly wing? (However, you are writing the book, not I—still, I am one of the people you are writing it for, you understand.) I only want to insist, in a friendly way, that the old man shall shed his sweet influence frequently upon the page—that is all.

The first time we called at the convent, Pere Jacopo was absent; the next (Just at this moment Miss Spaulding spoke up and said something about Pere Jacopo—there is more in this acting of one mind upon another than people think) time, he was there, and gave us preserved rose-leaves to eat, and talked about you, and Mrs. Howells, and Winnie, and brought out his photographs, and showed us a picture of "the library of your new house," but not so—it was the study in your Cambridge house. He was very sweet and good. He called on us next day; the day after that we left Venice, after a pleasant sojourn Of 3 or 4 weeks. He expects to spend this winter in Munich and will see us often, he said.

Pretty soon, I am going to write something, and when I finish it I shall know whether to put it to itself or in the "Contributors' Club." That "Contributors' Club" was a most happy idea. By the way, I think that the man who wrote the paragraph beginning at the bottom of page 643 has said a mighty sound and sensible thing. I wish his suggestion could be adopted.

It is lovely of you to keep that old pipe in such a place of honor.

While it occurs to me, I must tell you Susie's last. She is sorely badgered with dreams; and her stock dream is that she is being eaten up by bears. She is a grave and thoughtful child, as you will remember. Last night she had the usual dream. This morning she stood apart (after telling it,) for some time, looking vacantly at the floor, and absorbed in meditation. At last she looked up, and with the pathos of one who feels he has not been dealt by with even-handed fairness, said "But Mamma, the trouble is, that I am never the bear, but always the person."

It would not have occurred to me that there might be an advantage, even in a dream, in occasionally being the eater, instead of always the party eaten, but I easily perceived that her point was well taken.

I'm sending to Heidelberg for your letter and Winnie's, and I do hope they haven't been lost.

My wife and I send love to you all.

Yrs ever,

MARK.

The Howells story, running at this time in the Atlantic, and so much enjoyed by the Clemens party, was "The Lady of the Aroostook." The suggestions made for enlarging the part of the "old man" are eminently characteristic.

Mark Twain's forty-third birthday came in Munich, and in his letter conveying this fact to his mother we get a brief added outline of the daily life in that old Bavarian city. Certainly, it would seem to have been a quieter and more profitable existence than he had known amid the confusion of things left behind in, America.

To Mrs. Jane Clemens and Mrs. Moffett, in America:

*No. 1a Karlstrasse,*

*Dec. 1, MUNICH. 1878.*

MY DEAR MOTHER AND SISTER,—I broke the back of life yesterday and started down-hill toward old age. This fact has not produced any effect upon me that I can detect.

I suppose we are located here for the winter. I have a pleasant work-room a mile from here where I do my writing. The walk to and from that place gives me what exercise I need, and all I take. We staid three weeks in Venice, a week in Florence, a fortnight in Rome, and arrived here a couple of weeks ago. Livy and Miss Spaulding are studying drawing and German, and the children have a German day-governess. I cannot see but that the children speak German as well as they do English.

Susie often translates Livy's orders to the servants. I cannot work and study German at the same time: so I have dropped the latter, and do not even read the language, except in the morning paper to get the news.

We have all pretty good health, latterly, and have seldom had to call the doctor. The children have been in the open air pretty constantly for months now. In Venice they were on the water in the gondola most of the time, and were great friends with our gondolier; and in Rome and Florence they had long daily tramps, for Rosa is a famous hand to smell out the sights of a strange place. Here they wander less extensively.

The family all join in love to you all and to Orion and Mollie.

*Affly*

*Your son*

*SAM.*

## XIX. LETTERS 1879. RETURN TO AMERICA. THE GREAT GRANT REUNION

*Life went on very well in Munich. Each day the family fell more in love with Fraulein Dahlweiner and her house.*

*Mark Twain, however, did not settle down to his work readily. His "pleasant work-room" provided exercise, but no inspiration. When he discovered he could not find his Swiss note-book he was ready to give up his travel-writing altogether. In the letter that follows we find him much less enthusiastic concerning his own performances than over the story by Howells, which he was following in the Atlantic.*

*The "detective" chapter mentioned in this letter was not included in 'A Tramp Abroad.' It was published separately, as 'The Stolen White Elephant' in a volume bearing that title. The play, which he had now found "dreadfully witless and flat," was no other than "Simon Wheeler, Detective," which he had once regarded so highly. The "Stewart" referred to was the millionaire merchant, A. T. Stewart, whose body was stolen in the expectation of reward.*

To W. D. Howells, in Boston:

*MUNICH, Jan. 21, (1879)*

MY DEAR HOWELLS,—It's no use, your letter miscarried in some way and is lost. The consul has made a thorough search and says he has not been able to trace it. It is unaccountable, for all the letters I did not want arrived without a single grateful failure. Well, I have read-up, now, as far as you have got, that is, to where there's a storm at sea approaching,—and we three think you are clear, out-Howellsing Howells. If your literature has not struck perfection now we are not able to see what is lacking. It is all such truth—truth to the life; every where your pen falls it leaves a photograph. I did imagine that everything had been said about life at sea that could be said, but no matter, it was all a failure and lies, nothing but lies with a thin varnish of fact,—only you have stated it as it absolutely is. And only you see people and their ways, and their insides and outsides as they are, and make them talk as they do talk. I think you are the very greatest artist in these tremendous mysteries that ever lived. There doesn't seem to be anything that can be concealed from your awful all-seeing eye. It must be a cheerful thing for one to live with you and be aware that you are going up and down in him like another conscience all the time. Possibly you will not be a fully accepted classic until you have been dead a hundred years,—it is the fate of the Shakespeares and of all genuine prophets,—but then your books will be as common as Bibles, I believe. You're not a weed, but an oak; not a summer-house, but a cathedral. In that day I shall still be in the Cyclopedias, too, thus: "Mark Twain; history and occupation unknown—but he was personally acquainted with Howells." There—I could sing your praises all day, and feel and believe every bit of it.

My book is half finished; I wish to heaven it was done. I have given up writing a detective novel—can't write a novel, for I lack the faculty; but when the detectives were nosing around after Stewart's loud remains, I threw a chapter into my present book in which I have very extravagantly burlesqued the detective business—if it is possible to burlesque that business extravagantly. You know I was going to send you that detective play, so that you could re-write it. Well I didn't do it because I couldn't find a single idea in it that could be useful to you. It was dreadfully witless and flat. I knew it would sadden you and unfit you for work.

I have always been sorry we threw up that play embodying Orion which you began. It was a mistake to do that. Do keep that MS and tackle it again. It will work out all right; you will see. I don't believe that that character exists in literature in so well-developed a condition as it exists in Orion's person. Now won't you put Orion in a story? Then he will go handsomely into a play afterwards. How deliciously you could paint him—it would make fascinating reading—the sort that makes a reader laugh and cry at the same time, for Orion is as good and ridiculous a soul as ever was.

Ah, to think of Bayard Taylor! It is too sad to talk about. I was so glad there was not a single sting and so many good praiseful words in the Atlantic's criticism of Deukalion.

*Love to you all*

*Yrs Ever*

*MARK*

We remain here till middle of March.

*In 'A Tramp Abroad' there is an incident in which the author describes himself as hunting for a lost sock in the dark, in a vast hotel bedroom at Heilbronn. The account of the real incident, as written to Twichell, seems even more amusing.*

*The "Yarn About the Limburger Cheese and the Box of Guns," like "The Stolen White Elephant," did not find place in the travel-book, but was published in the same volume with the elephant story, added to the rambling notes of "An Idle Excursion."*

*With the discovery of the Swiss note-book, work with Mark Twain was going better. His letter reflects his enthusiasm.*

To Rev. J. H. Twichell, in Hartford:

*MUNICH, Jan 26 '79.*

DEAR OLD JOE,—Sunday. Your delicious letter arrived exactly at the right time. It was laid by my plate as I was finishing breakfast at 12 noon. Livy and Clara, (Spaulding) arrived from church 5 minutes later; I took a pipe and spread myself out on the sofa, and Livy sat by and read, and I warmed to that butcher the moment he began to swear. There is more than one way of praying, and I like the butcher's way because the petitioner is so apt to be in earnest. I was peculiarly alive to his performance just at this time, for another reason, to wit: Last night I awoke at 3 this morning, and after raging to my self for 2 interminable hours, I gave it up. I rose, assumed a catlike stealthiness, to keep from waking Livy, and proceeded to dress in the pitch dark. Slowly but surely I got on garment after garment—all down to one sock; I had one slipper on and the other in my hand. Well, on my hands and knees I crept softly around, pawing and feeling and scooping along the carpet, and among chair-legs for that missing sock; I kept that up; and still kept it up and kept it up. At first I only said to myself, "Blame that sock," but that soon ceased to answer; my expletives grew steadily stronger and stronger,—and at last, when I found I was lost, I had to sit flat down on the floor and take hold of something to keep from lifting the roof off with the profane explosion that was trying to get out of me. I could see the dim blur of the window, but of course it was in the wrong place and could give me no information as to where I was. But I had one comfort—I had not waked Livy; I believed I could find that sock in silence if the night lasted long enough. So I started again and softly pawed all over the place,—and sure enough at the end of half an hour I laid my hand on the missing article. I rose joyfully up and butted the wash-bowl and pitcher off the stand and simply raised——so to speak. Livy screamed, then said, "Who is that? what is the matter?" I said "There ain't anything the matter—I'm hunting for my sock." She said, "Are you hunting for it with a club?"

I went in the parlor and lit the lamp, and gradually the fury subsided and the ridiculous features of the thing began to suggest themselves. So I lay on the sofa, with note-book and pencil, and transferred the adventure to our big room in the hotel at Heilbronn, and got it on paper a good deal to my satisfaction.

I found the Swiss note-book, some time ago. When it was first lost I was glad of it, for I was getting an idea that I had lost my faculty of writing sketches of travel; therefore the loss of that note-book would render the writing of this one simply impossible, and let me gracefully out; I was about to write to Bliss and propose some other book, when the confounded thing turned up, and down went my heart into my boots. But there was now no excuse, so I went solidly to work—tore up a great part of the MS written in Heidelberg,—wrote and tore up,—continued to write and tear up,—and at last, reward of patient and noble persistence, my pen got the old swing again!

Since then I'm glad Providence knew better what to do with the Swiss note-book than I did, for I like my work, now, exceedingly, and often turn out over 30 MS pages a day and then quit sorry that Heaven makes the days so short.

One of my discouragements had been the belief that my interest in this tour had been so slender that I couldn't gouge matter enough out of it to make a book. What a mistake. I've got 900 pages written (not a word in it about the sea voyage) yet I stepped my foot out of Heidelberg for the first time yesterday,—and then only to take our party of four on our first pedestrian tour—to Heilbronn. I've got them dressed elaborately in walking costume—knapsacks, canteens, field-glasses, leather leggings, patent walking shoes, muslin folds around their hats, with long tails hanging down behind, sun umbrellas, and Alpenstocks. They go all the way to Wimpfen by rail-thence to Heilbronn in a chance vegetable cart drawn by a donkey and a cow; I shall fetch them home on a raft; and if other people shall perceive that that was no pedestrian excursion, they themselves shall not be conscious of it.—This trip will take 100 pages or more,—oh, goodness knows how many! for the mood is everything, not the material, and I already seem to see 300 pages rising before me on that trip. Then, I propose to leave Heidelberg for good. Don't you see, the book (1800 MS pages,) may really be finished before I ever get to Switzerland?

But there's one thing; I want to tell Frank Bliss and his father to be charitable toward me in,—that is, let me tear up all the MS I want to, and give me time to write more. I shan't waste the time—I haven't the slightest desire to loaf, but a consuming desire to work, ever since I got back my swing. And you see this book is either going to be compared with the Innocents Abroad, or contrasted with it, to my disadvantage. I think I can make a book that will be no dead corpse of a thing and I mean to do my level best to accomplish that.

My crude plans are crystalizing. As the thing stands now, I went to Europe for three purposes. The first you know, and must keep secret, even from the Blisses; the second is to study Art; and the third to acquire a critical knowledge of the German language. My MS already shows that the two latter objects are accomplished. It shows that I am moving about as an Artist and a Philologist, and unaware that there is any immodesty in assuming these titles. Having three definite objects has had the effect of seeming to enlarge my domain and give me the freedom of a loose costume. It is three strings to my bow, too.

Well, your butcher is magnificent. He won't stay out of my mind.—I keep trying to think of some way of getting your account of him into my book without his being offended—and yet confound him there isn't anything you have said which he would see any offense in,—I'm only thinking of his friends—they are the parties who busy themselves with seeing things for people. But I'm bound to have him in. I'm putting in the yarn about the Limburger cheese and the box of guns, too—mighty glad Howells declined it. It seems to gather richness and flavor with age. I have very nearly killed several companies with that narrative,—the American Artists Club, here, for instance, and Smith and wife and Miss Griffith (they were here in this house a week or two.) I've got other chapters that pretty nearly destroyed the same parties, too.

O, Switzerland! the further it recedes into the enriching haze of time, the more intolerably delicious the charm of it and the cheer of it and the glory and majesty and solemnity and pathos of it grow. Those mountains had a soul; they thought; they spoke,—one couldn't hear it with the ears of the body, but what a voice it was!—and how real. Deep down in my memory it is sounding yet. Alp calleth unto Alp!—that stately old Scriptural wording is the right one for God's Alps and God's ocean. How puny we were in that awful presence—and how painless it was to be so; how fitting and right it seemed, and how stingless was the sense of our unspeakable insignificance. And Lord how pervading were the repose and peace and blessedness that poured out of the heart of the invisible Great Spirit of the Mountains.

Now what is it? There are mountains and mountains and mountains in this world—but only these take you by the heart-strings. I wonder what the secret of it is. Well, time and time again it has seemed to me that I must drop everything and flee to Switzerland once more. It is a longing—a deep, strong, tugging longing—that is the word. We must go again, Joe.—October days, let us get up at dawn and breakfast at the tower. I should like that first rate.

Livy and all of us send deluges of love to you and Harmony and all the children. I dreamed last night that I woke up in the library at home and your children were frolicing around me and Julia was sitting in my lap; you and Harmony and both families of Warners had finished their welcomes and were filing out through the conservatory door, wrecking Patrick's flower pots with their dress skirts as they went. Peace and plenty abide with you all!

*MARK.*

I want the Blisses to know their part of this letter, if possible. They will see that my delay was not from choice.

> *Following the life of Mark Twain, whether through his letters or along the sequence of detailed occurrence, we are never more than a little while, or a little distance, from his brother Orion. In one form or another Orion is ever present, his inquiries, his proposals, his suggestions, his plans for improving his own fortunes, command our attention. He was one of the most human creatures that ever lived; indeed, his humanity excluded every form of artificiality*

*—everything that needs to be acquired. Talented, trusting, child-like, carried away by the impulse of the moment, despite a keen sense of humor he was never able to see that his latest plan or project was not bound to succeed. Mark Twain loved him, pitied him—also enjoyed him, especially with Howells. Orion's new plan to lecture in the interest of religion found its way to Munich, with the following result:*

To W. D. Howells, in Boston:

*MUNICH, Feb. 9. (1879)*

MY DEAR HOWELLS,—I have just received this letter from Orion—take care of it, for it is worth preserving. I got as far as 9 pages in my answer to it, when Mrs. Clemens shut down on it, and said it was cruel, and made me send the money and simply wish his lecture success. I said I couldn't lose my 9 pages—so she said send them to you. But I will acknowledge that I thought I was writing a very kind letter.

Now just look at this letter of Orion's. Did you ever see the grotesquely absurd and the heart-breakingly pathetic more closely joined together? Mrs. Clemens said "Raise his monthly pension." So I wrote to Perkins to raise it a trifle.

Now only think of it! He still has 100 pages to write on his lecture, yet in one inking of his pen he has already swooped around the United States and invested the result!

You must put him in a book or a play right away. You are the only man capable of doing it. You might die at any moment, and your very greatest work would be lost to the world. I could write Orion's simple biography, and make it effective, too, by merely stating the bald facts—and this I will do if he dies before I do; but you must put him into romance. This was the understanding you and I had the day I sailed.

Observe Orion's career—that is, a little of it: (1) He has belonged to as many as five different religious denominations; last March he withdrew from the deaconship in a Congregational Church and the Superintendency of its Sunday School, in a speech in which he said that for many months (it runs in my mind that he said 13 years,) he had been a confirmed infidel, and so felt it to be his duty to retire from the flock.

2. After being a republican for years, he wanted me to buy him a democratic newspaper. A few days before the Presidential election, he came out in a speech and publicly went over to the democrats; he prudently "hedged" by voting for 6 state republicans, also.

The new convert was made one of the secretaries of the democratic meeting, and placed in the list of speakers. He wrote me jubilantly of what a ten-strike he was going to make with that speech. All right—but think of his innocent and pathetic candor in writing me something like this, a week later:

"I was more diffident than I had expected to be, and this was increased by the silence with which I was received when I came forward; so I seemed unable to get the fire into my speech which I had calculated upon, and presently they began to get up and go out; and in a few minutes they all rose up and went away."

How could a man uncover such a sore as that and show it to another? Not a word of complaint, you see—only a patient, sad surprise.

3. His next project was to write a burlesque upon Paradise Lost.

4. Then, learning that the Times was paying Harte $100 a column for stories, he concluded to write some for the same price. I read his first one and persuaded him not to write any more.

5. Then he read proof on the N. Y. Eve. Post at $10 a week and meekly observed that the foreman swore at him and ordered him around "like a steamboat mate."

6. Being discharged from that post, he wanted to try agriculture—was

sure he could make a fortune out of a chicken farm. I gave him $900 and he went to a ten-house village a miles above Keokuk on the river bank—this place was a railway station. He soon asked for money to buy a horse and light wagon,—because the trains did not run at church time on Sunday and his wife found it rather far to walk.

For a long time I answered demands for "loans" and by next mail always received his check for the interest due me to date. In the most guileless way he let it leak out that he did not underestimate the value of his custom to me, since it was not likely that any other customer of mine paid his interest quarterly, and this enabled me to use my capital twice in 6 months instead of only once. But alas, when the debt at last reached $1800 or $2500 (I have forgotten which) the interest ate too formidably into his borrowings, and so he quietly ceased to pay it or speak of it. At the end of two years I found that the chicken farm had long ago been abandoned, and he had moved into Keokuk. Later in one of his casual moments, he observed that there was no money in fattening a chicken on 65 cents worth of corn and then selling it for 50.

7. Finally, if I would lend him $500 a year for two years, (this was 4 or 5 years ago,) he knew he could make a success as a lawyer, and would prove it. This is the pension which we have just increased to $600. The first year his legal business brought him $5. It also brought him an unremunerative case where some villains were trying to chouse some negro orphans out of $700. He still has this case. He has waggled it around through various courts and made some booming speeches on it. The negro children have grown up and married off, now, I believe, and their litigated town-lot has been dug up and carted off by somebody—but Orion still infests the courts with his documents and makes the welkin ring with his venerable case. The second year, he didn't make anything. The third he made $6, and I made Bliss put a case in his hands—about half an hour's work. Orion charged $50 for it—Bliss paid him $15. Thus four or five years of slaving has brought him $26, but this will doubtless be increased when he gets done lecturing and buys that "law library." Meantime his office rent has been $60 a year, and he has stuck to that lair day by day as patiently as a spider.

8. Then he by and by conceived the idea of lecturing around America as "Mark Twain's Brother"—that to be on the bills. Subject of proposed lecture, "On the Formation of Character."

9. I protested, and he got on his warpaint, couched his lance, and ran a bold tilt against total abstinence and the Red Ribbon fanatics. It raised a fine row among the virtuous Keokukians.

10. I wrote to encourage him in his good work, but I had let a mail intervene; so by the time my letter reached him he was already winning laurels as a Red Ribbon Howler.

11. Afterward he took a rabid part in a prayer-meeting epidemic; dropped that to travesty Jules Verne; dropped that, in the middle of the last chapter, last March, to digest the matter of an infidel book which he proposed to write; and now he comes to the surface to rescue our "noble and beautiful religion" from the sacrilegious talons of Bob Ingersoll.

Now come! Don't fool away this treasure which Providence has laid at your feet, but take it up and use it. One can let his imagination run riot in portraying Orion, for there is nothing so extravagant as to be out of character with him.

Well-good-bye, and a short life and a merry one be yours. Poor old Methusaleh, how did he manage to stand it so long?

*Yrs ever,*

*MARK.*

To Orion Clemens Unsent and inclosed with the foregoing, to W. D. Howells:

*MUNICH, Feb. 9, (1879)*

MY DEAR BRO.,—Yours has just arrived. I enclose a draft on Hartford for $25. You will have abandoned the project you wanted it for, by the time it arrives,—but no matter, apply it to your newer and present project, whatever it is. You see I have an ineradicable faith in your unsteadfastness,—but mind you, I didn't invent that faith, you conferred it on me yourself. But fire away, fire away! I don't see why a changeable man shouldn't get as much enjoyment out of his changes, and transformations and transfigurations as a steadfast man gets out of standing still and pegging at the same old monotonous thing all the time. That is to say, I don't see why a kaleidoscope shouldn't enjoy itself as much as a telescope, nor a grindstone have as good a time as a whetstone, nor a barometer as good a time as a yardstick. I don't feel like girding at you any more about fickleness of purpose, because I recognize and realize at last that it is incurable; but before I learned to accept this truth, each new weekly project of yours possessed the power of throwing me into the most exhausting and helpless convulsions of profanity. But fire away, now! Your magic has lost its might. I am able to view your inspirations dispassionately and judicially, now, and say "This one or that one or the other one is not up to your average flight, or is above it, or below it."

And so, without passion, or prejudice, or bias of any kind, I sit in judgment upon your lecture project, and say it was up to your average, it was indeed above it, for it had possibilities in it, and even practical ones. While I was not sorry you abandoned it, I should not be sorry if you had stuck to it and given it a trial. But on the whole you did the wise thing to lay it aside, I think, because a lecture is a most easy thing to fail in; and at your time of life, and in your own town, such a failure would make a deep and cruel wound in your heart and in your pride. It was decidedly unwise in you to think for a moment of coming before a community who knew you, with such a course of lectures; because Keokuk is not unaware that you have been a Swedenborgian, a Presbyterian, a Congregationalist, and a Methodist (on probation), and that just a year ago you were an infidel. If Keokuk had gone to your lecture course, it would have gone to be amused, not instructed, for when a man is known to have no settled convictions of his own he can't convince other people. They would have gone to be amused and that would have been a deep humiliation to you. It could have been safe for you to appear only where you were unknown—then many of your hearers would think you were in earnest. And they would be right. You are in earnest while your convictions are new. But taking it by and large, you probably did best to discard that project altogether. But I leave you to judge of that, for you are the worst judge I know of.

(Unfinished.)

*That Mark Twain in many ways was hardly less child-like than his brother is now and again revealed in his letters. He was of steadfast purpose, and he possessed the driving power which Orion Clemens lacked; but the importance to him of some of the smaller matters of life, as shown in a letter like the following, bespeaks a certain simplicity of nature which he never outgrew:*

To Rev. J. H. Twichell, in Hartford:

*MUNICH, Feb. 24. (1879)*

DEAR OLD JOE,—It was a mighty good letter, Joe—and that idea of yours is a rattling good one. But I have not sot down here to answer your letter,—for it is down at my study,—but only to impart some information.

For a months I had not shaved without crying. I'd spend 3/4 of an hour whetting away on my hand—no use, couldn't get an edge. Tried a razor strop-same result. So I sat down and put in an hour thinking out the mystery. Then it seemed plain—to wit: my hand can't give a razor an edge, it can only smooth and refine an edge that has already been given. I judge that a razor fresh from the hone is this shape V—the long point being the continuation of the edge—and that after much use the shape is this V—the attenuated edge all worn off and gone. By George I knew that was the explanation. And I knew that a freshly honed and freshly strapped razor won't cut, but after strapping on the hand as a final operation, it will cut.—So I sent out for an oil-stone; none to be had, but messenger brought back a little piece of rock the size of a Safety-match box—(it was bought in a shoemaker's shop) bad flaw in middle of it, too, but I put 4 drops of fine Olive oil on it, picked out the razor marked "Thursday" because it was never any account and would be no loss if I spoiled it—gave it a brisk and reckless honing for 10 minutes, then tried it on a hair—it wouldn't cut. Then I trotted it through a vigorous 20-minute course on a razor-strap and tried it on a hair-it wouldn't cut—tried it on my face—it made me cry—gave it a 5-minute stropping on my hand, and my land, what an edge she had! We thought we knew what sharp razors were when we were tramping in Switzerland, but it was a mistake—they were dull beside this old Thursday razor of mine—which I mean to name Thursday October Christian, in gratitude. I took my whetstone, and in 20 minutes I put two more of my razors in splendid condition—but I leave them in the box—I never use any but Thursday O. C., and shan't till its edge is gone—and then I'll know how to restore it without any delay.

We all go to Paris next Thursday—address, Monroe & Co., Bankers.

*With love*

*Ys Ever*

*MARK.*

*In Paris they found pleasant quarters at the Hotel Normandy, but it was a chilly, rainy spring, and the travelers gained a rather poor impression of the French capital. Mark Twain's work did not go well, at first, because of the noises of the street. But then he found a quieter corner in the hotel and made better progress. In a brief note to Aldrich he said: "I sleep like a lamb and write like a lion—I mean the kind of a lion that writes—if any such." He expected to finish the book in six weeks; that is to say, before returning to America. He was looking after its illustrations himself, and a letter to Frank Bliss, of The American Publishing Company, refers to the frontpiece, which, from time to time, has caused question as to its origin. To Bliss he says: "It is a thing which I manufactured by pasting a popular comic picture into the middle of a celebrated Biblical one—shall attribute it to Titian. It needs to be engraved by a master."*

*The weather continued bad in France and they left there in July to find it little better in England. They had planned a journey to Scotland to visit Doctor Brown, whose health was not very good. In after years Mark Twain blamed himself harshly for not making the trip, which he declared would have meant so much to Mrs. Clemens. He had forgotten by that time the real reasons for not going—the continued storms and uncertainty of trains (which made it barely possible for them to reach Liverpool in time for their sailing-date), and with characteristic self-reproach vowed that only perversity and obstinacy on his part had prevented the journey to Scotland. From Liverpool, on the eve of sailing, he sent Doctor Brown a good-by word.*

To Dr. John Brown, in Edinburgh:

*WASHINGTON HOTEL, LIME STREET, LIVERPOOL.*

*Aug. (1879)*

MY DEAR MR. BROWN,—During all the 15 months we have been spending on the continent, we have been promising ourselves a sight of you as our latest and most prized delight in a foreign land—but our hope has failed, our plan has miscarried. One obstruction after another intruded itself, and our short sojourn of three or four weeks on English soil was thus frittered gradually away, and we were at last obliged to give up the idea of seeing you at all. It is a great disappointment, for we wanted to show you how much "Megalopis" has grown (she is 7 now) and what a fine creature her sister is, and how prettily they both speak German. There are six persons in my party, and they are as difficult to cart around as nearly any other menagerie would be. My wife and Miss Spaulding are along, and you may imagine how they take to heart this failure of our long promised Edinburgh trip. We never even wrote you, because we were always so sure, from day to day, that our affairs would finally so shape themselves as to let us get to Scotland. But no,—everything went wrong we had only flying trips here and there in place of the leisurely ones which we had planned.

We arrived in Liverpool an hour ago very tired, and have halted at this hotel (by the advice of misguided friends)—and if my instinct and experience are worth anything, it is the very worst hotel on earth, without any exception. We shall move to another hotel early in the morning to spend to-morrow. We sail for America next day in the "Gallic."

We all join in the sincerest love to you, and in the kindest remembrance to "Jock"—[Son of Doctor Brown.]—and your sister.

*Truly yours,*

*S. L. CLEMENS.*

*It was September 3, 1879, that Mark Twain returned to America by the steamer Gallic. In the seventeen months of his absence he had taken on a "traveled look" and had added gray hairs. A New York paper said of his arrival that he looked older than when he went to Germany, and that his hair had turned quite gray.*

*Mark Twain had not finished his book of travel in Paris—in fact, it seemed to him far from complete—and he settled down rather grimly to work on it at Quarry Farm. When, after a few days no word of greeting came from Howells, Clemens wrote to ask if he were dead or only sleeping. Howells hastily sent a line to say that he had been sleeping "The sleep of a torpid conscience. I will feign that I did not know where to write you; but I love you and all of yours, and I am tremendously glad that you are home again. When and where shall we meet? Have you come home with your pockets full of Atlantic papers?" Clemens, toiling away at his book, was, as usual, not without the prospect of other plans. Orion, as literary material, never failed to excite him.*

To W. D. Howells, in Boston:

*ELMIRA, Sept. 15, 1879.*

MY DEAR HOWELLS,—When and where? Here on the farm would be an elegant place to meet, but of course you cannot come so far. So we will say Hartford or Belmont, about the beginning of November. The date of our return to Hartford is uncertain, but will be three or four weeks hence, I judge. I hope to finish my book here before migrating.

I think maybe I've got some Atlantic stuff in my head, but there's none in MS, I believe.

Say—a friend of mine wants to write a play with me, I to furnish the broad-comedy cuss. I don't know anything about his ability, but his letter serves to remind me of our old projects. If you haven't used Orion or Old Wakeman, don't you think you and I can get together and grind out a play with one of those fellows in it? Orion is a field which grows richer and richer the more he mulches it with each new top-dressing of religion or other guano. Drop me an immediate line about this, won't you? I imagine I see Orion on the stage, always gentle, always melancholy, always changing his politics and religion, and trying to reform the world, always inventing something, and losing a limb by a new kind of explosion at the end of each of the four acts. Poor old chap, he is good material. I can imagine his wife or his sweetheart reluctantly adopting each of his new religious in turn, just in time to see him waltz into the next one and leave her isolated once more.

(Mem. Orion's wife has followed him into the outer darkness, after 30 years' rabid membership in the Presbyterian Church.)

Well, with the sincerest and most abounding love to you and yours, from all this family, I am,

*Yrs ever*

*MARK.*

*The idea of the play interested Howells, but he had twinges of conscience in the matter of using Orion as material. He wrote: "More than once I have taken the skeleton of that comedy of ours and viewed it with tears..... I really have a compunction or two about helping to put your brother into drama. You can say that he is your brother, to do what you like with him, but the alien hand might inflict an incurable hurt on his tender heart."*

*As a matter of fact, Orion Clemens had a keen appreciation of his own shortcomings, and would have enjoyed himself in a play as much as any observer of it. Indeed, it is more than likely that he would have been pleased at the thought of such distinguished dramatization. From the next letter one might almost conclude that he had received a hint of this plan, and was bent upon supplying rich material.*

To W. D. Howells, in Boston:

*ELMIRA, Oct. 9 '79.*

MY DEAR HOWELLS,—Since my return, the mail facilities have enabled Orion to keep me informed as to his intentions. Twenty-eight days ago it was his purpose to complete a work aimed at religion, the preface to which he had already written. Afterward he began to sell off his furniture, with the idea of hurrying to Leadville and tackling silver-mining—threw up his law den and took in his sign. Then he wrote to Chicago and St. Louis newspapers asking for a situation as "paragrapher"—enclosing a taste of his quality in the shape of two stanzas of "humorous rhymes." By a later mail on the same day he applied to New York and Hartford insurance companies for copying to do.

However, it would take too long to detail all his projects. They comprise a removal to south-west Missouri; application for a reporter's berth on a Keokuk paper; application for a compositor's berth on a St. Louis paper; a re-hanging of his attorney's sign, "though it only creaks and catches no flies;" but last night's letter informs me that he has retackled the religious question, hired a distant den to write in, applied to my mother for $50 to re-buy his furniture, which has advanced in value since the sale—purposes buying $25 worth of books necessary to his labors which he had previously been borrowing, and his first chapter is already on its way to me for my decision as to whether it has enough ungodliness in it or not. Poor Orion!

Your letter struck me while I was meditating a project to beguile you, and John Hay and Joe Twichell, into a descent upon Chicago which I dream of making, to witness the re-union of the great Commanders of the Western Army Corps on the 9th of next month. My sluggish soul needs a fierce upstirring, and if it would not get it when Grant enters the meeting place I must doubtless "lay" for the final resurrection. Can you and Hay go? At the same time, confound it, I doubt if I can go myself, for this book isn't done yet. But I would give a heap to be there. I mean to heave some holiness into the Hartford primaries when I go back; and if there was a solitary office in the land which majestic ignorance and incapacity, coupled with purity of heart, could fill, I would run for it. This naturally reminds me of Bret Harte—but let him pass.

We propose to leave here for New York Oct. 21, reaching Hartford 24th or 25th. If, upon reflection, you Howellses find, you can stop over here on your way, I wish you would do it, and telegraph me. Getting pretty hungry to see you. I had an idea that this was your shortest way home, but like as not my geography is crippled again—it usually is.

*Yrs ever*

*MARK.*

*The "Reunion of the Great Commanders," mentioned in the foregoing, was a welcome to General Grant after his journey around the world. Grant's trip had been one continuous ovation—a triumphal march. In '79 most of his old commanders were still alive, and they had planned to assemble in Chicago to do him honor. A Presidential year was coming on, but if there was anything political in the project there were no surface indications. Mark Twain, once a Confederate soldier, had long since been completely "desouthernized"—at least to the point where he felt that the sight of old comrades paying tribute to the Union commander would stir his blood as perhaps it had not been stirred, even in that earlier time, when that same commander had chased him through the Missouri swamps. Grant, indeed, had long since become a hero to Mark Twain, though it is highly unlikely that Clemens favored the idea of a third term. Some days following the preceding letter an invitation came for him to be present at the Chicago reunion; but by this time he had decided not to go. The letter he wrote has been preserved.*

To Gen. William E. Strong, in Chicago:

*FARMINGTON AVENUE, HARTFORD.*

*Oct. 28, 1879.*

GEN. WM. E. STRONG, CH'M, AND GENTLEMEN OF THE COMMITTEE:

I have been hoping during several weeks that it might be my good fortune to receive an invitation to be present on that great occasion in Chicago; but now that my desire is accomplished my business matters have so shaped themselves as to bar me from being so far from home in the first half of November. It is with supreme regret that I lost this chance, for I have not had a thorough stirring up for some years, and I judged that if I could be in the banqueting hall and see and hear the veterans of the Army of the Tennessee at the moment that their old commander entered the room, or rose in his place to speak, my system would get the kind of upheaval it needs. General Grant's progress across the continent is of the marvelous nature of the returning Napoleon's progress from Grenoble to Paris; and as the crowning spectacle in the one case was the meeting with the Old Guard, so, likewise, the crowning spectacle in the other will be our great captain's meeting with his Old Guard—and that is the very climax which I wanted to witness.

Besides, I wanted to see the General again, any way, and renew the acquaintance. He would remember me, because I was the person who did not ask him for an office. However, I consume your time, and also wander from the point—which is, to thank you for the courtesy of your invitation, and yield up my seat at the table to some other guest who may possibly grace it better, but will certainly not appreciate its privileges more, than I should.

*With great respect,*

*I am, Gentlemen,*

*Very truly yours,*

*S. L. CLEMENS.*

Private:—I beg to apologize for my delay, gentlemen, but the card of invitation went to Elmira, N. Y. and hence has only just now reached me.

*This letter was not sent. He reconsidered and sent an acceptance, agreeing to speak, as the committee had requested. Certainly there was something picturesque in the idea of the Missouri private who had been chased for a rainy fortnight through the swamps of Ralls County being selected now to join in welcome to his ancient enemy.*

*The great reunion was to be something more than a mere banquet. It would continue for several days, with processions, great assemblages, and much oratory.*

*Mark Twain arrived in Chicago in good season to see it all. Three letters to Mrs. Clemens intimately present his experiences: his enthusiastic enjoyment and his own personal triumph.*

*The first was probably written after the morning of his arrival. The Doctor Jackson in it was Dr. A. Reeves Jackson, the guide-dismaying "Doctor" of Innocents Abroad.*

To Mrs. Clemens, in Hartford:

*PALMER HOUSE, CHICAGO, Nov. 11.*

Livy darling, I am getting a trifle leg-weary. Dr. Jackson called and dragged me out of bed at noon, yesterday, and then went off. I went down stairs and was introduced to some scores of people, and among them an elderly German gentleman named Raster, who said his wife owed her life to me—hurt in Chicago fire and lay menaced with death a long time, but the Innocents Abroad kept her mind in a cheerful attitude, and so, with the doctor's help for the body she pulled through.... They drove me to Dr. Jackson's and I had an hour's visit with Mrs. Jackson. Started to walk down Michigan Avenue, got a few steps on my way and met an erect, soldierly looking young gentleman who offered his hand; said, "Mr. Clemens, I believe—I wish to introduce myself—you were pointed out to me yesterday as I was driving down street—my name is Grant."

"Col. Fred Grant?"

"Yes. My house is not ten steps away, and I would like you to come and have a talk and a pipe, and let me introduce my wife."

So we turned back and entered the house next to Jackson's and talked something more than an hour and smoked many pipes and had a sociable good time. His wife is very gentle and intelligent and pretty, and they have a cunning little girl nearly as big as Bay but only three years old. They wanted me to come in and spend an evening, after the banquet, with them and Gen. Grant, after this grand pow-wow is over, but I said I was going home Friday. Then they asked me to come Friday afternoon, when they and the general will receive a few friends, and I said I would. Col. Grant said he and Gen. Sherman used the Innocents Abroad as their guide book when they were on their travels.

I stepped in next door and took Dr. Jackson to the hotel and we played billiards from 7 to 11.30 P.M. and then went to a beer-mill to meet some twenty Chicago journalists—talked, sang songs and made speeches till 6 o'clock this morning. Nobody got in the least degree "under the influence," and we had a pleasant time. Read awhile in bed, slept till 11, shaved, went to breakfast at noon, and by mistake got into the servants' hall. I remained there and breakfasted with twenty or thirty male and female servants, though I had a table to myself.

A temporary structure, clothed and canopied with flags, has been erected at the hotel front, and connected with the second-story windows of a drawing-room. It was for Gen. Grant to stand on and review the procession. Sixteen persons, besides reporters, had tickets for this place, and a seventeenth was issued for me. I was there, looking down on the packed and struggling crowd when Gen. Grant came forward and was saluted by the cheers of the multitude and the waving of ladies' handkerchiefs—for the windows and roofs of all neighboring buildings were massed full of life. Gen. Grant bowed to the people two or three times, then approached my side of the platform and the mayor pulled me forward and introduced me. It was dreadfully conspicuous. The General said a word or so—I replied, and then said, "But I'll step back, General, I don't want to interrupt your speech."

"But I'm not going to make any—stay where you are—I'll get you to make it for me."

General Sherman came on the platform wearing the uniform of a full General, and you should have heard the cheers. Gen. Logan was going to introduce me, but I didn't want any more conspicuousness.

When the head of the procession passed it was grand to see Sheridan, in his military cloak and his plumed chapeau, sitting as erect and rigid as a statue on his immense black horse—by far the most martial figure I ever saw. And the crowd roared again.

It was chilly, and Gen. Deems lent me his overcoat until night. He came a few minutes ago—5.45 P.M., and got it, but brought Gen. Willard, who lent me his for the rest of my stay, and will get another for himself when he goes home to dinner. Mine is much too heavy for this warm weather.

I have a seat on the stage at Haverley's Theatre, tonight, where the Army of the Tennessee will receive Gen. Grant, and where Gen. Sherman will make a speech. At midnight I am to attend a meeting of the Owl Club.

I love you ever so much, my darling, and am hoping to get a word from you yet.

*SAML.*

*Following the procession, which he describes, came the grand ceremonies of welcome at Haverley's Theatre. The next letter is written the following morning, or at least soiree time the following day, after a night of ratification.*

To Mrs. Clemens, in Hartford:

*CHICAGO, Nov. 12, '79.*

Livy darling, it was a great time. There were perhaps thirty people on the stage of the theatre, and I think I never sat elbow-to-elbow with so many historic names before. Grant, Sherman, Sheridan, Schofield, Pope, Logan, Augur, and so on. What an iron man Grant is! He sat facing the house, with his right leg crossed over his left and his right boot-sole tilted up at an angle, and his left hand and arm reposing on the arm of his chair—you note that position? Well, when glowing references were made to other grandees on the stage, those grandees always showed a trifle of nervous consciousness—and as these references came frequently, the nervous change of position and attitude were also frequent. But Grant!—he was under a tremendous and ceaseless bombardment of praise and gratulation, but as true as I'm sitting here he never moved a muscle of his body for a single instant, during 30 minutes! You could have played him on a stranger for an effigy. Perhaps he never would have moved, but at last a speaker made such a particularly ripping and blood-stirring remark about him that the audience rose and roared and yelled and stamped and clapped an entire minute—Grant sitting as serene as ever—when Gen. Sherman stepped to him, laid his hand affectionately on his shoulder, bent respectfully down and whispered in his ear. Gen. Grant got up and bowed, and the storm of applause swelled into a hurricane. He sat down, took about the same position and froze to it till by and by there was another of those deafening and protracted roars, when Sherman made him get up and bow again. He broke up his attitude once more—the extent of something more than a hair's breadth—to indicate me to Sherman when the house was keeping up a determined and persistent call for me, and poor bewildered Sherman, (who did not know me), was peering abroad over the packed audience for me, not knowing I was only three feet from him and most conspicuously located, (Gen. Sherman was Chairman.)

One of the most illustrious individuals on that stage was "Ole Abe," the historic war eagle. He stood on his perch—the old savage-eyed rascal—three or four feet behind Gen. Sherman, and as he had been in nearly every battle that was mentioned by the orators his soul was probably stirred pretty often, though he was too proud to let on.

Read Logan's bosh, and try to imagine a burly and magnificent Indian, in General's uniform, striking a heroic attitude and getting that stuff off in the style of a declaiming school-boy.

Please put the enclosed scraps in the drawer and I will scrap-book them.

I only staid at the Owl Club till 3 this morning and drank little or nothing. Went to sleep without whisky. Ich liebe dish.

*SAML.*

*But it is in the third letter that we get the climax. On the same day he wrote a letter to Howells, which, in part, is very similar in substance and need not be included here.*

*A paragraph, however, must not be omitted.*

*"Imagine what it was like to see a bullet-shredded old battle-flag reverently unfolded to the gaze of a thousand middle-aged soldiers, most of whom hadn't seen it since they saw it advancing over victorious fields, when they were in their prime. And imagine what it was like when Grant, their first commander, stepped into view while they were still going mad over the flag, and then right in the*

*midst of it all somebody struck up, 'When we were marching through Georgia.' Well, you should have heard the thousand voices lift that chorus and seen the tears stream down. If I live a hundred years I shan't ever forget these things, nor be able to talk about them.... Grand times, my boy, grand times!"*

*At the great banquet Mark Twain's speech had been put last on the program, to hold the house. He had been invited to respond to the toast of "The Ladies," but had replied that he had already responded to that toast more than once. There was one class of the community, he said, commonly overlooked on these occasions—the babies—he would respond to that toast. In his letter to Howells he had not been willing to speak freely of his personal triumph, but to Mrs. Clemens he must tell it all, and with that child-like ingenuousness which never failed him to his last day.*

To Mrs. Clemens, in Hartford:

*CHICAGO, Nov. 14 '79.*

A little after 5 in the morning.

I've just come to my room, Livy darling, I guess this was the memorable night of my life. By George, I never was so stirred since I was born. I heard four speeches which I can never forget. One by Emory Storrs, one by Gen. Vilas (O, wasn't it wonderful!) one by Gen. Logan (mighty stirring), one by somebody whose name escapes me, and one by that splendid old soul, Col. Bob Ingersoll,—oh, it was just the supremest combination of English words that was ever put together since the world began. My soul, how handsome he looked, as he stood on that table, in the midst of those 500 shouting men, and poured the molten silver from his lips! Lord, what an organ is human speech when it is played by a master! All these speeches may look dull in print, but how the lightning glared around them when they were uttered, and how the crowd roared in response! It was a great night, a memorable night. I am so richly repaid for my journey—and how I did wish with all my whole heart that you were there to be lifted into the very seventh heaven of enthusiasm, as I was. The army songs, the military music, the crashing applause—Lord bless me, it was unspeakable.

Out of compliment they placed me last in the list—No. 15—I was to "hold the crowd"—and bless my life I was in awful terror when No. 14. rose, at a o'clock this morning and killed all the enthusiasm by delivering the flattest, insipidest, silliest of all responses to "Woman" that ever a weary multitude listened to. Then Gen. Sherman (Chairman) announced my toast, and the crowd gave me a good round of applause as I mounted on top of the dinner table, but it was only on account of my name, nothing more—they were all tired and wretched. They let my first sentence go in silence, till I paused and added "we stand on common ground"—then they burst forth like a hurricane and I saw that I had them! From that time on, I stopped at the end of each sentence, and let the tornado of applause and laughter sweep around me—and when I closed with "And if the child is but the prophecy of the man, there are mighty few who will doubt that he succeeded," I say it who oughtn't to say it, the house came down with a crash. For two hours and a half, now, I've been shaking hands and listening to congratulations. Gen. Sherman said, "Lord bless you, my boy, I don't know how you do it—it's a secret that's beyond me—but it was great—give me your hand again."

And do you know, Gen. Grant sat through fourteen speeches like a graven image, but I fetched him! I broke him up, utterly! He told me he laughed till the tears came and every bone in his body ached. (And do you know, the biggest part of the success of the speech lay in the fact that the audience saw that for once in his life he had been knocked out of his iron serenity.)

Bless your soul, 'twas immense. I never was so proud in my life. Lots and lots of people—hundreds I might say—told me my speech was the triumph of the evening—which was a lie. Ladies, Tom, Dick and Harry—even the policemen—captured me in the halls and shook hands, and scores of army officers said "We shall always be grateful to you for coming." General Pope came to bunt me up—I was afraid to speak to him on that theatre stage last night, thinking it might be presumptuous to tackle a man so high up in military history. Gen. Schofield, and other historic men, paid their compliments. Sheridan was ill and could not come, but I'm to go with a General of his staff and see him before I go to Col. Grant's. Gen. Augur—well, I've talked with them all, received invitations from them all—from people living everywhere—and as I said before, it's a memorable night. I wouldn't have missed it for anything in the world.

But my sakes, you should have heard Ingersoll's speech on that table! Half an hour ago he ran across me in the crowded halls and put his arms about me and said "Mark, if I live a hundred years, I'll always be grateful for your speech—Lord what a supreme thing it was." But I told him it wasn't any use to talk, he had walked off with the honors of that occasion by something of a majority. Bully boy is Ingersoll—traveled with him in the cars the other day, and you can make up your mind we had a good time.

Of course I forgot to go and pay for my hotel car and so secure it, but the army officers told me an hour ago to rest easy, they would go at once, at this unholy hour of the night and compel the railways to do their duty by me, and said "You don't need to request the Army of the Tennessee to do your desires—you can command its services."

Well, I bummed around that banquet hall from 8 in the evening till 2 in the morning, talking with people and listening to speeches, and I never ate a single bite or took a sup of anything but ice water, so if I seem excited now, it is the intoxication of supreme enthusiasm. By George, it was a grand night, a historical night.

And now it is a quarter past 6 A.M.—so good bye and God bless you and the Bays,—[Family word for babies]—my darlings

*SAML.*

Show it to Joe if you want to—I saw some of his friends here.

Mark Twain's admiration for Robert Ingersoll was very great, and we may believe that he was deeply impressed by the Chicago speech, when we find him, a few days later, writing to Ingersoll for a perfect copy to read to a young girls' club in Hartford. Ingersoll sent the speech, also some of his books, and the next letter is Mark Twain's acknowledgment.

To Col. Robert G. Ingersoll:

*HARTFORD, Dec. 14.*

MY DEAR INGERSOLL,—Thank you most heartily for the books—I am devouring them—they have found a hungry place, and they content it and satisfy it to a miracle. I wish I could hear you speak these splendid chapters before a great audience—to read them by myself and hear the boom of the applause only in the ear of my imagination, leaves a something wanting—and there is also a still greater lack, your manner, and voice, and presence.

The Chicago speech arrived an hour too late, but I was all right anyway, for I found that my memory had been able to correct all the errors. I read it to the Saturday Club (of young girls) and told them to remember that it was doubtful if its superior existed in our language.

*Truly Yours,*

*S. L. CLEMENS.*

*The reader may remember Mark Twain's Whittier dinner speech of 1877, and its disastrous effects. Now, in 1879, there was to be another Atlantic gathering: a breakfast to Dr. Oliver Wendell Holmes, to which Clemens was invited. He was not eager to accept; it would naturally recall memories of two years before, but being urged by both Howells and Warner, he agreed to attend if they would permit him to speak. Mark Twain never lacked courage and he wanted to redeem himself. To Howells he wrote:*

To W. D. Howells, in Boston:

*HARTFORD, Nov. 28, 1879.*

MY DEAR HOWELLS,—If anybody talks, there, I shall claim the right to say a word myself, and be heard among the very earliest—else it would be confoundedly awkward for me—and for the rest, too. But you may read what I say, beforehand, and strike out whatever you choose.

Of course I thought it wisest not to be there at all; but Warner took the opposite view, and most strenuously.

Speaking of Johnny's conclusion to become an outlaw, reminds me of Susie's newest and very earnest longing—to have crooked teeth and glasses—"like Mamma."

I would like to look into a child's head, once, and see what its processes are.

*Yrs ever,*

*S. L. CLEMENS.*

*The matter turned out well. Clemens, once more introduced by Howells—this time conservatively, it may be said—delivered a delicate and fitting tribute to Doctor Holmes, full of graceful humor and grateful acknowledgment, the kind of speech he should have given at the Whittier dinner of two years before. No reference was made to his former disaster, and this time he came away covered with glory, and fully restored in his self-respect.*

## XX. LETTERS OF 1880, CHIEFLY TO HOWELLS. "THE PRINCE AND THE PAUPER." MARK TWAIN MUGWUMP SOCIETY.

*The book of travel,—[A Tramp Abroad.]—which Mark Twain had hoped to finish in Paris, and later in Elmira, for some reason would not come to an end. In December, in Hartford, he was still working on it, and he would seem to have finished it, at last, rather by a decree than by any natural process of authorship. This was early in January, 1880. To Howells he reports his difficulties, and his drastic method of ending them.*

To W. D. Howells, in Boston:

*HARTFORD, Jan. 8, '80.*

MY DEAR HOWELLS,—Am waiting for Patrick to come with the carriage. Mrs. Clemens and I are starting (without the children) to stay indefinitely in Elmira. The wear and tear of settling the house broke her down, and she has been growing weaker and weaker for a fortnight. All that time—in fact ever since I saw you—I have been fighting a life-and-death battle with this infernal book and hoping to get done some day. I required 300 pages of MS, and I have written near 600 since I saw you—and tore it all up except 288. This I was about to tear up yesterday and begin again, when Mrs. Perkins came up to the billiard room and said, "You will never get any woman to do the thing necessary to save her life by mere persuasion; you see you have wasted your words for three weeks; it is time to use force; she must have a change; take her home and leave the children here."

I said, "If there is one death that is painfuller than another, may I get it if I don't do that thing."

So I took the 288 pages to Bliss and told him that was the very last line I should ever write on this book. (A book which required 2600 pages of MS, and I have written nearer four thousand, first and last.)

I am as soary (and flighty) as a rocket, to-day, with the unutterable joy of getting that Old Man of the Sea off my back, where he has been roosting for more than a year and a half. Next time I make a contract before writing the book, may I suffer the righteous penalty and be burnt, like the injudicious believer.

I am mighty glad you are done your book (this is from a man who, above all others, feels how much that sentence means) and am also mighty glad you have begun the next (this is also from a man who knows the felicity of that, and means straightway to enjoy it.) The Undiscovered starts off delightfully—I have read it aloud to Mrs. C. and we vastly enjoyed it.

Well, time's about up—must drop a line to Aldrich.

*Yrs ever,*

*MARK.*

*In a letter which Mark Twain wrote to his brother Orion at this period we get the first hint of a venture which was to play an increasingly important part in the Hartford home and fortunes during the next ten or a dozen years. This was the type-setting machine investment, which, in the end, all but wrecked Mark Twain's finances. There is but a brief mention of it in the letter to Orion, and the letter itself is not worth preserving, but as references to the "machine" appear with increasing frequency, it seems proper to record here its first mention. In the same letter he suggests to his brother that he undertake an absolutely truthful autobiography, a confession in which nothing is to be withheld. He cites the value of Casanova's memories, and the confessions of Rousseau. Of course, any literary suggestion from "Brother Sam" was gospel to Orion, who began at once piling up manuscript at a great rate.*

*Meantime, Mark Twain himself, having got 'A Tramp Abroad' on the presses, was at work with enthusiasm on a story begun nearly three years before at Quarry Farm-a story for children-its name, as he called it then, "The Little Prince and The Little Pauper." He was presently writing to Howells his delight in the new work.*

To W. D. Howells, in Boston:

*HARTFORD, Mch. 11, '80.*

MY DEAR HOWELLS,—... I take so much pleasure in my story that I am loth to hurry, not wanting to get it done. Did I ever tell you the plot of it? It begins at 9 a.m., Jan. 27, 1547, seventeen and a half hours before Henry VIII's death, by the swapping of clothes and place, between the prince of Wales and a pauper boy of the same age and countenance (and half as much learning and still more genius and imagination) and after that, the rightful small King has a rough time among tramps and ruffians in the country parts of Kent, whilst the small bogus King has a gilded and worshipped and dreary and restrained and cussed time of it on the throne—and this all goes on for three weeks—till the midst of the coronation grandeurs in Westminster Abbey, Feb. 20, when the ragged true King forces his way in but cannot prove his genuineness—until the bogus King, by a remembered incident of the first day is able to prove it for him—whereupon clothes are changed and the coronation proceeds under the new and rightful conditions.

My idea is to afford a realizing sense of the exceeding severity of the laws of that day by inflicting some of their penalties upon the King himself and allowing him a chance to see the rest of them applied to others—all of which is to account for certain mildnesses which distinguished Edward VI's reign from those that preceded and followed it.

Imagine this fact—I have even fascinated Mrs. Clemens with this yarn for youth. My stuff generally gets considerable damning with faint praise out of her, but this time it is all the other way. She is become the horseleech's daughter and my mill doesn't grind fast enough to suit her. This is no mean triumph, my dear sir.

Last night, for the first time in ages, we went to the theatre—to see Yorick's Love. The magnificence of it is beyond praise. The language is so beautiful, the passion so fine, the plot so ingenious, the whole thing so stirring, so charming, so pathetic! But I will clip from the Courant—it says it right.

And what a good company it is, and how like live people they all acted! The "thee's" and the "thou's" had a pleasant sound, since it is the language of the Prince and the Pauper. You've done the country a service in that admirable work....

*Yrs Ever,*

*MARK.*

*The play, "Yorick's Love," mentioned in this letter, was one which Howells had done for Lawrence Barrett.*

*Onion Clemens, meantime, was forwarding his manuscript, and for once seems to have won his brother's approval, so much so that Mark Twain was willing, indeed anxious, that Howells should run the "autobiography" in the Atlantic. We may imagine how Onion prized the words of commendation which follow:*

To Orion Clemens:

*May 6, '80.*

MY DEAR BROTHER,—It is a model autobiography.

Continue to develop your character in the same gradual inconspicuous and apparently unconscious way. The reader, up to this time, may have his doubts, perhaps, but he can't say decidedly, "This writer is not such a simpleton as he has been letting on to be." Keep him in that state of mind. If, when you shall have finished, the reader shall say, "The man is an ass, but I really don't know whether he knows it or not," your work will be a triumph.

Stop re-writing. I saw places in your last batch where re-writing had done formidable injury. Do not try to find those places, else you will mar them further by trying to better them. It is perilous to revise a book while it is under way. All of us have injured our books in that foolish way.

Keep in mind what I told you—when you recollect something which belonged in an earlier chapter, do not go back, but jam it in where you are. Discursiveness does not hurt an autobiography in the least.

I have penciled the MS here and there, but have not needed to make any criticisms or to knock out anything.

The elder Bliss has heart disease badly, and thenceforth his life hangs upon a thread.

*Yr Bro*

*SAM.*

*But Howells could not bring himself to print so frank a confession as Orion had been willing to make. "It wrung my heart," he said, "and I felt haggard after I had finished it. The writer's soul is laid bare; it is shocking." Howells added that the best touches in it were those which made one acquainted with the writer's brother;*

*that is to say, Mark Twain, and that these would prove valuable material hereafter—a true prophecy, for Mark Twain's early biography would have lacked most of its vital incident, and at least half of its background, without those faithful chapters, fortunately preserved. Had Onion continued, as he began, the work might have proved an important contribution to literature, but he went trailing off into by-paths of theology and discussion where the interest was lost. There were, perhaps, as many as two thousand pages of it, which few could undertake to read.*

*Mark Twain's mind was always busy with plans and inventions, many of them of serious intent, some semi-serious, others of a purely whimsical character. Once he proposed a "Modest Club," of which the first and main qualification for membership was modesty. "At present," he wrote, "I am the only member; and as the modesty required must be of a quite aggravated type, the enterprise did seem for a time doomed to stop dead still with myself, for lack of further material; but upon reflection I have come to the conclusion that you are eligible. Therefore, I have held a meeting and voted to offer you the distinction of membership. I do not know that we can find any others, though I have had some thought of Hay, Warner, Twichell, Aldrich, Osgood, Fields, Higginson, and a few more —together with Mrs. Howells, Mrs. Clemens, and certain others of the sex."*

*Howells replied that the only reason he had for not joining the Modest Club was that he was too modest—too modest to confess his modesty. "If I could get over this difficulty I should like to join, for I approve highly of the Club and its object.... It ought to be given an annual dinner at the public expense. If you think I am not too modest you may put my name down and I will try to think the same of you. Mrs. Howells applauded the notion of the club from the very first. She said that she knew one thing: that she was modest enough, anyway. Her manner of saying it implied that the other persons you had named were not, and created a painful impression in my mind. I have sent your letter and the rules to Hay, but I doubt his modesty. He will think he has a right to belong to it as much as you or I; whereas, other people ought only to be admitted on sufferance."*

*Our next letter to Howells is, in the main, pure foolery, but we get in it a hint what was to become in time one of Mask Twain's strongest interests, the matter of copyright. He had both a personal and general interest in the subject. His own books were constantly pirated in Canada, and the rights of foreign authors were not respected in America. We have already seen how he had drawn a petition which Holmes, Lowell, Longfellow, and others were to sign, and while nothing had come of this plan he had never ceased to formulate others. Yet he hesitated when he found that the proposed* *protection was likely to work a hardship to readers of the poorer class. Once he wrote: "My notions have mightily changed lately.... I can buy a lot of the copyright classics, in paper, at from three to thirty cents apiece. These things must find their way into the very kitchens and hovels of the country..... And even if the treaty will kill Canadian piracy, and thus save me an average of $5,000 a year, I am down on it anyway, and I'd like cussed well to write an article opposing the treaty."*

To W. D. Howells, in Belmont, Mass.:

*Thursday, June 6th, 1880.*

MY DEAR HOWELLS,—There you stick, at Belmont, and now I'm going to Washington for a few days; and of course, between you and Providence that visit is going to get mixed, and you'll have been here and gone again just about the time I get back. Bother it all, I wanted to astonish you with a chapter or two from Orion's latest book—not the seventeen which he has begun in the last four months, but the one which he began last week.

Last night, when I went to bed, Mrs. Clemens said, "George didn't take the cat down to the cellar—Rosa says he has left it shut up in the conservatory." So I went down to attend to Abner (the cat.) About 3 in the morning Mrs. C. woke me and said, "I do believe I hear that cat in the drawing-room—what did you do with him?" I answered up with the confidence of a man who has managed to do the right thing for once, and said "I opened the conservatory doors, took the library off the alarm, and spread everything open, so that there wasn't any obstruction between him and the cellar." Language wasn't capable of conveying this woman's disgust. But the sense of what she said, was, "He couldn't have done any harm in the conservatory—so you must go and make the entire house free to him and the burglars, imagining that he will prefer the coal-bins to the drawing-room. If you had had Mr. Howells to help you,

I should have admired but not been astonished, because I should know that together you would be equal to it; but how you managed to contrive such a stately blunder all by yourself, is what I cannot understand."

So, you see, even she knows how to appreciate our gifts.

Brisk times here.—Saturday, these things happened: Our neighbor Chas. Smith was stricken with heart disease, and came near joining the majority; my publisher, Bliss, ditto, ditto; a neighbor's child died; neighbor Whitmore's sixth child added to his five other cases of measles; neighbor Niles sent for, and responded; Susie Warner down, abed; Mrs. George Warner threatened with death during several hours; her son Frank, whilst imitating the marvels in Barnum's circus bills, thrown from his aged horse and brought home insensible: Warner's friend Max Yortzburgh, shot in the back by a locomotive and broken into 32 distinct pieces and his life threatened; and Mrs. Clemens, after writing all these cheerful things to Clara Spaulding, taken at midnight, and if the doctor had not been pretty prompt the contemplated Clemens would have called before his apartments were ready.

However, everybody is all right, now, except Yortzburg, and he is mending—that is, he is being mended. I knocked off, during these stirring times, and don't intend to go to work again till we go away for the Summer, 3 or 6 weeks hence. So I am writing to you not because I have anything to say, but because you don't have to answer and I need something to do this afternoon.....

I have a letter from a Congressman this morning, and he says Congress couldn't be persuaded to bother about Canadian pirates at a time like this when all legislation must have a political and Presidential bearing, else Congress won't look at it. So have changed my mind and my course; I go north, to kill a pirate. I must procure repose some way, else I cannot get down to work again.

Pray offer my most sincere and respectful approval to the President—is approval the proper word? I find it is the one I most value here in the household and seldomest get.

With our affection to you both.

*Yrs ever*

*MARK.*

*It was always dangerous to send strangers with letters of introduction to Mark Twain. They were so apt to arrive at the wrong time, or to find him in the wrong mood. Howells was willing to risk it, and that the result was only amusing instead of tragic is the best proof of their friendship.*

To W. D. Howells, in Belmont, Mass.:

*June 9, '80.*

Well, old practical joker, the corpse of Mr. X——has been here, and I have bedded it and fed it, and put down my work during 24 hours and tried my level best to make it do something, or say something, or appreciate something—but no, it was worse than Lazarus. A kind-hearted, well-meaning corpse was the Boston young man, but lawsy bless me, horribly dull company. Now, old man, unless you have great confidence in Mr. X's judgment, you ought to make him submit his article to you before he prints it. For only think how true I was to you: Every hour that he was here I was saying, gloatingly, "O G— d—- you, when you are in bed and your light out, I will fix you" (meaning to kill him)...., but then the thought would follow—"No, Howells sent him—he shall be spared, he shall be respected he shall travel hell-wards by his own route."

Breakfast is frozen by this time, and Mrs. Clemens correspondingly hot. Good bye.

*Yrs ever,*

*MARK.*

*"I did not expect you to ask that man to live with you," Howells*

*answered. "What I was afraid of was that you would turn him out of doors, on sight, and so I tried to put in a good word for him. After this when I want you to board people, I'll ask you. I am sorry for your suffering. I suppose I have mostly lost my smell for bores; but yours is preternaturally keen. I shall begin to be afraid I bore you. (How does that make you feel?)"*

*In a letter to Twichell—a remarkable letter—when baby Jean Clemens was about a month old, we get a happy hint of conditions at Quarry Farm, and in the background a glimpse of Mark Twain's unfailing tragic reflection.*

To Rev. Twichell, in Hartford:

*QUARRY FARM, Aug. 29 ['80].*

DEAR OLD JOE,—Concerning Jean Clemens, if anybody said he "didn't see no pints about that frog that's any better'n any other frog," I should think he was convicting himself of being a pretty poor sort of observer.... I will not go into details; it is not necessary; you will soon be in Hartford, where I have already hired a hall; the admission fee will be but a trifle.

It is curious to note the change in the stock-quotation of the Affection Board brought about by throwing this new security on the market. Four weeks ago the children still put Mamma at the head of the list right along, where she had always been. But now:

*Jean*

*Mamma*

*Motley [a cat]*

*Fraulein [another]*

*Papa*

That is the way it stands, now Mamma is become No. 2; I have dropped from No. 4., and am become No. 5. Some time ago it used to be nip and tuck between me and the cats, but after the cats "developed" I didn't stand any more show.

I've got a swollen ear; so I take advantage of it to lie abed most of the day, and read and smoke and scribble and have a good time. Last evening Livy said with deep concern, "O dear, I believe an abscess is forming in your ear."

I responded as the poet would have done if he had had a cold in the head—

*"Tis said that abscess conquers love,*

*But O believe it not."*

This made a coolness.

Been reading Daniel Webster's Private Correspondence. Have read a hundred of his diffuse, conceited, "eloquent," bathotic (or bathostic) letters written in that dim (no, vanished) Past when he was a student; and Lord, to think that this boy who is so real to me now, and so booming with fresh young blood and bountiful life, and sappy cynicisms about girls, has since climbed the Alps of fame and stood against the sun one brief tremendous moment with the world's eyes upon him, and then—f-z-t-! where is he? Why the only long thing, the only real thing about the whole shadowy business is the sense of the lagging dull and hoary lapse of time that has drifted by since then; a vast empty level, it seems, with a formless spectre glimpsed fitfully through the smoke and mist that lie along its remote verge.

Well, we are all getting along here first-rate; Livy gains strength daily, and sits up a deal; the baby is five weeks old and—but no more of this; somebody may be reading this letter 80 years hence. And so, my friend (you pitying snob, I mean, who are holding this yellow paper in your hand in 1960,) save yourself the trouble of looking further; I know how pathetically trivial our small concerns will seem to you, and I will not let your eye profane them. No, I keep my news; you keep your compassion. Suffice it you to know, scoffer and ribald, that the little child is old and blind, now, and once more toothless; and the rest of us are shadows, these many, many years. Yes, and your time cometh!

*MARK.*

*At the Farm that year Mark Twain was working on The Prince and the Pauper, and, according to a letter to Aldrich, brought it to an end September 19th. It is a pleasant letter, worth preserving. The book by Aldrich here mentioned was 'The Stillwater Tragedy.'*

To T. B. Aldrich, in Ponkapog, Mass.:

*ELMIRA, Sept. 15, '80.*

MY DEAR ALDRICH,—Thank you ever so much for the book—I had already finished it, and prodigiously enjoyed it, in the periodical of the notorious Howells, but it hits Mrs. Clemens just right, for she is having a reading holiday, now, for the first time in same months; so between-times, when the new baby is asleep and strengthening up for another attempt to take possession of this place, she is going to read it. Her strong friendship for you makes her think she is going to like it.

I finished a story yesterday, myself. I counted up and found it between sixty and eighty thousand words—about the size of your book. It is for boys and girls—been at work at it several years, off and on.

I hope Howells is enjoying his journey to the Pacific. He wrote me that you and Osgood were going, also, but I doubted it, believing he was in liquor when he wrote it. In my opinion, this universal applause over his book is going to land that man in a Retreat inside of two months. I notice the papers say mighty fine things about your book, too. You ought to try to get into the same establishment with Howells. But applause does not affect me—I am always calm—this is because I am used to it.

Well, good-bye, my boy, and good luck to you. Mrs. Clemens asks me to send her warmest regards to you and Mrs. Aldrich—which I do, and add those of

*Yrs ever*

*MARK.*

*While Mark Twain was a journalist in San Francisco, there was a middle-aged man named Soule, who had a desk near him on the Morning Call. Soule was in those days highly considered as a poet by his associates, most of whom were younger and less gracefully poetic. But Soule's gift had never been an important one. Now, in his old age, he found his fame still local, and he yearned for wider recognition. He wished to have a volume of poems issued by a publisher of recognized standing. Because Mark Twain had been one of Soule's admirers and a warm friend in the old days, it was natural that Soule should turn to him now, and equally natural that Clemens should turn to Howells.*

To W. D. Howells, in Boston:

*Sunday, Oct. 2 '80.*

MY DEAR HOWELLS,—Here's a letter which I wrote you to San Francisco the second time you didn't go there.... I told Soule he needn't write you, but simply send the MS. to you. O dear, dear, it is dreadful to be an unrecognized poet. How wise it was in Charles Warren Stoddard to take in his sign and go for some other calling while still young.

I'm laying for that Encyclopedical Scotchman—and he'll need to lock the door behind him, when he comes in; otherwise when he hears my proposed tariff his skin will probably crawl away with him. He is accustomed to seeing the publisher impoverish the author—that spectacle must be getting stale to him—if he contracts with the undersigned he will experience a change in that programme that will make the enamel peel off his teeth for very surprise—and joy. No, that last is what Mrs. Clemens thinks—but it's not so. The proposed work is growing, mightily, in my estimation, day by day; and I'm not going to throw it away for any mere trifle. If I make a contract with the canny Scot, I will then tell him the plan which you and I have devised (that of taking in the humor of all countries)—otherwise I'll keep it to myself, I think. Why should we assist our fellowman for mere love of God?

*Yrs ever*

*MARK.*

*One wishes that Howells might have found value enough in the verses of Frank Soule to recommend them to Osgood. To Clemens he wrote: "You have touched me in regard to him, and I will deal gently with his poetry. Poor old fellow! I can imagine him, and how he must have to struggle not to be hard or sour."*

*The verdict, however, was inevitable. Soule's graceful verses proved to be not poetry at all. No publisher of standing could afford to give them his imprint.*

*The "Encyclopedical Scotchman" mentioned in the preceding letter was the publisher Gebbie, who had a plan to engage Howells and Clemens to prepare some sort of anthology of the world's literature. The idea came to nothing, though the other plan mentioned—for a library of humor—in time grew into a book.*

*Mark Twain's contracts with Bliss for the publication of his books on the subscription plan had been made on a royalty basis, beginning with 5 per cent. on 'The Innocents Abroad' increasing to 7 per cent. on 'Roughing It,' and to 10 per cent. on later books. Bliss had held that these later percentages fairly represented one half the profits. Clemens, however, had never been fully satisfied, and his brother Onion had more than once urged him to demand a specific contract on the half-profit basis. The agreement for the publication of 'A Tramp Abroad' was made on these terms. Bliss died before Clemens received his first statement of sales. Whatever may have been the facts under earlier conditions, the statement proved to Mark Twain's satisfaction; at least, that the half-profit arrangement was to his advantage. It produced another result; it gave Samuel Clemens an excuse to place his brother Onion in a position of independence.*

To Onion Clemens, in Keokuk, Iowa:

*Sunday, Oct 24 '80.*

MY DEAR BRO.,—Bliss is dead. The aspect of the balance-sheet is enlightening. It reveals the fact, through my present contract, (which is for half the profits on the book above actual cost of paper, printing and binding,) that I have lost considerably by all this nonsense—sixty thousand dollars, I should say—and if Bliss were alive I would stay with the concern and get it all back; for on each new book I would require a portion of that back pay; but as it is (this in the very strictest confidence,) I shall probably go to a new publisher 6 or 8 months hence, for I am afraid Frank, with his poor health, will lack push and drive.

Out of the suspicions you bred in me years ago, has grown this result,—to wit, that I shall within the twelvemonth get $40,000 out of this "Tramp" instead Of $20,000. Twenty thousand dollars, after taxes and other expenses are stripped away, is worth to the investor about $75 a month—so I shall tell Mr. Perkins to make your check that amount per month, hereafter, while our income is able to afford it. This ends the loan business; and hereafter you can reflect that you are living not on borrowed money but on money which you have squarely earned, and which has no taint or savor of charity about it—and you can also reflect that the money you have been receiving of me all these years is interest charged against the heavy bill which the next publisher will have to stand who gets a book of mine.

Jean got the stockings and is much obliged; Mollie wants to know whom she most resembles, but I can't tell; she has blue eyes and brown hair, and three chins, and is very fat and happy; and at one time or another she has resembled all the different Clemenses and Langdons, in turn, that have ever lived.

Livy is too much beaten out with the baby, nights, to write, these times; and I don't know of anything urgent to say, except that a basket full of letters has accumulated in the 7 days that I have been whooping and cursing over a cold in the head—and I must attack the pile this very minute.

*With love from us*

*Y aff*

*SAM*

*$25 enclosed.*

*On the completion of The Prince and Pauper story, Clemens had naturally sent it to Howells for consideration. Howells wrote: "I have read the two P's and I like it immensely, it begins well and it ends well." He pointed out some things that might be changed or omitted, and added: "It is such a book as I would expect from you, knowing what a bottom of fury there is to your fun." Clemens had thought somewhat of publishing the story anonymously, in the fear that it would not be accepted seriously over his own signature.*

*The "bull story" referred to in the next letter is the one later used in the Joan of Arc book, the story told Joan by "Uncle Laxart," how he rode a bull to a funeral.*

To W. D. Howells, in Boston:

*Xmas Eve, 1880.*

MY DEAR HOWELLS,—I was prodigiously delighted with what you said about the book—so, on the whole, I've concluded to publish intrepidly, instead of concealing the authorship. I shall leave out that bull story.

I wish you had gone to New York. The company was small, and we had a first-rate time. Smith's an enjoyable fellow. I liked Barrett, too. And the oysters were as good as the rest of the company. It was worth going there to learn how to cook them.

Next day I attended to business—which was, to introduce Twichell to Gen. Grant and procure a private talk in the interest of the Chinese Educational Mission here in the U. S. Well, it was very funny. Joe had been sitting up nights building facts and arguments together into a mighty and unassailable array and had studied them out and got them by heart—all with the trembling half-hearted hope of getting Grant to add his signature to a sort of petition to the Viceroy of China; but Grant took in the whole situation in a jiffy, and before Joe had more than fairly got started, the old man said: "I'll write the Viceroy a Letter—a separate letter—and bring strong reasons to bear upon him; I know him well, and what I say will have weight with him; I will attend to it right away. No, no thanks—I shall be glad to do it—it will be a labor of love."

So all Joe's laborious hours were for naught! It was as if he had come to borrow a dollar, and been offered a thousand before he could unfold his case....

But it's getting dark. Merry Christmas to all of you.

*Yrs Ever,*

*MARK.*

*The Chinese Educational Mission, mentioned in the foregoing, was a thriving Hartford institution, projected eight years before by a Yale graduate named Yung Wing. The mission was now threatened, and Yung Wing, knowing the high honor in which General Grant was held in China, believed that through him it might be saved. Twichell, of course, was deeply concerned and naturally overjoyed at Grant's interest. A day or two following the return to Hartford, Clemens received a letter from General Grant, in which he wrote: "Li Hung Chang is the most powerful and most influential Chinaman in his country. He professed great friendship for me when I was there, and I have had assurances of the same thing since. I hope, if he is strong enough with his government, that the decision to withdraw the Chinese students from this country may be changed."*

*But perhaps Li Hung Chang was experiencing one of his partial eclipses just then, or possibly he was not interested, for the Hartford Mission did not survive.*

## XXI. LETTERS 1881, TO HOWELLS AND OTHERS. ASSISTING A YOUNG SCULPTOR. LITERARY PLANS.

*With all of Mark Twain's admiration for Grant, he had opposed him as a third-term President and approved of the nomination of Garfield. He had made speeches for Garfield during the campaign just ended, and had been otherwise active in his support. Upon Garfield's election, however, he felt himself entitled to no special favor, and the single request which he preferred at length could hardly be classed as, personal, though made for a "personal friend."*

To President-elect James A. Garfield, in Washington:

*HARTFORD, Jany. 12, '81.*

GEN. GARFIELD

DEAR SIR,—Several times since your election persons wanting office have asked me "to use my influence" with you in their behalf.

To word it in that way was such a pleasant compliment to me that I never complied. I could not without exposing the fact that I hadn't any influence with you and that was a thing I had no mind to do.

It seems to me that it is better to have a good man's flattering estimate of my influence—and to keep it—than to fool it away with trying to get him an office. But when my brother—on my wife's side—Mr. Charles J. Langdon—late of the Chicago Convention—desires me to speak a word for Mr. Fred Douglass, I am not asked "to use my influence" consequently I am not risking anything. So I am writing this as a simple citizen. I am not drawing on my fund of influence at all. A simple citizen may express a desire with all propriety, in the matter of a recommendation to office, and so I beg permission to hope that you will retain Mr. Douglass in his present office of Marshall of the District of Columbia, if such a course will not clash with your own preferences or with the expediencies and interest of your administration. I offer this petition with peculiar pleasure and strong desire, because I so honor this man's high and blemishless character and so admire his brave, long crusade for the liberties and elevation of his race.

He is a personal friend of mine, but that is nothing to the point, his history would move me to say these things without that, and I feel them too.

*With great respect*

*I am, General,*

*Yours truly,*

*S. L. CLEMENS.*

*Clemens would go out of his way any time to grant favor to the colored race. His childhood associations were partly accountable for this, but he also felt that the white man owed the negro a debt for generations of enforced bondage. He would lecture any time in a colored church, when he would as likely as not refuse point-blank to speak for a white congregation. Once, in Elmira, he received a request, poorly and none too politely phrased, to speak for one of the churches. He was annoyed and about to send a brief refusal, when Mrs. Clemens, who was present, said:*

*"I think I know that church, and if so this preacher is a colored man; he does not know how to write a polished letter—how should*

*he?" Her husband's manner changed so suddenly that she added: "I will give you a motto, and it will be useful to you if you will adopt it: Consider every man colored until he is proved white."*

To W. D. Howells, in Boston:

*HARTFORD, Feb. 27, 1881.*

MY DEAR HOWELLS,—I go to West Point with Twichell tomorrow, but shall be back Tuesday or Wednesday; and then just as soon thereafter as you and Mrs. Howells and Winny can come you will find us ready and most glad to see you—and the longer you can stay the gladder we shall be. I am not going to have a thing to do, but you shall work if you want to. On the evening of March 10th, I am going to read to the colored folk in the African Church here (no whites admitted except such as I bring with me), and a choir of colored folk will sing jubilee songs. I count on a good time, and shall hope to have you folks there, and Livy. I read in Twichell's chapel Friday night and had a most rattling high time—but the thing that went best of all was Uncle Remus's Tar Baby. I mean to try that on my dusky audience. They've all heard that tale from childhood—at least the older members have.

I arrived home in time to make a most noble blunder—invited Charley Warner here (in Livy's name) to dinner with the Gerhardts, and told him Livy had invited his wife by letter and by word of mouth also. I don't know where I got these impressions, but I came home feeling as one does who realizes that he has done a neat thing for once and left no flaws or loop-holes. Well, Livy said she had never told me to invite Charley and she hadn't dreamed of inviting Susy, and moreover there wasn't any dinner, but just one lean duck. But Susy Warner's intuitions were correct—so she choked off Charley, and staid home herself—we waited dinner an hour and you ought to have seen that duck when he was done drying in the oven.

*MARK.*

*Clemens and his wife were always privately assisting worthy and ambitious young people along the way of achievement. Young actors were helped through dramatic schools; young men and women were assisted through college and to travel abroad. Among others Clemens paid the way of two colored students, one through a Southern institution and another through the Yale law school.*

*The mention of the name of Gerhardt in the preceding letter introduces the most important, or at least the most extensive, of these benefactions. The following letter gives the beginning of the story:*

To W. D. Howells, in Boston:

Private and Confidential.

*HARTFORD, Feb. 21, 1881.*

MY DEAR HOWELLS,—Well, here is our romance.

It happened in this way. One morning, a month ago—no, three weeks—Livy, and Clara Spaulding and I were at breakfast, at 10 A.M., and I was in an irritable mood, for the barber was up stairs waiting and his hot water getting cold, when the colored George returned from answering the bell and said: "There's a lady in the drawing-room wants to see you." "A book agent!" says I, with heat. "I won't see her; I will die in my tracks, first."

Then I got up with a soul full of rage, and went in there and bent scowling over that person, and began a succession of rude and raspy questions—and without even offering to sit down.

Not even the defendant's youth and beauty and (seeming) timidity were able to modify my savagery, for a time—and meantime question and answer were going on. She had risen to her feet with the first question; and there she stood, with her pretty face bent floorward whilst I inquired, but always with her honest eyes looking me in the face when it came her turn to answer.

And this was her tale, and her plea-diffidently stated, but straightforwardly; and bravely, and most winningly simply and earnestly: I put it in my own fashion, for I do not remember her words:

Mr. Karl Gerhardt, who works in Pratt & Whitney's machine shops, has made a statue in clay, and would I be so kind as to come and look at it, and tell him if there is any promise in it? He has none to go to, and he would be so glad.

"O, dear me," I said, "I don't know anything about art—there's nothing I could tell him."

But she went on, just as earnestly and as simply as before, with her plea—and so she did after repeated rebuffs; and dull as I am, even I began by and by to admire this brave and gentle persistence, and to perceive how her heart of hearts was in this thing, and how she couldn't give it up, but must carry her point. So at last I wavered, and promised in general terms that I would come down the first day that fell idle—and as I conducted her to the door, I tamed more and more, and said I would come during the very next week—"We shall be so glad—but—but, would you please come early in the week?—the statue is just finished and we are so anxious—and—and—we did hope you could come this week—and"—well, I came down another peg, and said I would come Monday, as sure as death; and before I got to the dining room remorse was doing its work and I was saying to myself, "Damnation, how can a man be such a hound? why didn't I go with her now?" Yes, and how mean I should have felt if I had known that out of her poverty she had hired a hack and brought it along to convey me. But luckily for what was left of my peace of mind, I didn't know that.

Well, it appears that from here she went to Charley Warner's. There was a better light, there, and the eloquence of her face had a better chance to do its office. Warner fought, as I had done; and he was in the midst of an article and very busy; but no matter, she won him completely. He laid aside his MS and said, "Come, let us go and see your father's statue. That is—is he your father?" "No, he is my husband." So this child was married, you see.

This was a Saturday. Next day Warner came to dinner and said "Go!—go tomorrow—don't fail." He was in love with the girl, and with her husband too, and said he believed there was merit in the statue. Pretty crude work, maybe, but merit in it.

Patrick and I hunted up the place, next day; the girl saw us driving up, and flew down the stairs and received me. Her quarters were the second story of a little wooden house—another family on the ground floor. The husband was at the machine shop, the wife kept no servant, she was there alone. She had a little parlor, with a chair or two and a sofa; and the artist-husband's hand was visible in a couple of plaster busts, one of the wife, and another of a neighbor's child; visible also in a couple of water colors of flowers and birds; an ambitious unfinished portrait of his wife in oils: some paint decorations on the pine mantel; and an excellent human ear, done in some plastic material at 16.

Then we went into the kitchen, and the girl flew around, with enthusiasm, and snatched rag after rag from a tall something in the corner, and presently there stood the clay statue, life size—a graceful girlish creature, nude to the waist, and holding up a single garment with one hand the expression attempted being a modified scare—she was interrupted when about to enter the bath.

Then this young wife posed herself alongside the image and so remained—a thing I didn't understand. But presently I did—then I said:

"O, it's you!"

"Yes," she said, "I was the model. He has no model but me. I have stood for this many and many an hour—and you can't think how it does tire one! But I don't mind it. He works all day at the shop; and then, nights and Sundays he works on his statue as long as I can keep up."

She got a big chisel, to use as a lever, and between us we managed to twist the pedestal round and round, so as to afford a view of the statue from all points. Well, sir, it was perfectly charming, this girl's innocence and purity—

exhibiting her naked self, as it were, to a stranger and alone, and never once dreaming that there was the slightest indelicacy about the matter. And so there wasn't; but it will be many along day before I run across another woman who can do the like and show no trace of self-consciousness.

Well, then we sat down, and I took a smoke, and she told me all about her people in Massachusetts—her father is a physician and it is an old and respectable family—(I am able to believe anything she says.) And she told me how "Karl" is 26 years old; and how he has had passionate longings all his life toward art, but has always been poor and obliged to struggle for his daily bread; and how he felt sure that if he could only have one or two lessons in—

"Lessons? Hasn't he had any lessons?"

No. He had never had a lesson.

And presently it was dinner time and "Karl" arrived—a slender young fellow with a marvelous head and a noble eye—and he was as simple and natural, and as beautiful in spirit as his wife was. But she had to do the talking—mainly—there was too much thought behind his cavernous eyes for glib spccch.

I went home enchanted. Told Livy and Clara Spaulding all about the paradise down yonder where those two enthusiasts are happy with a yearly expense of $350. Livy and Clara went there next day and came away enchanted. A few nights later the Gerhardts kept their promise and came here for the evening. It was billiard night and I had company and so was not down; but Livy and Clara became more charmed with these children than ever.

Warner and I planned to get somebody to criticise the statue whose judgment would be worth something. So I laid for Champney, and after two failures I captured him and took him around, and he said "this statue is full of faults—but it has merits enough in it to make up for them"—whereat the young wife danced around as delighted as a child. When we came away, Champney said, "I did not want to say too much there, but the truth is, it seems to me an extraordinary performance for an untrained hand. You ask if there is promise enough there to justify the Hartford folk in going to an expense of training this young man. I should say, yes, decidedly; but still, to make everything safe, you had better get the judgment of a sculptor."

Warner was in New York. I wrote him, and he said he would fetch up Ward—which he did. Yesterday they went to the Gerhardts and spent two hours, and Ward came away bewitched with those people and marveling at the winning innocence of the young wife, who dropped naturally into model-attitude beside the statue (which is stark naked from head to heel, now—G. had removed the drapery, fearing Ward would think he was afraid to try legs and hips) just as she has always done before.

Livy and I had two long talks with Ward yesterday evening. He spoke strongly. He said, "if any stranger had told me that this apprentice did not model that thing from plaster casts, I would not have believed it." He said "it is full of crudities, but it is full of genius, too. It is such a statue as the man of average talent would achieve after two years training in the schools. And the boldness of the fellow, in going straight to nature! He is an apprentice—his work shows that, all over; but the stuff is in him, sure. Hartford must send him to Paris—two years; then if the promise holds good, keep him there three more—and warn him to study, study, work, work, and keep his name out of the papers, and neither ask for orders nor accept them when offered."

Well, you see, that's all we wanted. After Ward was gone Livy came out with the thing that was in her mind. She said, "Go privately and start the Gerhardts off to Paris, and say nothing about it to any one else."

So I tramped down this morning in the snow-storm—and there was a stirring time. They will sail a week or ten days from now.

As I was starting out at the front door, with Gerhardt beside me and the young wife dancing and jubilating behind, this latter cried out impulsively, "Tell Mrs. Clemens I want to hug her—I want to hug you both!"

I gave them my old French book and they were going to tackle the language, straight off.

Now this letter is a secret—keep it quiet—I don't think Livy would mind my telling you these things, but then she might, you know, for she is a queer girl.

*Yrs ever,*

*MARK.*

*Champney was J. Wells Champney, a portrait-painter of distinction; Ward was the sculptor, J. Q. A. Ward.*

*The Gerhardts were presently off to Paris, well provided with means to make their dreams reality; in due time the letters will report them again.*

*The Uncle Remus tales of Joel Chandler Harris gave Mark Twain great pleasure. He frequently read them aloud, not only at home but in public. Finally, he wrote Harris, expressing his warm appreciation, and mentioning one of the negro stories of his own childhood, "The Golden Arm," which he urged Harris to look up and add to his collection.*

*"You have pinned a proud feather in Uncle-Remus's cap," replied Harris. "I do not know what higher honor he could have than to appear before the Hartford public arm in arm with Mark Twain." He disclaimed any originality for the stories, adding, "I understand that my relations toward Uncle Remus are similar to those that exist between an almanac maker and the calendar." He had not heard the "Golden Arm" story and asked for the outlines; also for some publishing advice, out of Mark Twain's long experience.*

To Joel Chandler Harris, in Atlanta:

*ELMIRA, N.Y., Aug. 10.*

MY DEAR MR. HARRIS,—You can argue yourself into the delusion that the principle of life is in the stories themselves and not in their setting; but you will save labor by stopping with that solitary convert, for he is the only intelligent one you will bag. In reality the stories are only alligator pears—one merely eats them for the sake of the salad-dressing. Uncle Remus is most deftly drawn, and is a lovable and delightful creation; he, and the little boy, and their relations with each other, are high and fine literature, and worthy to live, for their own sakes; and certainly the stories are not to be credited with them. But enough of this; I seem to be proving to the man that made the multiplication table that twice one are two.

I have been thinking, yesterday and to-day (plenty of chance to think, as I am abed with lumbago at our little summering farm among the solitudes of the Mountaintops,) and I have concluded that I can answer one of your questions with full confidence—thus: Make it a subscription book. Mighty few books that come strictly under the head of literature will sell by subscription; but if Uncle Remus won't, the gift of prophecy has departed out of me. When a book will sell by subscription, it will sell two or three times as many copies as it would in the trade; and the profit is bulkier because the retail price is greater.....

You didn't ask me for a subscription-publisher. If you had, I should have recommended Osgood to you. He inaugurates his subscription department with my new book in the fall.....

Now the doctor has been here and tried to interrupt my yarn about "The Golden Arm," but I've got through, anyway.

Of course I tell it in the negro dialect—that is necessary; but I have not written it so, for I can't spell it in your matchless way. It is marvelous the way you and Cable spell the negro and creole dialects.

Two grand features are lost in print: the weird wailing, the rising and falling cadences of the wind, so easily mimicked with one's mouth; and the impressive pauses and eloquent silences, and subdued utterances, toward the end of the yarn (which chain the attention of the children hand and foot, and they sit with parted lips and breathless, to be wrenched limb from limb with the sudden and appalling "You got it").

Old Uncle Dan'l, a slave of my uncle's' aged 60, used to tell us children yarns every night by the kitchen fire (no other light;) and the last yarn demanded, every night, was this one. By this time there was but a ghastly blaze or two flickering about the back-log. We would huddle close about the old man, and begin to shudder with the first familiar words; and under the spell of his impressive delivery we always fell a prey to that climax at the end when the rigid black shape in the twilight sprang at us with a shout.

When you come to glance at the tale you will recollect it—it is as common and familiar as the Tar Baby. Work up the atmosphere with your customary skill and it will "go" in print.

Lumbago seems to make a body garrulous—but you'll forgive it.

*Truly yours*

*S. L. CLEMENS*

*The "Golden Arm" story was one that Clemens often used in his public readings, and was very effective as he gave it.*

*In his sketch, "How to Tell a Story," it appears about as he used to tell it. Harris, receiving the outlines of the old Missouri tale, presently announced that he had dug up its Georgia relative, an interesting variant, as we gather from Mark Twain's reply.*

To Joel Chandler Harris, in Atlanta:

*HARTFORD, '81.*

MY DEAR MR. HARRIS,—I was very sure you would run across that Story somewhere, and am glad you have. A Drummond light—no, I mean a Brush light—is thrown upon the negro estimate of values by his willingness to risk his soul and his mighty peace forever for the sake of a silver sev'm-punce. And this form of the story seems rather nearer the true field-hand standard than that achieved by my Florida, Mo., negroes with their sumptuous arm of solid gold.

I judge you haven't received my new book yet—however, you will in a day or two. Meantime you must not take it ill if I drop Osgood a hint about your proposed story of slave life.....

When you come north I wish you would drop me a line and then follow it in person and give me a day or two at our house in Hartford. If you will, I will snatch Osgood down from Boston, and you won't have to go there at all unless you want to. Please to bear this strictly in mind, and don't forget it.

*Sincerely yours*

*S. L. CLEMENS.*

*Charles Warren Stoddard, to whom the next letter is written, was one of the old California literary crowd, a graceful writer of verse and prose, never quite arriving at the success believed by his friends to be his due. He was a gentle, irresponsible soul, well loved by all who knew him, and always, by one or another, provided against want. The reader may remember that during Mark Twain's great lecture engagement in London, winter of 1873-74, Stoddard lived with him, acting as his secretary. At a later period in his life he lived for several years with the great telephone magnate, Theodore N. Vail. At the time of this letter, Stoddard had decided that in the warm light and comfort of the Sandwich Islands he could survive on his literary earnings.*

To Charles Warren Stoddard, in the Sandwich Islands:

*HARTFORD, Oct. 26 '81.*

MY DEAR CHARLIE,—Now what have I ever done to you that you should not only slide off to Heaven before you have earned a right to go, but must add the gratuitous villainy of informing me of it?...

The house is full of carpenters and decorators; whereas, what we really need here, is an incendiary. If the house would only burn down, we would pack up the cubs and fly to the isles of the blest, and shut ourselves up in the healing solitudes of the crater of Haleakala and get a good rest; for the mails do not intrude there, nor yet the telephone and the telegraph. And after resting, we would come down the mountain a piece and board with a godly, breech-clouted native, and eat poi and dirt and give thanks to whom all thanks belong, for these privileges, and never house-keep any more.

I think my wife would be twice as strong as she is, but for this wearing and wearying slavery of house-keeping. However, she thinks she must submit to it for the sake of the children; whereas, I have always had a tenderness for parents too, so, for her sake and mine, I sigh for the incendiary. When the evening comes and the gas is lit and the wear and tear of life ceases, we want to keep house always; but next morning we wish, once more, that we were free and irresponsible boarders.

Work?—one can't you know, to any purpose. I don't really get anything done worth speaking of, except during the three or four months that we are away in the Summer. I wish the Summer were seven years long. I keep three or four books on the stocks all the time, but I seldom add a satisfactory chapter to one of them at home. Yes, and it is all because my time is taken up with answering the letters of strangers. It can't be done through a short hand amanuensis—I've tried that—it wouldn't work—I couldn't learn to dictate. What does possess strangers to write so many letters? I never could find that out. However, I suppose I did it myself when I was a stranger. But I will never do it again.

Maybe you think I am not happy? the very thing that gravels me is that I am. I don't want to be happy when I can't work; I am resolved that hereafter I won't be. What I have always longed for, was the privilege of living forever away up on one of those mountains in the Sandwich Islands overlooking the sea.

*Yours ever*

*MARK.*

That magazine article of yours was mighty good: up to your very best I think. I enclose a book review written by Howells.

To W. D. Howells, in Boston:

*HARTFORD, Oct. 26 '81.*

MY DEAR HOWELLS,—I am delighted with your review, and so is Mrs. Clemens. What you have said, there, will convince anybody that reads it; a body cannot help being convinced by it. That is the kind of a review to have; the doubtful man; even the prejudiced man, is persuaded and succumbs.

What a queer blunder that was, about the baronet. I can't quite see how I ever made it. There was an opulent abundance of things I didn't know; and consequently no need to trench upon the vest-pocketful of things I did know, to get material for a blunder.

Charley Warren Stoddard has gone to the Sandwich Islands permanently. Lucky devil. It is the only supremely delightful place on earth. It does seem that the more advantage a body doesn't earn, here, the more of them God throws at his head. This fellow's postal card has set the vision of those gracious islands before my mind, again, with not a leaf withered, nor a rainbow vanished, nor a sun-flash missing from the waves, and now it will be months, I reckon, before I can drive it away again. It is beautiful company, but it makes one restless and dissatisfied.

With love and thanks,

*Yrs ever,*

*MARK.*

*The review mentioned in this letter was of The Prince and the Pauper. What the queer "blunder" about the baronet was, the present writer confesses he does not know; but perhaps a careful reader could find it, at least in the early edition; very likely it was corrected without loss of time.*

*Clemens now and then found it necessary to pay a visit to Canada in the effort to protect his copyright. He usually had a grand time on these trips, being lavishly entertained by the Canadian literary fraternity. In November, 1881, he made one of these journeys in the interest of The Prince and the Pauper, this time with Osgood, who was now his publisher. In letters written home we get a hint of his diversions. The Monsieur Frechette mentioned was a Canadian poet of considerable distinction. "Clara" was Miss Clara Spaulding, of Elmira, who had accompanied Mr. and Mrs. Clemens to Europe in 1873, and again in 1878. Later she became Mrs. John B. Staachfield, of New York City. Her name has already appeared in these letters many times.*

To Mrs. Clemens, in Hartford:

*MONTREAL, Nov. 28 '81.*

Livy darling, you and Clara ought to have been at breakfast in the great dining room this morning. English female faces, distinctive English costumes, strange and marvelous English gaits—and yet such honest, honorable, clean-souled countenances, just as these English women almost always have, you know. Right away—

But they've come to take me to the top of Mount Royal, it being a cold, dry, sunny, magnificent day. Going in a sleigh.

*Yours lovingly,*

*SAML.*

To Mrs. Clemens, in Hartford:

*MONTREAL, Sunday, November 27, 1881.*

Livy dear, a mouse kept me awake last night till 3 or 4 o'clock—so I am lying abed this morning. I would not give sixpence to be out yonder in the storm, although it is only snow.

[The above paragraph is written in the form of a rebus illustrated with various sketches.]

There—that's for the children—was not sure that they could read writing; especially jean, who is strangely ignorant in some things.

I can not only look out upon the beautiful snow-storm, past the vigorous blaze of my fire; and upon the snow-veiled buildings which I have sketched; and upon the churchward drifting umbrellas; and upon the buffalo-clad cabmen stamping their feet and thrashing their arms on the corner yonder: but I also look out upon the spot where the first white men stood, in the neighborhood of four hundred years ago, admiring the mighty stretch of leafy solitudes, and being admired and marveled at by an eager multitude of naked savages. The discoverer of this region, and namer of it, Jacques Cartier, has a square named for him in the city. I wish you were here; you would enjoy your birthday, I think.

I hoped for a letter, and thought I had one when the mail was handed in, a minute ago, but it was only that note from Sylvester Baxter. You must write—do you hear?—or I will be remiss myself.

Give my love and a kiss to the children, and ask them to give you my love and a kiss from

*SAML.*

To Mrs. Clemens, in Hartford:

*QUEBEC, Sunday. '81.*

Livy darling, I received a letter from Monsieur Frechette this morning, in which certain citizens of Montreal tendered me a public dinner next Thursday, and by Osgood's advice I accepted it. I would have accepted anyway, and very cheerfully but for the delay of two days—for I was purposing to go to Boston Tuesday and home Wednesday; whereas, now I go to Boston Friday and home Saturday. I have to go by Boston on account of business.

We drove about the steep hills and narrow, crooked streets of this old town during three hours, yesterday, in a sleigh, in a driving snow-storm. The people here don't mind snow; they were all out, plodding around on their affairs—especially the children, who were wallowing around everywhere, like snow images, and having a mighty good time. I wish I could describe the winter costume of the young girls, but I can't. It is grave and simple, but graceful and pretty—the top of it is a brimless fur cap. Maybe it is the costume that makes pretty girls seem so monotonously plenty here. It was a kind of relief to strike a homely face occasionally.

You descend into some of the streets by long, deep stairways; and in the strong moonlight, last night, these were very picturesque. I did wish you were here to see these things. You couldn't by any possibility sleep in these beds, though, or enjoy the food.

Good night, sweetheart, and give my respects to the cubs.

*SAML.*

*It had been hoped that W. D. Howells would join the Canadian excursion, but Howells was not very well that autumn. He wrote that he had been in bed five weeks, "most of the time recovering; so you see how bad I must have been to begin with. But now I am out of any first-class pain; I have a good appetite, and I am as abusive and peremptory as Guiteau." Clemens, returning to Hartford, wrote him a letter that explains itself.*

To W. D. Howells, in Boston:

*HARTFORD, Dec. 16 '81.*

MY DEAR HOWELLS,—It was a sharp disappointment—your inability to connect, on the Canadian raid. What a gaudy good time we should have had!

Disappointed, again, when I got back to Boston; for I was promising myself half an hour's look at you, in Belmont; but your note to Osgood showed that that could not be allowed out yet.

The Atlantic arrived an hour ago, and your faultless and delicious Police Report brought that blamed Joe Twichell powerfully before me. There's a man who can tell such things himself (by word of mouth,) and has as sure an eye for detecting a thing that is before his eyes, as any man in the world, perhaps—then why in the nation doesn't he report himself with a pen?

One of those drenching days last week, he slopped down town with his cubs, and visited a poor little beggarly shed where were a dwarf, a fat woman, and a giant of honest eight feet, on exhibition behind tawdry show-canvases, but with nobody to exhibit to. The giant had a broom, and was cleaning up and fixing around, diligently. Joe conceived the idea of getting some talk out of him. Now that never would have occurred to me. So he dropped in under the man's elbow, dogged him patiently around, prodding him with questions and getting irritated snarls in return which would have finished me early—but at last one of Joe's random shafts drove the centre of that giant's sympathies somehow, and fetched him. The fountains of his great deep were broken up, and he rained a flood of personal history that was unspeakably entertaining.

Among other things it turned out that he had been a Turkish (native) colonel, and had fought all through the Crimean war—and so, for the first time, Joe got a picture of the Charge of the Six Hundred that made him see the living spectacle, the flash of flag and tongue-flame, the rolling smoke, and hear the booming of the guns; and for the first time also, he heard the reasons for that wild charge delivered from the mouth of a master, and realized that nobody had "blundered," but that a cold, logical, military brain had perceived this one and sole way to win an already lost battle, and so gave the command and did achieve the victory.

And mind you Joe was able to come up here, days afterwards, and reproduce that giant's picturesque and admirable history. But dern him, he can't write it—which is all wrong, and not as it should be.

And he has gone and raked up the MS autobiography (written in 1848,) of Mrs. Phebe Brown, (author of "I Love to Steal a While Away,") who educated Yung Wing in her family when he was a little boy; and I came near not getting to bed at all, last night, on account of the lurid fascinations of it. Why in the nation it has never got into print, I can't understand.

But, by jings! the postman will be here in a minute; so, congratulations upon your mending health, and gratitude that it is mending; and love to you all.

*Yrs Ever*

*MARK.*

Don't answer—I spare the sick.

## XXII. LETTERS, 1882, MAINLY TO HOWELLS. WASTED FURY. OLD SCENES REVISITED. THE MISSISSIPPI BOOK.

*A man of Mark Twain's profession and prominence must necessarily be the subject of much newspaper comment. Jest, compliment, criticism —none of these things disturbed him, as a rule. He was pleased that his books should receive favorable notices by men whose opinion he respected, but he was not grieved by adverse expressions. Jests at his expense, if well written, usually amused him; cheap jokes only made him sad; but sarcasms and innuendoes were likely to enrage him, particularly if he believed them prompted by malice. Perhaps among all the letters he ever wrote, there is none more characteristic than this confession of violence and eagerness for reprisal, followed by his acknowledgment of error and a manifest appreciation of his own weakness. It should be said that Mark Twain and Whitelaw Reid were generally very good friends, and perhaps for the moment this fact seemed to magnify the offense.*

To W. D. Howells, in Boston:

*HARTFORD, Jan. 28 '82.*

MY DEAR HOWELLS,—Nobody knows better than I, that there are times when swearing cannot meet the emergency. How sharply I feel that, at this moment. Not a single profane word has issued from my lips this mornin—I have not even had the impulse to swear, so wholly ineffectual would swearing have manifestly been, in the circumstances. But I will tell you about it.

About three weeks ago, a sensitive friend, approaching his revelation cautiously, intimated that the N. Y. Tribune was engaged in a kind of crusade against me. This seemed a higher compliment than I deserved; but no matter, it made me very angry. I asked many questions, and gathered, in substance, this: Since Reid's return from Europe, the Tribune had been flinging sneers and brutalities at me with such persistent frequency "as to attract general remark." I was an angered—which is just as good an expression, I take it, as an hungered. Next, I learned that Osgood, among the rest of the "general," was worrying over these constant and pitiless attacks. Next came the testimony of another friend, that the attacks were not merely "frequent," but "almost daily." Reflect upon that: "Almost daily" insults, for two months on a stretch. What would you have done?

As for me, I did the thing which was the natural thing for me to do, that is, I set about contriving a plan to accomplish one or the other of two things: 1. Force a peace; or 2. Get revenge. When I got my plan finished, it pleased me marvelously. It was in six or seven sections, each section to be used in its turn and by itself; the assault to begin at once with No. 1, and the rest to follow, one after the other, to keep the communication open while I wrote my biography of Reid. I meant to wind up with this latter great work, and then dismiss the subject for good.

Well, ever since then I have worked day and night making notes and collecting and classifying material. I've got collectors at work in England. I went to New York and sat three hours taking evidence while a stenographer set it down. As my labors grew, so also grew my fascination. Malice and malignity faded out of me—or maybe I drove them out of me, knowing that a malignant book would hurt nobody but the fool who wrote it. I got thoroughly in love with this work; for I saw that I was going to write a book which the very devils and angels themselves would delight to read, and which would draw disapproval from nobody but the hero of it, (and Mrs. Clemens, who was bitter against the whole thing.) One part of my plan was so delicious that I had to try my hand on it right away, just for the luxury of it. I set about it, and sure enough it panned out to admiration. I wrote that chapter most carefully, and I couldn't find a fault with it. (It was not for the biography—no, it belonged to an immediate and deadlier project.)

Well, five days ago, this thought came into my mind (from Mrs. Clemens's): "Wouldn't it be well to make sure that the attacks have been 'almost daily'?—and to also make sure that their number and character will justify me in doing what I am proposing to do?"

I at once set a man to work in New York to seek out and copy every unpleasant reference which had been made to me in the Tribune from Nov. 1st to date. On my own part I began to watch the current numbers, for I had subscribed for the paper.

The result arrived from my New York man this morning. O, what a pitiable wreck of high hopes! The "almost daily" assaults, for two months, consist of—1. Adverse criticism of P. & P. from an enraged idiot in the London Atheneum; 2. Paragraph from some indignant Englishman in the Pall Mall Gazette who pays me the vast compliment of gravely rebuking some imaginary ass who has set me up in the neighborhood of Rabelais; 3. A remark of the Tribune's about the Montreal dinner, touched with an almost invisible satire; 4. A remark of the Tribune's about refusal of Canadian copyright, not complimentary, but not necessarily malicious—and of course adverse criticism which is not malicious is a thing which none but fools irritate themselves about.

There—that is the prodigious bugaboo, in its entirety! Can you conceive of a man's getting himself into a sweat over so diminutive a provocation? I am sure I can't. What the devil can those friends of mine have been thinking about, to spread these 3 or 4 harmless things out into two months of daily sneers and affronts? The whole offense, boiled down, amounts to just this: one uncourteous remark of the Tribune about my book—not me between Nov. 1 and Dec. 20; and a couple of foreign criticisms (of my writings, not me,) between Nov. 1 and Jan. 26! If I can't stand that amount of friction, I certainly need reconstruction. Further boiled down, this vast outpouring of malice amounts to simply this: one jest from the Tribune (one can make nothing more serious than that out of it.) One jest—and that is all; for the foreign criticisms do not count, they being matters of news, and proper for publication in anybody's newspaper.

And to offset that one jest, the Tribune paid me one compliment Dec. 23, by publishing my note declining the New York New England dinner, while merely (in the same breath,) mentioning that similar letters were read from General Sherman and other men whom we all know to be persons of real consequence.

Well, my mountain has brought forth its mouse, and a sufficiently small mouse it is, God knows. And my three weeks' hard work have got to go into the ignominious pigeon-hole. Confound it, I could have earned ten thousand dollars with infinitely less trouble. However, I shouldn't have done it, for I am too lazy, now, in my sere and yellow leaf, to be willing to work for anything but love..... I kind of envy you people who are permitted for your righteousness' sake to dwell in a boarding house; not that I should always want to live in one, but I should like the change occasionally from this housekeeping slavery to that wild independence. A life of don't-care-a-damn in a boarding house is what I have asked for in many a secret prayer. I shall come by and by and require of you what you have offered me there.

*Yours ever,*

*MARK.*

*Howells, who had already known something of the gathering storm, replied: "Your letter was an immense relief to me, for although I had an abiding faith that you would get sick of your enterprise, I wasn't easy until I knew that you had given it up."*

*Joel Chandler Harris appears again in the letters of this period. Twichell, during a trip South about this time, had called on Harris with some sort of proposition or suggestion from Clemens that Harris appear with him in public, and tell, or read, the Remus stories from the platform. But Harris was abnormally diffident. Clemens later pronounced him "the shyest full-grown man" he had ever met, and the word which Twichell brought home evidently did not encourage the platform idea.*

To Joel Chandler Harris, in Atlanta:

*HARTFORD, Apl. 2, '82.*

Private.

MY DEAR MR. HARRIS,—Jo Twichell brought me your note and told me of his talk with you. He said you didn't believe you would ever be able to muster a sufficiency of reckless daring to make you comfortable and at ease before an audience. Well, I have thought out a device whereby I believe we can get around that difficulty. I will explain when I see you.

Jo says you want to go to Canada within a month or six weeks—I forget just exactly what he did say; but he intimated the trip could be delayed a while, if necessary. If this is so, suppose you meet Osgood and me in New Orleans early in May—say somewhere between the 1st and 6th?

It will be well worth your while to do this, because the author who goes to Canada unposted, will not know what course to pursue [to secure copyright] when he gets there; he will find himself in a hopeless confusion as to what is the correct thing to do. Now Osgood is the only man in America, who can lay out your course for you and tell you exactly what to do. Therefore, you just come to New Orleans and have a talk with him.

Our idea is to strike across lots and reach St. Louis the 20th of April—thence we propose to drift southward, stopping at some town a few hours or a night, every day, and making notes.

To escape the interviewers, I shall follow my usual course and use a fictitious name (C. L. Samuel, of New York.) I don't know what Osgood's name will be, but he can't use his own.

If you see your way to meet us in New Orleans, drop me a line, now, and as we approach that city I will telegraph you what day we shall arrive there.

I would go to Atlanta if I could, but shan't be able. We shall go back up the river to St. Paul, and thence by rail X-lots home.

(I am making this letter so dreadfully private and confidential because my movements must be kept secret, else I shan't be able to pick up the kind of book-material I want.)

If you are diffident, I suspect that you ought to let Osgood be your magazine-agent. He makes those people pay three or four times as much as an article is worth, whereas I never had the cheek to make them pay more than double.

*Yrs Sincerely*

*S. L. CLEMENS.*

*"My backwardness is an affliction," wrote Harris..... "The ordeal of appearing on the stage would be a terrible one, but my experience is that when a diffident man does become familiar with his surroundings he has more impudence than his neighbors. Extremes meet."*

*He was sorely tempted, but his courage became as water at the thought of footlights and assembled listeners. Once in New York he appears to have been caught unawares at a Tile Club dinner and made to tell a story, but his agony was such that at the prospect of a similar ordeal in Boston he avoided that city and headed straight for Georgia and safety.*

*The New Orleans excursion with Osgood, as planned by Clemens, proved a great success. The little party took the steamer Gold Dust from St. Louis down river toward New Orleans. Clemens was quickly recognized, of course, and his assumed name laid aside. The author of "Uncle Remus" made the trip to New Orleans. George W. Cable was there at the time, and we may believe that in the company of Mark Twain and Osgood those Southern authors passed two or three delightful days. Clemens also met his old teacher Bixby in New Orleans, and came back up the river with him, spending most of his time in the pilot-house, as in the old days. It was a glorious trip, and, reaching St. Louis, he continued it northward, stopping off at Hannibal and Quincy.'*

To Mrs. Clemens, in Hartford:

*QUINCY, ILL. May 17, '82.*

Livy darling, I am desperately homesick. But I have promised Osgood, and must stick it out; otherwise I would take the train at once and break for home.

I have spent three delightful days in Hannibal, loitering around all day long, examining the old localities and talking with the grey-heads who were boys and girls with me 30 or 40 years ago. It has been a moving time. I spent my nights with John and Helen Garth, three miles from town, in their spacious and beautiful house. They were children with me, and afterwards schoolmates. Now they have a daughter 19 or 20 years old. Spent an hour, yesterday, with A. W. Lamb, who was not married when I saw him last.

He married a young lady whom I knew. And now I have been talking with their grown-up sons and daughters. Lieutenant Hickman, the spruce young handsomely-uniformed volunteer of 1846, called on me—a grisly elephantine patriarch of 65 now, his grace all vanished.

That world which I knew in its blossoming youth is old and bowed and melancholy, now; its soft cheeks are leathery and wrinkled, the fire is gone out in its eyes, and the spring from its step. It will be dust and ashes when I come again. I have been clasping hands with the moribund—and usually they said, "It is for the last time."

Now I am under way again, upon this hideous trip to St. Paul, with a heart brimming full of thoughts and images of you and Susie and Bay and the peerless Jean. And so good night, my love.

*SAML.*

*Clemens's trip had been saddened by learning, in New Orleans, the news of the death of Dr. John Brown, of Edinburgh. To Doctor Brown's son, whom he had known as "Jock," he wrote immediately on his return to Hartford.*

To Mr. John Brown, in Edinburgh

*HARTFORD, June 1, 1882.*

MY DEAR MR. BROWN,—I was three thousand miles from home, at breakfast in New Orleans, when the damp morning paper revealed the sorrowful news among the cable dispatches. There was no place in America, however remote, or however rich, or poor or high or humble where words of mourning for your father were not uttered that morning, for his works had made him known and loved all over the land. To Mrs. Clemens and me, the loss is personal; and our grief the grief one feels for one who was peculiarly near and dear. Mrs. Clemens has never ceased to express regret that we came away from England the last time without going to see him, and often we have since projected a voyage across the Atlantic for the sole purpose of taking him by the hand and looking into his kind eyes once more before he should be called to his rest.

We both thank you greatly for the Edinburgh papers which you sent. My wife and I join in affectionate remembrances and greetings to yourself and your aunt, and in the sincere tender of our sympathies.

*Faithfully yours,*

*S. L. CLEMENS.*

Our Susie is still "Megalops." He gave her that name:

Can you spare a photograph of your father? We have none but the one taken in a group with ourselves.

*William Dean Howells, at the age of forty-five, reached what many still regard his highest point of achievement in American realism. His novel, The Rise of Silas Lapham, which was running as a Century serial during the summer of 1882, attracted wide attention, and upon its issue in book form took first place among his published novels. Mark Twain, to the end of his life, loved all that Howells wrote. Once, long afterward, he said: "Most authors give us glimpses of a radiant moon, but Howells's moon shines and sails all night long." When the instalments of The Rise of Silas Lapham began to appear, he overflowed in adjectives, the sincerity of which we need not doubt, in view of his quite open criticisms of the author's reading delivery.*

To W. D. Howells, in Belmont, Mass.:

MY DEAR HOWELLS,—I am in a state of wild enthusiasm over this July instalment of your story. It's perfectly dazzling—it's masterly—incomparable. Yet I heard you read it—without losing my balance. Well, the difference between your reading and your writing is-remarkable. I mean, in the effects produced and the impression left behind. Why, the one is to the other as is one of Joe Twichell's yarns repeated by a somnambulist. Goodness gracious, you read me a chapter, and it is a gentle, pearly dawn, with a sprinkle of faint stars in it; but by and by I strike it in print, and shout to myself, "God bless us, how has that pallid former spectacle been turned into these gorgeous sunset splendors!"

Well, I don't care how much you read your truck to me, you can't permanently damage it for me that way. It is always perfectly fresh and dazzling when I come on it in the magazine. Of course I recognize the form of it as being familiar—but that is all. That is, I remember it as pyrotechnic figures which you set up before me, dead and cold, but ready for the match—and now I see them touched off and all ablaze with blinding fires. You can read, if you want to, but you don't read worth a damn. I know you can read, because your readings of Cable and your repeatings of the German doctor's remarks prove that.

That's the best drunk scene—because the truest—that I ever read. There are touches in it that I never saw any writer take note of before. And they are set before the reader with amazing accuracy. How very drunk, and how recently drunk, and how altogether admirably drunk you must have been to enable you to contrive that masterpiece!

Why I didn't notice that that religious interview between Marcia and Mrs. Halleck was so deliciously humorous when you read it to me—but dear me, it's just too lovely for anything. (Wrote Clark to collar it for the "Library.")

Hang it, I know where the mystery is, now; when you are reading, you glide right along, and I don't get a chance to let the things soak home; but when I catch it in the magazine, I give a page 20 or 30 minutes in which to gently and thoroughly filter into me. Your humor is so very subtle, and elusive—(well, often it's just a vanishing breath of perfume which a body isn't certain he smelt till he stops and takes another smell) whereas you can smell other...

(Remainder obliterated.)

*Among Mark Twain's old schoolmates in Hannibal was little Helen Kercheval, for whom in those early days he had a very tender spot indeed. But she married another schoolmate, John Garth, who in time became a banker, highly respected and a great influence. John and Helen Garth have already been mentioned in the letter of May 17th.*

To John Garth, in Hannibal:

*HARTFORD, July 3 '82.*

DEAR JOHN,—Your letter of June 19 arrived just one day after we ought to have been in Elmira, N. Y. for the summer: but at the last moment the baby was seized with scarlet fever. I had to telegraph and countermand the order for special sleeping car; and in fact we all had to fly around in a lively way and undo the patient preparations of weeks—rehabilitate the dismantled house, unpack the trunks, and so on. A couple of days later, the eldest child was taken down with so fierce a fever that she was soon delirious—not scarlet fever, however. Next, I myself was stretched on the bed with three diseases at once, and all of them fatal. But I never did care for fatal diseases if I could only have privacy and room to express myself concerning them.

We gave early warning, and of course nobody has entered the house in all this time but one or two reckless old bachelors—and they probably wanted to carry the disease to the children of former flames of theirs. The house is still in quarantine and must remain so for a week or two yet—at which time we are hoping to leave for Elmira.

*Always your friend*

*S. L. CLEMENS.*

*By the end of summer Howells was in Europe, and Clemens, in Elmira, was trying to finish his Mississippi book, which was giving him a great deal of trouble. It was usually so with his non-fiction books; his interest in them was not cumulative; he was prone to grow weary of them, while the menace of his publisher's contract was maddening. Howells's letters, meant to be comforting, or at least entertaining, did not always contribute to his peace of mind. The Library of American Humor which they had planned was an added burden. Before sailing, Howells had written: "Do you suppose you can do your share of the reading at Elmira, while you are writing at the Mississippi book?"*

*In a letter from London, Howells writes of the good times he is having over there with Osgood, Hutton, John Hay, Aldrich, and Alma Tadema, excursioning to Oxford, feasting, especially "at the Mitre Tavern, where they let you choose your dinner from the joints hanging from the rafter, and have passages that you lose yourself in every time you try to go to your room.... Couldn't you and Mrs. Clemens step over for a little while?... We have seen lots of nice people and have been most pleasantly made of; but I would rather have you smoke in my face, and talk for half a day just for pleasure, than to go to the best house or club in London." The reader will gather that this could not be entirely soothing to a man shackled by a contract and a book that refused to come to an end.*

To W. D. Howells, in London:

*HARTFORD, CONN. Oct 30, 1882.*

MY DEAR HOWELLS,—I do not expect to find you, so I shan't spend many words on you to wind up in the perdition of some European dead-letter office. I only just want to say that the closing installments of the story are prodigious. All along I was afraid it would be impossible for you to keep up so splendidly to the end; but you were only, I see now, striking eleven. It is in these last chapters that you struck twelve. Go on and write; you can write good books yet, but you can never match this one. And speaking of the book, I inclose something which has been happening here lately.

We have only just arrived at home, and I have not seen Clark on our matters. I cannot see him or any one else, until I get my book finished. The weather turned cold, and we had to rush home, while I still lacked thirty thousand words. I had been sick and got delayed. I am going to write all day and two thirds of the night, until the thing is done, or break down at it. The spur and burden of the contract are intolerable to me. I can endure the irritation of it no longer. I went to work at nine o'clock yesterday morning, and went to bed an hour after midnight. Result of the day, (mainly stolen from books, tho' credit given,) 9500 words, so I reduced my burden by one third in one day. It was five days work in one. I have nothing more to borrow or steal; the rest must all be written. It is ten days work, and unless something breaks, it will be finished in five. We all send love to you and Mrs. Howells, and all the family.

*Yours as ever,*

*MARK.*

Again, from Villeneuve, on lake Geneva, Howells wrote urging him this time to spend the winter with them in Florence, where they would write their great American Comedy of 'Orme's Motor,' "which is to enrich us beyond the dreams of avarice.... We could have a lot of fun writing it, and you could go home with some of the good old Etruscan malaria in your bones, instead of the wretched pinch-beck Hartford article that you are suffering from now....

it's a great opportunity for you. Besides, nobody over there likes you half as well as I do."

It should be added that 'Orme's Motor' was the provisional title that Clemens and Howells had selected for their comedy, which was to be built, in some measure, at least, around the character, or rather from the peculiarities, of Orion Clemens. The Cable mentioned in Mark Twain's reply is, of course, George W. Cable, who only a little while before had come up from New Orleans to conquer the North with his wonderful tales and readings.

To W. D. Howells, in Switzerland:

*HARTFORD, Nov. 4th, 1882.*

MY DEAR HOWELLS,—Yes, it would be profitable for me to do that, because with your society to help me, I should swiftly finish this now apparently interminable book. But I cannot come, because I am not Boss here, and nothing but dynamite can move Mrs. Clemens away from home in the winter season.

I never had such a fight over a book in my life before. And the foolishest part of the whole business is, that I started Osgood to editing it before I had finished writing it. As a consequence, large areas of it are condemned here and there and yonder, and I have the burden of these unfilled gaps harassing me and the thought of the broken continuity of the work, while I am at the same time trying to build the last quarter of the book. However, at last I have said with sufficient positiveness that I will finish the book at no particular date; that I will not hurry it; that I will not hurry myself; that I will take things easy and comfortably, write when I choose to write, leave it alone when I so prefer. The printers must wait, the artists, the canvassers, and all the rest. I have got everything at a dead standstill, and that is where it ought to be, and that is where it must remain; to follow any other policy would be to make the book worse than it already is. I ought to have finished it before showing to anybody, and then sent it across the ocean to you to be edited, as usual; for you seem to be a great many shades happier than you deserve to be, and if I had thought of this thing earlier, I would have acted upon it and taken the tuck somewhat out of your joyousness.

In the same mail with your letter, arrived the enclosed from Orme the motor man. You will observe that he has an office. I will explain that this is a law office and I think it probably does him as much good to have a law office without anything to do in it, as it would another man to have one with an active business attached. You see he is on the electric light lay now. Going to light the city and allow me to take all the stock if I want to. And he will manage it free of charge. It never would occur to this simple soul how much less costly it would be to me, to hire him on a good salary not to manage it. Do you observe the same old eagerness, the same old hurry, springing from the fear that if he does not move with the utmost swiftness, that colossal opportunity will escape him? Now just fancy this same frantic plunging after vast opportunities, going on week after week with this same man, during fifty entire years, and he has not yet learned, in the slightest degree, that there isn't any occasion to hurry; that his vast opportunity will always wait; and that whether it waits or flies, he certainly will never catch it. This immortal hopefulness, fortified by its immortal and unteachable misjudgment, is the immortal feature of this character, for a play; and we will write that play. We should be fools else. That staccato postscript reads as if some new and mighty business were imminent, for it is slung on the paper telegraphically, all the small words left out. I am afraid something newer and bigger than the electric light is swinging across his orbit. Save this letter for an inspiration. I have got a hundred more.

Cable has been here, creating worshipers on all hands. He is a marvelous talker on a deep subject. I do not see how even Spencer could unwind a thought more smoothly or orderly, and do it in a cleaner, clearer, crisper English. He astounded Twichell with his faculty. You know when it comes down to moral honesty, limpid innocence, and utterly blemishless piety, the Apostles were mere policemen to Cable; so with this in mind you must imagine him at a midnight dinner in Boston the other night, where we gathered around the board of the Summerset Club; Osgood, full, Boyle O'Reilly, full, Fairchild responsively loaded, and Aldrich and myself possessing the floor, and properly fortified. Cable told Mrs. Clemens when he returned here, that he seemed to have been entertaining himself with horses, and had a dreamy idea that he must have gone to Boston in a cattle-car. It was a very large time. He called it an orgy. And no doubt it was, viewed from his standpoint.

I wish I were in Switzerland, and I wish we could go to Florence; but we have to leave these delights to you; there is no helping it. We all join in love to you and all the family.

*Yours as ever*

*MARK.*

## XXIII. LETTERS, 1883, TO HOWELLS AND OTHERS. A GUEST OF THE MARQUIS OF LORNE. THE HISTORY GAME. A PLAY BY HOWELLS AND MARK TWAIN.

*Mark Twain, in due season, finished the Mississippi book and placed it in Osgood's hands for publication. It was a sort of partnership arrangement in which Clemens was to furnish the money to make the book, and pay Osgood a percentage for handling it. It was, in fact, the beginning of Mark Twain's adventures as a publisher.*

*Howells was not as happy in Florence as he had hoped to be. The social life there overwhelmed him. In February he wrote: "Our two months in Florence have been the most ridiculous time that ever even half-witted people passed. We have spent them in chasing round after people for whom we cared nothing, and being chased by them. My story isn't finished yet, and what part of it is done bears the fatal marks of haste and distraction. Of course, I haven't put pen to paper yet on the play. I wring my hands and beat my breast when I think of how these weeks have been wasted; and how I have been forced to waste them by the infernal social circumstances from which I couldn't escape."*

*Clemens, now free from the burden of his own book, was light of heart and full of ideas and news; also of sympathy and appreciation.*

*Howells's story of this time was "A Woman's Reason." Governor Jewell, of this letter, was Marshall Jewell, Governor of Connecticut from 1871 to 1873. Later, he was Minister to Russia, and in 1874 was United States Postmaster-General.*

To W. D. Howells, in Florence:

*HARTFORD, March 1st, 1883.*

MY DEAR HOWELLS,—We got ourselves ground up in that same mill, once, in London, and another time in Paris. It is a kind of foretaste of hell. There is no way to avoid it except by the method which you have now chosen. One must live secretly and cut himself utterly off from the human race, or life in Europe becomes an unbearable burden and work an impossibility. I learned something last night, and maybe it may reconcile me to go to Europe again sometime. I attended one of the astonishingly popular lectures of a man by the name of Stoddard, who exhibits interesting stereopticon pictures and then knocks the interest all out of them with his comments upon them. But all the world go there to look and listen, and are apparently well satisfied. And they ought to be fully satisfied, if the lecturer would only keep still, or die in the first act. But he described how retired tradesmen and farmers in Holland load a lazy scow with the family and the household effects, and then loaf along the waterways of the low countries all the summer long, paying no visits, receiving none, and just lazying a heavenly life out in their own private unpestered society, and doing their literary work, if they have any, wholly uninterrupted. If you had hired such a boat and sent for us we should have a couple of satisfactory books ready for the press now with no marks of interruption, vexatious wearinesses, and other hellishnesses visible upon them anywhere. We shall have to do this another time. We have lost an opportunity for the present. Do you forget that Heaven is packed with a multitude of all nations and that these people are all on the most familiar how-the-hell-are-you footing with Talmage swinging around the circle to all eternity hugging the saints and patriarchs and archangels, and forcing you to do the same unless you choose to make yourself an object of remark if you refrain? Then why do you try to get to Heaven? Be warned in time.

We have all read your two opening numbers in the Century, and consider them almost beyond praise. I hear no dissent from this verdict. I did not know there was an untouched personage in American life, but I had forgotten the auctioneer. You have photographed him accurately.

I have been an utterly free person for a month or two; and I do not believe I ever so greatly appreciated and enjoyed—and realized the absence of the chains of slavery as I do this time. Usually my first waking thought in the morning is, "I have nothing to do to-day, I belong to nobody, I have ceased from being a slave." Of course the highest pleasure to be got out of freedom, and having nothing to do, is labor. Therefore I labor. But I take my time about it. I work one hour or four as happens to suit my mind, and quit when I please. And so these days are days of entire enjoyment. I told Clark the other day, to jog along comfortable and not get in a sweat. I said I believed you would not be able to enjoy editing that library over there, where you have your own legitimate work to do and be pestered to death by society besides; therefore I thought if he got it ready for you against your return, that that would be best and pleasantest.

You remember Governor Jewell, and the night he told about Russia, down in the library. He was taken with a cold about three weeks ago, and I stepped over one evening, proposing to beguile an idle hour for him with a yarn or two, but was received at the door with whispers, and the information that he was dying. His case had been dangerous during that day only and he died that night, two hours after I left. His taking off was a prodigious surprise, and his death has been most widely and sincerely regretted. Win. E. Dodge, the father-in-law of one of Jewell's daughters, dropped suddenly dead the day before Jewell died, but Jewell died without knowing that. Jewell's widow went down to New York, to Dodge's house, the day after Jewell's funeral, and was to return here day before yesterday, and she did—in a coffin. She fell dead, of heart disease, while her trunks were being packed for her return home. Florence Strong, one of Jewell's daughters, who lives in Detroit, started East on an urgent telegram, but missed a connection somewhere, and did not arrive here in time to see her father alive. She was his favorite child, and they had always been like lovers together. He always sent her a box of fresh flowers once a week to the day of his death; a custom which he never suspended even when he was in Russia. Mrs. Strong had only just reached her Western home again when she was summoned to Hartford to attend her mother's funeral.

I have had the impulse to write you several times. I shall try to remember better henceforth.

With sincerest regards to all of you,

*Yours as ever,*

*MARK.*

*Mark Twain made another trip to Canada in the interest of copyright —this time to protect the Mississippi book. When his journey was announced by the press, the Marquis of Lorne telegraphed an invitation inviting him to be his guest at Rideau Hall, in Ottawa. Clemens accepted, of course, and was handsomely entertained by the daughter of Queen Victoria and her husband, then Governor-General of Canada.*

*On his return to Hartford he found that Osgood had issued a curious little book, for which Clemens had prepared an introduction. It was an absurd volume, though originally issued with serious intent, its title being The New Guide of the Conversation in Portuguese and English.'—[The New Guide of the Conversation in Portuguese and English, by Pedro Caxolino, with an introduction by Mark Twain. Osgood, Boston, 1883. ]—Evidently the "New Guide" was prepared by some simple Portuguese soul with but slight knowledge of English beyond that which could be obtained from a dictionary, and his literal translation of English idioms are often startling, as, for instance, this one, taken at random:*

*"A little learneds are happies enough for to may to satisfy their fancies on the literature."*

*Mark Twain thought this quaint book might amuse his royal hostess, and forwarded a copy in what he considered to be the safe and proper form.*

To Col. De Winton, in Ottawa, Canada:

*HARTFORD, June 4, '83.*

DEAR COLONEL DE WINTON,—I very much want to send a little book to her Royal Highness—the famous Portuguese phrase book; but I do not know the etiquette of the matter, and I would not wittingly infringe any rule of propriety. It is a book which I perfectly well know will amuse her "some at most" if she has not seen it before, and will still amuse her "some at least," even if she has inspected it a hundred times already. So I will send the book to you, and you who know all about the proper observances will protect me from indiscretion, in case of need, by putting the said book in the fire, and remaining as dumb as I generally was when I was up there. I do not rebind the thing, because that would look as if I thought it worth keeping, whereas it is only worth glancing at and casting aside.

Will you please present my compliments to Mrs. De Winton and Mrs. Mackenzie?—and I beg to make my sincere compliments to you, also, for your infinite kindnesses to me. I did have a delightful time up there, most certainly.

*Truly yours*

*S. L. CLEMENS.*

P. S. Although the introduction dates a year back, the book is only just now issued. A good long delay.

*S. L. C.*

*Howells, writing from Venice, in April, manifested special interest in the play project: "Something that would run like Scheherazade, for a thousand and one nights," so perhaps his book was going better. He proposed that they devote the month of October to the work, and inclosed a letter from Mallory, who owned not only a religious paper, The Churchman, but also the Madison Square Theater, and was anxious for a Howells play. Twenty years before Howells had been Consul to Venice, and he wrote, now: "The idea of my being here is benumbing and silencing. I feel like the Wandering Jew, or the ghost of the Cardiff giant."*

*He returned to America in July. Clemens sent him word of welcome, with glowing reports of his own undertakings. The story on which he was piling up MS. was The Adventures of Huckleberry Finn, begun seven years before at Quarry Farm. He had no great faith in it then, and though he had taken it up again in 1880, his interest had not lasted to its conclusion. This time, however, he was in the proper spirit, and the story would be finished.*

To W. D. Howells, in Boston:

*ELMIRA, July 20, '83.*

MY DEAR HOWELLS,—We are desperately glad you and your gang are home again—may you never travel again, till you go aloft or alow. Charley Clark has gone to the other side for a run—will be back in August. He has been sick, and needed the trip very much.

Mrs. Clemens had a long and wasting spell of sickness last Spring, but she is pulling up, now. The children are booming, and my health is ridiculous, it's so robust, notwithstanding the newspaper misreports.

I haven't piled up MS so in years as I have done since we came here to the farm three weeks and a half ago. Why, it's like old times, to step right into the study, damp from the breakfast table, and sail right in and sail right on, the whole day long, without thought of running short of stuff or words.

I wrote 4000 words to-day and I touch 3000 and upwards pretty often, and don't fall below 1600 any working day. And when I get fagged out, I lie abed a couple of days and read and smoke, and then go it again for 6 or 7 days. I have finished one small book, and am away along in a big 433 one that I half-finished two or three years ago. I expect to complete it in a month or six weeks or two months more. And I shall like it, whether anybody else does or not.

It's a kind of companion to Tom Sawyer. There's a raft episode from it in second or third chapter of life on the Mississippi.....

I'm booming, these days—got health and spirits to waste—got an overplus; and if I were at home, we would write a play. But we must do it anyhow by and by.

We stay here till Sep. 10; then maybe a week at Indian Neck for sea air, then home.

We are powerful glad you are all back; and send love according.

*Yrs Ever*

*MARK*

To Onion Clemens and family, in Keokuk, Id.:

*ELMIRA, July 22, '83.*

*Private.*

DEAR MA AND ORION AND MOLLIE,—I don't know that I have anything new to report, except that Livy is still gaining, and all the rest of us flourishing. I haven't had such booming working-days for many years. I am piling up manuscript in a really astonishing way. I believe I shall complete, in two months, a book which I have been fooling over for 7 years. This summer it is no more trouble to me to write than it is to lie.

Day before yesterday I felt slightly warned to knock off work for one day. So I did it, and took the open air. Then I struck an idea for the instruction of the children, and went to work and carried it out. It took me all day. I measured off 817 feet of the road-way in our farm grounds, with a foot-rule, and then divided it up among the English reigns, from the Conqueror down to 1883, allowing one foot to the year. I whittled out a basket of little pegs and drove one in the ground at the beginning of each reign, and gave it that King's name—thus:

I measured all the reigns exactly as many feet to the reign as there were years in it. You can look out over the grounds and see the little pegs from the front door—some of them close together, like Richard II, Richard Cromwell, James II, &c., and some prodigiously wide apart, like Henry III, Edward III, George III, &c. It gives the children a realizing sense of the length or brevity of a reign. Shall invent a violent game to go with it.

And in bed, last night, I invented a way to play it indoors—in a far more voluminous way, as to multiplicity of dates and events—on a cribbage board.

*Hello, supper's ready.*

*Love to all.*

*Good bye.*

*SAML.*

*Onion Clemens would naturally get excited over the idea of the game and its commercial possibilities. Not more so than his brother, however, who presently employed him to arrange a quantity of historical data which the game was to teach. For a season, indeed, interest in the game became a sort of midsummer madness which pervaded the two households, at Keokuk and at Quarry Farm. Howells wrote his approval of the idea of "learning history by the running foot," which was a pun, even if unintentional, for in its out-door form it was a game of speed as well as knowledge.*

*Howells adds that he has noticed that the newspapers are exploiting Mark Twain's new invention of a history game, and we shall presently see how this happened.*

*Also, in this letter, Howells speaks of an English nobleman to whom he has given a letter of introduction. "He seemed a simple, quiet, gentlemanly man, with a good taste in literature, which he evinced by going about with my books in his pockets, and talking of yours."*

To W. D. Howells, in Boston:

MY DEAR HOWELLS,—How odd it seems, to sit down to write a letter with the feeling that you've got time to do it. But I'm done work, for this season, and so have got time. I've done two seasons' work in one, and haven't anything left to do, now, but revise. I've written eight or nine hundred MS pages in such a brief space of time that I mustn't name the number of days; I shouldn't believe it myself, and of course couldn't expect you to. I used to restrict myself to 4 or 5 hours a day and 5 days in the week, but this time I've wrought from breakfast till 5.15 p.m. six days in the week; and once or twice I smouched a Sunday when the boss wasn't looking. Nothing is half so good as literature hooked on Sunday, on the sly.

I wrote you and Twichell on the same night, about the game, and was appalled to get a note from him saying he was going to print part of my letter, and was going to do it before I could get a chance to forbid it. I telegraphed him, but was of course too late.

If you haven't ever tried to invent an indoor historical game, don't. I've got the thing at last so it will work, I guess, but I don't want any more tasks of that kind. When I wrote you, I thought I had it; whereas I was only merely entering upon the initiatory difficulties of it. I might have known it wouldn't be an easy job, or somebody would have invented a decent historical game long ago—a thing which nobody had done. I think I've got it in pretty fair shape—so I have caveated it.

Earl of Onston—is that it? All right, we shall be very glad to receive them and get acquainted with them. And much obliged to you, too. There's plenty of worse people than the nobilities. I went up and spent a week with the Marquis and the Princess Louise, and had as good a time as I want.

I'm powerful glad you are all back again; and we will come up there if our little tribe will give us the necessary furlough; and if we can't get it, you folks must come to us and give us an extension of time. We get home Sept. 11.

Hello, I think I see Waring coming!

Good-by-letter from Clark, which explains for him.

Love to you all from the

*CLEMENSES.*

No—it wasn't Waring. I wonder what the devil has become of that man. He was to spend to-day with us, and the day's most gone, now.

We are enjoying your story with our usual unspeakableness; and I'm right glad you threw in the shipwreck and the mystery—I like it. Mrs. Crane thinks it's the best story you've written yet. We—but we always think the last one is the best. And why shouldn't it be? Practice helps.

P. S. I thought I had sent all our loves to all of you, but Mrs. Clemens says I haven't. Damn it, a body can't think of everything; but a woman thinks you can. I better seal this, now—else there'll be more criticism.

I perceive I haven't got the love in, yet. Well, we do send the love of all the family to all the Howellses.

*S. L. C.*

*There had been some delay and postponement in the matter of the play which Howells and Clemens agreed to write. They did not put in the entire month of October as they had planned, but they did put in a portion of that month, the latter half, working out their old idea. In the end it became a revival of Colonel Sellers, or rather a caricature of that gentle hearted old visionary. Clemens had always complained that the actor Raymond had never brought out the finer shades of Colonel Sellers's character, but Raymond in his worst performance never belied his original as did Howells and Clemens in his dramatic revival. These two, working together, let their imaginations run riot with disastrous results. The reader can judge something of this himself, from The American Claimant the book which Mark Twain would later build from the play.*

*But at this time they thought it a great triumph. They had "cracked their sides" laughing over its construction, as Howells once said, and they thought the world would do the same over its performance. They decided to offer it to Raymond, but rather haughtily, indifferently, because any number of other actors would be waiting for it.*

*But this was a miscalculation. Raymond now turned the tables. Though favorable to the idea of a new play, he declared this one did not present his old Sellers at all, but a lunatic. In the end he returned the MS. with a brief note. Attempts had already been made to interest other actors, and would continue for some time.*

## XXIV. LETTERS, 1884, TO HOWELLS AND OTHERS. CABLE'S GREAT APRIL FOOL. "HUCK FINN" IN PRESS. MARK TWAIN FOR CLEVELAND. CLEMENS AND CABLE.

*Mark Twain had a lingering attack of the dramatic fever that winter. He made a play of the Prince and Pauper, which Howells pronounced "too thin and slight and not half long enough." He made another of Tom Sawyer, and probably destroyed it, for no trace of the MS. exists to-day. Howells could not join in these ventures, for he was otherwise occupied and had sickness in his household.*

To W. D. Howells, in Boston:

*Jan. 7, '84.*

MY DEAR HOWELLS,—"O my goodn's", as Jean says. You have now encountered at last the heaviest calamity that can befall an author. The scarlet fever, once domesticated, is a permanent member of the family. Money may desert you, friends forsake you, enemies grow indifferent to you, but the scarlet fever will be true to you, through thick and thin, till you be all saved or damned, down to the last one. I say these things to cheer you.

The bare suggestion of scarlet fever in the family makes me shudder; I believe I would almost rather have Osgood publish a book for me.

You folks have our most sincere sympathy. Oh, the intrusion of this hideous disease is an unspeakable disaster.

My billiard table is stacked up with books relating to the Sandwich Islands: the walls axe upholstered with scraps of paper penciled with notes drawn from them. I have saturated myself with knowledge of that unimaginably beautiful land and that most strange and fascinating people. And I have begun a story. Its hidden motive will illustrate a but-little considered fact in human nature; that the religious folly you are born in you will die in, no matter what apparently reasonabler religious folly may seem to have taken its place meanwhile, and abolished and obliterated it. I start Bill Ragsdale at 12 years of age, and the heroine at 4, in the midst of the ancient idolatrous system, with its picturesque and amazing customs and superstitions, 3 months before the arrival of the missionaries and the erection of a shallow Christianity upon the ruins of the old paganism. Then these two will become educated Christians, and highly civilized.

And then I will jump 15 years, and do Ragsdale's leper business. When we came to dramatize, we can draw a deal of matter from the story, all ready to our hand.

*Yrs Ever*

*MARK.*

*He never finished the Sandwich Islands story which he and Howells were to dramatize later. His head filled up with other projects, such as publishing plans, reading-tours, and the like. The type-setting machine does not appear in the letters of this period, but it was an important factor, nevertheless. It was costing several thousand dollars a month for construction and becoming a heavy drain on Mark Twain's finances. It was necessary to recuperate, and the anxiety for a profitable play, or some other adventure that would bring a quick and generous return, grew out of this need.*

*Clemens had established Charles L. Webster, his nephew by marriage, in a New York office, as selling agent for the Mississippi book and for his plays. He was also planning to let Webster publish the new book, Huck Finn.*

*George W. Cable had proven his ability as a reader, and Clemens saw possibilities in a reading combination, which was first planned to include Aldrich, and Howells, and a private car.*

*But Aldrich and Howells did not warm to the idea, and the car was eliminated from the plan. Cable came to visit Clemens in Hartford, and was taken with the mumps, so that the reading-trip was postponed.*

*The fortunes of the Sellers play were most uncertain and becoming daily more doubtful. In February, Howells wrote: "If you have got any comfort in regard to our play I wish you would heave it into my bosom."*

*Cable recovered in time, and out of gratitude planned a great April-fool surprise for his host. He was a systematic man, and did it in his usual thorough way. He sent a "private and confidential" suggestion to a hundred and fifty of Mark Twain's friends and admirers, nearly all distinguished literary men. The suggestion was that each one of them should send a request for Mark Twain's autograph, timing it so that it would arrive on the 1st of April. All seemed to have responded. Mark Twain's writing-table on April*

*Fool morning was heaped with letters, asking in every ridiculous fashion for his "valuable autograph." The one from Aldrich was a fair sample. He wrote: "I am making a collection of autographs of our distinguished writers, and having read one of your works, Gabriel Convoy, I would like to add your name to the list."*

*Of course, the joke in this was that Gabriel Convoy was by Bret Harte, who by this time was thoroughly detested by Mark Twain. The first one or two of the letters puzzled the victim; then he comprehended the size and character of the joke and entered into it thoroughly. One of the letters was from Bloodgood H. Cutter, the "Poet Lariat" of Innocents Abroad. Cutter, of course, wrote in "poetry," that is to say, doggerel. Mark Twain's April Fool was a most pleasant one.*

Rhymed letter by Bloodgood H. Cutter to Mark Twain:

*LITTLE NECK, LONG ISLAND.*

*LONG ISLAND FARMER, TO HIS FRIEND AND PILGRIM BROTHER,*

*SAMUEL L. CLEMENS, ESQ.*

*Friends, suggest in each one's behalf*

*To write, and ask your autograph.*

*To refuse that, I will not do,*

*After the long voyage had with you.*

*That was a memorable time You wrote in prose, I wrote in Rhyme To describe the wonders of each place, And the queer customs of each race.*

*That is in my memory yet*
*For while I live I'll not forget.*
*I often think of that affair*
*And the many that were with us there.*

*As your friends think it for the best*
*I ask your Autograph with the rest,*
*Hoping you will it to me send*
*'Twill please and cheer your dear old friend:*

*Yours truly,*

*BLOODGOOD H. CUTTER.*

To W. D. Howells, in Boston:

*HARTFORD, Apl 8, '84.*

MY DEAR HOWELLS, It took my breath away, and I haven't recovered it yet, entirely—I mean the generosity of your proposal to read the proofs of Huck Finn.

Now if you mean it, old man—if you are in earnest—proceed, in God's name, and be by me forever blest. I cannot conceive of a rational man deliberately piling such an atrocious job upon himself; but if there is such a man and you be that man, why then pile it on. It will cost me a pang every time I think of it, but this anguish will be eingebusst to me in the joy and comfort I shall get out of the not having to read the verfluchtete proofs myself. But if you have repented of your augenblichlicher Tobsucht and got back to calm cold reason again, I won't hold you to it unless I find I have got you down in writing somewhere. Herr, I would not read the proof of one of my books for any fair and reasonable sum whatever, if I could get out of it.

The proof-reading on the P & P cost me the last rags of my religion.

*M.*

*Howells had written that he would be glad to help out in the reading of the proofs of Huck Finn, which book Webster by this time had in hand. Replying to Clemens's eager and grateful acceptance now, he wrote: "It is all perfectly true about the generosity, unless I am going to read your proofs from one of the shabby motives which I always find at the bottom of my soul if I examine it." A characteristic utterance, though we may be permitted to believe that his shabby motives were fewer and less shabby than those of mankind in general.*

*The proofs which Howells was reading pleased him mightily. Once, during the summer, he wrote: "if I had written half as good a book as Huck Finn I shouldn't ask anything better than to read the proofs; even as it is, I don't, so send them on; they will always find me somewhere."*

*This was the summer of the Blaine-Cleveland campaign. Mark Twain, in company with many other leading men, had mugwumped, and was supporting Cleveland. From the next letter we gather something of the aspects of that memorable campaign, which was one of scandal and vituperation. We learn, too, that the young sculptor, Karl Gerhardt, having completed a three years' study in Paris, had returned to America a qualified artist.*

To W. D. Howells, in Boston:

*ELMIRA, Aug. 21, '84.*

MY DEAR HOWELLS,—This presidential campaign is too delicious for anything. Isn't human nature the most consummate sham and lie that was ever invented? Isn't man a creature to be ashamed of in pretty much all his aspects? Man, "know thyself "—and then thou wilt despise thyself, to a dead moral certainty. Take three quite good specimens—Hawley, Warner, and Charley Clark. Even I do not loathe Blaine more than they do; yet Hawley is howling for Blaine, Warner and Clark are eating their daily crow in the paper for him, and all three will vote for him. O Stultification, where is thy sting, O slave where is thy hickory!

I suppose you heard how a marble monument for which St. Gaudens was pecuniarily responsible, burned down in Hartford the other day, uninsured—for who in the world would ever think of insuring a marble shaft in a cemetery against a fire?—and left St. Gauden out of pocket $15,000.

It was a bad day for artists. Gerhardt finished my bust that day, and the work was pronounced admirable by all the kin and friends; but in putting it in plaster (or rather taking it out) next day it got ruined. It was four or five weeks hard work gone to the dogs. The news flew, and everybody on the farm flocked to the arbor and grouped themselves about the wreck in a profound and moving silence—the farm-help, the colored servants, the German nurse, the children, everybody—a silence interrupted at wide intervals by absent-minded ejaculations wising from unconscious breasts as the whole size of the disaster gradually worked its way home to the realization of one spirit after another.

Some burst out with one thing, some another; the German nurse put up her hands and said, "Oh, Schade! oh, schrecklich!" But Gerhardt said nothing; or almost that. He couldn't word it, I suppose. But he went to work, and by dark had everything thoroughly well under way for a fresh start in the morning; and in three days' time had built a new bust which was a trifle better than the old one—and to-morrow we shall put the finishing touches on it, and it will be about as good a one as nearly anybody can make.

*Yrs Ever*

*MARK.*

If you run across anybody who wants a bust, be sure and recommend Gerhardt on my say-so.

*But Howells was determinedly for Blaine. "I shall vote for Blaine," he replied. "I do not believe he is guilty of the things they accuse him of, and I know they are not proved against him. As for Cleveland, his private life may be no worse than that of most men, but as an enemy of that contemptible, hypocritical, lop-sided morality which says a woman shall suffer all the shame of unchastity and man none, I want to see him destroyed politically by his past. The men who defend him would take their wives to the White House if he were president, but if he married his concubine—'made her an honest woman' they would not go near him. I can't stand that."*

*Certainly this was sound logic, in that day, at least. But it left Clemens far from satisfied.*

To W. D. Howells, in Boston:

*ELMIRA, Sept. 17, '84.*

MY DEAR HOWELLS,—Somehow I can't seem to rest quiet under the idea of your voting for Blaine. I believe you said something about the country and the party. Certainly allegiance to these is well; but as certainly a man's first duty is to his own conscience and honor—the party or the country come second to that, and never first. I don't ask you to vote at all—I only urge you to not soil yourself by voting for Blaine.

When you wrote before, you were able to say the charges against him were not proven. But you know now that they are proven, and it seems to me that that bars you and all other honest and honorable men (who are independently situated) from voting for him.

It is not necessary to vote for Cleveland; the only necessary thing to do, as I understand it, is that a man shall keep himself clean, (by withholding his vote for an improper man) even though the party and the country go to destruction in consequence. It is not parties that make or save countries or that build them to greatness—it is clean men, clean ordinary citizens, rank and file, the masses. Clean masses are not made by individuals standing back till the rest become clean.

As I said before, I think a man's first duty is to his own honor; not to his country and not to his party. Don't be offended; I mean no offence. I am not so concerned about the rest of the nation, but—well, good-bye.

*Ys Ever*

*MARK.*

*There does not appear to be any further discussion of the matter between Howells and Clemens. Their letters for a time contained no suggestion of politics.*

*Perhaps Mark Twain's own political conscience was not entirely clear in his repudiation of his party; at least we may believe from his next letter that his Cleveland enthusiasm was qualified by a willingness to support a Republican who would command his admiration and honor. The idea of an eleventh-hour nomination was rather startling, whatever its motive.*

To Mr. Pierce, in Boston:

*HARTFORD, Oct. 22, '84.*

MY DEAR MR. PIERCE,—You know, as well as I do, that the reason the majority of republicans are going to vote for Blaine is because they feel that they cannot help themselves. Do not you believe that if Mr. Edmunds would consent to run for President, on the Independent ticket—even at this late day—he might be elected?

Well, if he wouldn't consent, but should even strenuously protest and say he wouldn't serve if elected, isn't it still wise and fair to nominate him and vote for him? since his protest would relieve him from all responsibility; and he couldn't surely find fault with people for forcing a compliment upon him. And do not you believe that his name thus compulsorily placed at the head of the Independent column would work absolutely certain defeat to Blain and save the country's honor?

Politicians often carry a victory by springing some disgraceful and rascally mine under the feet of the adversary at the eleventh hour; would it not be wholesome to vary this thing for once and spring as formidable a mine of a better sort under the enemy's works?

If Edmunds's name were put up, I would vote for him in the teeth of all the protesting and blaspheming he could do in a month; and there are lots of others who would do likewise.

If this notion is not a foolish and wicked one, won't you just consult with some chief Independents, and see if they won't call a sudden convention and whoop the thing through? To nominate Edmunds the 1st of November, would be soon enough, wouldn't it?

With kindest regards to you and the Aldriches,

*Yr Truly*

*S. L. CLEMENS.*

*Clemens and Cable set out on their reading-tour in November. They were a curiously-assorted pair: Cable was of orthodox religion, exact as to habits, neat, prim, all that Clemens was not. In the beginning Cable undertook to read the Bible aloud to Clemens each evening, but this part of the day's program was presently omitted by request. If they spent Sunday in a town, Cable was up bright and early visiting the various churches and Sunday-schools, while Mark Twain remained at the hotel, in bed, reading or asleep.*

## XXV. THE GREAT YEAR OF 1885. CLEMENS AND CABLE. PUBLICATION OF "HUCK FINN." THE GRANT MEMOIRS. MARK TWAIN AT FIFTY.

*The year 1885 was in some respects the most important, certainly the most pleasantly exciting, in Mark Twain's life. It was the year in which he entered fully into the publishing business and launched one of the most spectacular of all publishing adventures, The Personal Memoirs of General U. S. Grant. Clemens had not intended to do general publishing when he arranged with Webster to become sales-agent for the Mississippi book, and later general agent for Huck Finn's adventures; he had intended only to handle his own books, because he was pretty thoroughly dissatisfied with other publishing arrangements. Even the Library of Humor, which Howells, with Clark, of the Courant, had put together for him, he left with Osgood until that publisher failed, during the spring of 1885. Certainly he never dreamed of undertaking anything of the proportions of the Grant book.*

*He had always believed that Grant could make a book. More than once, when they had met, he had urged the General to prepare his memoirs for publication. Howells, in his 'My Mark Twain', tells of going with Clemens to see Grant, then a member of the ill-fated firm of Grant and Ward, and how they lunched on beans, bacon and coffee brought in from a near-by restaurant. It was while they were eating this soldier fare that Clemens—very likely abetted by Howells—especially urged the great commander to prepare his memoirs. But Grant had become a financier, as he believed, and the prospect of literary earnings, however large, did not appeal to him. Furthermore, he was convinced that he was without literary ability and that a book by him would prove a failure.*

*But then, by and by, came a failure more disastrous than anything he had foreseen—the downfall of his firm through the Napoleonic rascality of Ward. General Grant was utterly ruined; he was left without income and apparently without the means of earning one. It was the period when the great War Series was appeasing in the Century Magazine. General Grant, hard-pressed, was induced by the editors to prepare one or more articles, and, finding that he could write them, became interested in the idea of a book. It is unnecessary to repeat here the story of how the publication of this important work passed into the hands of Mark Twain; that is to say, the firm of Charles L. Webster & Co., the details having been fully given elsewhere.—[See Mark Twain: A Biography, chap. cliv.]—*

*We will now return for the moment to other matters, as reported in order by the letters. Clemens and Cable had continued their reading-tour into Canada, and in February found themselves in*

*Montreal. Here they were invited by the Toque Bleue Snow-shoe Club to join in one of their weekly excursions across Mt. Royal. They could not go, and the reasons given by Mark Twain are not without interest. The letter is to Mr. George Iles, author of Flame, Electricity, and the Camera, and many other useful works.*

To George Iles, far the Toque Blew Snow-shoe Club, Montreal:

*DETROIT, February 12, 1885.*

*Midnight, P.S.*

MY DEAR ILES,—I got your other telegram a while ago, and answered it, explaining that I get only a couple of hours in the middle of the day for social life. I know it doesn't seem rational that a man should have to lie abed all day in order to be rested and equipped for talking an hour at night, and yet in my case and Cable's it is so. Unless I get a great deal of rest, a ghastly dulness settles down upon me on the platform, and turns my performance into work, and hard work, whereas it ought always to be pastime, recreation, solid enjoyment. Usually it is just this latter, but that is because I take my rest faithfully, and prepare myself to do my duty by my audience.

I am the obliged and appreciative servant of my brethren of the Snow-shoe Club, and nothing in the world would delight me more than to come to their house without naming time or terms on my own part—but you see how it is. My cast iron duty is to my audience—it leaves me no liberty and no option.

With kindest regards to the Club, and to you,

*I am Sincerely yours*

*S. L. CLEMENS.*

*In the next letter we reach the end of the Clemens-Cable venture and get a characteristic summing up of Mark Twain's general attitude toward the companion of his travels. It must be read only in the clear realization of Mark Twain's attitude toward orthodoxy, and his habit of humor. Cable was as rigidly orthodox as Mark Twain was revolutionary. The two were never anything but the best of friends.*

To W. D. Howells, in Boston:

*PHILADA. Feb. 27, '85.*

MY DEAR HOWELLS,—To-night in Baltimore, to-morrow afternoon and night in Washington, and my four-months platform campaign is ended at last. It has been a curious experience. It has taught me that Cable's gifts of mind are greater and higher than I had suspected. But—

That "But" is pointing toward his religion. You will never, never know, never divine, guess, imagine, how loathsome a thing the Christian religion can be made until you come to know and study Cable daily and hourly. Mind you, I like him; he is pleasant company; I rage and swear at him sometimes, but we do not quarrel; we get along mighty happily together; but in him and his person I have learned to hate all religions. He has taught me to abhor and detest the Sabbath-day and hunt up new and troublesome ways to dishonor it.

Nat Goodwin was on the train yesterday. He plays in Washington all the coming week. He is very anxious to get our Sellers play and play it under changed names. I said the only thing I could do would be to write to you. Well, I've done it.

*Ys Ever*

*MARK.*

*Clemens and Webster were often at the house of General Grant during these early days of 1885, and it must have been Webster who was present with Clemens on the great occasion described in the following telegram. It was on the last day and hour of President Arthur's administration that the bill was passed which placed Ulysses S. Grant as full General with full pay on the retired list, and it is said that the congressional clock was set back in order that this enactment might become a law before the administration changed. General Grant had by this time developed cancer and was already in feeble health.*

Telegram to Mrs. Clemens, in Hartford:

*NEW YORK, Mar. 4, 1885.*

To MRS. S. L. CLEMENS, We were at General Grant's at noon and a telegram arrived that the last act of the expiring congress late this morning retired him with full General's rank and accompanying emoluments. The effect upon him was like raising the dead. We were present when the telegram was put in his hand.

*S. L. CLEMENS.*

*Something has been mentioned before of Mark Twain's investments and the generally unprofitable habit of them. He had a trusting nature, and was usually willing to invest money on any plausible recommendation. He was one of thousands such, and being a person of distinction he now and then received letters of inquiry, complaint, or condolence. A minister wrote him that he had bought some stocks recommended by a Hartford banker and advertised in a religious paper. He added, "After I made that purchase they wrote me that you had just bought a hundred shares and that you were a 'shrewd' man."*

*The writer closed by asking for further information. He received it, as follows:*

To the Rev. J——, in Baltimore:

*WASHINGTON, Mch. 2,'85.*

MY DEAR SIR,—I take my earliest opportunity to answer your favor of Feb. B—— was premature in calling me a "shrewd man." I wasn't one at that time, but am one now—that is, I am at least too shrewd to ever again invest in anything put on the market by B——. I know nothing whatever about the Bank Note Co., and never did know anything about it. B—— sold me about $4,000 or $5,000 worth of the stock at $110, and I own it yet. He sold me $10,000 worth of another rose-tinted stock about the same time. I have got that yet, also. I judge that a peculiarity of B——'s stocks is that they are of the staying kind. I think you should have asked somebody else whether I was a shrewd man or not for two reasons: the stock was advertised in a religious paper, a circumstance which was very suspicious; and the compliment came to you from a man who was interested to make a purchaser of you. I am afraid you deserve your loss. A financial scheme advertised in any religious paper is a thing which any living person ought to know enough to avoid; and when the factor is added that M. runs that religious paper, a dead person ought to know enough to avoid it.

*Very Truly Yours*

*S. L. CLEMENS.*

*The story of Huck Finn was having a wide success. Webster handled it skillfully, and the sales were large. In almost every quarter its welcome was enthusiastic. Here and there, however, could be found an exception; Huck's morals were not always approved of by library reading-committees. The first instance of this kind was reported from Concord; and would seem not to have depressed the author-publisher.*

To Chas. L. Webster, in New York:

*Mch 18, '85.*

DEAR CHARLEY,—The Committee of the Public Library of Concord, Mass, have given us a rattling tip-top puff which will go into every paper in the country. They have expelled Huck from their library as "trash and suitable only for the slums." That will sell 25,000 copies for us sure.

*S. L. C.*

*Perhaps the Concord Free Trade Club had some idea of making amends to Mark Twain for the slight put upon his book by their librarians, for immediately after the Huck Finn incident they notified him of his election to honorary membership.*

*Those were the days of "authors' readings," and Clemens and Howells not infrequently assisted at these functions, usually given as benefits of one kind or another. From the next letter, written following an entertainment given for the Longfellow memorial, we gather that Mark Twain's opinion of Howells's reading was steadily improving.*

To W. D. Howells, in Boston:

*HARTFORD, May 5, '85.*

MY DEAR HOWELLS,—.... Who taught you to read? Observation and thought, I guess. And practice at the Tavern Club?—yes; and that was the best teaching of all:

Well, you sent even your daintiest and most delicate and fleeting points home to that audience—absolute proof of good reading. But you couldn't read worth a damn a few years ago. I do not say this to flatter. It is true I looked around for you when I was leaving, but you had already gone.

Alas, Osgood has failed at last. It was easy to see that he was on the very verge of it a year ago, and it was also easy to see that he was still on the verge of it a month or two ago; but I continued to hope—but not expect that he would pull through. The Library of Humor is at his dwelling house, and he will hand it to you whenever you want it.

To save it from any possibility of getting mixed up in the failure, perhaps you had better send down and get it. I told him, the other day, that an order of any kind from you would be his sufficient warrant for its delivery to you.

In two days General Grant has dictated 50 pages of foolscap, and thus the Wilderness and Appomattox stand for all time in his own words. This makes the second volume of his book as valuable as the first.

He looks mighty well, these latter days.

*Yrs Ever*

*MARK.*

*"I am exceedingly glad," wrote Howells, "that you approve of my reading, for it gives me some hope that I may do something on the platform next winter.... but I would never read within a hundred miles of you, if I could help it. You simply straddled down to the footlights and took that house up in the hollow of your hand and tickled it."*

To W. D. Howells, in Boston:

*ELMIRA, July 21, 1885.*

MY DEAR HOWELLS,—You are really my only author; I am restricted to you, I wouldn't give a damn for the rest.

I bored through Middlemarch during the past week, with its labored and tedious analyses of feelings and motives, its paltry and tiresome people, its unexciting and uninteresting story, and its frequent blinding flashes of single-sentence poetry, philosophy, wit, and what not, and nearly died from the overwork. I wouldn't read another of those books for a farm. I did try to read one other—Daniel Deronda. I dragged through three chapters, losing flesh all the time, and then was honest enough to quit, and confess to myself that I haven't any romance literature appetite, as far as I can see, except for your books.

But what I started to say, was, that I have just read Part II of Indian Summer, and to my mind there isn't a waste line in it, or one that could be improved. I read it yesterday, ending with that opinion; and read it again to-day, ending with the same opinion emphasized. I haven't read Part I yet, because that number must have reached Hartford after we left; but we are going to send down town for a copy, and when it comes I am to read both parts aloud to the family. It is a beautiful story, and makes a body laugh all the time, and cry inside, and feel so old and so forlorn; and gives him gracious glimpses of his lost youth that fill him with a measureless regret, and build up in him a cloudy sense of his having been a prince, once, in some enchanted far-off land, and of being an exile now, and desolate—and Lord, no chance ever to get back there again! That is the thing that hurts. Well, you have done it with marvelous facility and you make all the motives and feelings perfectly clear without analyzing the guts out of them, the way George Eliot does. I can't stand George Eliot and Hawthorne and those people; I see what they are at a hundred years before they get to it and they just tire me to death. And as for "The Bostonians," I would rather be damned to John Bunyan's heaven than read that.

*Yrs Ever*

*MARK*

*It is as easy to understand Mark Twain's enjoyment of Indian Summer as his revolt against Daniel Deronda and The Bostonians. He cared little for writing that did not convey its purpose in the simplest and most direct terms. It is interesting to note that in thanking Clemens for his compliment Howells wrote: "What people cannot see is that I analyze as little as possible; they go on talking about the analytical school, which I am supposed to belong to, and I want to thank you for using your eyes..... Did you ever read De Foe's 'Roxana'? If not, then read it, not merely for some of the deepest insights into the lying, suffering, sinning, well-meaning human soul, but for the best and most natural English that a book was ever written in."*

*General Grant worked steadily on his book, dictating when he could, making brief notes on slips of paper when he could no longer speak. Clemens visited him at Mt. McGregor and brought the dying soldier the comforting news that enough of his books were already sold to provide generously for his family, and that the sales would aggregate at least twice as much by the end of the year.*

*This was some time in July. On the 23d of that month General Grant died. Immediately there was a newspaper discussion as to the most suitable place for the great chieftain to lie. Mark Twain's contribution to this debate, though in the form of an open letter, seems worthy of preservation here.*

To the New York "Sun," on the proper place for Grant's Tomb:

To THE EDITOR OP' THE SUN:—SIR,—The newspaper atmosphere is charged with objections to New York as a place of sepulchre for General Grant, and the objectors are strenuous that Washington is the right place. They offer good reasons—good temporary reasons—for both of these positions.

But it seems to me that temporary reasons are not mete for the occasion. We need to consider posterity rather than our own generation. We should select a grave which will not merely be in the right place now, but will still be in the right place 500 years from now.

How does Washington promise as to that? You have only to hit it in one place to kill it. Some day the west will be numerically strong enough to move the seat of government; her past attempts are a fair warning that when the day comes she will do it. Then the city of Washington will lose its consequence and pass out of the public view and public talk. It is quite within the possibilities that, a century hence, people would wonder and say, "How did your predecessors come to bury their great dead in this deserted place?"

But as long as American civilisation lasts New York will last. I cannot but think she has been well and wisely chosen as the guardian of a grave which is destined to become almost the most conspicuous in the world's history. Twenty centuries from now New York will still be New York, still a vast city, and the most notable object in it will still be the tomb and monument of General Grant.

*I observe that the common and strongest objection to New York is that she is not "national ground." Let us give ourselves no uneasiness about that. Wherever General Grant's body lies, that is national ground.*

*S. L. CLEMENS.*

*ELMIRA, July 27.*

*The letter that follows is very long, but it seems too important and too interesting to be omitted in any part. General Grant's early indulgence in liquors had long been a matter of wide, though not very definite, knowledge. Every one had heard how Lincoln, on being told that Grant drank, remarked something to the effect that he would like to know what kind of whisky Grant used so that he might get some of it for his other generals. Henry Ward Beecher, selected to deliver a eulogy on the dead soldier, and doubtless wishing neither to ignore the matter nor to make too much of it, naturally turned for information to the publisher of Grant's own memoirs, hoping from an advance copy to obtain light.*

To Henry Ward Beecher, Brooklyn:

*ELMIRA, N. Y. Sept. 11, '85.*

MY DEAR MR. BEECHER,—My nephew Webster is in Europe making contracts for the Memoirs. Before he sailed he came to me with a writing, directed to the printers and binders, to this effect:

"Honor no order for a sight or copy of the Memoirs while I am absent, even though it be signed by Mr. Clemens himself."

I gave my permission. There were weighty reasons why I should not only give my permission, but hold it a matter of honor to not dissolve the order or modify it at any time. So I did all of that—said the order should stand undisturbed to the end. If a principal could dissolve his promise as innocently as he can dissolve his written order unguarded by his promise, I would send you a copy of the Memoirs instantly. I did not foresee you, or I would have made an exception.

..........................

My idea gained from army men, is that the drunkenness (and sometimes pretty reckless spreeing, nights,) ceased before he came East to be Lt. General.

(Refer especially to Gen. Wm. B. Franklin—[If you could see Franklin and talk with him—then he would unbosom,]) It was while Grant was still in the West that Mr. Lincoln said he wished he could find out what brand of whisky that fellow used, so he could furnish it to some of the other generals. Franklin saw Grant tumble from his horse drunk, while reviewing troops in New Orleans. The fall gave him a good deal of a hurt. He was then on the point of leaving for the Chattanooga region. I naturally put "that and that together" when I read Gen. O. O. Howards's article in the Christian Union, three or four weeks ago—where he mentions that the new General arrived lame from a recent accident. (See that article.) And why not write Howard?

Franklin spoke positively of the frequent spreeing. In camp—in time of war.

.........................

Captain Grant was frequently threatened by the Commandant of his Oregon post with a report to the War Department of his conduct unless he modified his intemperance. The report would mean dismissal from the service. At last the report had to be made out; and then, so greatly was the captain beloved, that he was privately informed, and was thus enabled to rush his resignation to Washington ahead of the report. Did the report go, nevertheless? I don't know. If it did, it is in the War Department now, possibly, and seeable. I got all this from a regular army man, but I can't name him to save me.

The only time General Grant ever mentioned liquor to me was about last April or possibly May. He said:

"If I could only build up my strength! The doctors urge whisky and champagne; but I can't take them; I can't abide the taste of any kind of liquor."

Had he made a conquest so complete that even the taste of liquor was become an offense? Or was he so sore over what had been said about his habit that he wanted to persuade others and likewise himself that he hadn't even ever had any taste for it? It sounded like the latter, but that's no evidence.

He told me in the fall of '84 that there was something the matter with his throat, and that at the suggestion of his physicians he had reduced his smoking to one cigar a day. Then he added, in a casual fashion, that he didn't care for that one, and seldom smoked it.

I could understand that feeling. He had set out to conquer not the habit but the inclination—the desire. He had gone at the root, not the trunk. It's the perfect way and the only true way (I speak from experience.) How I do hate those enemies of the human race who go around enslaving God's free people with pledges—to quit drinking instead of to quit wanting to drink.

But Sherman and Van Vliet know everything concerning Grant; and if you tell them how you want to use the facts, both of them will testify. Regular army men have no concealments about each other; and yet they make their awful statements without shade or color or malice with a frankness and a child-like naivety, indeed, which is enchanting-and stupefying. West Point seems to teach them that, among other priceless things not to be got in any other college in this world. If we talked about our guild-mates as I have heard Sherman, Grant, Van Vliet and others talk about theirs—mates with whom they were on the best possible terms—we could never expect them to speak to us again.

......................

I am reminded, now, of another matter. The day of the funeral I sat an hour over a single drink and several cigars with Van Vliet and Sherman and Senator Sherman; and among other things Gen. Sherman said, with impatient scorn:

"The idea of all this nonsense about Grant not being able to stand rude language and indelicate stories! Why Grant was full of humor, and full of the appreciation of it. I have sat with him by the hour listening to Jim Nye's yarns, and I reckon you know the style of Jim Nye's histories, Clemens. It makes me sick—that newspaper nonsense. Grant was no namby-pamby fool, he was a man—all over—rounded and complete."

I wish I had thought of it! I would have said to General Grant: "Put the drunkenness in the Memoirs—and the repentance and reform. Trust the people."

But I will wager there is not a hint in the book. He was sore, there. As much of the book as I have read gives no hint, as far as I recollect.

The sick-room brought out the points of Gen. Grant's character—some of them particularly, to wit:

His patience; his indestructible equability of temper; his exceeding gentleness, kindness, forbearance, lovingness, charity; his loyalty: to friends, to convictions, to promises, half-promises, infinitesimal fractions and shadows of promises; (There was a requirement of him which I considered an atrocity, an injustice, an outrage; I wanted to implore him to repudiate it; Fred Grant said, "Save your labor, I know him; he is in doubt as to whether he made that half-promise or not—and, he will give the thing the benefit of the doubt; he will fulfill that half-promise or kill himself trying;" Fred Grant was right—he did fulfill it;) his aggravatingly trustful nature; his genuineness, simplicity, modesty, diffidence, self-depreciation, poverty in the quality of vanity-and, in no contradiction of this last, his simple pleasure in the flowers and general ruck sent to him by Tom, Dick and Harry from everywhere—a pleasure that suggested a perennial surprise that he should be the object of so much fine attention—he was the most lovable great child in the world; (I mentioned his loyalty: you remember Harrison, the colored body-servant? the whole family hated him, but that did not make any difference, the General always stood at his back, wouldn't allow him to be scolded; always excused his failures and deficiencies with the one unvarying formula, "We are responsible for these things in his race—it is not fair to visit our fault upon them—let him alone;" so they did let him alone, under compulsion, until the great heart that was his shield was taken away; then—well they simply couldn't stand him, and so they were excusable for determining to discharge him—a thing which they mortally hated to do, and by lucky accident were saved from the necessity of doing;) his toughness as a bargainer when doing business for other people or for his country (witness his "terms" at Donelson, Vicksburg, etc.; Fred Grant told me his father wound up an estate for the widow and orphans of a friend in St. Louis—it took several years; at the end every complication had been straightened out, and the property put upon a prosperous basis; great sums had passed through his hands, and when he handed over the papers there were vouchers to show what had been done with every penny) and his trusting, easy, unexacting fashion when doing business for himself (at that same time he was paying out money in driblets to a man who was running his farm for him—and in his first Presidency he paid every one of those driblets again (total, $3,000 F. said,) for he hadn't a scrap of paper to show that he had ever paid them before; in his dealings with me he would not listen to terms which would place my money at risk and leave him protected—the thought plainly gave him pain, and he put it from him, waved it off with his hands, as one does accounts of crushings and mutilations—wouldn't listen, changed the subject;) and his fortitude! He was under, sentence of death last spring; he sat thinking, musing, several days—nobody knows what about; then he pulled himself together and set to work to finish that book, a colossal task for a dying man. Presently his hand gave out; fate seemed to have got him checkmated. Dictation was suggested. No, he never could do that; had never tried it; too old to learn, now. By and by—if he could only do Appomattox-well. So he sent for a stenographer, and dictated 9,000 words at a single sitting!—never pausing, never hesitating for a word, never repeating—and in the written-out copy he made hardly a correction. He dictated again, every two or three days—the intervals were intervals of exhaustion and slow recuperation—and at last he was able to tell me that he had written more matter than could be got into the book. I then enlarged the book—had to. Then he lost his voice. He was not quite done yet, however:—there was no end of little plums and spices to be stuck in, here and there; and this work he patiently continued, a few lines a day, with pad and pencil, till far into July, at Mt. McGregor. One day he put his pencil aside, and said he was done—there was nothing more to do. If I had been there I could have foretold the shock that struck the world three days later.

Well, I've written all this, and it doesn't seem to amount to anything. But I do want to help, if I only could. I will enclose some scraps from my Autobiography—scraps about General Grant—they may be of some trifle of use, and they may not—they at least verify known traits of his character. My Autobiography is pretty freely dictated, but my idea is to jack-plane it a little before I die, some day or other; I mean the rude construction and rotten grammar. It is the only dictating I ever did, and it was most troublesome and awkward work. You may return it to Hartford.

*Sincerely Yours*

*S. L. CLEMENS.*

*The old long-deferred Library of Humor came up again for discussion, when in the fall of 1885 Howells associated himself with Harper & Brothers. Howells's contract provided that his name was not to appear on any book not published by the Harper firm. He wrote, therefore, offering to sell out his interest in the enterprise for two thousand dollars, in addition to the five hundred which he had already received—an amount considered to be less than he was to have received as joint author and compiler. Mark Twain's answer pretty fully covers the details of this undertaking.*

To W. D. Howells, in Boston:

*HARTFORD, Oct. 18, 1885.*

Private.

MY DEAR HOWELLS,—I reckon it would ruin the book that is, make it necessary to pigeon-hole it and leave it unpublished. I couldn't publish it without a very responsible name to support my own on the title page, because it has so much of my own matter in it. I bought Osgood's rights for $3,000 cash, I have paid Clark $800 and owe him $700 more, which must of course be paid whether I publish or not. Yet I fully recognize that I have no sort of moral right to let that ancient and procrastinated contract hamper you in any way, and I most certainly won't. So, it is my decision,—after thinking over and rejecting the idea of trying to buy permission of the Harpers for $2,500 to use your name, (a proposition which they would hate to refuse to a man in a perplexed position, and yet would naturally have to refuse it,) to pigeon-hole the "Library": not destroy it, but merely pigeon-hole it and wait a few years and see what new notion Providence will take concerning it. He will not desert us now, after putting in four licks to our one on this book all this time. It really seems in a sense discourteous not to call it "Providence's Library of Humor."

Now that deal is all settled, the next question is, do you need and must you require that $2,000 now? Since last March, you know, I am carrying a mighty load, solitary and alone—General Grant's book—and must carry it till the first volume is 30 days old (Jan. 1st) before the relief money will begin to flow in. From now till the first of January every dollar is as valuable to me as it could be to a famishing tramp. If you can wait till then—I mean without discomfort, without inconvenience—it will be a large accommodation to me; but I will not allow you to do this favor if it will discommode you. So, speak right out, frankly, and if you need the money I will go out on the highway and get it, using violence, if necessary.

Mind, I am not in financial difficulties, and am not going to be. I am merely a starving beggar standing outside the door of plenty—obstructed by a Yale time-lock which is set for Jan. 1st. I can stand it, and stand it perfectly well; but the days do seem to fool along considerable slower than they used to.

I am mighty glad you are with the Harpers. I have noticed that good men in their employ go there to stay.

Yours ever,

*MARK.*

*In the next letter we begin to get some idea of the size of Mark Twain's first publishing venture, and a brief summary of results may not be out of place here.*

*The Grant Life was issued in two volumes. In the early months of the year when the agents' canvass was just beginning, Mark Twain, with what seems now almost clairvoyant vision, prophesied a sale of three hundred thousand sets. The actual sales ran somewhat more than this number. On February 27, 1886, Charles L. Webster & Co. paid to Mrs. Grant the largest single royalty check in the history of book-publishing. The amount of it was two hundred thousand dollars. Subsequent checks increased the aggregate return to considerably more than double this figure. In a memorandum made by Clemens in the midst of the canvass he wrote.*

*"During 100 consecutive days the sales (i. e., subscriptions) of General Grant's book averaged 3,000 sets (6,000 single volumes) per day: Roughly stated, Mrs. Grant's income during all that time was $5,000 a day."*

To W. D. Howells, in Boston:

*HOTEL NORMANDIE*

*NEW YORK, Dec. 2, '85.*

MY DEAR HOWELLS,—I told Webster, this afternoon, to send you that $2,000; but he is in such a rush, these first days of publication, that he may possibly forget it; so I write lest I forget it too. Remind me, if he should forget. When I postponed you lately, I did it because I thought I should be cramped for money until January, but that has turned out to be an error, so I hasten to cut short the postponement.

I judge by the newspapers that you are in Auburndale, but I don't know it officially.

I've got the first volume launched safely; consequently, half of the suspense is over, and I am that much nearer the goal. We've bound and shipped 200,000 books; and by the 10th shall finish and ship the remaining 125,000 of the first edition. I got nervous and came down to help hump-up the binderies; and I mean to stay here pretty much all the time till the first days of March, when the second volume will issue. Shan't have so much trouble, this time, though, if we get to press pretty soon, because we can get more binderies then than are to be had in front of the holidays. One lives and learns. I find it takes 7 binderies four months to bind 325,000 books.

This is a good book to publish. I heard a canvasser say, yesterday, that while delivering eleven books he took 7 new subscriptions. But we shall be in a hell of a fix if that goes on—it will "ball up" the binderies again.

*Yrs ever*

*MARK.*

*November 30th that year was Mark Twain's fiftieth birthday, an event noticed by the newspapers generally, and especially observed by many of his friends. Warner, Stockton and many others sent letters; Andrew Lang contributed a fine poem; also Oliver Wendell. Holmes —the latter by special request of Miss Gilder—for the Critic. These attentions came as a sort of crowning happiness at the end of a golden year. At no time in his life were Mark Twain's fortunes and prospects brighter; he had a beautiful family and a perfect home. Also, he had great prosperity. The reading-tour with Cable had been a fine success. His latest book, The Adventures of Huckleberry Finn, had added largely to his fame and income. The publication of the Grant Memoirs had been a dazzling triumph. Mark Twain had become recognized, not only as America's most distinguished author, but as its most envied publisher. And now, with his fiftieth birthday, had come this laurel from Holmes, last of the Brahmins, to add a touch of glory to all the rest. We feel his exaltation in his note of acknowledgment.*

To Dr. Oliver Wendell Holmes, in Boston:

DEAR MR. HOLMES,—I shall never be able to tell you the half of how proud you have made me. If I could you would say you were nearly paid for the trouble you took. And then the family: If I can convey the electrical surprise and gratitude and exaltation of the wife and the children last night, when they happened upon that Critic where I had, with artful artlessness, spread it open and retired out of view to see what would happen—well, it was great and fine and beautiful to see, and made me feel as the victor feels when the shouting hosts march by; and if you also could have seen it you would have said the account was squared. For I have brought them up in your company, as in the company of a warm and friendly and beneficent but far distant sun; and so, for you to do this thing was for the sun to send down out of the skies the miracle of a special ray and transfigure me before their faces. I knew what that poem would be to them; I knew it would raise me up to remote and shining heights in their eyes, to very fellowship with the chambered Nautilus itself, and that from that fellowship they could never more dissociate me while they should live; and so I made sure to be by when the surprise should come.

Charles Dudley Warner is charmed with the poem for its own felicitous sake; and so indeed am I, but more because it has drawn the sting of my fiftieth year; taken away the pain of it, the grief of it, the somehow shame of it, and made me glad and proud it happened.

*With reverence and affection,*

*Sincerely yours,*

*S. L. CLEMENS.*

*Holmes wrote with his own hand: "Did Miss Gilder tell you I had twenty-three letters spread out for answer when her suggestion came about your anniversary? I stopped my correspondence and made my letters wait until the lines were done."*

# MARK TWAIN'S LETTERS—1853-1866

## VOLUME 4

## XXVI. LETTERS, 1886-87. JANE CLEMENS'S ROMANCE. UNMAILED LETTERS, ETC.

*When Clemens had been platforming with Cable and returned to Hartford for his Christmas vacation, the Warner and Clemens families had joined in preparing for him a surprise performance of The Prince and the Pauper. The Clemens household was always given to theatricals, and it was about this time that scenery and a stage were prepared—mainly by the sculptor Gerhardt—for these home performances, after which productions of The Prince and the Pauper were given with considerable regularity to audiences consisting of parents and invited friends. The subject is a fascinating one, but it has been dwelt upon elsewhere.—[In Mark Twain: A on***n, chaps. cliii and clx.]—We get a glimpse of one of these occasions as well as of Mark Twain's financial progress in the next brief*

To W. D. Howells; in Boston:

*Jan. 3, '86.*

MY DEAR HOWELLS,—The date set for the Prince and Pauper play is ten days hence—Jan. 13. I hope you and Pilla can take a train that arrives here during the day; the one that leaves Boston toward the end of the afternoon would be a trifle late; the performance would have already begun when you reached the house.

I'm out of the woods. On the last day of the year I had paid out $182,000 on the Grant book and it was totally free from debt.

*Yrs ever*

*MARK.*

*Mark Twain's mother was a woman of sturdy character and with a keen sense of humor and tender sympathies. Her husband, John Marshall Clemens, had been a man of high moral character, honored by all who knew him, respected and apparently loved by his wife. No one would ever have supposed that during all her years of marriage, and almost to her death, she carried a secret romance that would only be told at last in the weary disappointment of old age. It is a curious story, and it came to light in this curious way:*

To W. D. Howells, in Boston:

*HARTFORD, May 19, '86.*

MY DEAR HOWELLS,—..... Here's a secret. A most curious and pathetic romance, which has just come to light. Read these things, but don't mention them. Last fall, my old mother—then 82—took a notion to attend a convention of old settlers of the Mississippi Valley in an Iowa town. My brother's wife was astonished; and represented to her the hardships and fatigues of such a trip, and said my mother might possibly not even survive them; and said there could be no possible interest for her in such a meeting and such a crowd. But my mother insisted, and persisted; and finally gained her point. They started; and all the way my mother was young again with excitement, interest, eagerness, anticipation. They reached the town and the hotel. My mother strode with the same eagerness in her eye and her step, to the counter, and said:

"Is Dr. Barrett of St. Louis, here?"

"No. He was here, but he returned to St. Louis this morning."

"Will he come again?"

"No."

My mother turned away, the fire all gone from her, and said, "Let us go home."

They went straight back to Keokuk. My mother sat silent and thinking for many days—a thing which had never happened before. Then one day she said:

"I will tell you a secret. When I was eighteen, a young medical student named Barrett lived in Columbia (Ky.) eighteen miles away; and he used to ride over to see me. This continued for some time. I loved him with my whole heart, and I knew that he felt the same toward me, though no words had been spoken. He was too bashful to speak—he could not do it. Everybody supposed we were engaged—took it for granted we were—but we were not. By and by there was to be a party in a neighboring town, and he wrote my uncle telling him his feelings, and asking him to drive me over in his buggy and let him (Barrett) drive me back, so that he might have that opportunity to propose. My uncle should have done as he was asked, without explaining anything to me; but instead, he read me the letter; and then, of course, I could not go—and did not. He (Barrett) left the country presently, and I, to stop the clacking tongues, and to show him that I did not care, married, in a pet. In all these sixty-four years I have not seen him since. I saw in a paper that he was going to attend that Old Settlers' Convention. Only three hours before we reached that hotel, he had been standing there!"

Since then, her memory is wholly faded out and gone; and now she writes letters to the school-mates who had been dead forty years, and wonders why they neglect her and do not answer.

Think of her carrying that pathetic burden in her old heart sixty-four years, and no human being ever suspecting it!

*Yrs ever,*

*MARK.*

*We do not get the idea from this letter that those two long ago sweethearts quarreled, but Mark Twain once spoke of their having done so, and there may have been a disagreement, assuming that there was a subsequent meeting. It does not matter, now. In speaking of it, Mark Twain once said: "It is as pathetic a romance as any that has crossed the field of my personal experience in a long lifetime."—[When Mark Twain: A Biography was written this letter had not come to light, and the matter was stated there in accordance with Mark Twain's latest memory of it.]*

*Howells wrote: "After all, how poor and hackneyed all the inventions are compared with the simple and stately facts. Who could have imagined such a heart-break as that? Yet it went along with the fulfillment of everyday duty and made no more noise than a grave under foot. I doubt if fiction will ever get the knack of such things."*

*Jane Clemens now lived with her son Orion and his wife, in Keokuk, where she was more contented than elsewhere. In these later days her memory had become erratic, her realization of events about her uncertain, but there were times when she was quite her former self, remembering clearly and talking with her old-time gaiety of spirit. Mark Twain frequently sent her playful letters to amuse her, letters full of such boyish gaiety as had amused her long years before. The one that follows is a fair example. It was written after a visit which Clemens and his family had paid to Keokuk.*

To Jane Clemens, in Keokuk:

*ELMIRA, Aug. 7, '86.*

DEAR MA,—I heard that Molly and Orion and Pamela had been sick, but I see by your letter that they are much better now, or nearly well. When we visited you a month ago, it seemed to us that your Keokuk weather was pretty hot; Jean and Clara sat up in bed at Mrs. McElroy's and cried about it, and so did I; but I judge by your letter that it has cooled down, now, so that a person is comparatively comfortable, with his skin off. Well it did need cooling; I remember that I burnt a hole in my shirt, there, with some ice cream that fell on it; and Miss Jenkins told me they never used a stove, but cooked their meals on a marble-topped table in the drawing-room, just with the natural heat. If anybody else had told me, I would not have believed it. I was told by the Bishop of Keokuk that he did not allow crying at funerals, because it scalded the furniture. If Miss Jenkins had told me that, I would have believed it. This reminds me that you speak of Dr. Jenkins and his family as if they were strangers to me. Indeed they are not. Don't you suppose I remember gratefully how tender the doctor was with Jean when she hurt her arm, and how quickly he got the pain out of the hurt, whereas I supposed it was going to last at least an hour? No, I don't forget some things as easily as

I do others.

Yes, it was pretty hot weather. Now here, when a person is going to die, he is always in a sweat about where he is going to; but in Keokuk of course they don't care, because they are fixed for everything. It has set me reflecting, it has taught me a lesson. By and by, when my health fails, I am going to put all my affairs in order, and bid good-bye to my friends here, and kill all the people I don't like, and go out to Keokuk and prepare for death.

They are all well in this family, and we all send love.

*Affly Your Son*

*SAM.*

*The ways of city officials and corporations are often past understanding, and Mark Twain sometimes found it necessary to write picturesque letters of protest. The following to a Hartford lighting company is a fair example of these documents.*

To a gas and electric-lighting company, in Hartford:

GENTLEMEN,—There are but two places in our whole street where lights could be of any value, by any accident, and you have measured and appointed your intervals so ingeniously as to leave each of those places in the centre of a couple of hundred yards of solid darkness. When I noticed that you were setting one of your lights in such a way that I could almost see how to get into my gate at night, I suspected that it was a piece of carelessness on the part of the workmen, and would be corrected as soon as you should go around inspecting and find it out. My judgment was right; it is always right, when you axe concerned. For fifteen years, in spite of my prayers and tears, you persistently kept a gas lamp exactly half way between my gates, so that I couldn't find either of them after dark; and then furnished such execrable gas that I had to hang a danger signal on the lamp post to keep teams from running into it, nights. Now I suppose your present idea is, to leave us a little more in the dark.

Don't mind us—out our way; we possess but one vote apiece, and no rights which you are in any way bound to respect. Please take your electric light and go to—but never mind, it is not for me to suggest; you will probably find the way; and any way you can reasonably count on divine assistance if you lose your bearings.

*S. L. CLEMENS.*

[Etext Editor's Note: Twain wrote another note to Hartford Gas and Electric, which he may not have mailed and which Paine does not include in these volumes:

"Gentleman:—Someday you are going to move me almost to the point of irritation with your God-damned chuckle headed fashion of turning off your God-damned gas without giving notice to your God-damned parishioners—and you did it again last night—" D.W.]

*Frequently Clemens did not send letters of this sort after they were written. Sometimes he realized the uselessness of such protest, sometimes the mere writing of them had furnished the necessary relief, and he put, the letter away, or into the wastebasket, and wrote something more temperate, or nothing at all. A few such letters here follow.*

*Clemens was all the time receiving application from people who wished him to recommend one article or another; books, plays, tobacco, and what not. They were generally persistent people, unable to accept a polite or kindly denial. Once he set down some remarks on this particular phase of correspondence. He wrote:*

I

No doubt Mr. Edison has been offered a large interest in many and many an electrical project, for the use of his name to float it withal. And no doubt all men who have achieved for their names, in any line of activity whatever, a sure market value, have been familiar with this sort of solicitation. Reputation is a hall-mark: it can remove doubt from pure silver, and it can also make the plated article pass for pure.

And so, people without a hall-mark of their own are always trying to get the loan of somebody else's.

As a rule, that kind of a person sees only one side of the case. He sees that his invention or his painting or his book is—apparently—a trifle better than you yourself can do, therefore why shouldn't you be willing to put your hall-mark on it? You will be giving the purchaser his full money's worth; so who is hurt, and where is the harm? Besides, are you not helping a struggling fellow-craftsman, and is it not your duty to do that?

That side is plenty clear enough to him, but he can't and won't see the other side, to-wit: that you are a rascal if you put your hall-mark upon a thing which you did not produce yourself, howsoever good it may be. How simple that is; and yet there are not two applicants in a hundred who can, be made to see it.

When one receives an application of this sort, his first emotion is an indignant sense of insult; his first deed is the penning of a sharp answer. He blames nobody but that other person. That person is a very base being; he must be; he would degrade himself for money, otherwise it would not occur to him that you would do such a thing. But all the same, that application has done its work, and taken you down in your own estimation. You recognize that everybody hasn't as high an opinion of you as you have of yourself; and in spite of you there ensues an interval during which you are not, in your own estimation as fine a bird as you were before.

However, being old and experienced, you do not mail your sharp letter, but leave it lying a day. That saves you. For by that time you have begun to reflect that you are a person who deals in exaggerations—and exaggerations are lies. You meant yours to be playful, and thought you made them unmistakably so. But you couldn't make them playfulnesses to a man who has no sense of the playful and can see nothing but the serious side of things. You rattle on quite playfully, and with measureless extravagance, about how you wept at the tomb of Adam; and all in good time you find to your astonishment that no end of people took you at your word and believed you. And presently they find out that you were not in earnest. They have been deceived; therefore, (as they argue—and there is a sort of argument in it,) you are a deceiver. If you will deceive in one way, why shouldn't you in another? So they apply for the use of your trade-mark. You are amazed and affronted. You retort that you are not that kind of person. Then they are amazed and affronted; and wonder "since when?"

By this time you have got your bearings. You realize that perhaps there is a little blame on both sides. You are in the right frame, now. So you write a letter void of offense, declining. You mail this one; you pigeon-hole the other.

That is, being old and experienced, you do, but early in your career, you don't: you mail the first one.

II

An enthusiast who had a new system of musical notation, wrote to me and suggested that a magazine article from me, contrasting the absurdities of the old system with the simplicities of his new one, would be sure to make a "rousing hit." He shouted and shouted over the marvels wrought by his system, and quoted the handsome compliments which had been paid it by famous musical people; but he forgot to tell me what his notation was like, or what its simplicities consisted in. So I could not have written the article if I had wanted to—which I didn't; because I hate strangers with axes to grind. I wrote him a courteous note explaining how busy I was—I always explain how busy I am—and casually drooped this remark:

"I judge the X-X notation to be a rational mode of representing music, in place of the prevailing fashion, which was the invention of an idiot."

Next mail he asked permission to print that meaningless remark. I answered, no—courteously, but still, no; explaining that I could not afford to be placed in the attitude of trying to influence people with a mere worthless guess. What a scorcher I got, next mail! Such irony! such sarcasm, such caustic praise of my superhonorable loyalty to the public! And withal, such compassion for my stupidity, too, in not being able to understand my own language. I cannot remember the words of this letter broadside, but there was about a page used up in turning this idea round and round and exposing it in different lights.

*Unmailed Answer:*

DEAR SIR,—What is the trouble with you? If it is your viscera, you cannot have them taken out and reorganized a moment too soon. I mean, if they are inside. But if you are composed of them, that is another matter. Is it your brain? But it could not be your brain. Possibly it is your skull: you want to look out for that. Some people, when they get an idea, it pries the structure apart. Your system of notation has got in there, and couldn't find room, without a doubt that is what the trouble is. Your skull was not made to put ideas in, it was made to throw potatoes at.

*Yours Truly.*

*Mailed Answer:*

DEAR SIR,—Come, come—take a walk; you disturb the children.

*Yours Truly.*

There was a day, now happily nearly over, when certain newspapers made a practice of inviting men distinguished in any walk of life to give their time and effort without charge to express themselves on some subject of the day, or perhaps they were asked to send their favorite passages in prose or verse, with the reasons why. Such symposiums were "features" that cost the newspapers only the writing of a number of letters, stationery, and postage. To one such invitation Mark Twain wrote two replies. They follow herewith:

*Unmailed Answer:*

DEAR SIR,—I have received your proposition—which you have

imitated from a pauper London periodical which had previously imitated the idea of this sort of mendicancy from seventh-rate American journalism, where it originated as a variation of the inexpensive "interview."

Why do you buy Associated Press dispatches? To make your paper the more salable, you answer. But why don't you try to beg them? Why do you discriminate? I can sell my stuff; why should I give it to you? Why don't you ask me for a shirt? What is the difference between asking me for the worth of a shirt and asking me for the shirt itself? Perhaps you didn't know you were begging. I would not use that argument—it makes the user a fool. The passage of poetry—or prose, if you will—which has taken deepest root in my thought, and which I oftenest return to and dwell upon with keenest no matter what, is this: That the proper place for journalists who solicit literary charity is on the street corner with their hats in their hands.

*Mailed Answer:*

DEAR SIR,—Your favor of recent date is received, but I am obliged by press of work to decline.

*The manager of a traveling theatrical company wrote that he had taken the liberty of dramatizing Tom Sawyer, and would like also the use of the author's name—the idea being to convey to the public that it was a Mark Twain play. In return for this slight favor the manager sent an invitation for Mark Twain to come and see the play —to be present on the opening night, as it were, at his (the manager's) expense. He added that if the play should be a go in the cities there might be some "arrangement" of profits. Apparently these inducements did not appeal to Mark Twain. The long unmailed reply is the more interesting, but probably the briefer one that follows it was quite as effective.*

*Unmailed Answer:*

*HARTFORD, Sept. 8, '87.*

DEAR SIR,—And so it has got around to you, at last; and you also have "taken the liberty." You are No. 1365. When 1364 sweeter and better people, including the author, have "tried" to dramatize Tom Sawyer and did not arrive, what sort of show do you suppose you stand? That is a book, dear sir, which cannot be dramatized. One might as well try to dramatize any other hymn. Tom Sawyer is simply a hymn, put into prose form to give it a worldly air.

Why the pale doubt that flitteth dim and nebulous athwart the forecastle of your third sentence? Have no fears. Your piece will be a Go. It will go out the back door on the first night. They've all done it—the 1364. So will 1365. Not one of us ever thought of the simple device of half-soling himself with a stove-lid. Ah, what suffering a little hindsight would have saved us. Treasure this hint.

How kind of you to invite me to the funeral. Go to; I have attended a thousand of them. I have seen Tom Sawyer's remains in all the different kinds of dramatic shrouds there are. You cannot start anything fresh. Are you serious when you propose to pay my expence—if that is the Susquehannian way of spelling it? And can you be aware that I charge a hundred dollars a mile when I travel for pleasure? Do you realize that it is 432 miles to Susquehanna? Would it be handy for you to send me the $43,200 first, so I could be counting it as I come along; because railroading is pretty dreary to a sensitive nature when there's nothing sordid to buck at for Zeitvertreib.

Now as I understand it, dear and magnanimous 1365, you are going to recreate Tom Sawyer dramatically, and then do me the compliment to put me in the bills as father of this shady offspring. Sir, do you know that this kind of a compliment has destroyed people before now? Listen.

Twenty-four years ago, I was strangely handsome. The remains of it are still visible through the rifts of time. I was so handsome that human activities ceased as if spellbound when I came in view, and even inanimate things stopped to look—like locomotives, and district messenger boys and so-on. In San Francisco, in the rainy season I was often mistaken for fair weather. Upon one occasion I was traveling in the Sonora region, and stopped for an hour's nooning, to rest my horse and myself. All the town came out to look. The tribes of Indians gathered to look. A Piute squaw named her baby for me,—a voluntary compliment which pleased me greatly. Other attentions were paid me. Last of all arrived the president and faculty of Sonora University and offered me the post of Professor of Moral Culture and the Dogmatic Humanities; which I accepted gratefully, and entered at once upon my duties. But my name had pleased the Indians, and in the deadly kindness of their hearts they went on naming their babies after me. I tried to stop it, but the Indians could not understand why I should object to so manifest a compliment. The thing grew and grew and spread and spread and became exceedingly embarrassing. The University stood it a couple of years; but then for the sake of the college they felt obliged to call a halt, although I had the sympathy of the whole faculty. The president himself said to me, "I am as sorry as I can be for you, and would still hold out if there were any hope ahead; but you see how it is: there are a hundred and thirty-two of them already, and fourteen precincts to hear from. The circumstance has brought your name into most wide and unfortunate renown. It causes much comment—I believe that that is not an over-statement. Some of this comment is palliative, but some of it—by patrons at a distance, who only know the statistics without the explanation,—is offensive, and in some cases even violent. Nine students have been called home. The trustees of the college have been growing more and more uneasy all these last months—steadily along with the implacable increase in your census—and I will not conceal from you that more than once they have touched upon the expediency of a change in the Professorship of Moral Culture. The coarsely sarcastic editorial in yesterday's Alta, headed Give the Moral Acrobat a Rest—has brought things to a crisis, and I am charged with the unpleasant duty of receiving your resignation."

I know you only mean me a kindness, dear 1365, but it is a most deadly mistake. Please do not name your Injun for me. Truly Yours.

*Mailed Answer:*

*NEW YORK, Sept. 8. 1887.*

DEAR SIR,—Necessarily I cannot assent to so strange a proposition. And I think it but fair to warn you that if you put the piece on the stage, you must take the legal consequences.

*Yours respectfully,*

*S. L. CLEMENS.*

*Before the days of international copyright no American author's books were pirated more freely by Canadian publishers than those of Mark Twain. It was always a sore point with him that these books, cheaply printed, found their way into the United States, and were sold in competition with his better editions. The law on the subject seemed to be rather hazy, and its various interpretations exasperating. In the next unmailed letter Mark Twain relieves himself to a misguided official. The letter is worth reading today, if for no other reason, to show the absurdity of copyright conditions which prevailed at that time.*

*Unmailed Letter to H. C. Christiancy, on book Piracy:*

*HARTFORD, Dec. 18, '87.*

H. C. CHRISTIANCY, ESQ.

DEAR SIR,—As I understand it, the position of the U. S. Government is this: If a person be captured on the border with counterfeit bonds in his hands—bonds of the N. Y. Central Railway, for instance—the procedure in his case shall be as follows:

1. If the N. Y. C. have not previously filed in the several police offices

along the border, proof of ownership of the originals of the bonds, the government officials must collect a duty on the counterfeits, and then let them go ahead and circulate in this country.

2. But if there is proof already on file, then the N. Y. C. may pay the duty and take the counterfeits.

But in no case will the United States consent to go without its share of the swag. It is delicious. The biggest and proudest government on earth turned sneak-thief; collecting pennies on stolen property, and pocketing them with a greasy and libidinous leer; going into partnership with foreign thieves to rob its own children; and when the child escapes the foreigner, descending to the abysmal baseness of hanging on and robbing the infant all alone by itself! Dear sir, this is not any more respectable than for a father to collect toll on the forced prostitution of his own daughter; in fact it is the same thing. Upon these terms, what is a U. S. custom house but a "fence?" That is all it is: a legalized trader in stolen goods.

And this nasty law, this filthy law, this unspeakable law calls itself a "regulation for the protection of owners of copyright!" Can sarcasm go further than that? In what way does it protect them? Inspiration itself could not furnish a rational answer to that question. Whom does it protect, then? Nobody, as far as I can see, but the foreign thief—sometimes—and his fellow-footpad the U. S. government, all the time. What could the Central Company do with the counterfeit bonds after it had bought them of the star spangled banner Master-thief? Sell them at a dollar apiece and fetch down the market for the genuine hundred-dollar bond? What could I do with that 20-cent copy of "Roughing It" which the United States has collared on the border and is waiting to release to me for cash in case I am willing to come down to its moral level and help rob myself? Sell it at ten or fifteen cents—duty added—and destroy the market for the original $3,50 book? Who ever did invent that law? I would like to know the name of that immortal jackass.

Dear sir, I appreciate your courtesy in stretching your authority in the desire to do me a kindness, and I sincerely thank you for it. But I have no use for that book; and if I were even starving for it I would not pay duty on in either to get it or suppress it. No doubt there are ways in which I might consent to go into partnership with thieves and fences, but this is not one of them. This one revolts the remains of my self-respect; turns my stomach. I think I could companion with a highwayman who carried a shot-gun and took many risks; yes, I think I should like that if I were younger; but to go in with a big rich government that robs paupers, and the widows and orphans of paupers and takes no risk—why the thought just gags me.

Oh, no, I shall never pay any duties on pirated books of mine. I am much too respectable for that—yet awhile. But here—one thing that grovels me is this: as far as I can discover—while freely granting that the U. S. copyright laws are far and away the most idiotic that exist anywhere on the face of the earth—they don't authorize the government to admit pirated books into this country, toll or no toll. And so I think that that regulation is the invention of one of those people—as a rule, early stricken of God, intellectually—the departmental interpreters of the laws, in Washington. They can always be depended on to take any reasonably good law and interpret the common sense all out of it. They can be depended on, every time, to defeat a good law, and make it inoperative—yes, and utterly grotesque, too, mere matter for laughter and derision. Take some of the decisions of the Post-office Department, for instance—though I do not mean to suggest that that asylum is any worse than the others for the breeding and nourishing of incredible lunatics—I merely instance it because it happens to be the first to come into my mind. Take that case of a few years ago where the P. M. General suddenly issued an edict requiring you to add the name of the State after Boston, New York, Chicago, &c, in your superscriptions, on pain of having your letter stopped and forwarded to the dead-letter office; yes, and I believe he required the county, too. He made one little concession in favor of New York: you could say "New York City," and stop there; but if you left off the "city," you must add "N. Y." to your "New York." Why, it threw the business of the whole country into chaos and brought commerce almost to a stand-still. Now think of that! When that man goes to—to—well, wherever he is going to—we shan't want the microscopic details of his address. I guess we can find him.

Well, as I was saying, I believe that this whole paltry and ridiculous swindle is a pure creation of one of those cabbages that used to be at the head of one of those Retreats down there—Departments, you know—and that you will find it so, if you will look into it. And moreover—but land, I reckon we are both tired by this time.

*Truly Yours,*

*MARK TWAIN.*

## XXVII. MISCELLANEOUS LETTERS OF 1887. LITERARY ARTICLES. PEACEFUL DAYS AT THE FARM. FAVORITE READING. APOLOGY TO MRS. CLEVELAND, ETC.

We have seen in the preceding chapter how unknown aspirants in one field or another were always seeking to benefit by Mark Twain's reputation. Once he remarked, "The symbol of the human race ought to be an ax; every human being has one concealed about him somewhere." He declared when a stranger called on him, or wrote to him, in nine cases out of ten he could distinguish the gleam of the ax almost immediately. The following letter is closely related to those of the foregoing chapter, only that this one was mailed—not once, but many times, in some form adapted to the specific applicant. It does not matter to whom it was originally written, the name would not be recognized.

To Mrs. T. Concerning unearned credentials, etc.

*HARTFORD, 1887.*

MY DEAR MADAM,—It is an idea which many people have had, but it is of no value. I have seen it tried out many and many a time. I have seen a lady lecturer urged and urged upon the public in a lavishly complimentary document signed by Longfellow, Whittier, Holmes and some others of supreme celebrity, but—there was nothing in her and she failed. If there had been any great merit in her she never would have needed those men's help and (at her rather mature age,) would never have consented to ask for it.

There is an unwritten law about human successes, and your sister must bow to that law, she must submit to its requirements. In brief this law is:

1. *No occupation without an apprenticeship.*

2. *No pay to the apprentice.*

This law stands right in the way of the subaltern who wants to be a General before he has smelt powder; and it stands (and should stand) in everybody's way who applies for pay or position before he has served his apprenticeship and proved himself. Your sister's course is perfectly plain. Let her enclose this letter to Maj. J. B. Pond, and offer to lecture a year for $10 a week and her expenses, the contract to be annullable by him at any time, after a month's notice, but not annullable by her at all. The second year, he to have her services, if he wants them, at a trifle under the best price offered her by anybody else.

She can learn her trade in those two years, and then be entitled to remuneration—but she can not learn it in any less time than that, unless she is a human miracle.

Try it, and do not be afraid. It is the fair and right thing. If she wins, she will win squarely and righteously, and never have to blush.

*Truly yours,*

*S. L. CLEMENS.*

*Howells wrote, in February, offering to get a publisher to take the Library of Humor off Mark Twain's hands. Howells had been paid twenty-six hundred dollars for the work on it, and his conscience hurt him when he reflected that the book might never be used. In this letter he also refers to one of the disastrous inventions in which Clemens had invested—a method of casting brass dies for stamping book-covers and wall-paper. Howells's purpose was to introduce something of the matter into his next story. Mark Twain's reply gives us a light on this particular invention.*

*HARTFORD, Feb. 15, '87.*

DEAR HOWELLS,—I was in New York five days ago, and Webster mentioned the Library, and proposed to publish it a year or a year and half hence. I have written him your proposition to-day. (The Library is part of the property of the C. L. W. & Co. firm.)

I don't remember what that technical phrase was, but I think you will find it in any Cyclopedia under the head of "Brass." The thing I best remember is, that the self-styled "inventor" had a very ingenious way of keeping me from seeing him apply his invention: the first appointment was spoiled by his burning down the man's shop in which it was to be done, the night before; the second was spoiled by his burning down his own shop the night before. He unquestionably did both of these things. He really had no invention; the whole project was a blackmailing swindle, and cost me several thousand dollars.

The slip you sent me from the May "Study" has delighted Mrs. Clemens and me to the marrow. To think that thing might be possible to many; but to be brave enough to say it is possible to you only, I certainly believe. The longer I live the clearer I perceive how unmatchable, how unapproachable, a compliment one pays when he says of a man "he has the courage (to utter) his convictions." Haven't you had reviewers talk Alps to you, and then print potato hills?

I haven't as good an opinion of my work as you hold of it, but I've always done what I could to secure and enlarge my good opinion of it. I've always said to myself, "Everybody reads it and that's something—it surely isn't pernicious, or the most acceptable people would get pretty tired of it." And when a critic said by implication that it wasn't high and fine, through the remark "High and fine literature is wine" I retorted (confidentially, to myself,) "yes, high and fine literature is wine, and mine is only water; but everybody likes water."

You didn't tell me to return that proof-slip, so I have pasted it into my private scrap-book. None will see it there. With a thousand thanks.

*Ys Ever*

*MARK.*

*Our next letter is an unmailed answer, but it does not belong with the others, having been withheld for reasons of quite a different sort. Jeanette Gilder, then of the Critic, was one of Mark Twain's valued friends. In the comment which he made, when it was shown to him twenty-two years later, he tells us why he thinks this letter was not sent. The name, "Rest-and-be-Thankful," was the official title given to the summer place at Elmira, but it was more often known as "Quarry."*

To Jeannette Gilder (not mailed):

*HARTFORD, May 14, '87.*

MY DEAR MISS GILDER,—We shall spend the summer at the same old place-the remote farm called "Rest-and-be-Thankful," on top of the hills three miles from Elmira, N. Y. Your other question is harder to answer. It is my habit to keep four or five books in process of erection all the time, and every summer add a few courses of bricks to two or three of them; but I cannot forecast which of the two or three it is going to be. It takes seven years to complete a book by this method, but still it is a good method: gives the public a rest. I have been accused of "rushing into print" prematurely, moved thereto by greediness for money; but in truth I have never done that. Do you care for trifles of information? (Well, then, "Tom Sawyer" and "The Prince and the Pauper" were each on the stocks two or three years, and "Old Times on the Mississippi" eight.) One of my unfinished books has been on the stocks sixteen years; another seventeen. This latter book could have been finished in a day, at any time during the past five years. But as in the first of these two narratives all the action takes place in Noah's ark, and as in the other the action takes place in heaven, there seemed to be no hurry, and so I have not hurried. Tales of stirring adventure in those localities do not need to be rushed to publication lest they get stale by waiting. In twenty-one years, with all my time at my free disposal I have written and completed only eleven books, whereas with half the labor that a journalist does I could have written sixty in that time. I do not greatly mind being accused of a proclivity for rushing into print, but at the same time I don't believe that the charge is really well founded. Suppose I did write eleven books, have you nothing to be grateful for? Go to—-remember the forty-nine which I didn't write.

*Truly Yours*

*S. L. CLEMENS.*

*Notes (added twenty-two years later):*

Stormfield, April 30, 1909. It seems the letter was not sent. I probably feared she might print it, and I couldn't find a way to say so without running a risk of hurting her. No one would hurt Jeannette Gilder purposely, and no one would want to run the risk of doing it unintentionally. She is my neighbor, six miles away, now, and I must ask her about this ancient letter.

I note with pride and pleasure that I told no untruths in my unsent answer. I still have the habit of keeping unfinished books lying around years and years, waiting. I have four or five novels on hand at present in a half-finished condition, and it is more than three years since I have looked at any of them. I have no intention of finishing them. I could complete all of them in less than a year, if the impulse should come powerfully upon me: Long, long ago money-necessity furnished that impulse once, ("Following the Equator"), but mere desire for money has never furnished it, so far as I remember. Not even money-necessity was able to overcome me on a couple of occasions when perhaps I ought to have allowed it to succeed. While I was a bankrupt and in debt two offers were made me for weekly literary contributions to continue during a year, and they would have made a debtless man of me, but I declined them, with my wife's full approval, for I had known of no instance where a man had pumped himself out once a week and failed to run "emptyings" before the year was finished.

As to that "Noah's Ark" book, I began it in Edinburgh in 1873;—[This is not quite correct. The "Noah's Ark" book was begun in Buffalo in 1870.] I don't know where the manuscript is now. It was a Diary, which professed to be the work of Shem, but wasn't. I began it again several months ago, but only for recreation; I hadn't any intention of carrying it to a finish—or even to the end of the first chapter, in fact.

As to the book whose action "takes place in Heaven." That was a small thing, ("Captain Stormfield's Visit to Heaven.") It lay in my pigeon-holes 40 years, then I took it out and printed it in Harper's Monthly last year.

*S. L. C.*

In the next letter we get a pretty and peaceful picture of "Rest-and-be-Thankful." These were Mark Twain's balmy days. The financial drain of the type-machine was heavy but not yet exhausting, and the prospect of vast returns from it seemed to grow brighter each day. His publishing business, though less profitable, was still prosperous, his family life was ideal. How gratefully, then, he could enter into the peace of that "perfect day."

To Mrs. Orion Clemens, in Keokuk, Ia.:

*ON THE HILL NEAR ELMIRA, July 10, '87.*

DEAR MOLLIE,—This is a superb Sunday for weather—very cloudy, and the thermometer as low as 65. The city in the valley is purple with shade, as seen from up here at the study. The Cranes are reading and loafing in the canvas-curtained summer-house 50 yards away on a higher (the highest) point; the cats are loafing over at "Ellerslie" which is the children's estate and dwellinghouse in their own private grounds (by deed from Susie Crane) a hundred yards from the study, amongst the clover and young oaks and willows. Livy is down at the house, but I shall now go and bring her up to the Cranes to help us occupy the lounges and hammocks—whence a great panorama of distant hill and valley and city is seeable. The children have gone on a lark through the neighboring hills and woods. It is a perfect day indeed.

*With love to you all.*

*SAM.*

Two days after this letter was written we get a hint of what was the beginning of business trouble—that is to say, of the failing health of Charles L. Webster. Webster was ambitious, nervous, and not robust. He had overworked and was paying the penalty. His trouble was neurasthenia, and he was presently obliged to retire altogether from the business. The "Sam and Mary" mentioned were Samuel Moffet and his wife.

To Mrs. Pamela Moffett, in Fredonia, N. Y.

*ELMIRA, July 12, '87*

MY DEAR SISTER,—I had no idea that Charley's case was so serious. I knew it was bad, and persistent, but I was not aware of the full size of the matter.

I have just been writing to a friend in Hartford' who treated what I imagine was a similar case surgically last fall, and produced a permanent cure. If this is a like case, Charley must go to him.

If relief fails there, he must take the required rest, whether the business can stand it or not.

It is most pleasant to hear such prosperous accounts of Sam and Mary, I do not see how Sam could well be more advantageously fixed. He can grow up with that paper, and achieve a successful life.

It is not all holiday here with Susie and Clara this time. They have to put in some little time every day on their studies. Jean thinks she is studying too, but I don't know what it is unless it is the horses; she spends the day under their heels in the stables—and that is but a continuation of her Hartford system of culture.

With love from us all to you all.

*Affectionately*

*SAM.*

Mark Twain had a few books that he read regularly every year or two.

Among these were 'Pepys's Diary', Suetonius's 'Lives of the Twelve Caesars', and Thomas Carlyle's 'French Revolution'. He had a passion for history, biography, and personal memoirs of any sort. In his early life he had cared very little for poetry, but along in the middle eighties he somehow acquired a taste for Browning and became absorbed in it. A Browning club assembled as often as once a week at the Clemens home in Hartford to listen to his readings of the master. He was an impressive reader, and he carefully prepared himself for these occasions, indicating by graduated underscorings, the exact values he wished to give to words and phrases. Those were memorable gatherings, and they must have continued through at least two winters. It is one of the puzzling phases of Mark Twain's character that, notwithstanding his passion for direct and lucid expression, he should have found pleasure in the poems of Robert Browning.

To W. D. Howells, in Boston:

*ELMIRA, Aug. 22, '87.*

MY DEAR HOWELLS,—How stunning are the changes which age makes in a man while he sleeps. When I finished Carlyle's French Revolution in 1871, I was a Girondin; every time I have read it since, I have read it differently being influenced and changed, little by little, by life and environment (and Taine and St. Simon): and now I lay the book down once more, and recognize that I am a Sansculotte!—And not a pale, characterless Sansculotte, but a Marat. Carlyle teaches no such gospel so the change is in me—in my vision of the evidences.

People pretend that the Bible means the same to them at 50 that it did at all former milestones in their journey. I wonder how they can lie so. It comes of practice, no doubt. They would not say that of Dickens's or Scott's books. Nothing remains the same. When a man goes back to look at the house of his childhood, it has always shrunk: there is no instance of such a house being as big as the picture in memory and imagination call for. Shrunk how? Why, to its correct dimensions: the house hasn't altered; this is the first time it has been in focus.

Well, that's loss. To have house and Bible shrink so, under the disillusioning corrected angle, is loss-for a moment. But there are compensations. You tilt the tube skyward and bring planets and comets and corona flames a hundred and fifty thousand miles high into the field. Which I see you have done, and found Tolstoi. I haven't got him in focus yet, but I've got Browning....

*Ys Ever*

*MARK.*

*Mention has been made already of Mark Twain's tendency to absentmindedness. He was always forgetting engagements, or getting them wrong. Once he hurried to an afternoon party, and finding the mistress of the house alone, sat down and talked to her comfortably for an hour or two, not remembering his errand at all. It was only when he reached home that he learned that the party had taken place the week before. It was always dangerous for him to make engagements, and he never seemed to profit by sorrowful experience. We, however, may profit now by one of his amusing apologies.*

To Mrs. Grover Cleveland, in Washington:

*HARTFORD, Nov. 6, 1887.*

MY DEAR MADAM,—I do not know how it is in the White House, but in this house of ours whenever the minor half of the administration tries to run itself without the help of the major half it gets aground. Last night when I was offered the opportunity to assist you in the throwing open the Warner brothers superb benefaction in Bridgeport to those fortunate women, I naturally appreciated the honor done me, and promptly seized my chance. I had an engagement, but the circumstances washed it out of my mind. If I had only laid the matter before the major half of the administration on the spot, there would have been no blunder; but I never thought of that. So when I did lay it before her, later, I realized once more that it will not do for the literary fraction of a combination to try to manage affairs which properly belong in the office of the business bulk of it. I suppose the President often acts just like that: goes and makes an impossible promise, and you never find it out until it is next to impossible to break it up and set things straight again. Well, that is just our way, exactly-one half of the administration always busy getting the family into trouble, and the other half busy getting it out again. And so we do seem to be all pretty much alike, after all. The fact is, I had forgotten that we were to have a dinner party on that Bridgeport date—I thought it was the next day: which is a good deal of an improvement for me, because I am more used to being behind a day or two than ahead. But that is just the difference between one end of this kind of an administration and the other end of it, as you have noticed, yourself—the other end does not forget these things. Just so with a funeral; if it is the man's funeral, he is most always there, of course—but that is no credit to him, he wouldn't be there if you depended on him to remember about it; whereas, if on the other hand—but I seem to have got off from my line of argument somehow; never mind about the funeral. Of course I am not meaning to say anything against funerals—that is, as occasions—mere occasions—for as diversions I don't think they amount to much But as I was saying—if you are not busy I will look back and see what it was I was saying.

I don't seem to find the place; but anyway she was as sorry as ever anybody could be that I could not go to Bridgeport, but there was no help for it. And I, I have been not only sorry but very sincerely ashamed of having made an engagement to go without first making sure that I could keep it, and I do not know how to apologize enough for my heedless breach of good manners.

*With the sincerest respect,*

*S. L. CLEMENS.*

*Samuel Clemens was one of the very few authors to copyright a book in England before the enactment of the international copyright law.*

*As early as 1872 he copyrighted 'Roughing It' in England, and piratical publishers there respected his rights. Finally, in 1887, the inland revenue office assessed him with income tax, which he very willingly paid, instructing his London publishers, Chatto & Windus, to pay on the full amount he had received from them. But when the receipt for his taxes came it was nearly a yard square with due postage of considerable amount. Then he wrote:*

To Mr. Chatto, of Chatto & Windus, in London:

*HARTFORD, Dec. 5, '87.*

MY DEAR CHATTO,—Look here, I don't mind paying the tax, but don't you let the Inland Revenue Office send me any more receipts for it, for the postage is something perfectly demoralizing. If they feel obliged to print a receipt on a horse-blanket, why don't they hire a ship and send it over at their own expense?

Wasn't it good that they caught me out with an old book instead of a new one? The tax on a new book would bankrupt a body. It was my purpose to go to England next May and stay the rest of the year, but I've found that tax office out just in time. My new book would issue in March, and they would tax the sale in both countries. Come, we must get up a compromise somehow. You go and work in on the good side of those revenue people and get them to take the profits and give me the tax. Then I will come over and we will divide the swag and have a good time.

I wish you to thank Mr. Christmas for me; but we won't resist. The country that allows me copyright has a right to tax me.

*Sincerely Yours*

*S. L. CLEMENS.*

*Another English tax assessment came that year, based on the report that it was understood that he was going to become an English resident, and had leased Buckenham Hall, Norwich, for a year. Clemens wrote his publishers: "I will explain that all that about Buckenham Hall was an English newspaper's mistake. I was not in England, and if I had been I wouldn't have been at Buckenham Hall, anyway, but at Buckingham Palace, or I would have endeavored to find out the reason why." Clemens made literature out of this tax experience. He wrote an open letter to Her Majesty Queen Victoria. Such a letter has no place in this collection. It was published in the "Drawer" of Harper's Magazine, December, 1887, and is now included in the uniform edition of his works under the title of, "A Petition to the Queen of England."*

*From the following letter, written at the end of the year, we gather that the type-setter costs were beginning to make a difference in the Clemens economies.*

To Mrs. Moffett, in Fredonia:

*HARTFORD, Dec. 18, '87.*

DEAR PAMELA,—will you take this $15 and buy some candy or some other trifle for yourself and Sam and his wife to remember that we remember you, by?

If we weren't a little crowded this year by the typesetter, I'd send a check large enough to buy a family Bible or some other useful thing like that.

However we go on and on, but the type-setter goes on forever—at $3,000 a month; which is much more satisfactory than was the case the first seventeen months, when the bill only averaged $2,000, and promised to take a thousand years. We'll be through, now, in 3 or 4 months, I reckon, and then the strain will let up and we can breathe freely once more, whether success ensues or failure.

Even with a type-setter on hand we ought not to be in the least scrimped—but it would take a long letter to explain why and who is to blame.

All the family send love to all of you and best Christmas wishes for your prosperity.

*Affectionately,*

*SAM.*

## XXVIII. LETTERS,1888. A YALE DEGREE. WORK ON "THE YANKEE." ON INTERVIEWING, ETC.

*Mark Twain received his first college degree when he was made Master of Arts by Yale, in June, 1888. Editor of the Courant, Charles H. Clarke, was selected to notify him of his new title. Clarke was an old friend to whom Clemens could write familiarly.*

To Charles H. Clarke, in Hartford:

*ELMIRA, July 2, '88.*

MY DEAR CHARLES,—Thanks for your thanks, and for your initiation intentions. I shall be ready for you. I feel mighty proud of that degree; in fact, I could squeeze the truth a little closer and say vain of it. And why shouldn't I be?—I am the only literary animal of my particular subspecies who has ever been given a degree by any College in any age of the world, as far as I know.

*Sincerely Yours*

*S. L. Clemens M. A.*

*Reply: Charles H. Clarke to S. L Clemens:*

MY DEAR FRIEND, You are "the only literary animal of your particular subspecies" in existence and you've no cause for humility in the fact. Yale has done herself at least as much credit as she has done you, and "Don't you forget it."

*C. H. C.*

*With the exception of his brief return to the river in 1882. Mark Twain had been twenty-seven years away from pilots and piloting.*

*Nevertheless, he always kept a tender place in his heart for the old times and for old river comrades. Major "Jack" Downing had been a Mississippi pilot of early days, but had long since retired from the river to a comfortable life ashore, in an Ohio town. Clemens had not heard from him for years when a letter came which invited the following answer.*

To Major "Jack" Downing, in Middleport Ohio:

*ELMIRA, N. Y.[no month] 1888.*

DEAR MAJOR,—And has it come to this that the dead rise up and speak? For I supposed that you were dead, it has been so long since I heard your name.

And how young you've grown! I was a mere boy when I knew you on the river, where you had been piloting for 35 years, and now you are only a year and a half older than I am! I mean to go to Hot Springs myself and get 30 or 40 years knocked off my age. It's manifestly the place that Ponce de Leon was striking for, but the poor fellow lost the trail.

Possibly I may see you, for I shall be in St. Louis a day or two in November. I propose to go down the river and "note the changes" once more before I make the long crossing, and perhaps you can come there. Will you? I want to see all the boys that are left alive.

And so Grant Marsh, too, is flourishing yet? A mighty good fellow, and smart too. When we were taking that wood flat down to the Chambers, which was aground, I soon saw that I was a perfect lubber at piloting such a thing. I saw that I could never hit the Chambers with it, so I resigned in Marsh's favor, and he accomplished the task to my admiration. We should all have gone to the mischief if I had remained in authority. I always had good judgement, more judgement than talent, in fact.

No; the nom de plume did not originate in that way. Capt. Sellers used the signature, "Mark Twain," himself, when he used to write up the antiquities in the way of river reminiscences for the New Orleans Picayune. He hated me for burlesquing them in an article in the True Delta; so four years later when he died, I robbed the corpse—that is I confiscated the nom de plume. I have published this vital fact 3,000 times now. But no matter, it is good practice; it is about the only fact that I can tell the same way every time. Very glad, indeed, to hear from you Major, and shall be gladder still to see you in November.

*Truly yours,*

*S. L. CLEMENS.*

*He did not make the journey down the river planned for that year. He had always hoped to make another steamboat trip with Bixby, but one thing and another interfered and he did not go again.*

*Authors were always sending their books to Mark Twain to read, and no busy man was ever more kindly disposed toward such offerings, more generously considerate of the senders. Louis Pendleton was a young unknown writer in 1888, but Clemens took time to read his story carefully, and to write to him about it a letter that cost precious time, thought, and effort. It must have rejoiced the young man's heart to receive a letter like that, from one whom all young authors held supreme.*

To Louis Pendleton, in Georgia:

*ELMIRA, N. Y., Aug. 4, '88.*

MY DEAR SIR,—I found your letter an hour ago among some others which had lain forgotten a couple of weeks, and I at once stole time enough to read Ariadne. Stole is the right word, for the summer "Vacation" is the only chance I get for work; so, no minute subtracted from work is borrowed, it is stolen. But this time I do not repent. As a rule, people don't send me books which I can thank them for, and so I say nothing—which looks uncourteous. But I thank you. Ariadne is a beautiful and satisfying story; and true, too—which is the best part of a story; or indeed of any other thing. Even liars have to admit that, if they are intelligent liars; I mean in their private [the word conscientious written but erased] intervals. (I struck that word out because a man's private thought can never be a lie; what he thinks, is to him the truth, always; what he speaks—but these be platitudes.)

If you want me to pick some flaws—very well—but I do it unwillingly. I notice one thing—which one may notice also in my books, and in all books whether written by man or God: trifling carelessness of statement or Expression. If I think that you meant that she took the lizard from the water which she had drawn from the well, it is evidence—it is almost proof—that your words were not as clear as they should have been. True, it is only a trifling thing; but so is mist on a mirror. I would have hung the pail on Ariadne's arm. You did not deceive me when you said that she carried it under her arm, for I knew she didn't; still it was not your right to mar my enjoyment of the graceful picture. If the pail had been a portfolio, I wouldn't be making these remarks. The engraver of a fine picture revises, and revises, and revises—and then revises, and revises, and revises; and then repeats. And always the charm of that picture grows, under his hand. It was good enough before—told its story, and was beautiful. True: and a lovely girl is lovely, with freckles; but she isn't at her level best with them.

This is not hypercriticism; you have had training enough to know that.

So much concerning exactness of statement. In that other not-small matter—selection of the exact single word—you are hard to catch. Still, I should hold that Mrs. Walker considered that there was no occasion for concealment; that "motive" implied a deeper mental search than she expended on the matter; that it doesn't reflect the attitude of her mind with precision. Is this hypercriticism? I shan't dispute it. I only say, that if Mrs. Walker didn't go so far as to have a motive, I had to suggest that when a word is so near the right one that a body can't quite tell whether it is or isn't, it's good politics to strike it out and go for the Thesaurus. That's all. Motive may stand; but you have allowed a snake to scream, and I will not concede that that was the best word.

I do not apologize for saying these things, for they are not said in the speck-hunting spirit, but in the spirit of want-to-help-if-I-can. They would be useful to me if said to me once a month, they may be useful to you, said once.

I save the other stories for my real vacation—which is nine months long, to my sorrow. I thank you again.

*Truly Yours*

*S. L. CLEMENS.*

*In the next letter we get a sidelight on the type-setting machine, the Frankenstein monster that was draining their substance and holding out false hopes of relief and golden return. The program here outlined was one that would continue for several years yet, with the end always in sight, but never quite attained.*

To Orion Clemens, in Keokuk, Ia.:

*Oct. 3, '88.*

Private.

Saturday 29th, by a closely calculated estimate, there were 85 days' work to do on the machine.

We can use 4 men, but not constantly. If they could work constantly it would complete the machine in 21 days, of course. They will all be on hand and under wages, and each will get in all the work there is opportunity for, but by how much they can reduce the 85 days toward the 21 days, nobody can tell.

To-day I pay Pratt & Whitney $10,000. This squares back indebtedness and everything to date. They began about May or April or March 1886—along there somewhere, and have always kept from a dozen to two dozen master-hands on the machine.

That outgo is done; 4 men for a month or two will close up that leak and caulk it. Work on the patents is also kind of drawing toward a conclusion.

Love to you both. All well here.

And give our love to Ma if she can get the idea.

*SAM.*

*Mark Twain that year was working pretty steadily on 'The Yankee at King Arthur's Court', a book which he had begun two years before. He had published nothing since the Huck Finn story, and his company was badly in need of a new book by an author of distinction. Also it was highly desirable to earn money for himself; wherefore he set to work to finish the Yankee story. He had worked pretty steadily that summer in his Elmira study, but on his return to Hartford found a good deal of confusion in the house, so went over to Twichell's, where carpenter work was in progress. He seems to have worked there successfully, though what improvement of conditions he found in that numerous, lively household, over those at home it would be difficult to say.*

To Theodore W. Crane, at Quarry Farm, Elmira, N. Y.

*Friday, Oct.,5, '88.*

DEAR THEO,—I am here in Twichell's house at work, with the noise of the children and an army of carpenters to help. Of course they don't help, but neither do they hinder. It's like a boiler-factory for racket, and in nailing a wooden ceiling onto the room under me the hammering tickles my feet amazingly sometimes, and jars my table a good deal; but I never am conscious of the racket at all, and I move my feet into position of relief without knowing when I do it. I began here Monday morning, and have done eighty pages since. I was so tired last night that I thought I would lie abed and rest, to-day; but I couldn't resist. I mean to try to knock off tomorrow, but it's doubtful if I do. I want to finish the day the machine finishes, and a week ago the closest calculations for that indicated Oct. 22—but experience teaches me that their calculations will miss fire, as usual.

The other day the children were projecting a purchase, Livy and I to furnish the money—a dollar and a half. Jean discouraged the idea. She said: "We haven't got any money. Children, if you would think, you would remember the machine isn't done."

It's billiards to-night. I wish you were here.

*With love to you both*

*S. L. C.*

P. S. I got it all wrong. It wasn't the children, it was Marie. She wanted a box of blacking, for the children's shoes. Jean reproved her—and said:

"Why, Marie, you mustn't ask for things now. The machine isn't done."

*S. L. C.*

*The letter that follows is to another of his old pilot friends, one who was also a schoolmate, Will Bowen, of Hannibal. There is today no means of knowing the occasion upon which this letter was written, but it does not matter; it is the letter itself that is of chief value.*

To Will Bowen, in Hannibal, Mo.:

*HARTFORD, Nov 4, '88.*

DEAR WILL,—I received your letter yesterday evening, just as I was starting out of town to attend a wedding, and so my mind was privately busy, all the evening, in the midst of the maelstrom of chat and chaff and laughter, with the sort of reflections which create themselves, examine themselves, and continue themselves, unaffected by surroundings—unaffected, that is understood, by the surroundings, but not uninfluenced by them. Here was the near presence of the two supreme events of life: marriage, which is the beginning of life, and death which is the end of it. I found myself seeking chances to shirk into corners where I might think, undisturbed; and the most I got out of my thought, was this: both marriage and death ought to be welcome: the one promises happiness, doubtless the other assures it. A long procession of people filed through my mind—people whom you and I knew so many years ago—so many centuries ago, it seems like-and these ancient dead marched to the soft marriage music of a band concealed in some remote room of the house; and the contented music and the dreaming shades seemed in right accord with each other, and fitting. Nobody else knew that a procession of the dead was passing though this noisy swarm of the living, but there it was, and to me there was nothing uncanny about it; Rio, they were welcome faces to me. I would have liked to bring up every creature we knew in those days—even the dumb animals—it would be bathing in the fabled Fountain of Youth.

We all feel your deep trouble with you; and we would hope, if we might, but your words deny us that privilege. To die one's self is a thing that must be easy, and of light consequence, but to lose a part of one's self—well, we know how deep that pang goes, we who have suffered that disaster, received that wound which cannot heal.

*Sincerely your friend*

*S. L. CLEMENS.*

*His next is of quite a different nature. Evidently the typesetting conditions had alarmed Orion, and he was undertaking some economies with a view of retrenchment. Orion was always reducing economy to science. Once, at an earlier date, he recorded that he had figured his personal living expenses down to sixty cents a week, but inasmuch as he was then, by his own confession, unable to earn the sixty cents, this particular economy was wasted. Orion was a trial, certainly, and the explosion that follows was not without excuse. Furthermore, it was not as bad as it sounds. Mark Twain's rages always had an element of humor in them, a fact which no one more than Orion himself would appreciate. He preserved this letter, quietly noting on the envelope, "Letter from Sam, about ma's nurse."*

*Letter to Orion Clemens, in Keokuk, Iowa:*

*NOV. 29, '88.*

Jesus Christ!—It is perilous to write such a man. You can go crazy on less material than anybody that ever lived. What in hell has produced all these maniacal imaginings? You told me you had hired an attendant for ma. Now hire one instantly, and stop this nonsense of wearing Mollie and yourself out trying to do that nursing yourselves. Hire the attendant, and tell me her cost so that I can instruct Webster & Co. to add it every month to what they already send. Don't fool away any more time about this. And don't write me any more damned rot about "storms," and inability to pay trivial sums of money and—and—hell and damnation! You see I've read only the first page of your letter; I wouldn't read the rest for a million dollars.

*Yr*

*SAM.*

P. S. Don't imagine that I have lost my temper, because I swear. I swear all day, but I do not lose my temper. And don't imagine that I am on my way to the poorhouse, for I am not; or that I am uneasy, for I am not; or that I am uncomfortable or unhappy—for I never am. I don't know what it is to be unhappy or uneasy; and I am not going to try to learn how, at this late day.

*SAM.*

*Few men were ever interviewed oftener than Mark Twain, yet he never welcomed interviewers and was seldom satisfied with them. "What I say in an interview loses it character in print," he often remarked, "all its life and personality. The reporter realizes this himself, and tries to improve upon me, but he doesn't help matters any."*

*Edward W. Bok, before he became editor of the Ladies Home Journal, was conducting a weekly syndicate column under the title of "Bok's Literary Leaves." It usually consisted of news and gossip of writers, comment, etc., literary odds and ends, and occasional interviews with distinguished authors. He went up to Hartford one day to interview Mark Twain. The result seemed satisfactory to Bok, but wishing to be certain that it would be satisfactory to Clemens, he sent him a copy for approval. The interview was not returned; in the place of it came a letter-not altogether disappointing, as the reader may believe.*

To Edward W. Bok, in New York:

MY DEAR MR. BOK,—No, no. It is like most interviews, pure twaddle and valueless.

For several quite plain and simple reasons, an "interview" must, as a rule, be an absurdity, and chiefly for this reason—It is an attempt to use a boat on land or a wagon on water, to speak figuratively. Spoken speech is one thing, written speech is quite another. Print is the proper vehicle for the latter, but it isn't for the former. The moment "talk" is put into print you recognize that it is not what it was when you heard it; you perceive that an immense something has disappeared from it. That is its soul. You have nothing but a dead carcass left on your hands. Color, play of feature, the varying modulations of the voice, the laugh, the smile, the informing inflections, everything that gave that body warmth, grace, friendliness and charm and commended it to your affections—or, at least, to your tolerance—is gone and nothing is left but a pallid, stiff and repulsive cadaver.

Such is "talk" almost invariably, as you see it lying in state in an "interview". The interviewer seldom tries to tell one how a thing was said; he merely puts in the naked remark and stops there. When one writes for print his methods are very different. He follows forms which have but little resemblance to conversation, but they make the reader understand what the writer is trying to convey. And when the writer is making a story and finds it necessary to report some of the talk of his characters observe how cautiously and anxiously he goes at that risky and difficult thing. "If he had dared to say that thing in my presence," said Alfred, "taking a mock heroic attitude, and casting an arch glance upon the company, blood would have flowed."

"If he had dared to say that thing in my presence," said Hawkwood, with that in his eye which caused more than one heart in that guilty assemblage to quake, "blood would have flowed."

"If he had dared to say that thing in my presence," said the paltry blusterer, with valor on his tongue and pallor on his lips, "blood would have flowed."

So painfully aware is the novelist that naked talk in print conveys no meaning that he loads, and often overloads, almost every utterance of his characters with explanations and interpretations. It is a loud confession that print is a poor vehicle for "talk"; it is a recognition that uninterpreted talk in print would result in confusion to the reader, not instruction.

Now, in your interview, you have certainly been most accurate; you have set down the sentences I uttered as I said them. But you have not a word of explanation; what my manner was at several points is not indicated. Therefore, no reader can possibly know where I was in earnest and where I was joking; or whether I was joking altogether or in earnest altogether. Such a report of a conversation has no value. It can convey many meanings to the reader, but never the right one. To add interpretations which would convey the right meaning is a something which would require—what? An art so high and fine and difficult that no possessor of it would ever be allowed to waste it on interviews.

No; spare the reader, and spare me; leave the whole interview out; it is rubbish. I wouldn't talk in my sleep if I couldn't talk better than that.

If you wish to print anything print this letter; it may have some value, for it may explain to a reader here and there why it is that in interviews, as a rule, men seem to talk like anybody but themselves.

*Very sincerely yours,*

*MARK TWAIN.*

## XXIX. LETTERS, 1889. THE MACHINE. DEATH OF MR. CRANE. CONCLUSION OF THE YANKEE.

In January, 1889, Clemens believed, after his long seven years of waiting, fruition had come in the matter of the type machine. Paige, the inventor, seemed at last to have given it its finishing touches. The mechanical marvel that had cost so much time, mental stress, and a fortune in money, stood complete, responsive to the human will and touch—the latest, and one of the greatest, wonders of the world. To George Standring, a London printer and publisher, Clemens wrote: "The machine is finished!" and added, "This is by far the most marvelous invention ever contrived by man. And it is not a thing of rags and patches; it is made of massive steel, and will last a century."

In his fever of enthusiasm on that day when he had actually seen it in operation, he wrote a number of exuberant letters. They were more or less duplicates, but as the one to his brother is of fuller detail and more intimate than the others, it has been selected for preservation here.

To Orion Clemens, in Keokuk:

*HARTFORD, Jan. 5, '89.*

DEAR ORION,—At 12.20 this afternoon a line of movable types was spaced and justified by machinery, for the first time in the history of the world! And I was there to see. It was done automatically—instantly—perfectly. This is indeed the first line of movable types that ever was perfectly spaced and perfectly justified on this earth.

This was the last function that remained to be tested—and so by long odds the most amazing and extraordinary invention ever born of the brain of man stands completed and perfect. Livy is down stairs celebrating.

But it's a cunning devil, is that machine!—and knows more than any man that ever lived. You shall see. We made the test in this way. We set up a lot of random letters in a stick—three-fourths of a line; then filled out the line with quads representing 14 spaces, each space to be 35/1000 of an inch thick. Then we threw aside the quads and put the letters into the machine and formed them into 15 two-letter words, leaving the words separated by two-inch vacancies. Then we started up the machine slowly, by hand, and fastened our eyes on the space-selecting pins. The first pin-block projected its third pin as the first word came traveling along the race-way; second block did the same; but the third block projected its second pin!

"Oh, hell! stop the machine—something wrong—it's going to set a 30/1000 space!"

General consternation. "A foreign substance has got into the spacing plates." This from the head mathematician.

"Yes, that is the trouble," assented the foreman.

Paige examined. "No—look in, and you can see that there's nothing of the kind." Further examination. "Now I know what it is—what it must be: one of those plates projects and binds. It's too bad—the first test is a failure." A pause. "Well, boys, no use to cry. Get to work—take the machine down.—No—Hold on! don't touch a thing! Go right ahead! We are fools, the machine isn't. The machine knows what it's about. There is a speck of dirt on one of those types, and the machine is putting in a thinner space to allow for it!"

That was just it. The machine went right ahead, spaced the line, justified it to a hair, and shoved it into the galley complete and perfect! We took it out and examined it with a glass. You could not tell by your eye that the third space was thinner than the others, but the glass and the calipers showed the difference. Paige had always said that the machine would measure invisible particles of dirt and allow for them, but even he had forgotten that vast fact for the moment.

All the witnesses made written record of the immense historical birth—the first justification of a line of movable type by machinery—and also set down the hour and the minute. Nobody had drank anything, and yet everybody seemed drunk. Well-dizzy, stupefied, stunned.

All the other wonderful inventions of the human brain sink pretty nearly into commonplace contrasted with this awful mechanical miracle. Telephones, telegraphs, locomotives, cotton gins, sewing machines, Babbage calculators, jacquard looms, perfecting presses, Arkwright's frames—all mere toys, simplicities! The Paige Compositor marches alone and far in the lead of human inventions.

In two or three weeks we shall work the stiffness out of her joints and have her performing as smoothly and softly as human muscles, and then we shall speak out the big secret and let the world come and gaze.

Return me this letter when you have read it.

*SAM.*

*Judge of the elation which such a letter would produce in Keokuk! Yet it was no greater than that which existed in Hartford—for a time.*

*Then further delays. Before the machine got "the stiffness out of her joints" that "cunning devil" manifested a tendency to break the types, and Paige, who was never happier than when he was pulling things to pieces and making improvements, had the type-setter apart again and the day of complete triumph was postponed.*

*There was sadness at the Elmira farm that spring. Theodore Crane, who had long been in poor health, seemed to grow daily worse. In February he had paid a visit to Hartford and saw the machine in operation, but by the end of May his condition was very serious. Remembering his keen sense of humor, Clemens reported to him cheering and amusing incidents.*

To Mrs. Theodore Crane. in Elmira, N. Y.:

*HARTFORD, May 28, '89.*

Susie dear, I want you to tell this to Theodore. You know how absent-minded Twichell is, and how desolate his face is when he is in that frame. At such times, he passes the word with a friend on the street and is not aware of the meeting at all. Twice in a week, our Clara had this latter experience with him within the past month. But the second instance was too much for her, and she woke him up, in his tracks, with a reproach. She said:

"Uncle Joe, why do you always look as if you were just going down into the grave, when you meet a person on the street?"—and then went on to reveal to him the funereal spectacle which he presented on such occasions. Well, she has met Twichell three times since then, and would swim the Connecticut to avoid meeting him the fourth. As soon as he sights her, no matter how public the place nor how far off she is, he makes a bound into the air, heaves arms and legs into all sorts of frantic gestures of delight, and so comes prancing, skipping and pirouetting for her like a drunken Indian entering heaven.

With a full invoice of love from us all to you and Theodore.

*S. L. C.*

*The reference in the next to the "closing sentence" in a letter written by Howells to Clemens about this time, refers to a heart-broken utterance of the former concerning his daughter Winnie, who had died some time before. She had been a gentle talented girl, but never of robust health. Her death had followed a long period of gradual decline.*

To W. D. Howells, in Boston:

*HARTFORD, Judy 13, '89.*

DEAR HOWELLS,—I came on from Elmira a day or two ago, where I left a house of mourning. Mr. Crane died, after ten months of pain and two whole days of dying, at the farm on the hill, the 3rd inst: A man who had always hoped for a swift death. Mrs. Crane and Mrs. Clemens and the children were in a gloom which brought back to me the days of nineteen years ago, when Mr. Langdon died. It is heart-breaking to see Mrs. Crane. Many a time, in the past ten days, the sight of her has reminded me, with a pang, of the desolation which uttered itself in the closing sentence of your last letter to me. I do see that there is an argument against suicide: the grief of the worshipers left behind; the awful famine in their hearts, these are too costly terms for the release.

I shall be here ten days yet, and all alone: nobody in the house but the servants. Can't Mrs. Howells spare you to me? Can't you come and stay with me? The house is cool and pleasant; your work will not be interrupted; we will keep to ourselves and let the rest of the world do the same; you can have your choice of three bedrooms, and you will find the Children's schoolroom (which was built for my study,) the perfection of a retired and silent den for work. There isn't a fly or a mosquito on the estate. Come—say you will.

With kindest regards to Mrs. Howells, and Pilla and John,

*Yours Ever*

*MARK.*

Howells was more hopeful. He wrote: "I read something in a strange book, The Physical Theory of Another Life, that consoles a little; namely, we see and feel the power of Deity in such fullness that we ought to infer the infinite justice and Goodness which we do not see or feel." And a few days later, he wrote: "I would rather see and talk with you than any other man in the world outside my own blood."

A Connecticut Yankee at King Arthur's Court was brought to an end that year and given to the artist and printer. Dan Beard was selected for the drawings, and was given a free hand, as the next letter shows.

To Fred J. Hall, Manager Charles L. Webster & Co.:

[Charles L. Webster, owing to poor health, had by this time retired from the firm.]

*ELMIRA, July 20, '89.*

DEAR MR. HALL,—Upon reflection—thus: tell Beard to obey his own inspiration, and when he sees a picture in his mind put that picture on paper, be it humorous or be it serious. I want his genius to be wholly unhampered, I shan't have fears as to the result. They will be better pictures than if I mixed in and tried to give him points on his own trade.

Send this note and he'll understand.

*Yr*

*S. L. C.*

*Clemens had made a good choice in selecting Beard for the illustrations. He was well qualified for the work, and being of a socialistic turn of mind put his whole soul into it. When the drawings were completed, Clemens wrote: "Hold me under permanent obligations. What luck it was to find you! There are hundreds of artists that could illustrate any other book of mine, but there was only one who could illustrate this one. Yes, it was a fortunate hour that I went netting for lightning bugs and caught a meteor. Live forever!"*

*Clemens, of course, was anxious for Howells to read The Yankee, and Mrs. Clemens particularly so. Her eyes were giving her trouble that summer, so that she could not read the MS. for herself, and she had grave doubts as to some of its chapters. It may be said here that the book to-day might have been better if Mrs. Clemens had been able to read it. Howells was a peerless critic, but the revolutionary subject-matter of the book so delighted him that he was perhaps somewhat blinded to its literary defects. However, this is premature. Howells did not at once see the story. He had promised to come to Hartford, but wrote that trivial matters had made his visit impossible. From the next letter we get the situation at this time. The "Mr. Church" mentioned was Frederick S. Church, the well-known artist.*

To W. D. Howells, in Boston:

*ELMIRA, July 24, '89.*

DEAR HOWELLS,—I, too, was as sorry as I could be; yes, and desperately disappointed. I even did a heroic thing: shipped my book off to New York lest I should forget hospitality and embitter your visit with it. Not that I think you wouldn't like to read it, for I think you would; but not on a holiday that's not the time. I see how you were situated—another familiarity of Providence and wholly wanton intrusion—and of course we could not help ourselves. Well, just think of it: a while ago, while Providence's attention was absorbed in disordering some time-tables so as to break up a trip of mine to Mr. Church's on the Hudson, that Johnstown dam got loose. I swear I was afraid to pray, for fear I should laugh. Well, I'm not going to despair; we'll manage a meet yet.

I expect to go to Hartford again in August and maybe remain till I have to come back here and fetch the family. And, along there in August, some time, you let on that you are going to Mexico, and I will let on that I am going to Spitzbergen, and then under cover of this clever stratagem we will glide from the trains at Worcester and have a time. I have noticed that Providence is indifferent about Mexico and Spitzbergen.

*Ys Ever*

*MARK.*

*Possibly Mark Twain was not particularly anxious that Howells should see his MS., fearing that he might lay a ruthless hand on some of his more violent fulminations and wild fancies. However this may be, further postponement was soon at an end. Mrs. Clemens's eyes troubled her and would not permit her to read, so she requested that the Yankee be passed upon by soberminded critics, such as Howells and Edmund Clarence Stedman. Howells wrote that even if he hadn't wanted to read the book for its own sake, or for the author's sake, he would still want to do it for Mrs. Clemens's. Whereupon the proofs were started in his direction.*

To W. D. Howells, in Boston:

*ELMIRA, Aug. 24, '89.*

DEAR HOWELLS,—If you should be moved to speak of my book in the Study, I shall be glad and proud—and the sooner it gets in, the better for the book; though I don't suppose you can get it in earlier than the November number—why, no, you can't get it in till a month later than that. Well, anyway I don't think I'll send out any other press copy—except perhaps to Stedman. I'm not writing for those parties who miscall themselves critics, and I don't care to have them paw the book at all. It's my swan-song, my retirement from literature permanently, and I wish to pass to the cemetery unclodded.

I judge that the proofs have begun to reach you about this time, as I had some (though not revises,) this morning. I'm sure I'm going to be charmed with Beard's pictures. Observe his nice take-off of Middle-Age art-dinner-table scene.

*Ys sincerely*

*MARK.*

*Howells's approval of the Yankee came almost in the form of exultant shouts, one after reading each batch of proof. First he wrote: "It's charming, original, wonderful! good in fancy and sound to the core in morals." And again, "It's a mighty great book, and it makes my heart burn with wrath. It seems God did not forget to put a soul into you. He shuts most literary men off with a brain, merely." Then, a few days later: "The book is glorious—simply noble; what masses of virgin truth never touched in print before!" and, finally, "Last night I read your last chapter. As Stedman says of the whole book, it's titanic."*

To W. D. Howells, in Boston:

*HARTFORD, Sept. 22, '89.*

DEAR HOWELLS,—It is immensely good of you to grind through that stuff for me; but it gives peace to Mrs. Clemens's soul; and I am as grateful to you as a body can be. I am glad you approve of what I say about the French Revolution. Few people will. It is odd that even to this day Americans still observe that immortal benefaction through English and other monarchical eyes, and have no shred of an opinion about it that they didn't get at second-hand.

Next to the 4th of July and its results, it was the noblest and the holiest thing and the most precious that ever happened in this earth. And its gracious work is not done yet—not anywhere in the remote neighborhood of it.

Don't trouble to send me all the proofs; send me the pages with your corrections on them, and waste-basket the rest. We issue the book Dec. 10; consequently a notice that appears Dec. 20 will be just in good time.

I am waiting to see your Study set a fashion in criticism. When that happens—as please God it must—consider that if you lived three centuries you couldn't do a more valuable work for this country, or a humaner.

As a rule a critic's dissent merely enrages, and so does no good; but by the new art which you use, your dissent must be as welcome as your approval, and as valuable. I do not know what the secret of it is, unless it is your attitude—man courteously reasoning with man and brother, in place of the worn and wearisome critical attitude of all this long time—superior being lecturing a boy.

Well, my book is written—let it go. But if it were only to write over again there wouldn't be so many things left out. They burn in me; and they keep multiplying and multiplying; but now they can't ever be said. And besides, they would require a library—and a pen warmed up in hell.

*Ys Ever*

*MARK.*

*The type-setting machine began to loom large in the background. Clemens believed it perfected by this time. Paige had got it together again and it was running steadily—or approximately so —setting type at a marvelous speed and with perfect accuracy. In time an expert operator would be able to set as high as eight thousand ems per hour, or about ten times as much as a good compositor could set and distribute by hand. Those who saw it were convinced—most of them—that the type-setting problem was solved by this great mechanical miracle. If there were any who doubted, it was because of its marvelously minute accuracy which the others only admired. Such accuracy, it was sometimes whispered, required absolutely perfect adjustment, and what would happen when the great inventor—"the poet in steel," as Clemens once called him—was no longer at hand to supervise and to correct the slightest variation. But no such breath of doubt came to Mark Twain; he believed the machine as reliable as a constellation.*

*But now there was need of capital to manufacture and market the wonder. Clemens, casting about in his mind, remembered Senator Jones, of Nevada, a man of great wealth, and his old friend, Joe Goodman, of Nevada, in whom Jones had unlimited confidence. He wrote to Goodman, and in this letter we get a pretty full exposition of the whole matter as it stood in the fall of 1889. We note in this communication that Clemens says that he has been at the machine three years and seven months, but this was only the period during which he had spent the regular monthly sum of three thousand dollars. His interest in the invention had begun as far back as 1880.*

To Joseph T. Goodman, in Nevada:

*Private. HARTFORD, Oct. 7, '89.*

DEAR JOE,—I had a letter from Aleck Badlam day before yesterday, and in answering him I mentioned a matter which I asked him to consider a secret except to you and John McComb,—[This is Col. McComb, of the

Alta-California, who had sent Mark Twain on the Quaker City excursion]—as I am not ready yet to get into the newspapers.

I have come near writing you about this matter several times, but it wasn't ripe, and I waited. It is ripe, now. It is a type-setting machine which I undertook to build for the inventor (for a consideration). I have been at it three years and seven months without losing a day, at a cost of $3,000 a month, and in so private a way that Hartford has known nothing about it. Indeed only a dozen men have known of the matter. I have reported progress from time to time to the proprietors of the N. Y. Sun, Herald, Times, World, Harper Brothers and John F. Trow; also to the proprietors of the Boston Herald and the Boston Globe. Three years ago I asked all these people to squelch their frantic desire to load up their offices with the Mergenthaler (N. Y. Tribune) machine, and wait for mine and then choose between the two. They have waited—with no very gaudy patience—but still they have waited; and I could prove to them to-day that they have not lost anything by it. But I reserve the proof for the present—except in the case of the N. Y. Herald; I sent an invitation there the other day—a courtesy due a paper which ordered $240,000 worth of our machines long ago when it was still in a crude condition. The Herald has ordered its foreman to come up here next Thursday; but that is the only invitation which will go out for some time yet.

The machine was finished several weeks ago, and has been running ever since in the machine shop. It is a magnificent creature of steel, all of Pratt & Whitney's super-best workmanship, and as nicely adjusted and as accurate as a watch. In construction it is as elaborate and complex as that machine which it ranks next to, by every right—Man—and in performance it is as simple and sure.

Anybody can set type on it who can read—and can do it after only 15 minutes' instruction. The operator does not need to leave his seat at the keyboard; for the reason that he is not required to do anything but strike the keys and set type—merely one function; the spacing, justifying, emptying into the galley, and distributing of dead matter is all done by the machine without anybody's help—four functions.

The ease with which a cub can learn is surprising. Day before yesterday I saw our newest cub set, perfectly space and perfectly justify 2,150 ems of solid nonpareil in an hour and distribute the like amount in the same hour—and six hours previously he had never seen the machine or its keyboard. It was a good hour's work for 3-year veterans on the other type-setting machines to do. We have 3 cubs. The dean of the trio is a school youth of 18. Yesterday morning he had been an apprentice on the machine 16 working days (8-hour days); and we speeded him to see what he could do in an hour. In the hour he set 5,900 ems solid nonpareil, and the machine perfectly spaced and justified it, and of course distributed the like amount in the same hour. Considering that a good fair compositor sets 700 and distributes 700 in the one hour, this boy did the work of about 8 x a compositors in that hour. This fact sends all other type-setting machines a thousand miles to the rear, and the best of them will never be heard of again after we publicly exhibit in New York.

We shall put on 3 more cubs. We have one school boy and two compositors, now,—and we think of putting on a type writer, a stenographer, and perhaps a shoemaker, to show that no special gifts or training are required with this machine. We shall train these beginners two or three months—or until some one of them gets up to 7,000 an hour—then we will show up in New York and run the machine 24 hours a day 7 days in the week, for several months—to prove that this is a machine which will never get out of order or cause delay, and can stand anything an anvil can stand. You know there is no other typesetting machine that can run two hours on a stretch without causing trouble and delay with its incurable caprices.

We own the whole field—every inch of it—and nothing can dislodge us.

Now then, above is my preachment, and here follows the reason and purpose of it. I want you to run over here, roost over the machine a week and satisfy yourself, and then go to John P. Jones or to whom you please, and sell me a hundred thousand dollars' worth of this property and take ten per cent in cash or the "property" for your trouble—the latter, if you are wise, because the price I ask is a long way short of the value.

What I call "property" is this. A small part of my ownership consists of a royalty of $500 on every machine marketed under the American patents. My selling-terms are, a permanent royalty of one dollar on every American-marketed machine for a thousand dollars cash to me in hand paid. We shan't market any fewer than 5,000 machines in 15 years—a return of fifteen thousand dollars for one thousand. A royalty is better than stock, in one way—it must be paid, every six months, rain or shine; it is a debt, and must be paid before dividends are declared. By and by, when we become a stock company I shall buy these royalties back for stock if I can get them for anything like reasonable terms.

I have never borrowed a penny to use on the machine, and never sold a penny's worth of the property until the machine was entirely finished and proven by the severest tests to be what she started out to be—perfect, permanent, and occupying the position, as regards all kindred machines, which the City of Paris occupies as regards the canvas-backs of the mercantile marine.

It is my purpose to sell two hundred dollars of my royalties at the above price during the next two months and keep the other $300.

Mrs. Clemens begs Mrs. Goodman to come with you, and asks pardon for not writing the message herself—which would be a pathetically-welcome spectacle to me; for I have been her amanuensis for 8 months, now, since her eyes failed her. Yours as always

*MARK.*

*While this letter with its amazing contents is on its way to astonish Joe Goodman, we will consider one of quite a different, but equally characteristic sort. We may assume that Mark Twain's sister Pamela had been visiting him in Hartford and was now making a visit in Keokuk.*

To Mrs. Moffett, in Keokuk:

*HARTFORD, Oct 9, '89.*

DEAR PAMELA,—An hour after you left I was suddenly struck with a realizing sense of the utter chuckle-headedness of that notion of mine: to send your trunk after you. Land! it was idiotic. None but a lunatic would, separate himself from his baggage.

Well, I am soulfully glad the baggage fetcher saved me from consummating my insane inspiration. I met him on the street in the afternoon and paid him again. I shall pay him several times more, as opportunity offers.

I declined the invitation to banquet with the visiting South American Congress, in a polite note explaining that I had to go to New York today. I conveyed the note privately to Patrick; he got the envelope soiled, and asked Livy to put on a clean one. That is why I am going to the banquet; also why I have disinvited the boys I thought I was going to punch billiards with, upstairs to-night.

Patrick is one of the injudiciousest people I ever struck. And I am the other.

*Your Brother*

*SAM.*

*The Yankee was now ready for publication, and advance sheets were already in the reviewers' hands. Just at this moment the Brazilian monarchy crumbled, and Clemens was moved to write Sylvester Baxter, of the Boston Herald, a letter which is of special interest in its prophecy of the new day, the dawn of which was even nearer than he suspected.*

DEAR MR. BAXTER, Another throne has gone down, and I swim in oceans of satisfaction. I wish I might live fifty years longer; I believe I should see the thrones of Europe selling at auction for old iron. I believe I should really see the end of what is surely the grotesquest of all the swindles ever invented by man-monarchy. It is enough to make a graven image laugh, to see apparently rational people, away down here in this wholesome and merciless slaughter-day for shams, still mouthing empty reverence for those moss-backed frauds and scoundrelisms, hereditary kingship and so-called "nobility." It is enough to make the monarchs and nobles themselves laugh—and in private they do; there can be no question about that. I think there is only one funnier thing, and that is the spectacle of these bastard Americans—these Hamersleys and Huntingtons and such—offering cash, encumbered by themselves, for rotten carcases and stolen titles. When our great brethren the disenslaved Brazilians frame their Declaration of Independence, I hope they will insert this missing link: "We hold these truths to be self-evident: that all monarchs are usurpers, and descendants of usurpers; for the reason that no throne was ever set up in this world by the will, freely exercised, of the only body possessing the legitimate right to set it up—the numerical mass of the nation."

You already have the advance sheets of my forthcoming book in your hands. If you will turn to about the five hundredth page, you will find a state paper of my Connecticut Yankee in which he announces the dissolution of King Arthur's monarchy and proclaims the English Republic. Compare it with the state paper which announces the downfall of the Brazilian monarchy and proclaims the Republic of the United States of Brazil, and stand by to defend the Yankee from plagiarism. There is merely a resemblance of ideas, nothing more. The Yankee's proclamation was already in print a week ago. This is merely one of those odd coincidences which are always turning up. Come, protect the Yank from that cheapest and easiest of all charges—plagiarism. Otherwise, you see, he will have to protect himself by charging approximate and indefinite plagiarism upon the official servants of our majestic twin down yonder, and then there might be war, or some similar annoyance.

Have you noticed the rumor that the Portuguese throne is unsteady, and that the Portuguese slaves are getting restive? Also, that the head slave-driver of Europe, Alexander III, has so reduced his usual monthly order for chains that the Russian foundries are running on only half time now? Also that other rumor that English nobility acquired an added stench the other day—and had to ship it to India and the continent because there wasn't any more room for it at home? Things are working. By and by there is going to be an emigration, may be. Of course we shall make no preparation; we never do. In a few years from now we shall have nothing but played-out kings and dukes on the police, and driving the horse-cars, and whitewashing fences, and in fact overcrowding all the avenues of unskilled labor; and then we shall wish, when it is too late, that we had taken common and reasonable precautions and drowned them at Castle Garden.

*There followed at this time a number of letters to Goodman, but as there is much of a sameness in them, we need not print them all. Clemens, in fact, kept the mails warm with letters bulging with schemes for capitalization, and promising vast wealth to all concerned. When the letters did not go fast enough he sent telegrams. In one of the letters Goodman is promised "five hundred thousand dollars out of the profits before we get anything ourselves." One thing we gather from these letters is that Paige has taken the machine apart again, never satisfied with its perfection, or perhaps getting a hint that certain of its perfections were not permanent. A letter at the end of November seems worth preserving here.*

To Joseph T. Goodman, in California:

*HARTFORD, Nov. 29, '89.*

DEAR JOE, Things are getting into better and more flexible shape every day. Papers are now being drawn which will greatly simplify the raising of capital; I shall be in supreme command; it will not be necessary for the capitalist to arrive at terms with anybody but me. I don't want to dicker with anybody but Jones. I know him; that is to say, I want to dicker with you, and through you with Jones. Try to see if you can't be here by the 15th of January.

The machine was as perfect as a watch when we took her apart the other day; but when she goes together again the 15th of January we expect her to be perfecter than a watch.

Joe, I want you to sell some royalties to the boys out there, if you can, for I want to be financially strong when we go to New York. You know the machine, and you appreciate its future enormous career better than any man I know. At the lowest conceivable estimate (2,000 machines a year,) we shall sell 34,000 in the life of the patent—17 years.

All the family send love to you—and they mean it, or they wouldn't say it.

*Yours ever*

*MARK.*

*The Yankee had come from the press, and Howells had praised it in the "Editor's Study" in Harper's Magazine. He had given it his highest commendation, and it seems that his opinion of it did not change with time. "Of all fanciful schemes of fiction it pleases me most," he in one place declared, and again referred to it as "a greatly imagined and symmetrically developed tale."*

*In more than one letter to Goodman, Clemens had urged him to come East without delay. "Take the train, Joe, and come along," he wrote early in December. And we judge from the following that Joe had decided to come.*

To W. D. Howells, in Boston:

*HARTFORD, Dec. 23, '89.*

DEAR HOWELLS,—The magazine came last night, and the Study notice is just great. The satisfaction it affords us could not be more prodigious if the book deserved every word of it; and maybe it does; I hope it does, though of course I can't realize it and believe it. But I am your grateful servant, anyway and always.

I am going to read to the Cadets at West Point Jan. 11. I go from here to New York the 9th, and up to the Point the 11th. Can't you go with me? It's great fun. I'm going to read the passages in the "Yankee" in which the Yankee's West Point cadets figure—and shall covertly work in a lecture on aristocracy to those boys. I am to be the guest of the Superintendent, but if you will go I will shake him and we will go to the hotel. He is a splendid fellow, and I know him well enough to take that liberty.

And won't you give me a day or two's visit toward the end of January? For two reasons: the machine will be at work again by that time, and we want to hear the rest of the dream-story; Mrs. Clemens keeps speaking about it and hankering for it. And we can have Joe Goodman on hand again by that time, and I want you to get to know him thoroughly. It's well worth it. I am going to run up and stay over night with you as soon as I can get a chance.

We are in the full rush of the holidays now, and an awful rush it is, too. You ought to have been here the other day, to make that day perfect and complete. All alone I managed to inflict agonies on Mrs. Clemens, whereas I was expecting nothing but praises. I made a party call the day after the party—and called the lady down from breakfast to receive it. I then left there and called on a new bride, who received me in her dressing-gown; and as things went pretty well, I stayed to luncheon. The error here was, that the appointed reception-hour was 3 in the afternoon, and not at the bride's house but at her aunt's in another part of the town. However, as I meant well, none of these disasters distressed me.

*Yrs ever*

*MARK.*

*The Yankee did not find a very hearty welcome in England. English readers did not fancy any burlesque of their Arthurian tales, or American strictures on their institutions. Mark Twain's publishers had feared this, and asked that the story be especially edited for the English edition. Clemens, however, would not listen to any suggestions of the sort.*

To Messrs. Chatto & Windus, in London, Eng.:

GENTLEMEN,—Concerning The Yankee, I have already revised the story twice; and it has been read critically by W. D. Howells and Edmund Clarence Stedman, and my wife has caused me to strike out several passages that have been brought to her attention, and to soften others. Furthermore, I have read chapters of the book in public where Englishmen were present and have profited by their suggestions.

Now, mind you, I have taken all this pains because I wanted to say a Yankee mechanic's say against monarchy and its several natural props, and yet make a book which you would be willing to print exactly as it comes to you, without altering a word.

We are spoken of (by Englishmen) as a thin-skinned people. It is you who are thin-skinned. An Englishman may write with the most brutal frankness about any man or institution among us and we republish him without dreaming of altering a line or a word. But England cannot stand that kind of a book written about herself. It is England that is thin-skinned. It causeth me to smile when I read the modifications of my language which have been made in my English editions to fit them for the sensitive English palate.

Now, as I say, I have taken laborious pains to so trim this book of offense that you might not lack the nerve to print it just as it stands. I am going to get the proofs to you just as early as I can. I want you to read it carefully. If you can publish it without altering a single word, go ahead. Otherwise, please hand it to J. R. Osgood in time for him to have it published at my expense.

This is important, for the reason that the book was not written for America; it was written for England. So many Englishmen have done their sincerest best to teach us something for our betterment that it seems to me high time that some of us should substantially recognize the good intent by trying to pry up the English nation to a little higher level of manhood in turn.

*Very truly yours,*

*S. L. CLEMENS.*

The English nation, at least a considerable portion of it, did not wish to be "pried up to a higher level of manhood" by a Connecticut Yankee. The papers pretty generally denounced the book as coarse; in fact, a vulgar travesty. Some of the critics concluded that England, after all, had made a mistake in admiring Mark Twain. Clemens stood this for a time and then seems to have decided that something should be done. One of the foremost of English critics was his friend and admirer; he would state the case to him fully and invite his assistance.

To Andrew Lang, in London:

[First page missing.]

*1889*

They vote but do not print. The head tells you pretty promptly whether the food is satisfactory or not; and everybody hears, and thinks the whole man has spoken. It is a delusion. Only his taste and his smell have been heard from—important, both, in a way, but these do not build up the man; and preserve his life and fortify it.

The little child is permitted to label its drawings "This is a cow this is a horse," and so on. This protects the child. It saves it from the sorrow and wrong of hearing its cows and its horses criticized as kangaroos and work benches. A man who is white-washing a fence is doing a useful thing, so also is the man who is adorning a rich man's house with costly frescoes; and all of us are sane enough to judge these performances by standards proper to each. Now, then, to be fair, an author ought to be allowed to put upon his book an explanatory line: "This is written for the Head;" "This is written for the Belly and the Members." And the critic ought to hold himself in honor bound to put away from him his ancient habit of judging all books by one standard, and thenceforth follow a fairer course.

The critic assumes, every time, that if a book doesn't meet the cultivated-class standard, it isn't valuable. Let us apply his law all around: for if it is sound in the case of novels, narratives, pictures, and such things, it is certainly sound and applicable to all the steps which lead up to culture and make culture possible. It condemns the spelling book, for a spelling book is of no use to a person of culture; it condemns all school books and all schools which lie between the child's primer and Greek, and between the infant school and the university; it condemns all the rounds of art which lie between the cheap terra cotta groups and the Venus de Medici, and between the chromo and the Transfiguration; it requires Whitcomb Riley to sing no more till he can sing like Shakespeare, and it forbids all amateur music and will grant its sanction to nothing below the "classic."

Is this an extravagant statement? No, it is a mere statement of fact. It is the fact itself that is extravagant and grotesque. And what is the result? This—and it is sufficiently curious: the critic has actually imposed upon the world the superstition that a painting by Raphael is more valuable to the civilizations of the earth than is a chromo; and the august opera than the hurdy-gurdy and the villagers' singing society; and Homer than the little everybody's-poet whose rhymes are in all mouths today and will be in nobody's mouth next generation; and the Latin classics than Kipling's far-reaching bugle-note; and Jonathan Edwards than the Salvation Army; and the Venus de Medici than the plaster-cast peddler; the superstition, in a word, that the vast and awful comet that trails its cold lustre through the remote abysses of space once a century and interests and instructs a cultivated handful of astronomers is worth more to the world than the sun which warms and cheers all the nations every day and makes the crops to grow.

If a critic should start a religion it would not have any object but to convert angels: and they wouldn't need it. The thin top crust of humanity—the cultivated—are worth pacifying, worth pleasing, worth coddling, worth nourishing and preserving with dainties and delicacies, it is true; but to be caterer to that little faction is no very dignified or valuable occupation, it seems to me; it is merely feeding the over-fed, and there must be small satisfaction in that. It is not that little minority who are already saved that are best worth trying to uplift, I should think, but the mighty mass of the uncultivated who are underneath. That mass will never see the Old Masters—that sight is for the few; but the chromo maker can lift them all one step upward toward appreciation of art; they cannot have the opera, but the hurdy-gurdy and the singing class lift them a little way toward that far light; they will never know Homer, but the passing rhymester of their day leaves them higher than he found them; they may never even hear of the Latin classics, but they will strike step with Kipling's drum-beat, and they will march; for all Jonathan Edwards's help they would die in their slums, but the Salvation Army will beguile some of them up to pure air and a cleaner life; they know no sculpture, the Venus is not even a name to them, but they are a grade higher in the scale of civilization by the ministrations of the plaster-cast than they were before it took its place upon then mantel and made it beautiful to their unexacting eyes.

Indeed I have been misjudged, from the very first. I have never tried in even one single instance, to help cultivate the cultivated classes. I was not equipped for it, either by native gifts or training. And I never had any ambition in that direction, but always hunted for bigger game—the masses. I have seldom deliberately tried to instruct them, but have done my best to entertain them. To simply amuse them would have satisfied my dearest ambition at any time; for they could get instruction elsewhere, and I had two chances to help to the teacher's one: for amusement is a good preparation for study and a good healer of fatigue after it. My audience is dumb, it has no voice in print, and so I cannot know whether I have won its approbation or only got its censure.

Yes, you see, I have always catered for the Belly and the Members, but have been served like the others—criticized from the culture-standard—to my sorrow and pain; because, honestly, I never cared what became of the cultured classes; they could go to the theatre and the opera—they had no use for me and the melodeon.

And now at last I arrive at my object and tender my petition, making supplication to this effect: that the critics adopt a rule recognizing the Belly and the Members, and formulate a standard whereby work done for them shall be judged. Help me, Mr. Lang; no voice can reach further than yours in a case of this kind, or carry greater weight of authority.

*Lang's reply was an article in the Illustrated London News on "The Art of Mark Twain." Lang had no admiration to express for the Yankee, which he confessed he had not cared to read, but he glorified Huck Finn to the highest. "I can never forget, nor be ungrateful for the exquisite pleasure with which I read Huckleberry Finn for the first time, years ago," he wrote; "I read it again last night, deserting Kenilworth for Huck. I never laid it down till I had finished it."*

*Lang closed his article by referring to the story of Huck as the "great American novel which had escaped the eyes of those who watched to see this new planet swim into their ken."*

## XXX. LETTERS, 1890, CHIEFLY TO JOS. T. GOODMAN. THE GREAT MACHINE ENTERPRISE

*Dr. John Brown's son, whom Mark Twain and his wife had known in 1873 as "Jock," sent copies of Dr. John Brown and His Sister Isabella, by E. T. McLaren. It was a gift appreciated in the Clemens home.*

To Mr. John Brown, in Edinburgh, Scotland:

*HARTFORD, Feby 11, 1890.*

DEAR MR. BROWN,—Both copies came, and we are reading and re-reading the one, and lending the other, to old time adorers of "Rab and his Friends." It is an exquisite book; the perfection of literary workmanship. It says in every line, "Don't look at me, look at him"—and one tries to be good and obey; but the charm of the painter is so strong that one can't keep his entire attention on the developing portrait, but must steal side-glimpses of the artist, and try to divine the trick of her felicitous brush. In this book the doctor lives and moves just as he was. He was the most extensive slave-holder of his time, and the kindest; and yet he died without setting one of his bondmen free. We all send our very, very kindest regards.

*Sincerely yours*

*S. L. CLEMENS.*

*If Mark Twain had been less interested in the type-setting machine he might possibly have found a profit that winter in the old Sellers play, which he had written with Howells seven years before. The play had eventually been produced at the Lyceum Theatre in New York, with A. P. Burbank in the leading role, and Clemens and Howells as financial backers. But it was a losing investment, nor did it pay any better when Clemens finally sent Burbank with it on the road. Now, however, James A. Herne, a well-known actor and playwright, became interested in the idea, after a discussion of the matter with Howells, and there seemed a probability that with changes made under Herne's advisement the play might be made sensible and successful.*

*But Mark Twain's greater interest was now all in the type-machine, and certainly he had no money to put into any other venture. His next letter to Goodman is illuminating—the urgency of his need for funds opposed to that conscientiousness which was one of the most positive forces of Mark Twain's body spiritual. The Mr. Arnot of this letter was an Elmira capitalist.*

To Jos. T. Goodman, in California:

*HARTFORD, March 31, '90.*

DEAR JOE,—If you were here, I should say, "Get you to Washington and beg Senator Jones to take the chances and put up about ten or "—no, I wouldn't. The money would burn a hole in my pocket and get away from me if the furnisher of it were proceeding upon merely your judgment and mine and without other evidence. It is too much of a responsibility.

But I am in as close a place to-day as ever I was; $3,000 due for the last month's machine-expenses, and the purse empty. I notified Mr. Arnot a month ago that I should want $5,000 to-day, and his check arrived last night; but I sent it back to him, because when he bought of me on the 9th of December I said that I would not draw upon him for 3 months, and that before that date Senator Jones would have examined the machine and approved, or done the other thing. If Jones should arrive here a week or ten days from now (as he expects to do,) and should not approve, and shouldn't buy any royalties, my deal with Arnot would not be symmetrically square, and then how could I refund? The surest way was to return his check.

I have talked with the madam, and here is the result. I will go down to the factory and notify Paige that I will scrape together $6,000 to meet the March and April expenses, and will retire on the 30th of April and return the assignment to him if in the meantime I have not found financial relief.

It is very rough; for the machine does at last seem perfect, and just a bird to go! I think she's going to be good for 8,000 ems an hour in the hands of a good ordinary man after a solid year's practice. I may be in error, but I most solidly believe it.

There's an improved Mergenthaler in New York; Paige and Davis and I watched it two whole afternoons.

*With the love of us all,*

*MARK.*

*Arnot wrote Clemens urging him to accept the check for five thousand dollars in this moment of need. Clemens was probably as sorely tempted to compromise with his conscience as he had ever been in his life, but his resolution field firm.*

To M. H. Arnot, in Elmira, N. Y.:

MR. M. H. ARNOT

DEAR SIR,—No—no, I could not think of taking it, with you unsatisfied; and you ought not to be satisfied until you have made personal examination of the machine and had a consensus of testimony of disinterested people, besides. My own perfect knowledge of what is required of such a machine, and my perfect knowledge of the fact that this is the only machine that can meet that requirement, make it difficult for me to realize that a doubt is possible to less well-posted men; and so I would have taken your money without thinking, and thus would have done a great wrong to you and a great one to myself. And now that I go back over the ground, I remember that where I said I could get along 3 months without drawing on you, that delay contemplated a visit from you to the machine in the interval, and your satisfaction with its character and prospects. I had forgotten all that. But I remember it now; and the fact that it was not "so nominated in the bond" does not alter the case or justify me in making my call so prematurely. I do not know that you regarded all that as a part of the bargain—for you were thoroughly and magnanimously unexacting—but I so regarded it, notwithstanding I have so easily managed to forget all about it.

You so gratified me, and did me so much honor in bonding yourself to me in a large sum, upon no evidence but my word and with no protection but my honor, that my pride in that is much stronger than my desire to reap a money advantage from it.

With the sincerest appreciation I am Truly yours

*S L. CLEMENS.*

P. S. I have written a good many words and yet I seem to have failed to say the main thing in exact enough language—which is, that the transaction between us is not complete and binding until you shall have convinced yourself that the machine's character and prospects are satisfactory.

I ought to explain that the grippe delayed us some weeks, and that we have since been waiting for Mr. Jones. When he was ready, we were not; and now we have been ready more than a month, while he has been kept in Washington by the Silver bill. He said the other day that to venture out of the Capitol for a day at this time could easily chance to hurt him if the bill came up for action, meantime, although it couldn't hurt the bill, which would pass anyway. Mrs. Jones said she would send me two or three days' notice, right after the passage of the bill, and that they would follow as soon as I should return word that their coming would not inconvenience us. I suppose I ought to go to New York without waiting for Mr. Jones, but it would not be wise to go there without money.

The bill is still pending.

*The Mergenthaler machine, like the Paige, was also at this time in the middle stages of experimental development. It was a slower machine, but it was simpler, less expensive, occupied less room. There was not so much about it to get out of order; it was not so delicate, not so human. These were immense advantages.*

*But no one at this time could say with certainty which typesetter would reap the harvest of millions. It was only sure that at least one of them would, and the Mergenthaler people were willing to trade stock for stock with the Paige company in order to insure financial success for both, whichever won. Clemens, with a faith that never faltered, declined this offer, a decision that was to cost him millions.*

*Winter and spring had gone and summer had come, but still there had been no financial conclusion with Jones, Mackay, and the other rich Californians who were to put up the necessary million for the machine's manufacture. Goodman was spending a large part of his time traveling back and forth between California and Washington, trying to keep business going at both ends. Paige spent most of his time working out improvements for the type-setter, delicate attachments which complicated its construction more and more.*

To Joe T. Goodman, in Washington:

*HARTFORD, June 22, '90.*

DEAR JOE,—I have been sitting by the machine 2 hours, this afternoon, and my admiration of it towers higher than ever. There is no sort of mistake about it, it is the Big Bonanza. In the 2 hours, the time lost by type-breakage was 3 minutes.

This machine is totally without a rival. Rivalry with it is impossible. Last Friday, Fred Whitmore (it was the 28th day of his apprenticeship on the machine) stacked up 49,700 ems of solid nonpareil in 8 hours, and the type-breaking delay was only 6 minutes for the day.

I claim yet, as I have always claimed, that the machine's market (abroad and here together,) is today worth $150,000,000 without saying anything about the doubling and trebling of this sum that will follow within the life of the patents. Now here is a queer fact: I am one of the wealthiest grandees in America—one of the Vanderbilt gang, in fact—and yet if you asked me to lend you a couple of dollars I should have to ask you to take my note instead.

It makes me cheerful to sit by the machine: come up with Mrs. Goodman and refresh yourself with a draught of the same.

*Ys ever*

*MARK.*

*The machine was still breaking the types now and then, and no doubt Paige was itching to take it to pieces, and only restrained by force from doing so. He was never thoroughly happy unless he was taking the machine apart or setting it up again. Finally, he was allowed to go at it—a disasterous permission, for it was just then that Jones decided to steal a day or two from the Silver Bill and watch the type-setter in operation. Paige already had it in parts when this word came from Goodman, and Jones's visit had to be called off.*

*His enthusiasm would seem to have weakened from that day. In July, Goodman wrote that both Mackay and Jones had become somewhat diffident in the matter of huge capitalization. He thought it partly due, at least, to "the fatal delays that have sicklied over the bloom of original enthusiasm." Clemens himself went down to Washington and perhaps warmed Jones with his eloquence; at least, Jones seemed to have agreed to make some effort in the matter a qualified promise, the careful word of a wary politician and capitalist. How many Washington trips were made is not certain, but certainly more than one. Jones would seem to have suggested forms of contracts, but if he came to the point of signing any there is no evidence of it to-day.*

*Any one who has read Mark Twain's, "A Connecticut Yankee in King Arthur's Court," has a pretty good idea of his opinion of kings in general, and tyrants in particular. Rule by "divine right," however liberal, was distasteful to him; where it meant oppression it stirred him to violence. In his article, "The Czar's Soliloquy," he gave himself loose rein concerning atrocities charged to the master of Russia, and in a letter which he wrote during the summer of 1890, he offered a hint as to remedies. The letter was written by editorial request, but was never mailed. Perhaps it seemed too openly revolutionary at the moment.*

*Yet scarcely more than a quarter of a century was needed to make it "timely." Clemens and his family were spending some weeks in the Catskills when it was written.*

An unpublished letter on the Czar.

*ONTEORA, 1890.*

TO THE EDITOR OF FREE RUSSIA,—I thank you for the compliment of your invitation to say something, but when I ponder the bottom paragraph on your first page, and then study your statement on your third page, of the objects of the several Russian liberation-parties, I do not quite know how to proceed. Let me quote here the paragraph referred to:

"But men's hearts are so made that the sight of one voluntary victim for a noble idea stirs them more deeply than the sight of a crowd submitting to a dire fate they cannot escape. Besides, foreigners could not see so clearly as the Russians how much the Government was responsible for the grinding poverty of the masses; nor could they very well realize the moral wretchedness imposed by that Government upon the whole of educated Russia. But the atrocities committed upon the defenceless prisoners are there in all their baseness, concrete and palpable, admitting of no excuse, no doubt or hesitation, crying out to the heart of humanity against Russian tyranny. And the Tzar's Government, stupidly confident in its apparently unassailable position, instead of taking warning from the first rebukes, seems to mock this humanitarian age by the aggravation of brutalities. Not satisfied with slowly killing its prisoners, and with burying the flower of our young generation in the Siberian desserts, the Government of Alexander III. resolved to break their spirit by deliberately submitting them to a regime of unheard-of brutality and degradation."

When one reads that paragraph in the glare of George Kennan's revelations, and considers how much it means; considers that all earthly figures fail to typify the Czar's government, and that one must descend into hell to find its counterpart, one turns hopefully to your statement of the objects of the several liberation-parties—and is disappointed. Apparently none of them can bear to think of losing the present hell entirely, they merely want the temperature cooled down a little.

I now perceive why all men are the deadly and uncompromising enemies of the rattlesnake: it is merely because the rattlesnake has not speech. Monarchy has speech, and by it has been able to persuade men that it differs somehow from the rattlesnake, has something valuable about it somewhere, something worth preserving, something even good and high and fine, when properly "modified," something entitling it to protection from the club of the first comer who catches it out of its hole. It seems a most strange delusion and not reconcilable with our superstition that man is a reasoning being. If a house is afire, we reason confidently that it is the first comer's plain duty to put the fire out in any way he can—drown it with water, blow it up with dynamite, use any and all means to stop the spread of the fire and save the rest of the city. What is the Czar of Russia but a house afire in the midst of a city of eighty millions of inhabitants? Yet instead of extinguishing him, together with his nest and system, the liberation-parties are all anxious to merely cool him down a little and keep him.

It seems to me that this is illogical—idiotic, in fact. Suppose you had this granite-hearted, bloody-jawed maniac of Russia loose in your house, chasing the helpless women and little children—your own. What would you do with him, supposing you had a shotgun? Well, he is loose in your house-Russia. And with your shotgun in your hand, you stand trying to think up ways to "modify" him.

Do these liberation-parties think that they can succeed in a project which has been attempted a million times in the history of the world and has never in one single instance been successful—the "modification" of a despotism by other means than bloodshed? They seem to think they can. My privilege to write these sanguinary sentences in soft security was bought for me by rivers of blood poured upon many fields, in many lands, but I possess not one single little paltry right or privilege that come to me as a result of petition, persuasion, agitation for reform, or any kindred method of procedure. When we consider that not even the most responsible English monarch ever yielded back a stolen public right until it was wrenched from them by bloody violence, is it rational to suppose that gentler methods can win privileges in Russia?

Of course I know that the properest way to demolish the Russian throne would be by revolution. But it is not possible to get up a revolution there; so the only thing left to do, apparently, is to keep the throne vacant by dynamite until a day when candidates shall decline with thanks. Then organize the Republic. And on the whole this method has some large advantages; for whereas a revolution destroys some lives which cannot well be spared, the dynamite way doesn't. Consider this: the conspirators against the Czar's life are caught in every rank of life, from the low to the high. And consider: if so many take an active part, where the peril is so dire, is this not evidence that the sympathizers who keep still and do not show their hands, are countless for multitudes? Can you break the hearts of thousands of families with the awful Siberian exodus every year for generations and not eventually cover all Russia from limit to limit with bereaved fathers and mothers and brothers and sisters who secretly hate the perpetrator of this prodigious crime and hunger and thirst for his life? Do you not believe that if your wife or your child or your father was exiled to the mines of Siberia for some trivial utterances wrung from a smarting spirit by the Czar's intolerable tyranny, and you got a chance to kill him and did not do it, that you would always be ashamed to be in your own society the rest of your life? Suppose that that refined and lovely Russian lady who was lately stripped bare before a brutal soldiery and whipped to death by the Czar's hand in the person of the Czar's creature had been your wife, or your daughter or your sister, and to-day the Czar should pass within reach of your hand, how would you feel—and what would you do? Consider, that all over vast Russia, from boundary to boundary, a myriad of eyes filled with tears when that piteous news came, and through those tears that myriad of eyes saw, not that poor lady, but lost darlings of their own whose fate her fate brought back with new access of grief out of a black and bitter past never to be forgotten or forgiven.

If I am a Swinburnian—and clear to the marrow I am—I hold human nature in sufficient honor to believe there are eighty million mute Russians that are of the same stripe, and only one Russian family that isn't.

*MARK TWAIN.*

*Type-setter matters were going badly. Clemens still had faith in Jones, and he had lost no grain of faith in the machine. The money situation, however, was troublesome. With an expensive establishment, and work of one sort or another still to be done on the machine, his income would not reach. Perhaps Goodman had already given up hope, for he does not seem to have returned from California after the next letter was written—a colorless letter —in which we feel a note of resignation. The last few lines are sufficient.*

To Joe T. Goodman, in California:

DEAR JOE,—...... I wish you could get a day off and make those two or three Californians buy those privileges, for I'm going to need money before long.

I don't know where the Senator is; but out on the Coast I reckon.

I guess we've got a perfect machine at last. We never break a type, now, and the new device for enabling the operator to touch the last letters and justify the line simultaneously works, to a charm.

*With love to you both,*

*MARK*

*The year closed gloomily enough. The type-setter seemed to be perfected, but capital for its manufacture was not forthcoming. The publishing business of Charles L. Webster & Co. was returning little or no profit. Clemens's mother had died in Keokuk at the end of October, and his wife's mother, in Elmira a month later. Mark Twain, writing a short business letter to his publishing manager, Fred J. Ball, closed it: "Merry Xmas to you!—and I wish to God I could have one myself before I die."*

## XXXI. LETTERS, 1891, TO HOWELLS, MRS. CLEMENS AND OTHERS. RETURN TO LITERATURE. AMERICAN CLAIMANT. LEAVING HARTFORD. EUROPE. DOWN THE RHINE.

*Clemens was still not without hope in the machine, at the beginning of the new year (1891) but it was a hope no longer active, and it presently became a moribund. Jones, on about the middle of February, backed out altogether, laying the blame chiefly on Mackay and the others, who, he said, had decided not to invest. Jones "let his victim down easy" with friendly words, but it was the end, for the present, at least, of machine financiering.*

*It was also the end of Mark Twain's capital. His publishing business was not good. It was already in debt and needing more money. There was just one thing for him to do and he did it at once, not stopping to cry over spilt milk, but with good courage and the old enthusiasm that never failed him, he returned to the trade of authorship. He dug out half-finished articles and stories, finished them and sold them, and within a week after the Jones collapse he was at work on a novel based an the old Sellers idea, which eight years before he and Howells had worked into a play. The brief letter in which he reported this news to Howells bears no marks of depression, though the writer of it was in his fifty-sixth year; he was by no means well, and his financial prospects were anything but golden.*

To W. D. Howells, in Boston:

*HARTFORD, Feb. 24, '91*

DEAR HOWELLS,—Mrs. Clemens has been sick abed for near two weeks, but is up and around the room now, and gaining. I don't know whether she has written Mrs. Howells or not—I only know she was going to—and will yet, if she hasn't. We are promising ourselves a whole world of pleasure in the visit, and you mustn't dream of disappointing us.

Does this item stir an interest in you? Began a novel four days ago, and this moment finished chapter four. Title of the book:

*"Colonel Mulberry Sellers.*

*American Claimant*

*Of the*

*Great Earldom of Rossmore'*

*in the*

*Peerage of Great Britain."*

*Ys Ever*

*MARK.*

Probably Mark Twain did not return to literary work reluctantly. He had always enjoyed writing and felt now that he was equipped better than ever for authorship, at least so far as material was concerned. There exists a fragmentary copy of a letter to some unknown correspondent, in which he recites his qualifications. It bears evidence of having been written just at this time and is of unusual interest at this point.

Fragment of Letter to ———, 1891:

.... I confine myself to life with which I am familiar when pretending to portray life. But I confined myself to the boy-life out on the Mississippi because that had a peculiar charm for me, and not because I was not familiar with other phases of life. I was a soldier two weeks once in the beginning of the war, and was hunted like a rat the whole time. Familiar? My splendid Kipling himself hasn't a more burnt-in, hard-baked, and unforgetable familiarity with that death-on-the-pale-horse-with-hell-following-after, which is a raw soldier's first fortnight in the field—and which, without any doubt, is the most tremendous fortnight and the vividest he is ever going to see.

Yes, and I have shoveled silver tailings in a quartz-mill a couple of weeks, and acquired the last possibilities of culture in that direction. And I've done "pocket-mining" during three months in the one little patch of ground in the whole globe where Nature conceals gold in pockets—or did before we robbed all of those pockets and exhausted, obliterated, annihilated the most curious freak Nature ever indulged in. There are not thirty men left alive who, being told there was a pocket hidden on the broad slope of a mountain, would know how to go and find it, or have even the faintest idea of how to set about it; but I am one of the possible 20 or 30 who possess the secret, and I could go and put my hand on that hidden treasure with a most deadly precision.

And I've been a prospector, and know pay rock from poor when I find it—just with a touch of the tongue. And I've been a silver miner and know how to dig and shovel and drill and put in a blast. And so I know the mines and the miners interiorly as well as Bret Harte knows them exteriorly.

And I was a newspaper reporter four years in cities, and so saw the inside of many things; and was reporter in a legislature two sessions and the same in Congress one session, and thus learned to know personally three sample bodies of the smallest minds and the selfishest souls and the cowardliest hearts that God makes.

And I was some years a Mississippi pilot, and familiarly knew all the different kinds of steam-boatmen—a race apart, and not like other folk.

And I was for some years a traveling "jour" printer, and wandered from city to city—and so I know that sect familiarly.

And I was a lecturer on the public platform a number of seasons and was a responder to toasts at all the different kinds of banquets—and so I know a great many secrets about audiences—secrets not to be got out of books, but only acquirable by experience.

And I watched over one dear project of mine for years, spent a fortune on it, and failed to make it go—and the history of that would make a large book in which a million men would see themselves as in a mirror; and they would testify and say, Verily, this is not imagination; this fellow has been there—and after would cast dust upon their heads, cursing and blaspheming.

And I am a publisher, and did pay to one author's widow (General Grant's) the largest copyright checks this world has seen—aggregating more than L80,000 in the first year.

And I have been an author for 20 years and an ass for 55.

Now then; as the most valuable capital or culture or education usable in the building of novels is personal experience I ought to be well equipped for that trade.

I surely have the equipment, a wide culture, and all of it real, none of it artificial, for I don't know anything about books.

*[No signature.]*

*Clemens for several years had been bothered by rheumatism in his shoulder. The return now to the steady use of the pen aggravated his trouble, and at times he was nearly disabled. The phonograph for commercial dictation had been tried experimentally, and Mark Twain was always ready for any innovation.*

To W. D. Howells, in Boston:

*HARTFORD, Feb. 28, '91.*

DEAR HOWELLS,—Won't you drop-in at the Boylston Building (New England Phonograph Co) and talk into a phonograph in an ordinary conversation-voice and see if another person (who didn't hear you do it) can take the words from the thing without difficulty and repeat them to you. If the experiment is satisfactory (also make somebody put in a message which you don't hear, and see if afterward you can get it out without difficulty) won't you then ask them on what terms they will rent me a phonograph for 3 months and furnish me cylinders enough to carry 75,000 words. 175 cylinders, ain't it?

I don't want to erase any of them. My right arm is nearly disabled by rheumatism, but I am bound to write this book (and sell 100,000 copies of it—no, I mean a million—next fall) I feel sure I can dictate the book into a phonograph if I don't have to yell. I write 2,000 words a day; I think I can dictate twice as many.

But mind, if this is going to be too much trouble to you—go ahead and do it, all the same.

*Ys ever*

*MARK.*

*Howells, always willing to help, visited the phonograph place, and a few days later reported results. He wrote: "I talked your letter into a fonograf in my usual tone at my usual gait of speech. Then the fonograf man talked his answer in at his wonted swing and swell. Then we took the cylinder to a type-writer in the next room, and she put the hooks into her ears and wrote the whole out. I send you the result. There is a mistake of one word. I think that if you have the cheek to dictate the story into the fonograf, all the rest is perfectly easy. It wouldn't fatigue me to talk for an hour as I did."*

*Clemens did not find the phonograph entirely satisfactory, at least not for a time, and he appears never to have used it steadily. His early experience with it, however, seems interesting.*

To W. D. Howells, in Boston:

*HARTFORD, Apl. 4, '91.*

DEAR HOWELLS,—I'm ashamed. It happened in this way. I was proposing to acknowledge the receipt of the play and the little book per phonograph, so that you could see that the instrument is good enough for mere letter-writing; then I meant to add the fact that you can't write literature with it, because it hasn't any ideas and it hasn't any gift for elaboration, or smartness of talk, or vigor of action, or felicity of expression, but is just matter-of-fact, compressive, unornamental, and as grave and unsmiling as the devil.

I filled four dozen cylinders in two sittings, then found I could have said about as much with the pen and said it a deal better. Then I resigned.

I believe it could teach one to dictate literature to a phonographer—and some time I will experiment in that line.

The little book is charmingly written, and it interested me. But it flies too high for me. Its concretest things are filmy abstractions to me, and when I lay my grip on one of them and open my hand, I feel as embarrassed as I use to feel when I thought I had caught a fly. I'm going to try to mail it back to you to-day—I mean I am going to charge my memory. Charging my memory is one of my chief industries....

With our loves and our kindest regards distributed among you according to the proprieties.

*Yrs ever*

*MARK.*

P. S.—I'm sending that ancient "Mental Telegraphy" article to Harper's—with a modest postscript. Probably read it to you years ago.

*S. L. C.*

*The "little book" mentioned in this letter was by Swedenborg, an author in whom the Boston literary set was always deeply interested. "Mental Telegraphy" appeared in Harper's Magazine, and is now included in the Uniform Edition of Mark Twain's books. It was written in 1878.*

*Joe Goodman had long since returned to California, it being clear that nothing could be gained by remaining in Washington. On receipt of the news of the type-setter's collapse he sent a consoling word. Perhaps he thought Clemens would rage over the unhappy circumstance, and possibly hold him in some measure to blame. But it was generally the smaller annoyances of life that made Mark Twain rage; the larger catastrophes were likely to stir only his philosophy.*

*The Library of American Literature, mentioned in the following letter, was a work in many volumes, edited by Edmund Clarence Stedman and Ellen Mackay Hutchinson.*

To Joe T. Goodman:

*April [?] 1891.*

DEAR JOE, Well, it's all right, anyway. Diplomacy couldn't have saved it—diplomacy of mine—at that late day. I hadn't any diplomacy in stock, anyway. In order to meet Jones's requirements I had to surrender the old contract (a contract which made me boss of the situation and gave me the whip-hand of Paige) and allow the new one to be drafted and put in its place. I was running an immense risk, but it was justified by Jones's promises—promises made to me not merely once but every time I tallied with him. When February arrived, I saw signs which were mighty plain reading. Signs which meant that Paige was hoping and praying that Jones would go back on me—which would leave Paige boss, and me robbed and out in the cold. His prayers were answered, and I am out in the cold. If I ever get back my nine-twentieths interest, it will be by law-suit—which will be instituted in the indefinite future, when the time comes.

I am at work again—on a book. Not with a great deal of spirit, but with enough—yes, plenty. And I am pushing my publishing house. It has turned the corner after cleaning $50,000 a year for three consecutive years, and piling every cent of it into one book—Library of American Literature—and from next January onward it will resume dividends. But I've got to earn $50,000 for it between now and then—which I will do if I keep my health. This additional capital is needed for that same book, because its prosperity is growing so great and exacting.

It is dreadful to think of you in ill health—I can't realize it; you are always to me the same that you were in those days when matchless health, and glowing spirits and delight in life were commonplaces with us. Lord save us all from old age and broken health and a hope-tree that has lost the faculty of putting out blossoms.

*With love to you both from us all.*

*MARK.*

*Mark Twain's residence in Hartford was drawing rapidly to a close. Mrs. Clemens was poorly, and his own health was uncertain. They believed that some of the European baths would help them.*

*Furthermore, Mark Twain could no longer afford the luxury of his Hartford home. In Europe life could be simpler and vastly cheaper. He was offered a thousand dollars apiece for six European letters, by the McClure syndicate and W. M. Laffan, of the Sun. This would at least give him a start on the other side. The family began immediately their sad arrangements for departure.*

To Fred J. Hall (manager Chas. L. Webster & Co.), N. Y.:

*HARTFORD, Apl. 14, '91.*

DEAR MR. HALL,—Privately—keep it to yourself—as you, are already aware, we are going to Europe in June, for an indefinite stay. We shall sell the horses and shut up the house. We wish to provide a place for our coachman, who has been with us a 21 years, and is sober, active, diligent, and unusually bright and capable. You spoke of hiring a colored man as engineer and helper in the packing room. Patrick would soon learn that trade and be very valuable. We will cease to need him by the middle or end of June. Have you made irrevocable arrangements with the colored man, or would you prefer to have Patrick, if he thinks he would like to try?

I have not said anything to him about it yet.

*Yours*

*S. L. C.*

*It was to be a complete breaking up of their beautiful establishment. Patrick McAleer, George the butler, and others of their household help had been like members of the family. We may guess at the heartbreak of it all, even though the letters remain cheerful.*

*Howells, strangely enough, seems to have been about the last one to be told of their European plans; in fact, he first got wind of it from the papers, and wrote for information. Likely enough Clemens had not until then had the courage to confess.*

To W. D. Howells, in Boston:

*HARTFORD, May 20, '91.*

DEAR HOWELLS,—For her health's sake Mrs. Clemens must try baths somewhere, and this it is that has determined us to go to Europe. The water required seems to be provided at a little obscure and little-visited nook up in the hills back of the Rhine somewhere and you get to it by Rhine traffic-boat and country stage-coach. Come, get "sick or sorry enough" and join us. We shall be a little while at that bath, and the rest of the summer at Annecy (this confidential to you) in Haute Savoie, 22 miles from Geneva. Spend the winters in Berlin. I don't know how long we shall be in Europe—I have a vote, but I don't cast it. I'm going to do whatever the others desire, with leave to change their mind, without prejudice, whenever they want to. Travel has no longer, any charm for me. I have seen all the foreign countries I want to see except heaven and hell, and I have only a vague curiosity as concerns one of those.

I found I couldn't use the play—I had departed too far from its lines when I came to look at it. I thought I might get a great deal of dialogue out of it, but I got only 15 loosely written pages—they saved me half a days work. It was the cursing phonograph. There was abundance of good dialogue, but it couldn't befitted into the new conditions of the story.

Oh, look here—I did to-day what I have several times in past years thought of doing: answered an interviewing proposition from a rich newspaper with the reminder that they had not stated the terms; that my time was all occupied with writing, at good pay, and that as talking was harder work I should not care to venture it unless I knew the pay was going to be proportionately higher. I wish I had thought of this the other day when Charley Stoddard turned a pleasant Englishman loose on me and I couldn't think of any rational excuse.

*Ys Ever*

*MARK.*

*Clemens had finished his Sellers book and had disposed of the serial rights to the McClure syndicate. The house in Hartford was closed early in June, and on the 6th the family, with one maid, Katie Leary, sailed on the Gascogne. Two weeks later they had begun a residence abroad which was to last for more than nine years.*

*It was not easy to get to work in Europe. Clemens's arm remained lame, and any effort at writing brought suffering. The Century Magazine proposed another set of letters, but by the end of July he had barely begun on those promised to McClure and Laffan. In August, however, he was able to send three: one from Aix about the baths there, another from Bayreuth concerning the Wagner festival, and a third from Marienbad, in Bohemia, where they rested for a time. He decided that he would arrange for no more European letters when the six were finished, but would gather material for a book. He would take a courier and a kodak and go tramping again in some fashion that would be interesting to do and to write.*

*The idea finally matured when he reached Switzerland and settled the family at the Hotel Beau Rivage, Ouchy, Lausanne, facing Lake Leman.*

*He decided to make a floating trip down the Rhone, and he engaged Joseph Very, a courier that had served him on a former European trip, to accompany him. The courier went over to Bourget and bought for five dollars a flat-bottomed boat and engaged its owner as their pilot. It was the morning of September 20, when they began their floating-trip down the beautiful historic river that flows through the loveliest and most romantic region of France. He wrote daily to Mrs. Clemens, and his letters tell the story of that drowsy, happy experience better than the notes made with a view to publication. Clemens had arrived at Lake Bourget on the evening before the morning of their start and slept on the Island of Chatillon, in an old castle of the same name. Lake Bourget connects with the Rhone by a small canal.*

Letters and Memoranda to Mrs. Clemens, in Ouchy, Switzerland:

*Sept. 20, 1891.*

*Sunday, 11 a.m.*

On the lake Bourget—just started. The castle of Chatillon high overhead showing above the trees. It was a wonderfully still place to sleep in. Beside us there was nobody in it but a woman, a boy and a dog. A Pope was born in the room I slept in. No, he became a Pope later.

The lake is smooth as glass—a brilliant sun is shining.

Our boat is comfortable and shady with its awning.

11.20 We have crossed the lake and are entering the canal. Shall presently be in the Rhone.

Noon. Nearly down to the Rhone. Passing the village of Chanaz.

3.15 p. m. Sunday. We have been in the Rhone 3 hours. It is unimaginably still and reposeful and cool and soft and breezy. No rowing or work of any kind to do—we merely float with the current—we glide noiseless and swift—as fast as a London cab-horse rips along—8 miles an hour—the swiftest current I've ever boated in. We have the entire river to ourselves—nowhere a boat of any kind.

*Good bye Sweetheart*

*S. L. C.*

*PORT DE GROLEE, Monday, 4.15 p.m.*

*[Sept. 21, 1891]*

Name of the village which we left five minutes ago.

We went ashore at 5 p. m. yesterday, dear heart, and walked a short mile to St. Geuix, a big village, and took quarters at the principal inn; had a good dinner and afterwards along walk out of town on the banks of the Guiers till 7.30.

Went to bed at 8.30 and continued to make notes and read books and newspapers till midnight. Slept until 8, breakfasted in bed, and lay till noon, because there had been a very heavy rain in the night and the day was still dark and lowering. But at noon the sun broke through and in 15 minutes we were tramping toward the river. Got afloat at 1 p. m. but at 2.40 we had to rush suddenly ashore and take refuge in the above village. Just as we got ourselves and traps safely housed in the inn, the rain let go and came down in great style. We lost an hour and a half there, but we are off again, now, with bright sunshine.

I wrote you yesterday my darling, and shall expect to write you every day.

Good-day, and love to all of you.

*SAML.*

*ON THE RHONE BELOW VILLEBOIS,*

*Tuesday noon.*

Good morning, sweetheart. Night caught us yesterday where we had to take quarters in a peasant's house which was occupied by the family and a lot of cows and calves—also several rabbits.—[His word for fleas.]—The latter had a ball, and I was the ball-room; but they were very friendly and didn't bite.

The peasants were mighty kind and hearty, and flew around and did their best to make us comfortable. This morning I breakfasted on the shore in the open air with two sociable dogs and a cat. Clean cloth, napkin and table furniture, white sugar, a vast hunk of excellent butter, good bread, first class coffee with pure milk, fried fish just caught. Wonderful that so much cleanliness should come out of such a phenomenally dirty house.

An hour ago we saw the Falls of the Rhone, a prodigiously rough and dangerous looking place; shipped a little water but came to no harm. It was one of the most beautiful pieces of piloting and boat-management I ever saw. Our admiral knew his business.

We have had to run ashore for shelter every time it has rained heretofore, but Joseph has been putting in his odd time making a water-proof sun-bonnet for the boat, and now we sail along dry although we had many heavy showers this morning.

With a word of love to you all and particularly you,

*SAML.*

*ON THE RHONE, BELOW VIENNA.*

I salute you, my darling. Your telegram reached me in Lyons last night and was very pleasant news indeed.

I was up and shaved before 8 this morning, but we got delayed and didn't sail from Lyons till 10.30—an hour and a half lost. And we've lost another hour—two of them, I guess—since, by an error. We came in sight of Vienne at 2 o'clock, several miles ahead, on a hill, and I proposed to walk down there and let the boat go ahead of us. So Joseph and I got out and struck through a willow swamp along a dim path, and by and by came out on the steep bank of a slough or inlet or something, and we followed that bank forever and ever trying to get around the head of that slough. Finally I noticed a twig standing up in the water, and by George it had a distinct and even vigorous quiver to it! I don't know when I have felt so much like a donkey. On an island! I wanted to drown somebody, but I hadn't anybody I could spare. However, after another long tramp we found a lonely native, and he had a scow and soon we were on the mainland—yes, and a blamed sight further from Vienne than we were when we started.

Notes—I make millions of them; and so I get no time to write to you. If you've got a pad there, please send it poste-restante to Avignon. I may not need it but I fear I shall.

**I'm straining to reach St. Pierre de Boef, but it's going to be a close fit, I reckon.**

*AFLOAT, Friday, 3 p.m., '91.*

Livy darling, we sailed from St. Pierre de Boef six hours ago, and are now approaching Tournon, where we shall not stop, but go on and make Valence, a City Of 25,000 people. It's too delicious, floating with the swift current under the awning these superb sunshiny days in deep peace and quietness. Some of these curious old historical towns strangely persuade me, but it is so lovely afloat that I don't stop, but view them from the outside and sail on. We get abundance of grapes and peaches for next to nothing.

Joseph is perfect. He is at his very best—and never was better in his life. I guess he gets discouraged and feels disliked and in the way when he is lying around—but here he is perfection, and brim full of useful alacrities and helps and ingenuities.

When I woke up an hour ago and heard the clock strike 4, I said "I seem to have been asleep an immensely long time; I must have gone to bed mighty early; I wonder what time I did go to bed." And I got up and lit a candle and looked at my watch to see.

*AFLOAT*

*2 HOURS BELOW BOURG ST. ANDEOL.*

*Monday, 11 a.m., Sept. 28.*

Livy darling, I didn't write yesterday. We left La Voulte in a driving storm of cold rain—couldn't write in it—and at 1 p. m. when we were not thinking of stopping, we saw a picturesque and mighty ruin on a high hill back of a village, and I was seized with a desire to explore it; so we landed at once and set out with rubbers and umbrella, sending the boat ahead to St. Andeol, and we spent 3 hours clambering about those cloudy heights among those worn and vast and idiotic ruins of a castle built by two crusaders 650 years ago. The work of these asses was full of interest, and we had a good time inspecting, examining and scrutinizing it. All the hills on both sides of the Rhone have peaks and precipices, and each has its gray and wasted pile of mouldy walls and broken towers. The Romans displaced the Gauls, the Visigoths displaced the Romans, the Saracens displaced the Visigoths, the Christians displaced the Saracens, and it was these pious animals who built these strange lairs and cut each other's throats in the name and for the glory of God, and robbed and burned and slew in peace and war; and the pauper and the slave built churches, and the credit of it went to the Bishop who racked the money out of them. These are pathetic shores, and they make one despise the human race.

We came down in an hour by rail, but I couldn't get your telegram till this morning, for it was Sunday and they had shut up the post office to go to the circus. I went, too. It was all one family—parents and 5 children—performing in the open air to 200 of these enchanted villagers, who contributed coppers when called on. It was a most gay and strange and pathetic show. I got up at 7 this morning to see the poor devils cook their poor breakfast and pack up their sordid fineries.

This is a 9 k-m. current and the wind is with us; we shall make Avignon before 4 o'clock. I saw watermelons and pomegranates for sale at St. Andeol.

*With a power of love, Sweetheart,*

*SAML.*

*HOTEL D'EUROPE, AVIGNON,*

*Monday, 6 p.m., Sept. 28.*

Well, Livy darling, I have been having a perfect feast of letters for an hour, and I thank you and dear Clam with all my heart. It's like hearing from home after a long absence.

It is early to be in bed, but I'm always abed before 9, on this voyage; and up at 7 or a trifle later, every morning. If I ever take such a trip again, I will have myself called at the first tinge of dawn and get to sea as soon after as possible. The early dawn on the water-nothing can be finer, as I know by old Mississippi experience. I did so long for you and Sue yesterday morning—the most superb sunrise!—the most marvelous sunrise! and I saw it all from the very faintest suspicion of the coming dawn all the way through to the final explosion of glory. But it had interest private to itself and not to be found elsewhere in the world; for between me and it, in the far distant-eastward, was a silhouette mountain-range in which I had discovered, the previous afternoon, a most noble face upturned to the sky, and mighty form out stretched, which I had named Napoleon Dreaming of Universal Empire—and now, this prodigious face, soft, rich, blue, spirituelle, asleep, tranquil, reposeful, lay against that giant conflagration of ruddy and golden splendors all rayed like a wheel with the upstreaming and far-reaching lances of the sun. It made one want to cry for delight, it was so supreme in its unimaginable majesty and beauty.

We had a curious experience today. A little after I had sealed and directed my letter to you, in which I said we should make Avignon before 4, we got lost. We ceased to encounter any village or ruin mentioned in our "particularizes" and detailed Guide of the Rhone—went drifting along by the hour in a wholly unknown land and on an uncharted river! Confound it, we stopped talking and did nothing but stand up in the boat and search the horizons with the glass and wonder what in the devil had happened. And at last, away yonder at 5 o'clock when some east towers and fortresses hove in sight we couldn't recognize them for Avignon—yet we knew by the broken bridge that it was Avignon.

Then we saw what the trouble was—at some time or other we had drifted down the wrong side of an island and followed a sluggish branch of the Rhone not frequented in modern times. We lost an hour and a half by it and missed one of the most picturesque and gigantic and history-sodden masses of castellated medieval ruin that Europe can show.

It was dark by the time we had wandered through the town and got the letters and found the hotel—so I went to bed.

We shall leave here at noon tomorrow and float down to Arles, arriving about dark, and there bid good bye to the boat, the river-trip finished. Between Arles and Nimes (and Avignon again,) we shall be till Saturday morning—then rail it through on that day to Ouchy, reaching the hotel at 11 at night if the train isn't late.

Next day (Sunday) if you like, go to Basel, and Monday to Berlin. But I shall be at your disposal, to do exactly as you desire and prefer.

*With no end of love to all of you and twice as much to you,*

*sweetheart,*

*SAML.*

I believe my arm is a trifle better than it was when I started.

*The mention in the foregoing letter of the Napoleon effigy is the beginning of what proved to be a rather interesting episode. Mark Twain thought a great deal of his discovery, as he called it—the giant figure of Napoleon outlined by the distant mountain range. In his note-book he entered memoranda telling just where it was to be seen, and added a pencil sketch of the huge profile. But then he characteristically forgot all about it, and when he recalled the incident ten years later, he could not remember the name of the village, Beauchastel, from which the great figure could be seen; also, that he had made a record of the place.*

*But he was by this time more certain than ever that his discovery was a remarkable one, which, if known, would become one of the great natural wonders, such as Niagara Falls. Theodore Stanton was visiting him at the time, and Clemens urged him, on his return to France, to make an excursion to the Rhone and locate the Lost Napoleon, as he now called it. But Clemens remembered the wonder as being somewhere between Arles and Avignon, instead of about a hundred miles above the last-named town. Stanton naturally failed to find it, and it remained for the writer of these notes, motoring up the Rhone one September day, exactly twenty-two years after the first discovery, to re-locate the vast reclining figure of the first consul of France, "dreaming of Universal Empire." The re-discovery was not difficult—with Mark Twain's memoranda as a guide—and it was worth while. Perhaps the Lost Napoleon is not so important a natural wonder as Mark Twain believed, but it is a striking picture, and on a clear day the calm blue face outlined against the sky will long hold the traveler's attention.*

To Clara Clemens, in Ouchy, Switzerland:

*AFLOAT, 11.20 a.m., Sept. 29, Tuesday.*

DEAR OLD BEN,—The vast stone masses and huge towers of the

ancient papal palace of Avignon are projected above an intervening wooded island a mile up the river behind me—for we are already on our way to Arles. It is a perfectly still morning, with a brilliant sun, and very hot—outside; but I am under cover of the linen hood, and it is cool and shady in here.

Please tell mamma I got her very last letter this morning, and I perceive by it that I do not need to arrive at Ouchy before Saturday midnight. I am glad, because I couldn't do the railroading I am proposing to do during the next two or three days and get there earlier. I could put in the time till Sunday midnight, but shall not venture it without telegraphic instructions from her to Nimes day after tomorrow, Oct. 1, care Hotel Manivet.

The only adventures we have is in drifting into rough seas now and then. They are not dangerous, but they go thro' all the motions of it. Yesterday when we shot the Bridge of the Holy Spirit it was probably in charge of some inexperienced deputy spirit for the day, for we were allowed to go through the wrong arch, which brought us into a tourbillon below which tried to make this old scow stand on its head. Of course I lost my temper and blew it off in a way to be heard above the roar of the tossing waters. I lost it because the admiral had taken that arch in deference to my opinion that it was the best one, while his own judgment told him to take the one nearest the other side of the river. I could have poisoned him I was so mad to think I had hired such a turnip. A boatman in command should obey nobody's orders but his own, and yield to nobody's suggestions.

It was very sweet of you to write me, dear, and I thank you ever so much. With greatest love and kisses,

*PAPA.*

To Mrs. Clemens, in Ouchy, Switzerland:

*ARLES, Sept. 30, noon.*

Livy darling, I hain't got no time to write today, because I am sight seeing industriously and imagining my chapter.

Bade good-bye to the river trip and gave away the boat yesterday evening. We had ten great days in her.

We reached here after dark. We were due about 4.30, counting by distance, but we couldn't calculate on such a lifeless current as we found.

*I love you, sweetheart.*

*SAML.*

*It had been a long time since Clemens had written to his old friend Twichell, but the Rhone trip must have reminded him of those days thirteen years earlier, when, comparatively young men, he and Twichell were tramping through the Black Forest and scaling Gemmi Pass. He sent Twichell a reminder of that happy time.*

To Rev. Joseph H. Twichell, in Hartford, Conn:

*NIMES, Oct. 1, '91.*

DEAR JOE,—I have been ten days floating down the Rhone on a raft, from Lake Bourget, and a most curious and darling kind of a trip it has been. You ought to have been along—I could have made room for you easily—and you would have found that a pedestrian tour in Europe doesn't begin with a raft-voyage for hilarity and mild adventure, and intimate contact with the unvisited native of the back settlements, and extinction from the world and newspapers, and a conscience in a state of coma, and lazy comfort, and solid happiness. In fact there's nothing that's so lovely.

But it's all over. I gave the raft away yesterday at Arles, and am loafing along back by short stages on the rail to Ouchy-Lausanne where the tribe are staying.

*Love to you all*

*MARK.*

*The Clemenses settled in Berlin for the winter, at 7 Kornerstrasse, and later at the Hotel Royal. There had been no permanent improvement in Mark Twain's arm and he found writing difficult.*

*Some of the letters promised to Laffan and McClure were still unfinished.*

*Young Hall, his publishing manager in America, was working hard to keep the business afloat, and being full of the optimism of his years did not fail to make as good a showing as he could. We may believe his letters were very welcome to Clemens and his wife, who found little enough in the general prospect to comfort them.*

To Mr. Hall, in New York:

*BERLIN, Nov. 27, '91.*

DEAR MR. HALL,—That kind of a statement is valuable. It came this morning. This is the first time since the business began that I have had a report that furnished the kind of information I wanted, and was really enlightening and satisfactory. Keep it up. Don't let it fall into desuetude.

Everything looks so fine and handsome with the business, now, that I feel a great let-up from depression. The rewards of your long and patient industry are on their way, and their arrival safe in port, presently, seems assured.

By George, I shall be glad when the ship comes in!

My arm is so much better that I was able to make a speech last night to 250 Americans. But when they threw my portrait on the screen it was a sorrowful reminder, for it was from a negative of 15 years ago, and hadn't a gray hair in it. And now that my arm is better, I have stolen a couple of days and finished up a couple of McClure letters that have been lying a long time.

I shall mail one of them to you next Tuesday—registered. Lookout for it.

I shall register and mail the other one (concerning the "Jungfrau") next Friday look out for it also, and drop me a line to let me know they have arrived.

I shall write the 6th and last letter by and by when I have studied Berlin sufficiently.

Yours in a most cheerful frame of mind, and with my and all the family's Thanksgiving greetings and best wishes,

*S. L. CLEMENS.*

*Postscript by Mrs. Clemens written on Mr. Clemens's letter:*

DEAR MR. HALL,—This is my birthday and your letter this morning was a happy addition to the little gifts on the breakfast table. I thought of going out and spending money for something unnecessary after it came, but concluded perhaps I better wait a little longer.

*Sincerely yours*

*O. L. CLEMENS.*

*"The German Chicago" was the last of the six McClure letters and was finished that winter in Berlin. It is now included in the Uniform Edition of Mark Twain's works, and is one of the best descriptive articles of the German capital ever written. He made no use of the Rhone notes further than to put them together in literary form. They did not seem to him to contain enough substance to warrant publication. A letter to Hall, written toward the end of December, we find rather gloomy in tone, though he is still able to extract comfort and even cheerfulness from one of Mr. Hall's reports.*

*Memorandum to Fred J. Hall, in New York:*

Among the MSS I left with you are a few that have a recent look and are written on rather stiff pale green paper. If you will have those type-writered and keep the originals and send me the copies (one per mail, not two.) I'll see if I can use them.

But tell Howells and other inquirers that my hopes of writing anything are very slender—I seem to be disabled for life.

Drop McClure a line and tell him the same. I can't dare to make an engagement now for even a single letter.

I am glad Howells is on a magazine, but sorry he gave up the Study. I shall have to go on a magazine myself if this L. A. L. continues to hold my nose down to the grind-stone much longer.

I'm going to hold my breath, now, for 30 days—then the annual statement will arrive and I shall know how we feel! Merry Xmas to you from us all.

*Sincerely,*

*S. L. C.*

P. S. Just finished the above and finished raging at the eternal German tax-gatherer, and so all the jubilant things which I was going to say about the past year's business got knocked out of me. After writing this present letter I was feeling blue about Huck Finn, but I sat down and overhauled your reports from now back to last April and compared them with the splendid Oct.-Nov. business, and went to bed feeling refreshed and fine, for certainly it has been a handsome year. Now rush me along the Annual Report and let's see how we feel!

*S. L. C.*

## XXXII. LETTERS, 1892, CHIEFLY TO MR. HALL AND MRS. CRANE. IN BERLIN, MENTONE, BAD-NAUHEIM, FLORENCE.

Mark Twain was the notable literary figure in Berlin that winter, the center of every great gathering. He was entertained by the Kaiser, and shown many special attentions by Germans of every rank. His books were as well known in Berlin as in New York, and at court assemblies and embassies he was always a chief center of interest.

He was too popular for his own good; the gaiety of the capital told on him. Finally, one night, after delivering a lecture in a hot room, he contracted a severe cold, driving to a ball at General von Versen's, and a few days later was confined to his bed with pneumonia. It was not a severe attack, but it was long continued. He could write some letters and even work a little, but he was not allowed to leave his bed for many weeks, a condition which he did not find a hardship, for no man ever enjoyed the loose luxury of undress and the comfort of pillows more than Mark Twain. In a memorandum of that time he wrote: "I am having a booming time all to myself."

Meantime, Hall, in America, was sending favorable reports of the publishing business, and this naturally helped to keep up his spirits. He wrote frequently to Hall, of course, but the letters for the most part are purely of a business nature and of little interest to the general reader.

To Fred J. Hall, in New York:

*HOTEL ROYAL, BERLIN, Feb. 12.*

DEAR MR. HALL,—Daly wants to get the stage rights of the "American Claimant." The foundation from which I wrote the story is a play of the same name which has been in A. P. Burbank's hands 5 or 6 years. That play cost me some money (helping Burbank stage it) but has never brought me any. I have written Burbank (Lotos Club) and asked him to give me back his rights in the old play so that I can treat with Daly and utilize this chance to even myself up. Burbank is a lovely fellow, and if he objects I can't urge him. But you run in at the Lotos and see him; and if he relinquishes his claim, then I would like you to conduct the business with Daly; or have Whitford or some other lawyer do it under your supervision if you prefer.

This morning I seem to have rheumatism in my right foot.

I am ordered south by the doctor and shall expect to be well enough to start by the end of this month.

*[No signature.]*

*It is curious, after Clemens and Howells had tried so hard and so long to place their "Sellers" Play, that now, when the story appeared in book form, Augustin Daly should have thought it worth dramatizing. Daly and Clemens were old friends, and it would seem that Daly could hardly have escaped seeing the play when it was going the rounds. But perhaps there is nothing more mysterious in the world than the ways and wants of theatrical managers. The matter came to nothing, of course, but the fact that Daly should have thought a story built from an old discarded play had a play in it seems interesting.*

*Clemens and his wife were advised to leave the cold of Berlin as soon as he was able to travel. This was not until the first of March, when, taking their old courier, Joseph Very, they left the children in good hands and journeyed to the south of France.*

To Susy Clemens, in Berlin:

*MENTONE, Mch 22, '92.*

SUSY DEAR,—I have been delighted to note your easy facility with your pen and proud to note also your literary superiorities of one kind and another—clearness of statement, directness, felicity of expression, photographic ability in setting forth an incident—style—good style—no barnacles on it in the way of unnecessary, retarding words (the Shipman scrapes off the barnacles when he wants his racer to go her best gait and straight to the buoy.) You should write a letter every day, long or short—and so ought I, but I don't.

Mamma says, tell Clara yes, she will have to write a note if the fan comes back mended.

We couldn't go to Nice to-day—had to give it up, on various accounts—and this was the last chance. I am sorry for Mamma—I wish she could have gone. She got a heavy fall yesterday evening and was pretty stiff and lame this morning, but is working it off trunk packing.

Joseph is gone to Nice to educate himself in Kodaking—and to get the pictures mounted which Mamma thinks she took here; but I noticed she didn't take the plug out, as a rule. When she did, she took nine pictures on top of each other—composites.

*With lots of love.*

*PAPA.*

*In the course of their Italian wanderings they reached Florence, where they were so comfortable and well that they decided to engage a villa for the next winter. Through Prof. Willard Fiske, they discovered the Villa Viviani, near Settignano, an old palace beautifully located on the hilltops east of Florence, commanding a wonderful view of the ancient city. Clemens felt that he could work there, and time proved that he was right.*

*For the summer, however, they returned to Germany, and located at Bad-Nauheim. Clemens presently decided to make a trip to America to give some personal attention to business matters. For one thing, his publishing-house, in spite of prosperity, seemed constantly to be requiring more capital, and then a Chicago company had been persuaded by Paige to undertake the manufacture of the type-setter. It was the beginning of a series of feverish trips which he would make back and forth across the ocean during the next two years.*

To Fred J. Hall, in New York:

*BAD-NAUHEIM, June 11, '92.*

*Saturday.*

DEAR MR. HALL,—If this arrives before I do, let it inform you that I am leaving Bremen for New York next Tuesday in the "Havel."

If you can meet me when the ship arrives, you can help me to get away from the reporters; and maybe you can take me to your own or some other lodgings where they can't find me.

But if the hour is too early or too late for you, I shall obscure myself somewhere till I can come to the office.

Yours sincerely S. L. C.

*Nothing of importance happened in America. The new Paige company had a factory started in Chicago and expected to manufacture fifty machines as a beginning. They claimed to have capital, or to be able to command it, and as the main control had passed from Clemens's hands, he could do no more than look over the ground and hope for the best. As for the business, about all that he could do was to sign certain notes necessary to provide such additional capital as was needed, and agree with Hall that hereafter they would concentrate their efforts and resist further temptation in the way of new enterprise. Then he returned to Bad-Nauheim and settled down to literature. This was the middle of July, and he must have worked pretty steadily, for he presently had a variety of MSS. ready to offer.*

To Fred J. Hall, in New York:

*Aug. 10, '92.*

DEAR MR. HALL,—I have dropped that novel I wrote you about, because I saw a more effective way of using the main episode—to wit: by telling it through the lips of Huck Finn. So I have started Huck Finn and Tom Sawyer (still 15 years old) and their friend the freed slave Jim around the world in a stray balloon, with Huck as narrator, and somewhere after the end of that great voyage he will work in the said episode and then nobody will suspect that a whole book has been written and the globe circumnavigated merely to get that episode in an effective (and at the same time apparently unintentional) way. I have written 12,000 words of this narrative, and find that the humor flows as easily as the adventures and surprises—so I shall go along and make a book of from 50,000 to 100,000 words.

It is a story for boys, of course, and I think will interest any boy between 8 years and 80.

When I was in New York the other day Mrs. Dodge, editor of St. Nicholas, wrote and, offered me $5,000 for (serial right) a story for boys 50,000 words long. I wrote back and declined, for I had other matter in my mind, then.

I conceive that the right way to write a story for boys is to write so that it will not only interest boys but will also strongly interest any man who has ever been a boy. That immensely enlarges the audience.

Now this story doesn't need to be restricted to a Childs magazine—it is proper enough for any magazine, I should think, or for a syndicate. I don't swear it, but I think so.

Proposed title of the story, "New Adventures of Huckleberry Finn."

*[No signature.]*

*The "novel" mentioned in the foregoing was The Extraordinary Twins, a story from which Pudd'nhead Wilson would be evolved later. It was a wildly extravagant farce—just the sort of thing that now and then Mark Twain plunged into with an enthusiasm that had to work itself out and die a natural death, or mellow into something worth while. Tom Sawyer Abroad, as the new Huck story was finally called, was completed and disposed of to St. Nicholas for serial publication.*

*The Twichells were in Europe that summer, and came to Bad-Nauheim. The next letter records a pleasant incident. The Prince of Wales of that day later became King Edward VII.*

To Mr. and Mrs. Orion Clemens, in Keokuk, Iowa.:

*Private. BAD-NAUHEIM, Aug. 23, '92.*

DEAR ORION AND MOLLIE,—("Private" because no newspaper-man or other gossip must get hold of it)

Livy is getting along pretty well, and the doctor thinks another summer here will cure her.

The Twichell's have been here four days and we have had good times with them. Joe and I ran over to Homburg, the great pleasure resort, Saturday, to dine with some friends, and in the morning I went walking in the promenade and met the British Ambassador to the Court of Berlin, and he introduced me to the Prince of Wales, and I found him a most unusually comfortable and unembarrassing Englishman to talk with—quick to see the obscurest point, and equipped with a laugh which is spontaneous and catching. Am invited by a near friend of his to meet him at dinner day after tomorrow, and there could be a good time, but the brass band will smash the talk and spoil everything.

We are expecting to move to Florence ten or twelve days hence, but if this hot weather continues we shall wait for cooler. I take Clara to Berlin for the winter-music, mainly, with German and French added. Thus far, Jean is our only glib French scholar.

We all send love to you all and to Pamela and Sam's family, and Annie.

*SAM*

*Clemens and family left Bad-Nauheim for Italy by way of Switzerland. In September Mrs. Clemens's sister, Mrs. Crane, who had been with them in Europe during the first year, had now returned to America. Mrs. Clemens had improved at the baths, though she had by no means recovered her health. We get a general report of conditions from the letter which Clemens wrote Mrs. Crane from Lucerne, Switzerland, where the party rested for several days. The "Phelps" mentioned in this letter was William Walter Phelps, United States Minister to Germany. The Phelps and Clemens families had been much associated in Berlin. "Mason" was Frank Mason, Consul General at Frankfort, and in later years at Paris. "Charlie and Ida" were Charles and Mrs. Langdon, of Elmira.*

To Mrs. Crane, in Elmira, N. Y.:

*LUCERNE, Sept. 18, '92.*

DEAR AUNT SUE,—Imagine how I felt to find that you had actually gone off without filling my traveling ink stand which you gave me! I found it out yesterday. Livy advised me to write you about it.

I have been driving this pen hard. I wrote 280 pages on a yarn called "Tom Sawyer Abroad," then took up the "Twins" again, destroyed the last half of the manuscript and re-wrote it in another form, and am going to continue it and finish it in Florence. "Tom Sawyer" seems rather pale to the family after the extravagances of the Twins, but they came to like it after they got used to it.

We remained in Nauheim a little too long. If we had left there four or five days earlier we should have made Florence in 3 days; but by the time we got started Livy had got smitten with what we feared might be erysipelas—greatly swollen neck and face, and unceasing headaches. We lay idle in Frankfort 4 days, doctoring. We started Thursday and made Bale. Hard trip, because it was one of those trains that gets tired every seven minutes and stops to rest three quarters of an hour. It took us 3 1/2 hours to get here, instead of the regulation 2.20. We reached here Friday evening and will leave tomorrow (Tuesday) morning. The rest has made the headaches better. We shall pull through to Milan tomorrow if possible. Next day we shall start at 10 a. m., and try to make Bologna, 5 hours. Next day (Thursday) Florence, D. V. Next year we will walk, for these excursions have got to be made over again. I've got seven trunks, and I undertook to be courier because I meant to express them to Florence direct, but we were a couple of days too late. All continental roads had issued a peremptory order that no baggage should travel a mile except in the company of the owner. (All over Europe people are howling; they are separated from their baggage and can't get it forwarded to them) I have to re-ship my trunks every day. It is very amusing—uncommonly so. There seemed grave doubts about our being able to get these trunks over the Italian frontier, but I've got a very handsome note from the Frankfort Italian

Consul General addressed to all Italian Customs Officers, and we shall get through if anybody does.

The Phelpses came to Frankfort and we had some great times—dinner at his hotel, the Masons, supper at our inn—Livy not in it. She was merely allowed a glimpse, no more. Of course, Phelps said she was merely pretending to be ill; was never looking so well and fine.

The children are all right. They paddle around a little, and drive-so do we all. Lucerne seems to be pretty full of tourists. The Fleulen boat went out crowded yesterday morning.

The Paris Herald has created a public interest by inoculating one of its correspondents with cholera. A man said yesterday he wished to God they would inoculate all of them. Yes, the interest is quite general and strong, and much hope is felt.

Livy says, I have said enough bad things, and better send all our loves to you and Charley and Ida and all the children and shut up. Which I do—and shut up.

*S. L. C.*

*They reached Florence on the 26th, and four days later we find Clemens writing again to Mrs. Crane, detailing everything at length. Little comment on this letter is required; it fully explains itself. Perhaps a word of description from one of his memoranda will not be out of place. Of the villa he wrote: "It is a plain, square building, like a box, and is painted light green and has green window-shutters. It stands in a commanding position on the artificial terrace of liberal dimensions, which is walled around with masonry. From the walls the vineyards and olive groves of the estate slant away toward the valley.... Roses overflow the retaining walls and the battered and mossy stone urn on the gate-post, in pink and yellow cataracts, exactly as they do on the drop-curtains in the theaters. The house is a very fortress for strength."*

*The Mrs. Ross in this letter was Janet Ross, daughter of Lady Duff Gordon, remembered to-day for her Egyptian letters. The Ross castle was but a little distance away.*

To Mrs. Crane, in Elmira:

*VILLA VIVIANI, SETTIGNANO, FLORENCE.*

*Sept. 30, 1892*

DEAR SUE,—We have been in the house several days, and certainly it is a beautiful place,—particularly at this moment, when the skies are a deep leaden color, the domes of Florence dim in the drizzling rain, and occasional perpendicular coils of lightning quivering intensely in the black sky about Galileo's Tower. It is a charming panorama, and the most conspicuous towers and domes down in the city look to-day just as they looked when Boccaccio and Dante used to contemplate them from this hillock five and six hundred years ago.

The Mademoiselle is a great help to Livy in the housekeeping, and is a cheery and cheerful presence in the house. The butler is equipped with a little French, and it is this fact that enables the house to go—but it won't go well until the family get some sort of facility with the Italian tongue, for the cook, the woman-of-all-work and the coachman understand only that. It is a stubborn and devilish language to learn, but Jean and the others will master it. Livy's German Nauheim girl is the worst off of anybody, as there is no market for her tongue at all among the help.

With the furniture in and the curtains up the house is very pretty, and not unhomelike. At mid-night last night we heard screams up stairs—Susy had set the lofty window curtains afire with a candle. This sounds kind of frightful, whereas when you come to think of it, a burning curtain or pile of furniture hasn't any element of danger about it in this fortress. There isn't any conceivable way to burn this house down, or enable a conflagration on one floor to climb to the next.

Mrs. Ross laid in our wood, wine and servants for us, and they are excellent. She had the house scoured from Cellar to rook the curtains washed and put up, all beds pulled to pieces, beaten, washed and put together again, and beguiled the Marchese into putting a big porcelain stove in the vast central hall. She is a wonderful woman, and we don't quite see how or when we should have gotten under way without her.

Observe our address above—the post delivers letters daily at the house.

Even with the work and fuss of settling the house Livy has improved—and the best is yet to come. There is going to be absolute seclusion here—a hermit life, in fact. We (the rest of us) shall run over to the Ross's frequently, and they will come here now and then and see Livy—that is all. Mr. Fiske is away—nobody knows where—and the work on his house has been stopped and his servants discharged. Therefore we shall merely go Rossing—as far as society is concerned—shan't circulate in Florence until Livy shall be well enough to take a share in it.

This present house is modern. It is not much more than two centuries old; but parts of it, and also its foundations are of high antiquity. The fine beautiful family portraits—the great carved ones in the large ovals over the doors of the big hall—carry one well back into the past. One of them is dated 1305—he could have known Dante, you see. Another is dated 1343—he could have known Boccaccio and spent his afternoons in Fiesole listening to the Decameron tales. Another is dated 1463—he could have met Columbus.....

Evening. The storm thundered away until night, and the rain came down in floods. For awhile there was a partial break, which furnished about such a sunset as will be exhibited when the Last Day comes and the universe tumbles together in wreck and ruin. I have never seen anything more spectacular and impressive.

One person is satisfied with the villa, anyway. Jean prefers it to all Europe, save Venice. Jean is eager to get at the Italian tongue again, now, and I see that she has forgotten little or nothing of what she learned of it in Rome and Venice last spring.

I am the head French duffer of the family. Most of the talk goes over my head at the table. I catch only words, not phrases. When Italian comes to be substituted I shall be even worse off than I am now, I suppose.

This reminds me that this evening the German girl said to Livy, "Man hat mir gesagt loss Sie una candella verlaught habe"—unconsciously dropping in a couple of Italian words, you see. So she is going to join the polyglots, too, it appears. They say it is good entertainment to hear her and the butler talk together in their respective tongues, piecing out and patching up with the universal sign-language as they go along. Five languages in use in the house (including the sign-language-hardest-worked of them all) and yet with all this opulence of resource we do seem to have an uncommonly tough time making ourselves understood.

What we lack is a cat. If we only had Germania! That was the most satisfactory all-round cat I have seen yet. Totally ungermanic in the raciness of his character and in the sparkle of his mind and the spontaneity of his movements. We shall not look upon his like again....

*S. L. C.*

*Clemens got well settled down to work presently. He found the situation, the climate, the background, entirely suited to literary production, and in a little while he had accomplished more than at any other time since his arrival in Europe. From letters to Mrs. Crane and to Mr. Hall we learn something of his employments and his satisfaction.*

To Mrs. Crane, in Elmira:

*VILLA VIVIANI*

*SETTIGNANO, FLORENCE. Oct. 22, '92.*

DEAR SUE,—We are getting wonted. The open fires have driven away the cold and the doubt, and now a cheery spirit pervades the place. Livy and the Kings and Mademoiselle having been taking their tea a number of times, lately, on the open terrace with the city and the hills and the sunset for company. I stop work, a few minutes, as a rule, when the sun gets down to the hilltops west of Florence, and join the tea-group to wonder and exclaim. There is always some new miracle in the view, a new and exquisite variation in the show, a variation which occurs every 15 minutes between dawn and night. Once early in the morning, a multitude of white villas not before perceived, revealed themselves on the far hills; then we recognized that all those great hills are snowed thick with them, clear to the summit.

The variety of lovely effects, the infinitude of change, is something not to be believed by any who has not seen it. No view that I am acquainted with in the world is at all comparable to this for delicacy, charm, exquisiteness, dainty coloring, and bewildering rapidity of change. It keeps a person drunk with pleasure all the time. Sometimes Florence ceases to be substantial, and becomes just a faint soft dream, with domes and towers of air, and one is persuaded that he might blow it away with a puff of his breath.

Livy is progressing admirably. This is just the place for her.

*[Remainder missing.]*

To Fred J. Hall, in New York:

*Dec. 12, '92.*

DEAR MR. HALL,—November check received.

I have lent the Californian's Story to Arthur Stedman for his Author Club Book, so your suggestion that my new spring-book bear that name arrives too late, as he probably would not want us to use that story in a book of ours until the Author book had had its run. That is for him to decide—and I don't want him hampered at all in his decision. I, for my part, prefer the "$1,000,000 Banknote and Other Stories" by Mark Twain as a title, but above my judgment I prefer yours. I mean this—it is not taffy.

I told Arthur to leave out the former squib or paragraph and use only the Californian's Story. Tell him this is because I am going to use that in the book I am now writing.

I finished "Those Extraordinary Twins" night before last makes 60 or 80,000 words—haven't counted.

The last third of it suits me to a dot. I begin, to-day, to entirely recast and re-write the first two-thirds—new plan, with two minor characters, made very prominent, one major character cropped out, and the Twins subordinated to a minor but not insignificant place.

The minor character will now become the chiefest, and I will name the story after him—"Puddn'head Wilson."

Merry Xmas to you, and great prosperity and felicity!

*S. L. CLEMENS.*

## XXXIII. LETTERS, 1893, TO MR. HALL, MRS. CLEMENS, AND OTHERS. FLORENCE. BUSINESS TROUBLES. "PUDD'NHEAD WILSON." "JOAN OF ARC." AT THE PLAYERS, NEW

YORK.

The reader may have suspected that young Mr. Hall in New York was having his troubles. He was by this time one-third owner in the business of Charles L. Webster & Co., as well as its general manager. The business had been drained of its capital one way and another-partly by the publication of unprofitable books; partly by the earlier demands of the typesetter, but more than all by the manufacturing cost and agents' commissions demanded by L. A. L.; that is to say, the eleven large volumes constituting the Library of American Literature, which Webster had undertaken to place in a million American homes. There was plenty of sale for it—indeed, that was just the trouble; for it was sold on payments—small monthly payments—while the cost of manufacture and the liberal agents' commissions were cash items, and it would require a considerable period before the dribble of collections would swell into a tide large enough to satisfy the steady outflow of expense. A sale of twenty-five sets a day meant prosperity on paper, but unless capital could be raised from some other source to make and market those books through a period of months, perhaps even years, to come, it meant bankruptcy in reality. It was Hall's job, with Clemens to back him, to keep their ship afloat on these steadily ebbing financial waters. It was also Hall's affair to keep Mark Twain cheerful, to look pleasant himself, and to show how they were steadily getting rich because orders were pouring in, though a cloud that resembled bankruptcy loomed always a little higher upon the horizon. If Hall had not been young and an optimist, he would have been frightened out of his boots early in the game. As it was, he made a brave steady fight, kept as cheerful and stiff an upper lip as possible, always hoping that something would happen—some grand sale of his other books, some unexpected inflow from the type-setter interests—anything that would sustain his ship until the L. A. L. tide should turn and float it into safety.

Clemens had faith in Hall and was fond of him. He never found fault with him; he tried to accept his encouraging reports at their face value. He lent the firm every dollar of his literary earnings not absolutely needed for the family's support; he signed new notes; he allowed Mrs. Clemens to put in such remnants of her patrimony as the type-setter had spared.

The situation in 1893 was about as here outlined. The letters to Hall of that year are frequent and carry along the story. To any who had formed the idea that Mark Twain was irascible, exacting, and faultfinding, they will perhaps be a revelation.

To Fred J. Hall, in New York:

*FLORENCE, Jan. 1, '93.*

DEAR MR. HALL,—Yours of Dec. 19 is to hand, and Mrs. Clemens is deeply distressed, for she thinks I have been blaming you or finding fault with you about something. But most surely that cannot be. I tell her that although I am prone to write hasty and regrettable things to other people, I am not a bit likely to write such things to you. I can't believe I have done anything so ungrateful. If I have, pile coals of fire on my head, for I deserve it!

I wonder if my letter of credit isn't an encumbrance? Do you have to deposit the whole amount it calls for? If that is so, it is an encumbrance, and we must withdraw it and take the money out of soak. I have never made drafts upon it except when compelled, because I thought you deposited nothing against it, and only had to put up money that I drew upon it; that therefore the less I drew the easier it would be for you.

I am dreadfully sorry I didn't know it would be a help to you to let my monthly check pass over a couple of months. I could have stood that by drawing what is left of Mrs. Clemens's letter of credit, and we would have done it cheerfully.

I will write Whitmore to send you the "Century" check for $1,000, and you can collect Mrs. Dodge's $2,000 (Whitmore has power of attorney which I think will enable him to endorse it over to you in my name.) If you need that $3,000 put it in the business and use it, and send Whitmore the Company's note for a year. If you don't need it, turn it over to Mr. Halsey and let him invest it for me.

I've a mighty poor financial head, and I may be all wrong—but tell me if I am wrong in supposing that in lending my own firm money at 6 per cent I pay 4 of it myself and so really get only a per cent? Now don't laugh if that is stupid.

Of course my friend declined to buy a quarter interest in the L. A. L. for $200,000. I judged he would. I hoped he would offer $100,000, but he didn't. If the cholera breaks out in America, a few months hence, we can't borrow or sell; but if it doesn't we must try hard to raise $100,000. I wish we could do it before there is a cholera scare.

I have been in bed two or three days with a cold, but I got up an hour ago, and I believe I am all right again.

How I wish I had appreciated the need of $100,000 when I was in New York last summer! I would have tried my best to raise it. It would make us able to stand 1,000 sets of L. A. L. per month, but not any more, I guess.

You have done magnificently with the business, and we must raise the money somehow, to enable you to reap the reward of all that labor.

*Sincerely Yours*

*S. L. CLEMENS.*

"Whitmore," in this letter, was F. G. Whitmore, of Hartford, Mark Twain's financial agent. The money due from Mrs. Dodge was a balance on Tom Sawyer Abroad, which had been accepted by St. Nicholas. Mr. Halsey was a down-town broker.

Clemens, who was growing weary of the constant demands of L. A. L., had conceived the idea that it would be well to dispose of a portion of it for enough cash to finance its manufacture.

We don't know who the friend was to whom he offered a quarter interest for the modest sum of two hundred thousand dollars. But in the next letter we discover designs on a certain very canny Scotchman of Skibo.

To Fred J. Hall, in New York:

*FLORENCE, Jan. 28, '92.*

DEAR MR. HALL,—I want to throw out a suggestion and see what you think of it. We have a good start, and solid ground under us; we have a valuable reputation; our business organization is practical, sound and well-devised; our publications are of a respect-worthy character and of a money-breeding species. Now then I think that the association with us of some one of great name and with capital would give our business a prodigious impetus—that phrase is not too strong.

As I look at it, it is not money merely that is needed; if that were all, the firm has friends enough who would take an interest in a paying venture; we need some one who has made his life a success not only from a business standpoint, but with that achievement back of him, has been great enough to make his power felt as a thinker and a literary man. It is a pretty usual thing for publishers to have this sort of partners. Now you see what a power Carnegie is, and how far his voice reaches in the several lines I speak of. Do you know him? You do by correspondence or purely business talks about his books—but personally, I mean? so that it would not be an intrusion for you to speak to him about this desire of mine—for I would like you to put it before him, and if you fail to interest him in it, you will probably get at least some valuable suggestions from him. I'll enclose a note of introduction—you needn't use it if you don't need to.

*Yours S. L. C.*

P. S. Yes, I think I have already acknowledged the Dec. $1,000 and the Jan. $500—and if another $500 was mailed 3 days ago there's no hiatus.

I think I also reminded you that the new letter of credit does not cover the unexpended balance of the old one but falls considerably short of it.

Do your best with Carnegie, and don't wait to consider any of my intermediate suggestions or talks about our raising half of the $200,000 ourselves. I mean, wait for nothing. To make my suggestion available I should have to go over and see Arnot, and I don't want to until I can mention Carnegie's name to him as going in with us.

My book is type-written and ready for print—"Pudd'nhead Wilson-a Tale." (Or, "Those Extraordinary Twins," if preferable.)

It makes 82,500 words—12,000 more than Huck Finn. But I don't know what to do with it. Mrs. Clemens thinks it wouldn't do to go to the Am. Pub. Co. or anywhere outside of our own house; we have no subscription machinery, and a book in the trade is a book thrown away, as far as money-profit goes. I am in a quandary. Give me a lift out of it.

I will mail the book to you and get you to examine it and see if it is good or if it is bad. I think it is good, and I thought the Claimant bad, when I saw it in print; but as for real judgment, I think I am destitute of it.

I am writing a companion to the Prince and Pauper, which is half done and will make 200,000 words; and I have had the idea that if it were gotten up in handsome style, with many illustrations and put at a high enough price maybe the L. A. L. canvassers would take it and run it with that book. Would they? It could be priced anywhere from $4 up to $10, according to how it was gotten up, I suppose.

I don't want it to go into a magazine.

*S. L. C.*

I am having several short things type-"writered." I will send them to you presently. I like the Century and Harper's, but I don't know that I have any business to object to the Cosmopolitan if they pay as good rates. I suppose a man ought to stick to one magazine, but that may be only superstition. What do you think?

*S. L. C.*

*"The companion to The Prince and the Pauper," mentioned in this letter, was the story of Joan of Arc, perhaps the most finished of Mark Twain's literary productions. His interest in Joan had been*

*first awakened when, as a printer's apprentice in Hannibal, he had found blowing along the street a stray leaf from some printed story of her life. That fragment of history had pictured Joan in prison, insulted and mistreated by ruffians. It had aroused all the sympathy and indignation in the boy, Sam Clemens; also, it had awakened his interest in history, and, indeed, in all literature.*

*His love for the character of Joan had grown with the years, until in time he had conceived the idea of writing her story. As far back as the early eighties he had collected material for it, and had begun to make the notes. One thing and another had interfered, and he had found no opportunity for such a story. Now, however, in Florence, in the ancient villa, and in the quiet garden, looking across the vineyards and olive groves to the dream city along the Arno, he felt moved to take up the tale of the shepherd girl of France, the soldier maid, or, as he called her, "The noble child, the most innocent, the most lovely, the most adorable the ages have produced." His surroundings and background would seem to have been perfect, and he must have written with considerable ease to have completed a hundred thousand words in a period of not more than six weeks.*

*Perhaps Hall did not even go to see Carnegie; at all events nothing seems to have come of the idea. Once, at a later time, Mask Twain himself mentioned the matter to Carnegie, and suggested to him that it was poor financiering to put all of one's eggs into one basket, meaning into iron. But Carnegie answered, "That's a mistake; put all your eggs into one basket and watch that basket."*

*It was March when Clemens felt that once more his presence was demanded in America. He must see if anything could be realized from the type-setter or L. A. L.*

To Fred J. Hall, in New York:

*March 13, '93.*

DEAR MR. HALL,—I am busy getting ready to sail the 22d, in the Kaiser Wilhelm II.

I send herewith 2 magazine articles.

The Story contains 3,800 to 4,000 words.

The "Diary" contains 3,800 words.

Each would make about 4 pages of the Century.

The Diary is a gem, if I do say it myself that shouldn't.

If the Cosmopolitan wishes to pay $600 for either of them or $1,200 for both, gather in the check, and I will use the money in America instead of breaking into your treasury.

If they don't wish to trade for either, send the articles to the Century, without naming a price, and if their check isn't large enough I will call and abuse them when I come.

I signed and mailed the notes yesterday.

*Yours*

*S. L. C.*

*Clemens reached New York on the 3d of April and made a trip to Chicago, but accomplished nothing, except to visit the World's Fair and be laid up with a severe cold. The machine situation had not progressed. The financial stringency of 1893 had brought everything to a standstill. The New York bank would advance Webster & Co. no more money. So disturbed were his affairs, so disordered was everything, that sometimes he felt himself as one walking amid unrealities. A fragment of a letter to Mrs. Crane conveys this:*

*"I dreamed I was born and grew up and was a pilot on the Mississippi and a miner and a journalist in Nevada and a pilgrim in the Quaker City, and had a wife and children and went to live in a villa at Florence—and this dream goes on and on and sometimes seems so real that I almost believe it is real. I wonder if it is? But there is no way to tell, for if one applies tests they would be part of the dream, too, and so would simply aid the deceit. I wish I knew whether it is a dream or real."*

*He saw Warner, briefly, in America; also Howells, now living in New York, but he had little time for visiting. On May 13th he sailed again for Europe on the Kaiser Wilhelm II. On the night before sailing he sent Howells a good-by word.*

To W. D. Howells, in New York City:

*MURRAY HILL HOTEL, NEW YORE, May 12, 1893.*

*Midnight.*

DEAR HOWELLS—I am so sorry I missed you.

I am very glad to have that book for sea entertainment, and I thank you ever so much for it.

I've had a little visit with Warner at last; I was getting afraid I wasn't going to have a chance to see him at all. I forgot to tell you how thoroughly I enjoyed your account of the country printing office, and how true it all was and how intimately recognizable in all its details. But Warner was full of delight over it, and that reminded me, and I am glad, for I wanted to speak of it.

You have given me a book; Annie Trumbull has sent me her book; I bought a couple of books; Mr. Hall gave me a choice German book; Laflan gave me two bottles of whisky and a box of cigars—I go to sea nobly equipped.

Good-bye and all good fortune attend you and yours—and upon you all I leave my benediction.

*MARK.*

*Mention has already been made of the Ross home being very near to Viviani, and the association of the Ross and Clemens families. There was a fine vegetable garden on the Ross estate, and it was in the interest of it that the next letter was written to the Secretary of Agriculture.*

To Hon. J. Sterling Morton, in Washington, D. C.: Editorial Department Century Magazine, Union Square,

*NEW YORK, April 6, 1893.*

TO THE HON. J. STERLING MORTON,—Dear Sir: Your petitioner, Mark Twain, a poor farmer of Connecticut—indeed, the poorest one there, in the opinion of many-desires a few choice breeds of seed corn (maize), and in return will zealously support the Administration in all ways honorable and otherwise.

To speak by the card, I want these things to hurry to Italy to an English lady. She is a neighbor of mine outside of Florence, and has a great garden and thinks she could raise corn for her table if she had the right ammunition. I myself feel a warm interest in this enterprise, both on patriotic grounds and because I have a key to that garden, which I got made from a wax impression. It is not very good soil, still I think she can grow enough for one table and I am in a position to select the table. If you are willing to aid and abet a countryman (and Gilder thinks you are,) please find the signature and address of your petitioner below.

Respectfully and truly yours.

*MARK TWAIN,*

67 Fifth Avenue, New York.

P. S.—A handful of choice (Southern) watermelon seeds would pleasantly add to that lady's employments and give my table a corresponding lift.

*His idea of business values had moderated considerably by the time he had returned to Florence. He was not hopeless yet, but he was clearly a good deal disheartened—anxious for freedom.*

To Fred J. Hall, in New York:

*FLORENCE May 30, '93*

DEAR MR. HALL,—You were to cable me if you sold any machine royalties—so I judge you have not succeeded.

This has depressed me. I have been looking over the past year's letters and statements and am depressed still more.

I am terribly tired of business. I am by nature and disposition unfitted for it and I want to get out of it. I am standing on the Mount Morris volcano with help from the machine a long way off—doubtless a long way further off than the Connecticut Co. imagines.

Now here is my idea for getting out.

The firm owes Mrs. Clemens and me—I do not know quite how much, but it is about $170,000 or $175,000, I suppose (I make this guess from the documents here, whose technicalities confuse me horribly.)

The firm owes other sums, but there is stock and cash assets to cover the entire indebtedness and $116,679.20 over. Is that it? In addition we have the L. A. L. plates and copyright, worth more than $130,000—is that correct?

That is to say, we have property worth about $250,000 above indebtedness, I suppose—or, by one of your estimates, $300,000? The greater part of the first debts to me is in notes paying 6 percent. The rest (the old $70,000 or whatever it is) pays no interest.

Now then, will Harper or Appleton, or Putnam give me $200,000 for those debts and my two-thirds interest in the firm? (The firm of course taking the Mount Morris and all such obligations off my hands and leaving me clear of all responsibility.)

I don't want much money. I only want first class notes—$200,000 worth of them at 6 per cent, payable monthly;—yearly notes, renewable annually for 3 years, with $5,000 of the principal payable at the beginning and middle of each year. After that, the notes renewable annually and (perhaps) a larger part of the principal payable semi-annually.

Please advise me and suggest alterations and emendations of the above scheme, for I need that sort of help, being ignorant of business and not able to learn a single detail of it.

Such a deal would make it easy for a big firm to pour in a big cash capital and jump L. A. L. up to enormous prosperity. Then your one-third would be a fortune—and I hope to see that day!

I enclose an authority to use with Whitmore in case you have sold any royalties. But if you can't make this deal don't make any. Wait a little and see if you can't make the deal. Do make the deal if you possibly can. And if any presence shall be necessary in order to complete it I will come over, though I hope it can be done without that.

Get me out of business!

And I will be yours forever gratefully,

*S. L. CLEMENS.*

My idea is, that I am offering my 2/3 of L. A. L. and the business for thirty or forty thousand dollars. Is that it?

P. S. S. The new firm could retain my books and reduce them to a 10 percent royalty.

*S. L. C.*

To Rev. Jos. H. Twichell, in Hartford:

*VILLA VIVIANI, SETTIGNANO (FLORENCE)*

*June 9, '93.*

DEAR JOE, The sea voyage set me up and I reached here May 27 in tolerable condition—nothing left but weakness, cough all gone.

Old Sir Henry Layard was here the other day, visiting our neighbor Janet Ross, daughter of Lady Duff Gordon, and since then I have been reading his account of the adventures of his youth in the far East. In a footnote he has something to say about a sailor which I thought might interest you—viz:

"This same quartermaster was celebrated among the English in Mesopotamia for an entry which he made in his log-book-after a perilous storm; 'The windy and watery elements raged. Tears and prayers was had recourse to, but was of no manner of use. So we hauled up the anchor and got round the point.'"

There—it isn't Ned Wakeman; it was before his day.

*With love,*

*MARK.*

*They closed Villa Viviani in June and near the end of the month arrived in Munich in order that Mrs. Clemens might visit some of the German baths. The next letter is written by her and shows her deep sympathy with Hall in his desperate struggle. There have been few more unselfish and courageous women in history than Mark Twain's wife.*

From Mrs. Clemens to Mr. Hall, in New York:

*June 27th 1893*

*MUNICH.*

DEAR MR. HALL,—Your letter to Mr. Clemens of June 16th has just reached here; as he has gone to Berlin for Clara I am going to send you just a line in answer to it.

Mr. Clemens did not realize what trouble you would be in when his letter should reach you or he would not have sent it just then. I hope you will not worry any more than you can help. Do not let our interests weigh on you too heavily. We both know you will, as you always have, look in every way to the best interests of all.

I think Mr. Clemens is right in feeling that he should get out of business, that he is not fitted for it; it worries him too much.

But he need be in no haste about it, and of course, it would be the very farthest from his desire to imperil, in the slightest degree, your interests in order to save his own.

I am sure that I voice his wish as well as mine when I say that he would simply like you to bear in mind the fact that he greatly desires to be released from his present anxiety and worry, at a time when it shall not endanger your interest or the safety of the business.

I am more sorry than I can express that this letter of Mr. Clemens' should have reached you when you were struggling under such terrible pressure. I hope now that the weight is not quite so heavy. He would not have written you about the money if he had known that it was an inconvenience for you to send it. He thought the book-keeper whose duty it is to forward it had forgotten.

We can draw on Mr. Langdon for money for a few weeks until things are a little easier with you. As Mr. Clemens wrote you we would say "do not send us any more money at present" if we were not afraid to do so. I will say, however, do not trouble yourself if for a few weeks you are not able to send the usual amount.

Mr. Clemens and I have the greatest possible desire, not to increase in any way your burdens, and sincerely wish we might aid you.

I trust my brother may be able, in his talk with you, to throw some helpful light on the situation.

Hoping you will see a change for the better and begin to reap the fruit of your long and hard labor.

*Believe me*

*Very Cordially yours*

*OLIVIA L. CLEMENS.*

Hall, naturally, did not wish to be left alone with the business. He realized that his credit would suffer, both at the bank and with the public, if his distinguished partner should retire. He wrote, therefore, proposing as an alternate that they dispose of the big subscription set that was swamping them. It was a good plan—if it would work—and we find Clemens entering into it heartily.

To Fred J. Hall, in New York:

*MUNICH, July 3, '93.*

DEAR MR. HALL,—You make a suggestion which has once or twice flitted dimly through my mind heretofore to wit, sell L. A. L.

I like that better than the other scheme, for it is no doubt feasible, whereas the other is perhaps not.

The firm is in debt, but L. A. L. is free—and not only free but has large money owing to it. A proposition to sell that by itself to a big house could be made without embarrassment we merely confess that we cannot spare capital from the rest of the business to run it on the huge scale necessary to make it an opulent success.

It will be selling a good thing—for somebody; and it will be getting rid of a load which we are clearly not able to carry. Whoever buys will have a noble good opening—a complete equipment, a well organized business, a capable and experienced manager, and enterprise not experimental but under full sail, and immediately able to pay 50 per cent a year on every dollar the publisher shall actually invest in it—I mean in making and selling the books.

I am miserably sorry to be adding bothers and torments to the over-supply which you already have in these hideous times, but I feel so troubled, myself, considering the dreary fact that we are getting deeper and deeper in debt and the L. A. L. getting to be a heavier and heavier burden all the time, that I must bestir myself and seek a way of relief.

It did not occur to me that in selling out I would injure you—for that I am not going to do. But to sell L. A. L. will not injure you it will put you in better shape.

*Sincerely Yours*

*S. L. CLEMENS.*

To Fred J. Hall, in New York:

*July 8, '92.*

DEAR MR. HALL,—I am sincerely glad you are going to sell L. A. L.

I am glad you are shutting off the agents, and I hope the fatal book will be out of our hands before it will be time to put them on again. With nothing but our non-existent capital to work with the book has no value for us, rich a prize as it will be to any competent house that gets it.

I hope you are making an effort to sell before you discharge too many agents, for I suppose the agents are a valuable part of the property.

We have been stopping in Munich for awhile, but we shall make a break for some country resort in a few days now.

*Sincerely Yours*

*S. L. C.*

*July 8*

P. S. No, I suppose I am wrong in suggesting that you wait a moment before discharging your L. A. L. agents—in fact I didn't mean that. I judge your only hope of salvation is in discharging them all at once, since it is their commissions that threaten to swamp us. It is they who have eaten up the $14,000 I left with you in such a brief time, no doubt.

I feel panicky.

I think the sale might be made with better advantage, however, now, than later when the agents have got out of the purchaser's reach.

*S. L. C.*

P. S. No monthly report for many months.

*Those who are old enough to remember the summer of 1893 may recall it as a black financial season. Banks were denying credit, businesses were forced to the wall. It was a poor time to float any costly enterprise. The Chicago company who was trying to build the machines made little progress. The book business everywhere was bad. In a brief note following the foregoing letters Clemens wrote*

*Hall:*

*"It is now past the middle of July and no cablegram to say the machine is finished. We are afraid you are having miserable days and worried nights, and we sincerely wish we could relieve you, but it is all black with us and we don't know any helpful thing to say or do."*

*He inclosed some kind of manuscript proposition for John Brisben Walker, of the Cosmopolitan, with the comment: "It is my ingenious scheme to protect the family against the alms-house for one more year—and after that—well, goodness knows! I have never felt so desperate in my life—and good reason, for I haven't got a penny to my name, and Mrs. Clemens hasn't enough laid up with Langdon to keep us two months."*

*It was like Mark Twain, in the midst of all this turmoil, to project an entirely new enterprise; his busy mind was always visioning success in unusual undertakings, regardless of immediate conditions and the steps necessary to achievement.*

To Fred J. Hall, in New York:

*July 26, '93.*

DEAR MR. HALL,—..... I hope the machine will be finished this month; but it took me four years and cost me $100,000 to finish the other machine after it was apparently entirely complete and setting type like a house-afire.

I wonder what they call "finished." After it is absolutely perfect it can't go into a printing-office until it has had a month's wear, running night and day, to get the bearings smooth, I judge.

I may be able to run over about mid-October. Then if I find you relieved of L. A. L. we will start a magazine inexpensive, and of an entirely unique sort. Arthur Stedman and his father editors of it. Arthur could do all the work, merely submitting it to his father for approval.

The first number should pay—and all subsequent ones—25 cents a number. Cost of first number (20,000 copies) $2,000. Give most of them away, sell the rest. Advertising and other expenses—cost unknown. Send one to all newspapers—it would get a notice—favorable, too.

But we cannot undertake it until L. A. L, is out of the way. With our hands free and some capital to spare, we could make it hum.

Where is the Shelley article? If you have it on hand, keep it and I will presently tell you what to do with it.

Don't forget to tell me.

*Yours Sincerely*

*S. L. C.*

*The Shelley article mentioned in this letter was the "Defense of Harriet Sheller," one of the very best of his essays. How he could have written this splendid paper at a time of such distraction passes comprehension. Furthermore, it is clear that he had revised, indeed rewritten, the long story of Pudd'nhead Wilson.*

To Fred J. Hall, in New York:

*July 30, '93.*

DEAR MR. HALL,—This time "Pudd'nhead Wilson" is a success! Even

Mrs. Clemens, the most difficult of critics, confesses it, and without reserves or qualifications. Formerly she would not consent that it be published either before or after my death. I have pulled the twins apart and made two individuals of them; I have sunk them out of sight, they are mere flitting shadows, now, and of no importance; their story has disappeared from the book. Aunt Betsy Hale has vanished wholly, leaving not a trace behind; aunt Patsy Cooper and her daughter Rowena have almost disappeared—they scarcely walk across the stage. The whole story is centered on the murder and the trial; from the first chapter the movement is straight ahead without divergence or side-play to the murder and the trial; everything that is done or said or that happens is a preparation for those events. Therefore, 3 people stand up high, from beginning to end, and only 3—Pudd'nhead, "Tom" Driscoll, and his nigger mother, Roxana; none of the others are important, or get in the way of the story or require the reader's attention. Consequently, the scenes and episodes which were the strength of the book formerly are stronger than ever, now.

When I began this final reconstruction the story contained 81,500 words, now it contains only 58,000. I have knocked out everything that delayed the march of the story—even the description of a Mississippi steamboat. There's no weather in, and no scenery—the story is stripped for flight!

Now, then what is she worth? The amount of matter is but 3,000 words short of the American Claimant, for which the syndicate paid $12,500. There was nothing new in that story, but the finger-prints in this one is virgin ground—absolutely fresh, and mighty curious and interesting to everybody.

I don't want any more syndicating—nothing short of $20,000, anyway, and that I can't get—but won't you see how much the Cosmopolitan will stand?

Do your best for me, for I do not sleep these nights, for visions of the poor-house.

This in spite of the hopeful tone of yours of 11th to Langdon (just received) for in me hope is very nearly expiring. Everything does look so blue, so dismally blue!

By and by I shall take up the Rhone open-boat voyage again, but not now—we are going to be moving around too much. I have torn up some of it, but still have 15,000 words that Mrs. Clemens approves of, and that I like. I may go at it in Paris again next winter, but not unless I know I can write it to suit me.

Otherwise I shall tackle Adam once more, and do him in a kind of a friendly and respectful way that will commend him to the Sunday schools. I've been thinking out his first life-days to-day and framing his childish and ignorant impressions and opinions for him.

Will ship Pudd'nhead in a few days. When you get it cable

*Mark Twain*

*Care Brownship, London*

*Received.*

I mean to ship "Pudd'nhead Wilson" to you-say, tomorrow. It'll furnish me hash for awhile I reckon. I am almost sorry it is finished; it was good entertainment to work at it, and kept my mind away from things.

We leave here in about ten days, but the doctors have changed our plans again. I think we shall be in Bohemia or thereabouts till near the end of September, then go to Paris and take a rest.

*Yours Sincerely*

*S. L. C.*

P. S. Mrs. Clemens has come in since, and read your letter and is deeply distressed. She thinks that in some letter of mine I must have reproached you. She says it is wonderful that you have kept the ship afloat in this storm that has seen fleets and fleets go down; that from what she learns of the American business-situation from her home letters you have accomplished a marvel in the circumstances, and that she cannot bear to have a word said to you that shall voice anything but praise and the heartiest appreciation—and not the shadow of a reproach will she allow.

I tell her I didn't reproach you and never thought of such a thing. And I said I would break open my letter and say so.

Mrs. Clemens says I must tell you not to send any money for a month or two—so that you may be afforded what little relief is in our power. All right—I'm willing; (this is honest) but I wish Brer Chatto would send along his little yearly contribution. I dropped him a line about another matter a week ago—asked him to subscribe for the Daily News for me—you see I wanted to remind him in a covert way that it was pay-up time—but doubtless I directed the letter to you or some one else, for I don't hear from him and don't get any Daily News either.

To Fred J. Hall, in New York:

*Aug. 6, '93.*

DEAR MR. HALL,—I am very sorry—it was thoughtless in me. Let the reports go. Send me once a month two items, and two only:

Cash liabilities—(so much) Cash assets—(so much)

I can perceive the condition of the business at a glance, then, and that will be sufficient.

Here we never see a newspaper, but even if we did I could not come anywhere near appreciating or correctly estimating the tempest you have been buffeting your way through—only the man who is in it can do that—but I have tried not to burden you thoughtlessly or wantonly. I have been wrought and unsettled in mind by apprehensions, and that is a thing that is not helpable when one is in a strange land and sees his resources melt down to a two months' supply and can't see any sure daylight beyond. The bloody machine offered but a doubtful outlook—and will still offer nothing much better for a long time to come; for when Davis's "three weeks" is up there's three months' tinkering to follow I guess. That is unquestionably the boss machine of the world, but is the toughest one on prophets, when it is in an incomplete state, that has ever seen the light. Neither Davis nor any other man can foretell with any considerable approach to certainty when it will be ready to get down to actual work in a printing office.

*[No signature.]*

*Three days after the foregoing letter was written he wrote, briefly: "Great Scott but it's a long year-for you and me! I never knew the almanac to drag so. At least since I was finishing that other machine.*

*"I watch for your letters hungrily—just as I used to watch for the cablegram saying the machine's finished; but when 'next week certainly' swelled into 'three weeks sure' I recognized the old familiar tune I used to hear so much. Ward don't know what sick-heartedness is—but he is in a way to find out."*

*Always the quaint form of his humor, no matter how dark the way. We may picture him walking the floor, planning, scheming, and smoking—always smoking—trying to find a way out. It was not the kind of scheming that many men have done under the circumstances; not scheming to avoid payment of debts, but to pay them.*

To Fred J. Hall, in New York:

*Aug. 14, '93*

DEAR MR. HALL,—I am very glad indeed if you and Mr. Langdon are able to see any daylight ahead. To me none is visible. I strongly advise that every penny that comes in shall be applied to paying off debts. I may be in error about this, but it seems to me that we have no other course open. We can pay a part of the debts owing to outsiders—none to the Clemenses. In very prosperous times we might regard our stock and copyrights as assets sufficient, with the money owing to us, to square up and quit even, but I suppose we may not hope for such luck in the present condition of things.

What I am mainly hoping for, is to save my royalties. If they come into danger I hope you will cable me, so that I can come over and try to save them, for if they go I am a beggar.

I would sail to-day if I had anybody to take charge of my family and help them through the difficult journeys commanded by the doctors. I may be able to sail ten days hence; I hope so, and expect so.

We can never resurrect the L. A. L. I would not spend any more money on that book. You spoke, a while back, of trying to start it up again as a preparation to disposing of it, but we are not in shape to venture that, I think. It would require more borrowing, and we must not do that.

*Yours Sincerely*

*S. L. C.*

Aug. 16. I have thought, and thought, but I don't seem to arrive in any very definite place. Of course you will not have an instant's safety until the bank debts are paid. There is nothing to be thought of but to hand over every penny as fast as it comes in—and that will be slow enough! Or could you secure them by pledging part of our cash assets and—

I am coming over, just as soon as I can get the family moved and settled.

*S. L. C.*

*Two weeks following this letter he could endure the suspense no longer, and on August 29th sailed once more for America. In New York, Clemens settled down at the Players Club, where he could live cheaply, and undertook some literary work while he was casting about for ways and means to relieve the financial situation. Nothing promising occurred, until one night at the Murray Hill Hotel he was introduced by Dr. Clarence C. Rice to Henry H. Rogers, of the Standard Oil group of financiers. Rogers had a keen sense of humor and had always been a great admirer of Mark Twain's work. It was a mirthful evening, and certainly an eventful one in Mark Twain's life. A day or two later Doctor Rice asked the millionaire to interest himself a little in Clemens's business affairs, which he thought a good deal confused. Just what happened is not remembered now, but from the date of the next letter we realize that a discussion of the matter by Clemens and Rogers must have followed pretty promptly.*

To Mrs. Clemens, in Europe:

*Oct. 18, '93.*

DEAR, DEAR SWEETHEART,—I don't seem to get even half a chance to write you, these last two days, and yet there's lots to say.

Apparently everything is at last settled as to the giveaway of L. A. L., and the papers will be signed and the transfer made to-morrow morning.

Meantime I have got the best and wisest man in the whole Standard Oil group of mufti-millionaires a good deal interested in looking into the type-setter (this is private, don't mention it.) He has been searching into that thing for three weeks, and yesterday he said to me, "I find the machine to be all you represented it—I have here exhaustive reports from my own experts, and I know every detail of its capacity, its immense value, its construction, cost, history, and all about its inventor's character. I know that the New York Co. and the Chicago Co. are both stupid, and that they are unbusinesslike people, destitute of money and in a hopeless boggle."

Then he told me the scheme he had planned, then said: "If I can arrange with these people on this basis—it will take several weeks to find out—I will see to it that they get the money they need. Then the thing will move right along and your royalties will cease to be waste paper. I will post you the minute my scheme fails or succeeds. In the meantime, you stop walking the floor. Go off to the country and try to be gay. You may have to go to walking again, but don't begin till I tell you my scheme has failed." And he added: "Keep me posted always as to where you are—for if I need you and can use you—I want to know where to put my hand on you."

If I should even divulge the fact that the Standard Oil is merely talking remotely about going into the type-setter, it would send my royalties up.

With worlds and worlds of love and kisses to you all,

*SAML.*

With so great a burden of care shifted to the broad financial shoulders of H. H. Rogers, Mark Twain's spirits went ballooning, soaring toward the stars. He awoke, too, to some of the social gaieties about him, and found pleasure in the things that in the hour of his gloom had seemed mainly mockery. We find him going to a Sunday evening at Howells's, to John Mackay's, and elsewhere.

To Mrs. Clemens, in Paris:

*Dec. 2, '93.*

LIVY DARLING,—Last night at John Mackay's the dinner consisted of soup, raw oysters, corned beef and cabbage, and something like a custard. I ate without fear or stint, and yet have escaped all suggestion of indigestion. The men present were old gray Pacific-coasters whom I knew when I and they were young and not gray. The talk was of the days when we went gypsying a long time ago—thirty years. Indeed it was a talk of the dead. Mainly that. And of how they looked, and the harum-scarum things they did and said. For there were no cares in that life, no aches and pains, and not time enough in the day (and three-fourths of the night) to work off one's surplus vigor and energy. Of the mid-night highway robbery joke played upon me with revolvers at my head on the windswept and desolate Gold Hill Divide, no witness is left but me, the victim. All the friendly robbers are gone. These old fools last night laughed till they cried over the particulars of that old forgotten crime.

John Mackay has no family here but a pet monkey—a most affectionate and winning little devil. But he makes trouble for the servants, for he is full of curiosity and likes to take everything out of the drawers and examine it minutely; and he puts nothing back. The examinations of yesterday count for nothing to-day—he makes a new examination every day. But he injures nothing.

I went with Laffan to the Racquet Club the other night and played, billiards two hours without starting up any rheumatism. I suppose it was all really taken out of me in Berlin.

Richard Harding Davis spoke yesterday of Clara's impersonations at Mrs. Van Rensselaer's here and said they were a wonderful piece of work.

Livy dear, I do hope you are comfortable, as to quarters and food at the Hotel Brighton. But if you're not don't stay there. Make one more effort—don't give it up. Dear heart, this is from one who loves you—which is Saml.

*It was decided that Rogers and Clemens should make a trip to Chicago to investigate personally the type-setter situation there. Clemens reports the details of the excursion to Mrs. Clemens in a long subdivided letter, most of which has no general interest and is here omitted. The trip, as a whole, would seem to have been satisfactory. The personal portions of the long Christmas letter may properly be preserved.*

To Mrs. Clemens, in Paris:

*THE PLAYERS, Xmas, 1893.*

*No. 1.*

Merry Xmas, my darling, and all my darlings! I arrived from Chicago close upon midnight last night, and wrote and sent down my Christmas cablegram before undressing: "Merry Xmas! Promising progress made in Chicago." It would get to the telegraph office toward 8 this morning and reach you at luncheon.

I was vaguely hoping, all the past week, that my Xmas cablegram would be definite, and make you all jump with jubilation; but the thought always intruded itself, "You are not going out there to negotiate with a man, but with a louse. This makes results uncertain."

I was asleep as Christmas struck upon the clock at mid night, and didn't wake again till two hours ago. It is now half past 10 Xmas morning; I have had my coffee and bread, and shan't get out of bed till it is time to dress for Mrs. Laflan's Christmas dinner this evening—where I shall meet Bram Stoker and must make sure about that photo with Irving's autograph. I will get the picture and he will attend to the rest. In order to remember and not forget—well, I will go there with my dress coat wrong side out; it will cause remark and then I shall remember.

*No. 2 and 3.*

I tell you it was interesting! The Chicago campaign, I mean. On the way out Mr. Rogers would plan out the campaign while I walked the floor and smoked and assented. Then he would close it up with a snap and drop it and we would totally change the subject and take up the scenery, etc.

(Here follows the long detailed report of the Chicago conference, of interest only to the parties directly concerned.)

*No. 4.*

We had nice tripe, going and coming. Mr. Rogers had telegraphed the Pennsylvania Railroad for a couple of sections for us in the fast train leaving at 2 p. m. the 22nd. The Vice President telegraphed back that every berth was engaged (which was not true—it goes without saying) but that he was sending his own car for us. It was mighty nice and comfortable. In its parlor it had two sofas, which could become beds at night. It had four comfortably-cushioned cane arm-chairs. It had a very nice bedroom with a wide bed in it; which I said I would take because I believed I was a little wider than Mr. Rogers—which turned out to be true; so I took it. It had a darling back-porch—railed, roofed and roomy; and there we sat, most of the time, and viewed the scenery and talked, for the weather was May weather, and the soft dream-pictures of hill and river and mountain and sky were clear and away beyond anything I have ever seen for exquisiteness and daintiness.

The colored waiter knew his business, and the colored cook was a finished artist. Breakfasts: coffee with real cream; beefsteaks, sausage, bacon, chops, eggs in various ways, potatoes in various—yes, and quite wonderful baked potatoes, and hot as fire. Dinners—all manner of things, including canvas-back duck, apollinaris, claret, champagne, etc.

We sat up chatting till midnight, going and coming; seldom read a line, day or night, though we were well fixed with magazines, etc.; then I finished off with a hot Scotch and we went to bed and slept till 9.30 a.m. I honestly tried to pay my share of hotel bills, fees, etc., but I was not allowed—and I knew the reason why, and respected the motive. I will explain when I see you, and then you will understand.

We were 25 hours going to Chicago; we were there 24 hours; we were 30 hours returning. Brisk work, but all of it enjoyable. We insisted on leaving the car at Philadelphia so that our waiter and cook (to whom Mr. R. gave $10 apiece,) could have their Christmas-eve at home.

Mr. Rogers's carriage was waiting for us in Jersey City and deposited me at the Players. There—that's all. This letter is to make up for the three letterless days. I love you, dear heart, I love you all.

*SAML.*

## XXXIV. LETTERS 1894. A WINTER IN NEW YORK. BUSINESS FAILURE. END OF THE MACHINE.

The beginning of the new year found Mark Twain sailing buoyantly on a tide of optimism. He believed that with H. H. Rogers as his financial pilot he could weather safely any storm or stress. He could divert himself, or rest, or work, and consider his business affairs with interest and amusement, instead of with haggard anxiety. He ran over to Hartford to see an amateur play; to Boston to give a charity reading; to Fair Haven to open the library which Mr. Rogers had established there; he attended gay dinners, receptions, and late studio parties, acquiring the name of the "Belle of New York." In the letters that follow we get the echo of some of these things. The Mrs. Rice mentioned in the next brief letter was the wife of Dr. Clarence C. Rice, who had introduced H. H. Rogers to Mark Twain.

To Mrs. Clemens, in Paris:

*Jan. 12, '94*

Livy darling, I came down from Hartford yesterday with Kipling, and he and Hutton and I had the small smoking compartment to ourselves and found him at last at his ease, and not shy. He was very pleasant company indeed. He is to be in the city a week, and I wish I could invite him to dinner, but it won't do. I should be interrupted by business, of course. The construction of a contract that will suit Paige's lawyer (not Paige) turns out to be very difficult. He is embarrassed by earlier advice to Paige, and hates to retire from it and stultify himself. The negotiations are being conducted, by means of tedious long telegrams and by talks over the long-distance telephone. We keep the wires loaded.

Dear me, dinner is ready. So Mrs. Rice says.

*With worlds of love,*

*SAML.*

Clemens and Oliver Wendell Holmes had met and become friends soon after the publication of Innocents Abroad, in 1869. Now, twenty-five years later, we find a record of what without doubt was their last meeting. It occurred at the home of Mrs. James T. Field.

To Mrs. Clemens, in Paris:

*BOSTON, Jan. 25, '94.*

Livy darling, I am caught out worse this time than ever before, in the matter of letters. Tuesday morning I was smart enough to finish and mail my long letter to you before breakfast—for I was suspecting that I would not have another spare moment during the day. It turned out just so.

In a thoughtless moment I agreed to come up here and read for the poor. I did not reflect that it would cost me three days. I could not get released. Yesterday I had myself called at 8 and ran out to Mr. Rogers's house at 9, and talked business until half past 10; then caught 11 o'clock train and arrived here at 6; was shaven and dressed by 7 and ready for dinner here in Mrs. Field's charming house.

Dr. Oliver Wendell Holmes never goes out now (he is in his 84th year,) but he came out this time—said he wanted to "have a time" once more with me.

Mrs. Fields said Aldrich begged to come and went away crying because she wouldn't let him. She allowed only her family (Sarah Orne Jewett and sister) to be present, because much company would overtax Dr. Holmes.

Well, he was just delightful! He did as brilliant and beautiful talking (and listening) as ever he did in his life, I guess. Fields and Jewett said he hadn't been in such splendid form in years. He had ordered his carriage for 9.

The coachman sent in for him at 9; but he said, "Oh, nonsense!—leave glories and grandeurs like these? Tell him to go away and come in an hour!"

At 10 he was called for again, and Mrs. Fields, getting uneasy, rose, but he wouldn't go—and so we rattled ahead the same as ever. Twice more Mrs. Fields rose, but he wouldn't go—and he didn't go till half past 10—

an unwarrantable dissipation for him in these days. He was prodigiously complimentary about some of my books, and is having Pudd'nhead read to him. I told him you and I used the Autocrat as a courting book and marked it all through, and that you keep it in the sacred green box with the love letters, and it pleased him.

Good-bye, my dear darling, it is 15 minutes to dinner and I'm not dressed yet. I have a reception to-night and will be out very late at that place and at Irving's Theatre where I have a complimentary box. I wish you were all here.

*SAML.*

*In the next letter we meet James J. Corbett—"Gentleman Jim," as he was sometimes called—the champion pugilist of that day.*

*The Howells incident so amusingly dramatized will perhaps be more appreciated if the reader remembers that Mark Twain himself had at intervals been a mind-healing enthusiast. Indeed, in spite of his strictures on Mrs. Eddy, his interest in the subject of mind-cure continued to the end of his life.*

To Mrs. Clemens, in Paris:

*Sunday, 9.30 a. m.*

Livy dear, when we got out to the house last night, Mrs. Rogers, who is up and around, now, didn't want to go down stairs to dinner, but Mr. R. persuaded her and we had a very good time indeed. By 8 o'clock we were down again and bought a fifteen-dollar box in the Madison Square Garden (Rogers bought it, not I,) then he went and fetched Dr. Rice while I (went) to the Players and picked up two artists—Reid and Simmons—and thus we filled 5 of the 6 seats. There was a vast multitude of people in the brilliant place. Stanford White came along presently and invited me to go to the

World-Champion's dressing room, which I was very glad to do. Corbett has a fine face and is modest and diffident, besides being the most perfectly and beautifully constructed human animal in the world. I said:

"You have whipped Mitchell, and maybe you will whip Jackson in June—but you are not done, then. You will have to tackle me."

He answered, so gravely that one might easily have thought him in earnest:

"No—I am not going to meet you in the ring. It is not fair or right to require it. You might chance to knock me out, by no merit of your own, but by a purely accidental blow; and then my reputation would be gone and you would have a double one. You have got fame enough and you ought not to want to take mine away from me."

Corbett was for a long time a clerk in the Nevada Bank in San Francisco.

There were lots of little boxing matches, to entertain the crowd: then at last Corbett appeared in the ring and the 8,000 people present went mad with enthusiasm. My two artists went mad about his form. They said they had never seen anything that came reasonably near equaling its perfection except Greek statues, and they didn't surpass it.

Corbett boxed 3 rounds with the middle-weight Australian champion—oh, beautiful to see!—then the show was over and we struggled out through a perfect wash of humanity. When we reached the street I found I had left my arctics in the box. I had to have them, so Simmons said he would go back and get them, and I didn't dissuade him. I couldn't see how he was going to make his way a single yard into that solid oncoming wave of people—yet he must plow through it full 50 yards. He was back with the shoes in 3 minutes!

How do you reckon he accomplished that miracle? By saying:

"Way, gentlemen, please—coming to fetch Mr. Corbett's overshoes."

The word flew from mouth to mouth, the Red Sea divided, and Simmons walked comfortably through and back, dry shod. Simmons (this was revealed to me under seal of secrecy by Reid) is the hero of "Gwen," and he and

Gwen's author were once engaged to marry. This is "fire-escape" Simmons, the inveterate talker, you know: "Exit—in case of Simmons."

I had an engagement at a beautiful dwelling close to the Players for 10.30; I was there by 10.45. Thirty cultivated and very musical ladies and gentlemen present—all of them acquaintances and many of them personal friends of mine. That wonderful Hungarian Band was there (they charge $500 for an evening.) Conversation and Band until midnight; then a bite of supper; then the company was compactly grouped before me and I told about Dr. B. E. Martin and the etchings, and followed it with the Scotch-Irish Christening. My, but the Martin is a darling story! Next, the head tenor from the Opera sang half a dozen great songs that set the company wild, yes, mad with delight, that nobly handsome young Damrosch accompanying on the piano.

Just a little pause—then the Band burst out into an explosion of weird and tremendous dance music, a Hungarian celebrity and his wife took the floor—I followed; I couldn't help it; the others drifted in, one by one, and it was Onteora over again.

By half past 4 I had danced all those people down—and yet was not tired; merely breathless. I was in bed at 5, and asleep in ten minutes. Up at 9 and presently at work on this letter to you. I think I wrote until 2 or half past. Then I walked leisurely out to Mr. Rogers's (it is called 3 miles but it is short of it) arriving at 3.30, but he was out—to return at 5.30—(and a person was in, whom I don't particularly like)—so I didn't stay, but dropped over and chatted with the Howellses until 6.

First, Howells and I had a chat together. I asked about Mrs. H. He said she was fine, still steadily improving, and nearly back to her old best health. I asked (as if I didn't know):

"What do you attribute this strange miracle to?"

"Mind-cure—simply mind-cure."

"Lord, what a conversion! You were a scoffer three months ago."

"I? I wasn't."

"You were. You made elaborate fun of me in this very room."

"I did not, Clemens."

"It's a lie, Howells, you did."

I detailed to him the conversation of that time—with the stately argument furnished by Boyesen in the fact that a patient had actually been killed by a mind-curist; and Howells's own smart remark that when the mind-curist is done with you, you have to call in a "regular" at last because the former can't procure you a burial permit.

At last he gave in—he said he remembered that talk, but had now been a mind-curist so long it was difficult for him to realize that he had ever been anything else.

Mrs. H. came skipping in, presently, the very person, to a dot, that she used to be, so many years ago.

Mrs. H. said: "People may call it what they like, but it is just hypnotism, and that's all it is—hypnotism pure and simple. Mind-cure!—the idea! Why, this woman that cured me hasn't got any mind. She's a good creature, but she's dull and dumb and illiterate and—"

"Now Eleanor!"

"I know what I'm talking about!—don't I go there twice a week? And Mr. Clemens, if you could only see her wooden and satisfied face when she snubs me for forgetting myself and showing by a thoughtless remark that to me weather is still weather, instead of being just an abstraction and a superstition—oh, it's the funniest thing you ever saw! A-n-d-when she tilts up her nose-well, it's—it's—Well it's that kind of a nose that—"

"Now Eleanor!—the woman is not responsible for her nose—" and so-on and so-on. It didn't seem to me that I had any right to be having this feast and you not there.

She convinced me before she got through, that she and William James are right—hypnotism and mind-cure are the same thing; no difference between them. Very well; the very source, the very center of hypnotism is Paris. Dr. Charcot's pupils and disciples are right there and ready to your hand without fetching poor dear old Susy across the stormy sea. Let Mrs. Mackay (to whom I send my best respects), tell you whom to go to to learn all you need to learn and how to proceed. Do, do it, honey. Don't lose a minute.

.... At 11 o'clock last night Mr. Rogers said:

"I am able to feel physical fatigue—and I feel it now. You never show any, either in your eyes or your movements; do you ever feel any?"

I was able to say that I had forgotten what that feeling was like. Don't you remember how almost impossible it was for me to tire myself at the Villa? Well, it is just so in New York. I go to bed unfatigued at 3, I get up fresh and fine six hours later. I believe I have taken only one daylight nap since I have been here.

When the anchor is down, then I shall say:

"Farewell—a long farewell—to business! I will never touch it again!"

I will live in literature, I will wallow in it, revel in it, I will swim in ink! Joan of Arc—but all this is premature; the anchor is not down yet.

To-morrow (Tuesday) I will add a P. S. if I've any to add; but, whether or no, I must mail this to morrow, for the mail steamer goes next day.

5.30 p. m. Great Scott, this is Tuesday! I must rush this letter into the mail instantly.

Tell that sassy Ben I've got her welcome letter, and I'll write her as soon as I get a daylight chance. I've most time at night, but I'd druther write daytimes.

*SAML.*

*The Reid and Simmons mentioned in the foregoing were Robert Reid and Edward Simmons, distinguished painter—the latter a brilliant, fluent, and industrious talker. The title; "Fire-escape Simmons," which Clemens gives him, originated when Oliver Herford, whose quaint wit has so long delighted New-Yorkers, one day pinned up by the back door of the Players the notice: "Exit in case of Simmons." Gwen, a popular novel of that day, was written by Blanche Willis Howard.*

*"Jamie" Dodge, in the next letter, was the son of Mrs. Mary Mapes Dodge, editor of St. Nicholas.*

To Clara Clemens, in Paris:

*MR. ROGERS'S OFFICE, Feb. 5, '94.*

Dear Benny—I was intending to answer your letter to-day, but I am away down town, and will simply whirl together a sentence or two for good-fellowship. I have bought photographs of Coquelin and Jane Hading and will ask them to sign them. I shall meet Coquelin tomorrow night, and if Hading is not present I will send her picture to her by somebody.

I am to breakfast with Madame Nordica in a few days, and meantime I hope to get a good picture of her to sign. She was of the breakfast company yesterday, but the picture of herself which she signed and gave me does not do her majestic beauty justice.

I am too busy to attend to the photo-collecting right, because I have to live up to the name which Jamie Dodge has given me—the "Belle of New York"—and it just keeps me rushing. Yesterday I had engagements to breakfast at noon, dine at 3, and dine again at 7. I got away from the long breakfast at 2 p. m., went and excused myself from the 3 o'clock dinner, then lunched with Mrs. Dodge in 58th street, returned to the Players and dressed, dined out at 9, and was back at Mrs. Dodge's at 10 p. m. where we had magic-lantern views of a superb sort, and a lot of yarns until an hour after midnight, and got to bed at 2 this morning—a good deal of a gain on my recent hours. But I don't get tired; I sleep as sound as a dead person, and always wake up fresh and strong—usually at exactly 9.

I was at breakfast lately where people of seven separate nationalities sat and the seven languages were going all the time. At my side sat a charming gentleman who was a delightful and active talker, and interesting. He talked glibly to those folks in all those seven languages and still had a language to spare! I wanted to kill him, for very envy.

*I greet you with love and kisses.*

*PAPA.*

To Mrs. Clemens, in Paris:

*Feb.—.*

Livy dear, last night I played billiards with Mr. Rogers until 11, then went to Robert Reid's studio and had a most delightful time until 4 this morning. No ladies were invited this time. Among the people present were—

*Coquelin;*

*Richard Harding Davis;*

*Harrison, the great out-door painter;*

*Wm. H. Chase, the artist;*

*Bettini, inventor of the new phonograph.*

*Nikola Tesla, the world-wide illustrious electrician; see article about him in Jan. or Feb. Century.*

*John Drew, actor;*

*James Barnes, a marvelous mimic; my, you should see him!*

*Smedley the artist;*

*Zorn the artist;*

*Zogbaum the artist;*

*Reinhart the artist;*

*Metcalf the artist;*

*Ancona, head tenor at the Opera;*

Oh, a great lot of others. Everybody there had done something and was in his way famous.

Somebody welcomed Coquelin in a nice little French speech; John Drew did the like for me in English, and then the fun began. Coquelin did some excellent French monologues—one of them an ungrammatical Englishman telling a colorless historiette in French. It nearly killed the fifteen or twenty people who understood it.

I told a yarn, Ancona sang half a dozen songs, Barnes did his darling imitations, Harding Davis sang the hanging of Danny Deever, which was of course good, but he followed it with that most fascinating (for what reason I don't know) of all Kipling's poems, "On the Road to Mandalay," sang it tenderly, and it searched me deeper and charmed me more than the Deever.

Young Gerrit Smith played some ravishing dance music and we all danced about an hour. There couldn't be a pleasanter night than that one was. Some of those people complained of fatigue but I don't seem to know what the sense of fatigue is.

Coquelin talks quite good English now. He said:

"I have a brother who has the fine mind—ah, a charming and delicate fancy, and he knows your writings so well, and loves them—and that is the same with me. It will stir him so when I write and tell him I have seen you!"

Wasn't that nice? We talked a good deal together. He is as winning as his own face. But he wouldn't sign that photograph for Clara. "That? No! She shall have a better one. I will send it to you."

He is much driven, and will forget it, but Reid has promised to get the picture for me, and I will try and keep him reminded.

Oh, dear, my time is all used up and your letters are not answered.

Mama, dear, I don't go everywhere—I decline most things. But there are plenty that I can't well get out of.

I will remember what you say and not make my yarning too common.

I am so glad Susy has gone on that trip and that you are trying the electric. May you both prosper. For you are mighty dear to me and in my thoughts always.

*SAML.*

*The affairs of the Webster Publishing Company were by this time getting into a very serious condition indeed. The effects of the panic of the year before could not be overcome. Creditors were pressing their claims and profits were negligible. In the following letter we get a Mark Twain estimate of the great financier who so cheerfully was willing to undertake the solving of Mark Twain's financial problems.*

To Mrs. Clemens, in Paris:

*THE PLAYERS, Feb. 15, '94. 11.30 p. m.*

Livy darling, Yesterday I talked all my various matters over with Mr. Rogers and we decided that it would be safe for me to leave here the 7th of March, in the New York. So his private secretary, Miss Harrison, wrote and ordered a berth for me and then I lost no time in cabling you that I should reach Southampton March 14, and Paris the 15th. Land, but it made my pulses leap, to think I was going to see you again!... One thing at a time. I never fully laid Webster's disastrous condition before Mr. Rogers until to-night after billiards. I did hate to burden his good heart and over-worked head with it, but he took hold with avidity and said it was no burden to work for his friends, but a pleasure. We discussed it from various standpoints, and found it a sufficiently difficult problem to solve; but he thinks that after he has slept upon it and thought it over he will know what to suggest.

You must not think I am ever rude with Mr. Rogers, I am not. He is not common clay, but fine—fine and delicate—and that sort do not call out the coarsenesses that are in my sort. I am never afraid of wounding him; I do not need to watch myself in that matter. The sight of him is peace.

He wants to go to Japan—it is his dream; wants to go with me—which means, the two families—and hear no more about business for awhile, and have a rest. And he needs it. But it is like all the dreams of all busy men—fated to remain dreams.

You perceive that he is a pleasant text for me. It is easy to write about him. When I arrived in September, lord how black the prospect was—how desperate, how incurably desperate! Webster and Co. had to have a small sum of money or go under at once. I flew to Hartford—to my friends—but they were not moved, not strongly interested, and I was ashamed that I went. It was from Mr. Rogers, a stranger, that I got the money and was by it saved. And then—while still a stranger—he set himself the task of saving my financial life without putting upon me (in his native delicacy) any sense that I was the recipient of a charity, a benevolence—and he has accomplished that task; accomplished it at a cost of three months of wearing and difficult labor. He gave that time to me—time which could not be bought by any man at a hundred thousand dollars a month—no, nor for three times the money.

Well, in the midst of that great fight, that long and admirable fight, George Warner came to me and said:

"There is a splendid chance open to you. I know a man—a prominent man—who has written a book that will go like wildfire; a book that arraigns the Standard Oil fiends, and gives them unmitigated hell, individual by individual. It is the very book for you to publish; there is a fortune in it, and I can put you in communication with the author."

I wanted to say:

"The only man I care for in the world; the only man I would give a damn for; the only man who is lavishing his sweat and blood to save me and mine from starvation and shame, is a Standard Oil fiend. If you know me, you know whether I want the book or not."

But I didn't say that. I said I didn't want any book; I wanted to get out of the publishing business and out of all business, and was here for that purpose and would accomplish it if I could.

But there's enough. I shall be asleep by 3, and I don't need much sleep, because I am never drowsy or tired these days. Dear, dear Susy my strength reproaches me when I think of her and you, my darling.

*SAML.*

*But even so able a man as Henry Rogers could not accomplish the impossible. The affairs of the Webster Company were hopeless, the business was not worth saving. By Mr. Rogers's advice an assignment was made April, 18, 1894. After its early spectacular success less than ten years had brought the business to failure. The publication of the Grant memoirs had been its only great achievement.*

*Clemens would seem to have believed that the business would resume, and for a time Rogers appears to have comforted him in his hope, but we cannot believe that it long survived. Young Hall, who had made such a struggle for its salvation, was eager to go on, but he must presently have seen the futility of any effort in that direction.*

*Of course the failure of Mark Twain's firm made a great stir in the country, and it is easy to understand that loyal friends would rally in his behalf.*

To Mrs. Clemens, in Paris:

*April 22, '94.*

Dear old darling, we all think the creditors are going to allow us to resume business; and if they do we shall pull through and pay the debts. I am prodigiously glad we made an assignment. And also glad that we did not make it sooner. Earlier we should have made a poor showing; but now we shall make a good one.

I meet flocks of people, and they all shake me cordially by the hand and say "I was so sorry to hear of the assignment, but so glad you did it. It was around, this long time, that the concern was tottering, and all your friends were afraid you would delay the assignment too long."

John Mackay called yesterday, and said, "Don't let it disturb you, Sam—we all have to do it, at one time or another; it's nothing to be ashamed of."

One stranger out in New York State sent me a dollar bill and thought he would like to get up a dollar-subscription for me. And Poultney Bigelow's note came promptly, with his check for $1,000. I had been meeting him every day at the Club and liking him better and better all the time. I couldn't take his money, of course, but I thanked him cordially for his good will.

Now and then a good and dear Joe Twichell or Susy Warner condoles with me and says "Cheer up—don't be downhearted," and some other friend says, "I am glad and surprised to see how cheerful you are and how bravely you stand it"—and none of them suspect what a burden has been lifted from me and how blithe I am inside. Except when I think of you, dear heart—then I am not blithe; for I seem to see you grieving and ashamed, and dreading to look people in the face. For in the thick of the fight there is cheer, but you are far away and cannot hear the drums nor see the wheeling squadrons. You only seem to see rout, retreat, and dishonored colors dragging in the dirt—whereas none of these things exist. There is temporary defeat, but no dishonor—and we will march again. Charley Warner said to-day, "Sho, Livy isn't worrying. So long as she's got you and the children she doesn't care what happens. She knows it isn't her affair." Which didn't convince me.

Good bye my darling, I love you and all of the kids—and you can tell Clara I am not a spitting gray kitten.

*SAML.*

*Clemens sailed for Europe as soon as his affairs would permit him to go. He must get settled where he could work comfortably. Type-setter prospects seemed promising, but meantime there was need of funds.*

*He began writing on the ship, as was his habit, and had completed his article on Fenimore Cooper by the time he reached London. In August we find him writing to Mr. Rogers from Etretat, a little Norman watering-place.*

To H. H. Rogers, in New York:

*ETRETAT, (NORMANDIE)*

*CHALET DES ABRIS*

*Aug. 25, '94.*

DEAR MR. ROGERS,—I find the Madam ever so much better in health and strength. The air is superb and soothing and wholesome, and the Chalet is remote from noise and people, and just the place to write in. I shall begin work this afternoon.

Mrs. Clemens is in great spirits on, account of the benefit which she has received from the electrical treatment in Paris and is bound to take it up again and continue it all the winter, and of course I am perfectly willing. She requires me to drop the lecture platform out of my mind and go straight ahead with Joan until the book is finished. If I should have to go home for even a week she means to go with me—won't consent to be separated again—but she hopes I won't need to go.

I tell her all right, "I won't go unless you send, and then I must."

She keeps the accounts; and as she ciphers it we can't get crowded for money for eight months yet. I didn't know that. But I don't know much anyway.

*Sincerely yours,*

*S. L. CLEMENS.*

*The reader may remember that Clemens had written the first half of his Joan of Arc book at the Villa Viviani, in Florence, nearly two years before. He had closed the manuscript then with the taking of Orleans, and was by no means sure that he would continue the story beyond that point. Now, however, he was determined to reach the tale's tragic conclusion.*

To H. H. Rogers, in New York:

*ETRETAT,*

*Sunday, Sept. 9, '94.*

DEAR MR. ROGERS, I drove the quill too hard, and I broke down—in my head. It has now been three days since I laid up. When I wrote you a week ago I had added 10,000 words or thereabout to Joan. Next day I added 1,500 which was a proper enough day's work though not a full one; but during Tuesday and Wednesday I stacked up an aggregate of 6,000 words—and that was a very large mistake. My head hasn't been worth a cent since.

However, there's a compensation; for in those two days I reached and passed—successfully—a point which I was solicitous about before I ever began the book: viz., the battle of Patay. Because that would naturally be the next to the last chapter of a work consisting of either two books or one. In the one case one goes right along from that point (as I shall do now); in the other he would add a wind-up chapter and make the book consist of Joan's childhood and military career alone.

I shall resume work to-day; and hereafter I will not go at such an intemperate' rate. My head is pretty cobwebby yet.

I am hoping that along about this time I shall hear that the machine is beginning its test in the Herald office. I shall be very glad indeed to know the result of it. I wish I could be there.

*Sincerely yours*

*S. L. CLEMENS.*

*Rouen, where Joan met her martyrdom, was only a short distance away, and they halted there en route to Paris, where they had arranged to spend the winter. The health of Susy Clemens was not good, and they lingered in Rouen while Clemens explored the old city and incidentally did some writing of another sort. In a note to Mr. Rogers he said: "To put in my odd time I am writing some articles about Paul Bourget and his Outre-Mer chapters—laughing at them and at some of our oracular owls who find them important. What the hell makes them important, I should like to know!"*

*He was still at Rouen two weeks later and had received encouraging news from Rogers concerning the type-setter, which had been placed for trial in the office of the Chicago Herald. Clemens wrote: "I can hardly keep from sending a hurrah by cable. I would certainly do it if I wasn't superstitious." His restraint, though wise, was wasted the end was near.*

To H. H. Rogers, in New York:

*169 RUE DE L'UNIVERSITE,*

*PARIS, Dec. 22; '94.*

DEAR MR. ROGERS,—I seemed to be entirely expecting your letter, and also prepared and resigned; but Lord, it shows how little we know ourselves and how easily we can deceive ourselves. It hit me like a thunder-clap. It knocked every rag of sense out of my head, and I went flying here and there and yonder, not knowing what I was doing, and only one clearly defined thought standing up visible and substantial out of the crazy storm-drift that my dream of ten years was in desperate peril, and out of the 60,000 or 90,000 projects for its rescue that came floating through my skull, not one would hold still long enough for me to examine it and size it up. Have you ever been like that? Not so much so, I reckon.

There was another clearly defined idea—I must be there and see it die. That is, if it must die; and maybe if I were there we might hatch up some next-to-impossible way to make it take up its bed and take a walk.

So, at the end of four hours I started, still whirling and walked over to the rue Scribe—4 P. M.—and asked a question or two and was told I should be running a big risk if I took the 9 P. M. train for London and Southampton; "better come right along at 6.52 per Havre special and step aboard the New York all easy and comfortable." Very! and I about two miles from home, with no packing done.

Then it occurred to me that none of these salvation-notions that were whirl-winding through my head could be examined or made available unless at least a month's time could be secured. So I cabled you, and said to myself that I would take the French steamer tomorrow (which will be Sunday).

By bedtime Mrs. Clemens had reasoned me into a fairly rational and contented state of mind; but of course it didn't last long. So I went on thinking—mixing it with a smoke in the dressing room once an hour—until dawn this morning. Result—a sane resolution; no matter what your answer to my cable might be, I would hold still and not sail until I should get an answer to this present letter which I am now writing, or a cable answer from you saying "Come" or "Remain."

I have slept 6 hours, my pond has clarified, and I find the sediment of my 70,000 projects to be of this character:

[Several pages of suggestions for reconstructing the machine follow.]

Don't say I'm wild. For really I'm sane again this morning.

......................

I am going right along with Joan, now, and wait untroubled till I hear from you. If you think I can be of the least use, cable me "Come." I can write Joan on board ship and lose no time. Also I could discuss my plan with the publisher for a deluxe Joan, time being an object, for some of the pictures could be made over here cheaply and quickly, but would cost much time and money in America.

......................

If the meeting should decide to quit business Jan. 4, I'd like to have Stoker stopped from paying in any more money, if Miss Harrison doesn't mind that disagreeable job. And I'll have to write them, too, of course.

*With love,*

*S. L. CLEMENS.*

*The "Stoker" of this letter was Bram Stoker, long associated with Sir Henry Irving. Irving himself had also taken stock in the machine. The address, 169 Rue de l'Universite, whence these letters are written, was the beautiful studio home of the artist Pomroy which they had taken for the winter.*

To H. H. Rogers, in New York:

*169 RUE DE L'UNIVERSITE,*

*PARIS, Dec. 27, '94.*

DEAR MR. ROGERS,—Notwithstanding your heart is "old and hard," you make a body choke up. I know you "mean every word you say" and I do take it "in the same spirit in which you tender it." I shall keep your regard while we two live—that I know; for I shall always remember what you have done for me, and that will insure me against ever doing anything that could forfeit it or impair it. I am 59 years old; yet I never had a friend before who put out a hand and tried to pull me ashore when he found me in deep waters.

It is six days or seven days ago that I lived through that despairing day, and then through a night without sleep; then settled down next day into my right mind (or thereabouts,) and wrote you. I put in the rest of that day till 7 P. M. plenty comfortably enough writing a long chapter of my book; then went to a masked ball blacked up as Uncle Remus, taking Clara along; and we had a good time. I have lost no day since and suffered no discomfort to speak of, but drove my troubles out of my mind and had good success in keeping them out—through watchfulness. I have done a good week's work and put the book a good way ahead in the Great Trial, which is the difficult part which requires the most thought and carefulness. I cannot see the end of the Trial yet, but I am on the road. I am creeping surely toward it.

"Why not leave them all to me." My business bothers? I take you by the hand! I jump at the chance!

I ought to be ashamed and I am trying my best to be ashamed—and yet I do jump at the chance in spite of it. I don't want to write Irving and I don't want to write Stoker. It doesn't seem as if I could. But I can suggest something for you to write them; and then if you see that I am unwise, you can write them something quite different. Now this is my idea:

1. *To return Stoker's $100 to him and keep his stock.*
2. *And tell Irving that when luck turns with me I will make good to him what the salvage from the dead Co. fails to pay him of his $500.*

P. S. Madam says No, I must face the music. So I enclose my effort to be used if you approve, but not otherwise.

There! Now if you will alter it to suit your judgment and bang away, I shall be eternally obliged.

We shall try to find a tenant for our Hartford house; not an easy matter, for it costs heavily to live in. We can never live in it again; though it would break the family's hearts if they could believe it.

Nothing daunts Mrs. Clemens or makes the world look black to her—which is the reason I haven't drowned myself.

We all send our deepest and warmest greetings to you and all of yours and a Happy New Year!

*S. L. CLEMENS.*

Enclosure:

MY DEAR STOKER,—I am not dating this because it is not to be mailed at present.

When it reaches you it will mean that there is a hitch in my machine-enterprise—a hitch so serious as to make it take to itself the aspect of a dissolved dream. This letter, then, will contain cheque for the $100 which you have paid. And will you tell Irving for me—I can't get up courage enough to talk about this misfortune myself, except to you, whom by good luck I haven't damaged yet that when the wreckage presently floats ashore he will get a good deal of his $500 back; and a dab at a time I will make up to him the rest.

I'm not feeling as fine as I was when I saw you there in your home. Please remember me kindly to Mrs. Stoker. I gave up that London lecture-project entirely. Had to—there's never been a chance since to find the time.

*Sincerely yours,*

*S. L. CLEMENS.*

## XXXV. LETTERS, 1895-96, TO H. H. ROGERS AND OTHERS. FINISHING "JOAN OF ARC." THE TRIP AROUND THE WORLD. DEATH OF SUSY CLEMENS.

To H. H. Rogers, in New York City:

*[No date.]*

DEAR MR. ROGERS,—Yours of Dec. 21 has arrived, containing the circular to stockholders and I guess the Co. will really quit—there doesn't seem to be any other wise course.

There's one thing which makes it difficult for me to soberly realize that my ten year dream is actually dissolved; and that is, that it reveries my horoscope. The proverb says, "Born lucky, always lucky," and I am very superstitious. As a small boy I was notoriously lucky. It was usual for one or two of our lads (per annum) to get drowned in the Mississippi or in Bear Creek, but I was pulled out in a 2/3 drowned condition 9 times before I learned to swim, and was considered to be a cat in disguise. When the "Pennsylvania" blew up and the telegraph reported my brother as fatally injured (with 60 others) but made no mention of me, my uncle said to my mother "It means that Sam was somewhere else, after being on that boat a year and a half—he was born lucky." Yes, I was somewhere else. I am so superstitious that I have always been afraid to have business dealings with certain relatives and friends of mine because they were unlucky people. All my life I have stumbled upon lucky chances of large size, and whenever they were wasted it was because of my own stupidity and carelessness. And so I have felt entirely certain that that machine would turn up trumps eventually. It disappointed me lots of times, but I couldn't shake off the confidence of a life-time in my luck.

Well, whatever I get out of the wreckage will be due to good luck—the good luck of getting you into the scheme—for, but for that, there wouldn't be any wreckage; it would be total loss.

I wish you had been in at the beginning. Then we should have had the good luck to step promptly ashore.

Miss Harrison has had a dream which promises me a large bank account, and I want her to go ahead and dream it twice more, so as to make the prediction sure to be fulfilled.

I've got a first rate subject for a book. It kept me awake all night, and I began it and completed it in my mind. The minute I finish Joan I will take it up.

*Love and Happy New Year to you all.*

*Sincerely yours,*

*S. L. CLEMENS.*

*This was about the end of the machine interests so far as Clemens was concerned. Paige succeeded in getting some new people interested, but nothing important happened, or that in any way affected Mark Twain. Characteristically he put the whole matter behind him and plunged into his work, facing comparative poverty and a burden of debts with a stout heart. The beginning of the new year found him really poorer in purse than he had ever been in his life, but certainly not crushed, or even discouraged—at least, not permanently—and never more industrious or capable.*

To H. H. Rogers, in New York City:

*169 RUE DE L'UNIVERSITE,*

*PARIS, Jan. 23, '95.*

DEAR MR. ROGERS,—After I wrote you, two or three days ago I thought I would make a holiday of the rest of the day—the second deliberate holiday since I had the gout. On the first holiday I wrote a tale of about

6,000 words, which was 3 days' work in one; and this time I did 8,000 before midnight. I got nothing out of that first holiday but the recreation of it, for I condemned the work after careful reading and some revision; but this time I fared better—I finished the Huck Finn tale that lies in your safe, and am satisfied with it.

The Bacheller syndicate (117 Tribune Building) want a story of 5,000 words (lowest limit of their London agent) for $1,000 and offer to plank the check on delivery, and it was partly to meet that demand that I took that other holiday. So as I have no short story that suits me (and can't and shan't make promises), the best I can do is to offer the longer one which I finished on my second holiday—"Tom Sawyer, Detective."

It makes 27 or 28,000 words, and is really written for grown folks, though I expect young folk to read it, too. It transfers to the banks of the Mississippi the incidents of a strange murder which was committed in Sweden in old times.

I'll refer applicants for a sight of the story to you or Miss Harrison.—[Secretary to Mr. Rogers.]

*Yours sincerely,*

*S. L. CLEMENS.*

To H. H. Rogers, in New York City:

*169 RUE DE L'UNIVERSITE,*

*Apr. 29, '95.*

DEAR MR. ROGERS,—Your felicitous delightful letter of the 15th arrived three days ago, and brought great pleasure into the house.

There is one thing that weighs heavily on Mrs. Clemens and me. That is Brusnahan's money. If he is satisfied to have it invested in the Chicago enterprise, well and good; if not, we would like to have the money paid back to him. I will give him as many months to decide in as he pleases—let him name 6 or 10 or 12—and we will let the money stay where it is in your hands till the time is up. Will Miss Harrison tell him so? I mean if you approve. I would like him to have a good investment, but would meantime prefer to protect him against loss.

At 6 minutes past 7, yesterday evening, Joan of Arc was burned at the stake.

With the long strain gone, I am in a sort of physical collapse today, but it will be gone tomorrow. I judged that this end of the book would be hard work, and it turned out so. I have never done any work before that cost so much thinking and weighing and measuring and planning and cramming, or so much cautious and painstaking execution. For I wanted the whole Rouen trial in, if it could be got in in such a way that the reader's interest would not flag—in fact I wanted the reader's interest to increase; and so I stuck to it with that determination in view—with the result that I have left nothing out but unimportant repetitions. Although it is mere history—history pure and simple—history stripped naked of flowers, embroideries, colorings, exaggerations, invention—the family agree that I have succeeded. It was a perilous thing to try in a tale, but I never believed it a doubtful one—provided I stuck strictly to business and didn't weaken and give up: or didn't get lazy and skimp the work. The first two-thirds of the book were easy; for I only needed to keep my historical road straight; therefore I used for reference only one French history and one English one—and shoveled in as much fancy work and invention on both sides of the historical road as I pleased. But on this last third I have constantly used five French sources and five English ones and I think no telling historical nugget in any of them has escaped me.

Possibly the book may not sell, but that is nothing—it was written for love.

There—I'm called to see company. The family seldom require this of me, but they know I am not working today.

*Yours sincerely,*

*S. L. CLEMENS.*

*"Brusnahan," of the foregoing letter, was an employee of the New York Herald, superintendent of the press-room—who had invested some of his savings in the type-setter.*

*In February Clemens returned to New York to look after matters connected with his failure and to close arrangements for a reading-tour around the world. He was nearly sixty years old, and time had not lessened his loathing for the platform. More than once, however, in earlier years, he had turned to it as a debt-payer, and never yet had his burden been so great as now. He concluded arrangements with Major Pond to take him as far as the Pacific Coast, and with R. S. Smythe, of Australia, for the rest of the tour. In April we find him once more back in Paris preparing to bring the family to America, He had returned by way of London, where he had visited Stanley the explorer—an old friend.*

To H. H. Rogers, in New York City:

*169 RUE DE L'UNIVERSITE,*

*Sunday, Apr. 7, '95.*

DEAR MR. ROGERS,—..... Stanley is magnificently housed in London, in a grand mansion in the midst of the official world, right off Downing Street and Whitehall. He had an extraordinary assemblage of brains and fame there to meet me—thirty or forty (both sexes) at dinner, and more than a hundred came in, after dinner. Kept it up till after midnight. There were cabinet ministers, ambassadors, admirals, generals, canons, Oxford professors, novelists, playwrights, poets, and a number of people equipped with rank and brains. I told some yarns and made some speeches. I promised to call on all those people next time I come to London, and show them the wife and the daughters. If I were younger and very strong I would dearly love to spend a season in London—provided I had no work on hand, or no work more exacting than lecturing. I think I will lecture there a month or two when I return from Australia.

There were many delightful ladies in that company. One was the wife of His Excellency Admiral Bridge, Commander-in Chief of the Australian Station, and she said her husband was able to throw wide all doors to me in that part of the world and would be glad to do it, and would yacht me and my party around, and excursion us in his flag-ship and make us have a great time; and she said she would write him we were coming, and we would find him ready. I have a letter from her this morning enclosing a letter of introduction to the Admiral. I already know the Admiral commanding in the China Seas and have promised to look in on him out there. He sleeps with my books under his pillow. P'raps it is the only way he can sleep.

According to Mrs. Clemens's present plans—subject to modification, of course—we sail in May; stay one day, or two days in New York, spend June, July and August in Elmira and prepare my lectures; then lecture in San Francisco and thereabouts during September and sail for Australia before the middle of October and open the show there about the middle of November. We don't take the girls along; it would be too expensive and they are quite willing to remain behind anyway.

Mrs. C. is feeling so well that she is not going to try the New York doctor till we have gone around the world and robbed it and made the finances a little easier.

*With a power of love to you all,*

*S. L. CLEMENS.*

*There would come moments of depression, of course, and a week later he wrote: "I am tired to death all the time:" To a man of less vitality, less vigor of mind and body, it is easy to believe that under such circumstances this condition would have remained permanent. But perhaps, after all, it was his comic outlook on things in general that was his chief life-saver.*

To H. H. Rogers, in New York City:

*169 RUE DE L'UNIVERSITE, Apr. 29, '95.*

DEAR MR. ROGERS,—I have been hidden an hour or two, reading proof of Joan and now I think I am a lost child. I can't find anybody on the place. The baggage has all disappeared, including the family. I reckon that in the hurry and bustle of moving to the hotel they forgot me. But it is no matter. It is peacefuller now than I have known it for days and days and days.

In these Joan proofs which I have been reading for the September Harper I find a couple of tip-top platform readings—and I mean to read them on our trip. If the authorship is known by then; and if it isn't, I will reveal it. The fact is, there is more good platform-stuff in Joan than in any previous book of mine, by a long sight.

Yes, every danged member of the tribe has gone to the hotel and left me lost. I wonder how they can be so careless with property. I have got to try to get there by myself now.

All the trunks are going over as luggage; then I've got to find somebody on the dock who will agree to ship 6 of them to the Hartford Customhouse. If it is difficult I will dump them into the river. It is very careless of Mrs. Clemens to trust trunks and things to me.

*Sincerely yours,*

*S. L. CLEMENS.*

*By the latter part of May they were at Quarry Farm, and Clemens, laid up there with a carbuncle, was preparing for his long tour.*

*The outlook was not a pleasant one. To Mr. Rogers he wrote: "I sha'n't be able to stand on the platform before we start west. I sha'n't get a single chance to practice my reading; but will have to appear in Cleveland without the essential preparation. Nothing in this world can save it from being a shabby, poor disgusting performance. I've got to stand; I can't do it and talk to a house, and how in the nation am I going to sit? Land of Goshen, it's this night week! Pray for me."*

*The opening at Cleveland July 15th appears not to have been much of a success, though from another reason, one that doubtless seemed amusing to him later.*

To H. H. Rogers, in New York City:

*(Forenoon)*

*CLEVELAND, July 16, '95.*

DEAR MR. ROGERS,—Had a roaring success at the Elmira reformatory Sunday night. But here, last night, I suffered defeat—There were a couple of hundred little boys behind me on the stage, on a lofty tier of benches which made them the most conspicuous objects in the house. And there was nobody to watch them or keep them quiet. Why, with their scufflings and horse-play and noise, it was just a menagerie. Besides, a concert of amateurs had been smuggled into the program (to precede me,) and their families and friends (say ten per cent of the audience) kept encoring them and they always responded. So it was 20 minutes to 9 before I got the platform in front of those 2,600 people who had paid a dollar apiece for a chance to go to hell in this fashion.

I got started magnificently, but inside of half an hour the scuffling boys had the audience's maddened attention and I saw it was a gone case; so I skipped a third of my program and quit. The newspapers are kind, but between you and me it was a defeat. There ain't going to be any more concerts at my lectures. I care nothing for this defeat, because it was not my fault. My first half hour showed that I had the house, and I could have kept it if I hadn't been so handicapped.

*Yours sincerely,*

*S. L. CLEMENS.*

P. S. Had a satisfactory time at Petoskey. Crammed the house and turned away a crowd. We had $548 in the house, which was $300 more than it had ever had in it before. I believe I don't care to have a talk go off better than that one did.

*Mark Twain, on this long tour, was accompanied by his wife and his daughter Clara—Susy and Jean Clemens remaining with their aunt at Quarry Farm. The tour was a financial success from the start. By the time they were ready to sail from Vancouver five thousand dollars had been remitted to Mr. Rogers against that day of settlement when the debts of Webster & Co. were to be paid. Perhaps it should be stated here that a legal settlement had been arranged on a basis of fifty cents on the dollar, but neither Clemens nor his wife consented to this as final. They would pay in full.*

*They sailed from Vancouver August 23, 1895. About the only letter of this time is an amusing note to Rudyard Kipling, written at the moment of departure.*

To Rudyard Kipling, in England:

*August, 1895.*

DEAR KIPLING,—It is reported that you are about to visit India. This has moved me to journey to that far country in order that I may unload from my conscience a debt long due to you. Years ago you came from India to Elmira to visit me, as you said at the time. It has always been my purpose to return that visit and that great compliment some day. I shall arrive next January and you must be ready. I shall come riding my ayah with his tusks adorned with silver bells and ribbons and escorted by a troop of native howdahs richly clad and mounted upon a herd of wild bungalows; and you must be on hand with a few bottles of ghee, for I shall be thirsty.

*Affectionately,*

*S. L. CLEMENS.*

*Clemens, platforming in Australia, was too busy to write letters. Everywhere he was welcomed by great audiences, and everywhere lavishly entertained. He was beset by other carbuncles, but would seem not to have been seriously delayed by them. A letter to his old friend Twichell carries the story.*

To Rev. Jos. H. Twichell, in Hartford:

*FRANK MOELLER'S MASONIC HOTEL,*

*NAPIER, NEW ZEALAND,*

*November 29, '95.*

DEAR JOE,—Your welcome letter of two months and five days ago has just arrived, and finds me in bed with another carbuncle. It is No. 3. Not a serious one this time. I lectured last night without inconvenience, but the doctors thought best to forbid to-night's lecture. My second one kept me in bed a week in Melbourne.

... We are all glad it is you who is to write the article, it delights us all through.

I think it was a good stroke of luck that knocked me on my back here at Napier, instead of some hotel in the centre of a noisy city. Here we have the smooth and placidly-complaining sea at our door, with nothing between us and it but 20 yards of shingle—and hardly a suggestion of life in that space to mar it or make a noise. Away down here fifty-five degrees south of the Equator this sea seems to murmur in an unfamiliar tongue—a foreign tongue—tongue bred among the ice-fields of the Antarctic—a murmur with a note of melancholy in it proper to the vast unvisited solitudes it has come from. It was very delicious and solacing to wake in the night and find it still pulsing there. I wish you were here—land, but it would be fine!

Livy and Clara enjoy this nomadic life pretty well; certainly better than one could have expected they would. They have tough experiences, in the way of food and beds and frantic little ships, but they put up with the worst that befalls with heroic endurance that resembles contentment.

No doubt I shall be on the platform next Monday. A week later we shall reach Wellington; talk there 3 nights, then sail back to Australia. We sailed for New Zealand October 30.

Day before yesterday was Livy's birthday (under world time), and tomorrow will be mine. I shall be 60—no thanks for it.

I and the others send worlds and worlds of love to all you dear ones.

*MARK.*

*The article mentioned in the foregoing letter was one which Twichell had been engaged by Harper's Magazine to write concerning the home life and characteristics of Mark Twain. By the time the Clemens party had completed their tour of India—a splendid, triumphant tour, too full of work and recreation for letter-writing—and had reached South Africa, the article had appeared, a satisfactory one, if we may judge by Mark Twain's next.*

*This letter, however, has a special interest in the account it gives of Mark Twain's visit to the Jameson raiders, then imprisoned at Pretoria.*

To Rev. Jos. H. Twichell, in Hartford:

*PRETORIA, SOUTH AFRICAN REPUBLIC,*

*The Queen's Birthday, '96.*

*(May 24)*

DEAR OLD JOE,—Harper for May was given to me yesterday in Johannesburg by an American lady who lives there, and I read your article on me while coming up in the train with her and an old friend and fellow-Missourian of mine, Mrs. John Hays Hammond, the handsome and spirited wife of the chief of the 4 Reformers, who lies in prison here under a 15-year sentence, along with 50 minor Reformers who are in for 1 and 5-year terms. Thank you a thousand times Joe, you have praised me away above my deserts, but I am not the man to quarrel with you for that; and as for Livy, she will take your very hardiest statements at par, and be grateful to you to the bottom of her heart. Between you and Punch and Brander Matthews, I am like to have my opinion of myself raised sufficiently high; and I guess the children will be after you, for it is the study of their lives to keep my self-appreciation down somewhere within bounds.

I had a note from Mrs. Rev. Gray (nee Tyler) yesterday, and called on her to-day. She is well.

Yesterday I was allowed to enter the prison with Mrs. Hammond. A Boer guard was at my elbow all the time, but was courteous and polite, only he barred the way in the compound (quadrangle or big open court) and wouldn't let me cross a white mark that was on the ground—the "death-line" one of the prisoners called it. Not in earnest, though, I think. I found that I had met Hammond once when he was a Yale senior and a guest of Gen. Franklin's. I also found that I had known Capt. Mein intimately 32 years ago. One of the English prisoners had heard me lecture in London 23 years ago. After being introduced in turn to all the prisoners, I was allowed to see some of the cells and examine their food, beds, etc. I was told in Johannesburg that Hammond's salary of $150,000 a year is not stopped, and that the salaries of some of the others are still continued. Hammond was looking very well indeed, and I can say the same of all the others. When the trouble first fell upon them it hit some of them very hard; several fell sick (Hammond among them), two or three had to be removed to the hospital, and one of the favorites lost his mind and killed himself, poor fellow, last week. His funeral, with a sorrowing following of 10,000, took the place of the public demonstration the Americans were getting up for me.

These prisoners are strong men, prominent men, and I believe they are all educated men. They are well off; some of them are wealthy. They have a lot of books to read, they play games and smoke, and for awhile they will be able to bear up in their captivity; but not for long, not for very long, I take it. I am told they have times of deadly brooding and depression. I made them a speech—sitting down. It just happened so. I don't prefer that attitude. Still, it has one advantage—it is only a talk, it doesn't take the form of a speech. I have tried it once before on this trip. However, if a body wants to make sure of having "liberty," and feeling at home, he had better stand up, of course. I advised them at considerable length to stay where they were—they would get used to it and like it presently; if they got out they would only get in again somewhere else, by the look of their countenances; and I promised to go and see the President and do what I could to get him to double their jail-terms.

We had a very good sociable time till the permitted time was up and a little over, and we outsiders had to go. I went again to-day, but the Rev. Mr. Gray had just arrived, and the warden, a genial, elderly Boer named Du Plessis—explained that his orders wouldn't allow him to admit saint and sinner at the same time, particularly on a Sunday. Du Plessis—descended from the Huguenot fugitives, you see, of 200 years ago—but he hasn't any French left in him now—all Dutch.

It gravels me to think what a goose I was to make Livy and Clara remain in Durban; but I wanted to save them the 30-hour railway trip to Johannesburg. And Durban and its climate and opulent foliage were so lovely, and the friends there were so choice and so hearty that I sacrificed myself in their interests, as I thought. It is just the beginning of winter, and although the days are hot, the nights are cool. But it's lovely weather in these regions, too; and the friends are as lovely as the weather, and Johannesburg and Pretoria are brimming with interest. I talk here twice more, then return to Johannesburg next Wednesday for a fifth talk there; then to the Orange Free State capital, then to some town on the way to Port Elizabeth, where the two will join us by sea from Durban; then the gang will go to Kimberley and presently to the Cape—and so, in the course of time, we shall get through and sail for England; and then we will hunt up a quiet village and I will write and Livy edit, for a few months, while Clara and Susy and Jean study music and things in London.

We have had noble good times everywhere and every day, from Cleveland, July 15, to Pretoria, May 24, and never a dull day either on sea or land, notwithstanding the carbuncles and things. Even when I was laid up 10 days at Jeypore in India we had the charmingest times with English friends. All over India the English well, you will never know how good and fine they are till you see them.

Midnight and after! and I must do many things to-day, and lecture tonight.

A world of thanks to you, Joe dear, and a world of love to all of you.

*MARK.*

*Perhaps for readers of a later day a word as to what constituted the Jameson raid would not be out of place here. Dr. Leander Starr*

*Jameson was an English physician, located at Kimberley. President Kruger (Oom Paul), head of the South African Republic, was one of his patients; also, Lobengula, the Matabele chief. From Lobengula concessions were obtained which led to the formation of the South African Company. Jameson gave up his profession and went in for conquest, associating himself with the projects of Cecil Rhodes. In time he became administrator of Rhodesia. By the end of 1894. he was in high feather, and during a visit to England was feted as a sort of romantic conqueror of the olden time. Perhaps this turned his head; at all events at the end of 1895 came the startling news that "Dr. Jim," as he was called, at the head of six hundred men, had ridden into the Transvaal in support of a Rhodes scheme for an uprising at Johannesburg. The raid was a failure. Jameson, and those other knights of adventure, were captured by the forces of "Oom Paul," and some of them barely escaped execution. The Boer president handed them over to the English Government for punishment, and they received varying sentences, but all were eventually released. Jameson, later, became again prominent in South-African politics, but there is no record of any further raids.*

.........................

*The Clemens party sailed from South Africa the middle of July, 1896, and on the last day of the month reached England. They had not planned to return to America, but to spend the winter in or near London in some quiet place where Clemens could write the book of his travels.*

*The two daughters in America, Susy and Jean, were expected to arrive August 12th, but on that day there came, instead, a letter saying that Susy Clemens was not well enough to sail. A cable inquiry was immediately sent, but the reply when it came was not satisfactory, and Mrs. Clemens and Clara sailed for America without further delay. This was on August 15th. Three days later, in the old home at Hartford, Susy Clemens died of cerebral fever. She had been visiting Mrs. Charles Dudley Warner, but by the physician's advice had been removed to the comfort and quiet of her own home, only a few steps away.*

*Mark Twain, returning from his triumphant tour of the world in the hope that soon, now, he might be free from debt, with his family happily gathered about him, had to face alone this cruel blow. There was no purpose in his going to America; Susy would be buried long before his arrival. He awaited in England the return of his broken family. They lived that winter in a quiet corner of Chelsea, No. 23 Tedworth Square.*

To Rev. Joseph H. Twichell, in Hartford, Conn.:

*Permanent address:*

*% CHATTO & WINDUS*

*111 T. MARTIN'S LANE, LONDON,*

*Sept. 27, '96.*

Through Livy and Katy I have learned, dear old Joe, how loyally you stood poor Susy's friend, and mine, and Livy's: how you came all the way down, twice, from your summer refuge on your merciful errands to bring the peace and comfort of your beloved presence, first to that poor child, and again to the broken heart of her poor desolate mother. It was like you; like your good great heart, like your matchless and unmatchable self. It was no surprise to me to learn that you stayed by Susy long hours, careless of fatigue and heat, it was no surprise to me to learn that you could still the storms that swept her spirit when no other could; for she loved you, revered you, trusted you, and "Uncle Joe" was no empty phrase upon her lips! I am grateful to you, Joe, grateful to the bottom of my heart, which has always been filled with love for you, and respect and admiration; and I would have chosen you out of all the world to take my place at Susy's side and Livy's in those black hours.

Susy was a rare creature; the rarest that has been reared in Hartford in this generation. And Livy knew it, and you knew it, and Charley Warner and George, and Harmony, and the Hillyers and the Dunhams and the Cheneys, and Susy and Lilly, and the Bunces, and Henry Robinson and Dick Burton, and perhaps others. And I also was of the number, but not in the same degree—for she was above my duller comprehension. I merely knew that she was my superior in fineness of mind, in the delicacy and subtlety of her intellect, but to fully measure her I was not competent. I know her better now; for I have read her private writings and sounded the deeps of her mind; and I know better, now, the treasure that was mine than I knew it when I had it. But I have this consolation: that dull as I was, I always knew enough to be proud when she commended me or my work—as proud as if Livy had done it herself—and I took it as the accolade from the hand of genius. I see now—as Livy always saw—that she had greatness in her; and that she herself was dimly conscious of it.

And now she is dead—and I can never tell her.

God bless you Joe—and all of your house.

*S. L. C.*

To Mr. Henry C. Robinson, Hartford, Conn.:

*LONDON, Sept. 28, '96.*

It is as you say, dear old friend, "the pathos of it" yes, it was a piteous thing—as piteous a tragedy as any the year can furnish. When we started westward upon our long trip at half past ten at night, July 14, 1895, at Elmira, Susy stood on the platform in the blaze of the electric light waving her good-byes to us as the train glided away, her mother throwing back kisses and watching her through her tears. One year, one month, and one week later, Clara and her mother having exactly completed the circuit of the globe, drew up at that platform at the same hour of the night, in the same train and the same car—and again Susy had come a journey and was near at hand to meet them. She was waiting in the house she was born in, in her coffin.

All the circumstances of this death were pathetic—my brain is worn to rags rehearsing them. The mere death would have been cruelty enough, without overloading it and emphasizing it with that score of harsh and wanton details. The child was taken away when her mother was within three days of her, and would have given three decades for sight of her.

In my despair and unassuageable misery I upbraid myself for ever parting with her. But there is no use in that. Since it was to happen it would have happened.

*With love*

*S. L. C.*

*The life at Tedworth Square that winter was one of almost complete privacy. Of the hundreds of friends which Mark Twain had in London scarcely half a dozen knew his address. He worked steadily on his book of travels, 'Following the Equator', and wrote few letters beyond business communications to Mr. Rogers. In one of these he said, "I am appalled! Here I am trying to load you up with work again after you have been dray-horsing over the same tiresome ground for a year. It's too bad, and I am ashamed of it."*

*But late in November he sent a letter of a different sort—one that was to have an important bearing on the life of a girl today of unique and world-wide distinction.*

To Mrs. H. H. Rogers, in New York City:

For and in behalf of Helen Keller, stone blind and deaf, and formerly dumb.

DEAR MRS. ROGERS,—Experience has convinced me that when one wishes to set a hard-worked man at something which he mightn't prefer to be bothered with, it is best to move upon him behind his wife. If she can't convince him it isn't worth while for other people to try.

Mr. Rogers will remember our visit with that astonishing girl at Lawrence Hutton's house when she was fourteen years old. Last July, in Boston, when she was 16 she underwent the Harvard examination for admission to Radcliffe College. She passed without a single condition. She was allowed the same amount of time that is granted to other applicants, and this was shortened in her case by the fact that the question papers had to be read to her. Yet she scored an average of 90 as against an average of 78 on the part of the other applicants.

It won't do for America to allow this marvelous child to retire from her studies because of poverty. If she can go on with them she will make a fame that will endure in history for centuries. Along her special lines she is the most extraordinary product of all the ages.

There is danger that she must retire from the struggle for a College degree for lack of support for herself and for Miss Sullivan, (the teacher who has been with her from the start—Mr. Rogers will remember her.) Mrs. Hutton writes to ask me to interest rich Englishmen in her case, and I would gladly try, but my secluded life will not permit it. I see nobody. Nobody knows my address. Nothing but the strictest hiding can enable me to write my long book in time.

So I thought of this scheme: Beg you to lay siege to your husband and get him to interest himself and Mess. John D. and William Rockefeller and the other Standard Oil chiefs in Helen's case; get them to subscribe an annual aggregate of six or seven hundred or a thousand dollars—and agree to continue this for three or four years, until she has completed her college course. I'm not trying to limit their generosity—indeed no, they may pile that Standard Oil, Helen Keller College Fund as high as they please, they have my consent.

Mrs. Hutton's idea is to raise a permanent fund the interest upon which shall support Helen and her teacher and put them out of the fear of want. I shan't say a word against it, but she will find it a difficult and disheartening job, and meanwhile what is to become of that miraculous girl?

No, for immediate and sound effectiveness, the thing is for you to plead with Mr. Rogers for this hampered wonder of your sex, and send him clothed with plenary powers to plead with the other chiefs—they have spent mountains of money upon the worthiest benevolences, and I think that the same spirit which moved them to put their hands down through their hearts into their pockets in those cases will answer "Here!" when its name is called in this one. 638

There—I don't need to apologize to you or to H. H. for this appeal that I am making; I know you too well for that.

Good-bye with love to all of you

*S. L. CLEMENS.*

Laurence Hutton is on the staff of Harper's Monthly—close by, and handy when wanted.

*The plea was not made in vain. Mr. and Mrs. Rogers interested themselves most liberally in Helen Keller's fortune, and certainly no one can say that any of those who contributed to her success ever had reason for disappointment.*

*In his letter of grateful acknowledgment, which follows, Clemens also takes occasion to thank Mr. Rogers for his further efforts in the matter of his own difficulties. This particular reference concerns the publishing, complications which by this time had arisen between the American Publishing Company, of Hartford, and the house in Franklin Square.*

*LONDON, Dec. 22, '96.*

DEAR MRS. ROGERS,—It is superb! And I am beyond measure grateful to you both. I knew you would be interested in that wonderful girl, and that Mr. Rogers was already interested in her and touched by her; and I was sure that if nobody else helped her you two would; but you have gone far and away beyond the sum I expected—may your lines fall in pleasant places here and Hereafter for it!

The Huttons are as glad and grateful as they can be, and I am glad for their sakes as well as for Helen's.

I want to thank Mr. Rogers for crucifying himself again on the same old cross between Bliss and Harper; and goodness knows I hope he will come to enjoy it above all other dissipations yet, seeing that it has about it the elements of stability and permanency. However, at any time that he says sign, we're going to do it.

*Ever sincerely Yours*

*S. L. CLEMENS.*

## XXXVI. LETTERS 1897. LONDON, SWITZERLAND, VIENNA

*Mark Twain worked steadily on his book that sad winter and managed to keep the gloom out of his chapters, though it is noticeable that 'Following the Equator' is more serious than his other books of travel. He wrote few letters, and these only to his three closest friends, Howells, Twichell, and Rogers. In the letter to Twichell, which follows, there is mention of two unfinished manuscripts which he expects to resume. One of these was a dream story, enthusiastically begun, but perhaps with insufficient plot to carry it through, for it never reached conclusion. He had already tried it in one or two forms and would begin it again presently. The identity of the other tale is uncertain.*

To Rev. J. H. Twichell, in Hartford:

*LONDON, Jan. 19, '97.*

DEAR JOE,—Do I want you to write to me? Indeed I do. I do not want most people to write, but I do want you to do it. The others break my heart, but you will not. You have a something divine in you that is not in other men. You have the touch that heals, not lacerates. And you know the secret places of our hearts. You know our life—the outside of it—as the others do—and the inside of it—which they do not. You have seen our whole voyage. You have seen us go to sea, a cloud of sail—and the flag at the peak; and you see us now, chartless, adrift—derelicts; battered, water-logged, our sails a ruck of rags, our pride gone. For it is gone. And there is nothing in its place. The vanity of life was all we had, and there is no more vanity left in us. We are even ashamed of that we had; ashamed that we trusted the promises of life and builded high—to come to this!

I did know that Susy was part of us; I did not know that she could go away; I did not know that she could go away, and take our lives with her, yet leave our dull bodies behind. And I did not know what she was. To me she was but treasure in the bank; the amount known, the need to look at it daily, handle it, weigh it, count it, realize it, not necessary; and now that I would do it, it is too late; they tell me it is not there, has vanished away in a night, the bank is broken, my fortune is gone, I am a pauper. How am I to comprehend this? How am I to have it? Why am I robbed, and who is benefited?

Ah, well, Susy died at home. She had that privilege. Her dying eyes rested upon nothing that was strange to them, but only upon things which they had known and loved always and which had made her young years glad; and she had you, and Sue, and Katy, and John, and Ellen. This was happy fortune—I am thankful that it was vouchsafed to her. If she had died in another house-well, I think I could not have borne that. To us, our house was not unsentient matter—it had a heart, and a soul, and eyes to see us with; and approvals, and solicitudes, and deep sympathies; it was of us, and we were in its confidence, and lived in its grace and in the peace of its benediction. We never came home from an absence that its face did not light up and speak out its eloquent welcome—and we could not enter it unmoved. And could we now, oh, now, in spirit we should enter it unshod.

I am trying to add to the "assets" which you estimate so generously. No, I am not. The thought is not in my mind. My purpose is other. I am working, but it is for the sake of the work—the "surcease of sorrow" that is found there. I work all the days, and trouble vanishes away when I use that magic. This book will not long stand between it and me, now; but that is no matter, I have many unwritten books to fly to for my preservation; the interval between the finishing of this one and the beginning of the next will not be more than an hour, at most. Continuances, I mean; for two of them are already well along—in fact have reached exactly the same stage in their journey: 19,000 words each. The present one will contain 180,000 words—130,000 are done. I am well protected; but Livy! She has nothing in the world to turn to; nothing but housekeeping, and doing things for the children and me. She does not see people, and cannot; books have lost their interest for her. She sits solitary; and all the day, and all the days, wonders how it all happened, and why. We others were always busy with our affairs, but Susy was her comrade—had to be driven from her loving persecutions—sometimes at 1 in the morning. To Livy the persecutions were welcome. It was heaven to her to be plagued like that. But it is ended now. Livy stands so in need of help; and none among us all could help her like you.

Some day you and I will walk again, Joe, and talk. I hope so. We could have such talks! We are all grateful to you and Harmony—how grateful it is not given to us to say in words. We pay as we can, in love; and in this coin practicing no economy.

*Good bye, dear old Joe!*

*MARK.*

*The letters to Mr. Rogers were, for the most part, on matters of business, but in one of them he said: "I am going to write with all my might on this book, and follow it up with others as fast as I can in the hope that within three years I can clear out the stuff that is in me waiting to be written, and that I shall then die in the promptest kind of a way and no fooling around." And in one he wrote: "You are the best friend ever a man had, and the surest."*

To W. D. Howells, in New York

*LONDON, Feb. 23, '97.*

DEAR HOWELLS,—I find your generous article in the Weekly, and I want to thank you for its splendid praises, so daringly uttered and so warmly. The words stir the dead heart of me, and throw a glow of color into a life which sometimes seems to have grown wholly wan. I don't mean that I am miserable; no—worse than that—indifferent. Indifferent to nearly everything but work. I like that; I enjoy it, and stick to it. I do it without purpose and without ambition; merely for the love of it.

This mood will pass, some day—there is history for it. But it cannot pass until my wife comes up out of the submergence. She was always so quick to recover herself before, but now there is no rebound, and we are dead people who go through the motions of life. Indeed I am a mud image, and it will puzzle me to know what it is in me that writes, and has comedy-fancies and finds pleasure in phrasing them. It is a law of our nature, of course, or it wouldn't happen; the thing in me forgets the presence of the mud image and goes its own way, wholly unconscious of it and apparently of no kinship with it. I have finished my book, but I go on as if the end were indefinitely away—as indeed it is. There is no hurry—at any rate there is no limit.

Jean's spirits are good; Clara's are rising. They have youth—the only thing that was worth giving to the race.

These are sardonic times. Look at Greece, and that whole shabby muddle. But I am not sorry to be alive and privileged to look on. If I were not a hermit I would go to the House every day and see those people scuffle over it and blether about the brotherhood of the human race. This has been a bitter year for English pride, and I don't like to see England humbled—that is, not too much. We are sprung from her loins, and it hurts me. I am for republics, and she is the only comrade we've got, in that. We can't count France, and there is hardly enough of Switzerland to count. Beneath the governing crust England is sound-hearted—and sincere, too, and nearly straight. But I am appalled to notice that the wide extension of the surface has damaged her manners, and made her rather Americanly uncourteous on the lower levels.

Won't you give our love to the Howellses all and particular?

*Sincerely yours*

*S. L. CLEMENS.*

*The travel-book did not finish easily, and more than once when he thought it completed he found it necessary to cut and add and change. The final chapters were not sent to the printer until the middle of May, and in a letter to Mr. Rogers he commented: "A successful book is not made of what is in it, but what is left out of it." Clemens was at the time contemplating a uniform edition of his books, and in one of his letters to Mr. Rogers on the matter he wrote, whimsically, "Now I was proposing to make a thousand sets at a hundred dollars a set, and do the whole canvassing myself..... I would load up every important jail and saloon in America with de luxe editions of my books. But Mrs. Clemens and the children object to this, I do not know why." And, in a moment of depression: "You see the lightning refuses to strike me—there is where the defect is. We have to do our own striking as Barney Barnato did. But nobody ever gets the courage until he goes crazy."*

*They went to Switzerland for the summer to the village of Weggis, on Lake Lucerne—"The charmingest place we ever lived in," he declared, "for repose, and restfulness, and superb scenery." It was here that he began work on a new story of Tom and Huck, and at least upon one other manuscript. From a brief note to Mr. Rogers we learn something of his employments and economies.*

To Henry H. Rogers, in New York:

*LUCERNE, August the something or other, 1897.*

DEAR MR. ROGERS,—I am writing a novel, and am getting along very well with it.

I believe that this place (Weggis, half an hour from Lucerne,) is the loveliest in the world, and the most satisfactory. We have a small house on the hillside all to ourselves, and our meals are served in it from the inn below on the lake shore. Six francs a day per head, house and food included. The scenery is beyond comparison beautiful. We have a row boat and some bicycles, and good roads, and no visitors. Nobody knows we are here. And Sunday in heaven is noisy compared to this quietness.

*Sincerely yours*

*S. L. C.*

To Rev. J. H. Twichell, in Hartford:

*LUCERNE, Aug. 22, '97.*

DEAR JOE,—Livy made a noble find on the Lucerne boat the other day on one of her shopping trips—George Williamson Smith—did I tell you about it? We had a lovely time with him, and such intellectual refreshment as we had not tasted in many a month.

And the other night we had a detachment of the jubilee Singers—6. I had known one of them in London 24 years ago. Three of the 6 were born in slavery, the others were children of slaves. How charming they were—in spirit, manner, language, pronunciation, enunciation, grammar, phrasing, matter, carriage, clothes—in every detail that goes to make the real lady and gentleman, and welcome guest. We went down to the village hotel and bought our tickets and entered the beer-hall, where a crowd of German and Swiss men and women sat grouped at round tables with their beer mugs in front of them—self-contained and unimpressionable looking people, an indifferent and unposted and disheartened audience—and up at the far end of the room sat the Jubilees in a row. The Singers got up and stood—the talking and glass jingling went on. Then rose and swelled out above those common earthly sounds one of those rich chords the secret of whose make only the Jubilees possess, and a spell fell upon that house. It was fine to see the faces light up with the pleased wonder and surprise of it. No one was indifferent any more; and when the singers finished, the camp was theirs. It was a triumph. It reminded me of Launcelot riding in Sir Kay's armor and astonishing complacent Knights who thought they had struck a soft thing. The Jubilees sang a lot of pieces. Arduous and painstaking cultivation has not diminished or artificialized their music, but on the contrary—to my surprise—has mightily reinforced its eloquence and beauty. Away back in the beginning—to my mind—their music made all other vocal music cheap; and that early notion is emphasized now. It is utterly beautiful, to me; and it moves me infinitely more than any other music can. I think that in the Jubilees and their songs America has produced the perfectest flower of the ages; and I wish it were a foreign product, so that she would worship it and lavish money on it and go properly crazy over it.

Now, these countries are different: they would do all that, if it were native. It is true they praise God, but that is merely a formality, and nothing in it; they open out their whole hearts to no foreigner.

The musical critics of the German press praise the Jubilees with great enthusiasm—acquired technique etc, included.

One of the jubilee men is a son of General Joe Johnson, and was educated by him after the war. The party came up to the house and we had a pleasant time.

This is paradise, here—but of course we have got to leave it by and by. The 18th of August—[Anniversary of Susy Clemens's death.]—has come and gone, Joe—and we still seem to live.

*With love from us all.*

*MARK.*

*Clemens declared he would as soon spend his life in Weggis "as anywhere else in the geography," but October found them in Vienna for the winter, at the Hotel Metropole. The Austrian capital was just then in a political turmoil, the character of which is hinted in the following:*

To Rev. J. H. Twichell, in Hartford:

*HOTEL METROPOLE,*

*VIENNA, Oct. 23, '97.*

DEAR JOE,—We are gradually getting settled down and wonted. Vienna is not a cheap place to live in, but I have made one small arrangement which: has a distinctly economical aspect. The Vice Consul made the contract for me yesterday-to-wit: a barber is to come every morning 8.30 and shave me and keep my hair trimmed for $2.50 a month. I used to pay $1.50 per shave in our house in Hartford.

Does it suggest to you reflections when you reflect that this is the most important event which has happened to me in ten days—unless I count—in my handing a cabman over to the police day before yesterday, with the proper formalities, and promised to appear in court when his case comes up.

If I had time to run around and talk, I would do it; for there is much politics agoing, and it would be interesting if a body could get the hang of it. It is Christian and Jew by the horns—the advantage with the superior man, as usual—the superior man being the Jew every time and in all countries. Land, Joe, what chance would the Christian have in a country where there were 3 Jews to 10 Christians! Oh, not the shade of a shadow of a chance. The difference between the brain of the average Christian and that of the average Jew—certainly in Europe—is about the difference between a tadpole's and an Archbishop's. It's a marvelous, race—by long odds the most marvelous that the world has produced, I suppose.

And there's more politics—the clash between Czech and Austrian. I wish I could understand these quarrels, but of course I can't.

With the abounding love of us all

*MARK.*

*In Following the Equator there was used an amusing picture showing Mark Twain on his trip around the world. It was a trick photograph made from a picture of Mark Twain taken in a steamer-chair, cut out and combined with a dilapidated negro-cart drawn by a horse and an ox. In it Clemens appears to be sitting luxuriously in the end of the disreputable cart. His companions are two negroes. To the creator of this ingenious effect Mark Twain sent a characteristic acknowledgment.*

To T. S. Frisbie

*VIENNA, Oct. 25, '97.*

MR. T. S. FRISBIE,—Dear Sir: The picture has reached me, and has moved me deeply. That was a steady, sympathetic and honorable team, and although it was not swift, and not showy, it pulled me around the globe successfully, and always attracted its proper share of attention, even in the midst of the most costly and fashionable turnouts. Princes and dukes and other experts were always enthused by the harness and could hardly keep from trying to buy it. The barouche does not look as fine, now, as it did earlier-but that was before the earthquake.

The portraits of myself and uncle and nephew are very good indeed, and your impressionist reproduction of the palace of the Governor General of India is accurate and full of tender feeling.

I consider that this picture is much more than a work of art. How much more, one cannot say with exactness, but I should think two-thirds more.

*Very truly yours*

*MARK TWAIN.*

*Following the Equator was issued by subscription through Mark Twain's old publishers, the Blisses, of Hartford. The sale of it was large, not only on account of the value of the book itself, but also because of the sympathy of the American people with Mark Twain's brave struggle to pay his debts. When the newspapers began to print exaggerated stories of the vast profits that were piling up, Bliss became worried, for he thought it would modify the sympathy. He cabled Clemens for a denial, with the following result:*

To Frank E. Bliss, in Hartford:

*VIENNA, Nov. 4, 1897.*

DEAR BLISS,—Your cablegram informing me that a report is in circulation which purports to come from me and which says I have recently made $82,000 and paid all my debts has just reached me, and I have cabled back my regret to you that it is not true. I wrote a letter—a private letter—a short time ago, in which I expressed the belief that I should be out of debt within the next twelvemonth. If you make as much as usual for me out of the book, that belief will crystallize into a fact, and I shall be wholly out of debt. I am encoring you now.

It is out of that moderate letter that the Eighty-Two Thousand-Dollar mare's nest has developed. But why do you worry about the various reports? They do not worry me. They are not unfriendly, and I don't see how they can do any harm. Be patient; you have but a little while to wait; the possible reports are nearly all in. It has been reported that I was seriously ill—it was another man; dying—it was another man; dead—the other man again. It has been reported that I have received a legacy it was another man; that I am out of debt—it was another man; and now comes this $82,000—still another man. It has been reported that I am writing books—for publication; I am not doing anything of the kind. It would surprise (and gratify) me if I should be able to get another book ready for the press within the next three years. You can see, yourself, that there isn't anything more to be reported—invention is exhausted. Therefore, don't worry, Bliss—the long night is breaking. As far as I can see, nothing remains to be reported, except that I have become a foreigner. When you hear it, don't you believe it. And don't take the trouble to deny it. Merely just raise the American flag on our house in Hartford, and let it talk.

*Truly yours,*

*MARK TWAIN.*

P. S. This is not a private letter. I am getting tired of private letters.

To Rev. J. H. Twichell, in Hartford:

*VIENNA*

*HOTEL METROPOLE, NOV. 19, '97.*

DEAR JOE,—Above is our private (and permanent) address for the winter. You needn't send letters by London.

I am very much obliged for Forrest's Austro-Hungarian articles. I have just finished reading the first one: and in it I find that his opinion and Vienna's are the same, upon a point which was puzzling me—the paucity (no, the absence) of Austrian Celebrities. He and Vienna both say the country cannot afford to allow great names to grow up; that the whole safety and prosperity of the Empire depends upon keeping things quiet; can't afford to have geniuses springing up and developing ideas and stirring the public soul. I am assured that every time a man finds himself blooming into fame, they just softly snake him down and relegate him to a wholesome obscurity. It is curious and interesting.

Three days ago the New York World sent and asked a friend of mine (correspondent of a London daily) to get some Christmas greetings from the celebrities of the Empire. She spoke of this. Two or three bright Austrians were present. They said "There are none who are known all over the world! none who have achieved fame; none who can point to their work and say it is known far and wide in the earth: there are no names; Kossuth (known because he had a father) and Lecher, who made the 12 hour speech; two names-nothing more. Every other country in the world, perhaps, has a giant or two whose heads are away up and can be seen, but ours. We've got the material—have always had it—but we have to suppress it; we can't afford to let it develop; our political salvation depends upon tranquillity—always has."

Poor Livy! She is laid up with rheumatism; but she is getting along now. We have a good doctor, and he says she will be out of bed in a couple of days, but must stay in the house a week or ten.

Clara is working faithfully at her music, Jean at her usual studies, and we all send love.

*MARK.*

*Mention has already been made of the political excitement in Vienna. The trouble between the Hungarian and German legislative bodies presently became violent. Clemens found himself intensely interested, and was present in one of the galleries when it was cleared by the police. All sorts of stories were circulated as to what happened to him, one of which was cabled to America. A letter to Twichell sets forth what really happened.*

To Rev. J. H. Twichell, in Hartford:

*HOTEL METROPOLE,*

*VIENNA, Dec. 10, '97.*

DEAR JOE,—Pond sends me a Cleveland paper with a cablegram from here in it which says that when the police invaded the parliament and expelled the 11 members I waved my handkerchief and shouted 'Hoch die Deutschen!' and got hustled out. Oh dear, what a pity it is that one's adventures never happen! When the Ordner (sergeant-at-arms) came up to our gallery and was hurrying the people out, a friend tried to get leave for me to stay, by saying, "But this gentleman is a foreigner—you don't need to turn him out—he won't do any harm."

"Oh, I know him very well—I recognize him by his pictures; and I should be very glad to let him stay, but I haven't any choice, because of the strictness of the orders."

And so we all went out, and no one was hustled. Below, I ran across the London Times correspondent, and he showed me the way into the first gallery and I lost none of the show. The first gallery had not misbehaved, and was not disturbed.

... We cannot persuade Livy to go out in society yet, but all the lovely people come to see her; and Clara and I go to dinner parties, and around here and there, and we all have a most hospitable good time. Jean's woodcarving flourishes, and her other studies.

Good-bye Joe—and we all love all of you.

*MARK.*

*Clemens made an article of the Austrian troubles, one of the best things he ever wrote, and certainly one of the clearest elucidations of the Austro-Hungarian confusions. It was published in Harper's Magazine, and is now included in his complete works.*

*Thus far none of the Webster Company debts had been paid—at least, none of importance. The money had been accumulating in Mr. Rogers's hands, but Clemens was beginning to be depressed by the heavy burden. He wrote asking for relief.*

Fragment of a letter to H. H. Rogers, in New York:

DEAR MR. ROGERS,—I throw up the sponge. I pull down the flag. Let us begin on the debts. I cannot bear the weight any longer. It totally unfits me for work. I have lost three entire months now. In that time I have begun twenty magazine articles and books—and flung every one of them aside in turn. The debts interfered every time, and took the spirit out of any work. And yet I have worked like a bond slave and wasted no time and spared no effort——

Rogers wrote, proposing a plan for beginning immediately upon the debts. Clemens replied enthusiastically, and during the next few weeks wrote every few days, expressing his delight in liquidation.

*Extracts from letters to H. H. Rogers, in New York:*

... We all delighted with your plan. Only don't leave B—out. Apparently that claim has been inherited by some women—daughters, no doubt. We don't want to see them lose any thing. B——- is an ass, and disgruntled, but I don't care for that. I am responsible for the money and must do the best I can to pay it..... I am writing hard—writing for the creditors.

*Dec. 29.*

Land we are glad to see those debts diminishing. For the first time in my life I am getting more pleasure out of paying money out than pulling it in.

*Jan. 2.*

Since we have begun to pay off the debts I have abundant peace of mind again—no sense of burden. Work is become a pleasure again—it is not labor any longer.

*March 7.*

Mrs. Clemens has been reading the creditors' letters over and over again and thanks you deeply for sending them, and says it is the only really happy day she has had since Susy died.

## XXXVII. LETTERS, 1898, TO HOWELLS AND TWICHELL. LIFE IN VIENNA. PAYMENT OF THE DEBTS. ASSASSINATION OF THE EMPRESS.

The end of January saw the payment of the last of Mark Twain's debts. Once more he stood free before the world—a world that sounded his praises. The latter fact rather amused him. "Honest men must be pretty scarce," he said, "when they make so much fuss over even a defective specimen." When the end was in sight Clemens wrote the news to Howells in a letter as full of sadness as of triumph.

To W. D. Howells, in New York:

*HOTEL METROPOLE,*

*VIENNA, Jan. 22, '98.*

DEAR HOWELLS,—Look at those ghastly figures. I used to write it "Hartford, 1871." There was no Susy then—there is no Susy now. And how much lies between—one long lovely stretch of scented fields, and meadows, and shady woodlands, and suddenly Sahara! You speak of the glorious days of that old time—and they were. It is my quarrel—that traps like that are set. Susy and Winnie given us, in miserable sport, and then taken away.

About the last time I saw you I described to you the culminating disaster in a book I was going to write (and will yet, when the stroke is further away)—a man's dead daughter brought to him when he had been through all other possible misfortunes—and I said it couldn't be done as it ought to be done except by a man who had lived it—it must be written with the blood out of a man's heart. I couldn't know, then, how soon I was to be made competent. I have thought of it many a time since. If you were here I think we could cry down each other's necks, as in your dream. For we are a pair of old derelicts drifting around, now, with some of our passengers gone and the sunniness of the others in eclipse.

I couldn't get along without work now. I bury myself in it up to the ears. Long hours—8 and 9 on a stretch, sometimes. And all the days, Sundays included. It isn't all for print, by any means, for much of it fails to suit me; 50,000 words of it in the past year. It was because of the deadness which invaded me when Susy died. But I have made a change lately—into dramatic work—and I find it absorbingly entertaining. I don't know that I can write a play that will play: but no matter, I'll write half a dozen that won't, anyway. Dear me, I didn't know there was such fun in it. I'll write twenty that won't play. I get into immense spirits as soon as my day is fairly started. Of course a good deal of this friskiness comes of my being in sight of land—on the Webster & Co. debts, I mean. (Private.) We've lived close to the bone and saved every cent we could, and there's no undisputed claim, now, that we can't cash. I have marked this "private" because it is for the friends who are attending to the matter for us in New York to reveal it when they want to and if they want to. There are only two claims which I dispute and which I mean to look into personally before I pay them. But they are small. Both together they amount to only $12,500. I hope you will never get the like of the load saddled onto you that was saddled onto me 3 years ago. And yet there is such a solid pleasure in paying the things that I reckon maybe it is worth while to get into that kind of a hobble, after all. Mrs. Clemens gets millions of delight out of it; and the children have never uttered one complaint about the scrimping, from the beginning.

We all send you and all of you our love.

*MARK.*

*Howells wrote: "I wish you could understand how unshaken you are, you old tower, in every way; your foundations are struck so deep that you will catch the sunshine of immortal years, and bask in the same light as Cervantes and Shakespeare."*

*The Clemens apartments at the Metropole became a sort of social clearing-house of the Viennese art and literary life, much more like an embassy than the home of a mere literary man. Celebrities in every walk of life, persons of social and official rank, writers for the press, assembled there on terms hardly possible in any other home in Vienna. Wherever Mark Twain appeared in public he was a central figure. Now and then he read or spoke to aid some benefit, and these were great gatherings attended by members of the royal family. It was following one such event that the next letter was written.*

(Private)

To Rev. J. H. Twichell, in Hartford:

*HOTEL METROPOLE,*

*VIENNA, Feb. 3, '98.*

DEAR JOE, There's that letter that I began so long ago—you see how it is: can't get time to finish anything. I pile up lots of work, nevertheless. There may be idle people in the world, but I'm not one of them. I say "Private" up there because I've got an adventure to tell, and you mustn't let a breath of it get out. First I thought I would lay it up along with a thousand others that I've laid up for the same purpose—to talk to you about, but—those others have vanished out of my memory; and that must not happen with this.

The other night I lectured for a Vienna charity; and at the end of it Livy and I were introduced to a princess who is aunt to the heir apparent of the imperial throne—a beautiful lady, with a beautiful spirit, and very cordial in her praises of my books and thanks to me for writing them; and glad to meet me face to face and shake me by the hand—just the kind of princess that adorns a fairy tale and makes it the prettiest tale there is.

Very well, we long ago found that when you are noticed by supremacies, the correct etiquette is to go, within a couple of days, and pay your respects in the quite simple form of writing your name in the Visitors' Book kept in the office of the establishment. That is the end of it, and everything is squared up and ship-shape.

So at noon today Livy and I drove to the Archducal palace, and got by the sentries all right, and asked the grandly-uniformed porter for the book and said we wished to write our names in it. And he called a servant in livery and was sending us up stairs; and said her Royal Highness was out but would soon be in. Of course Livy said "No—no—we only want the book;" but he was firm, and said, "You are Americans?"

"Yes."

"Then you are expected, please go up stairs."

"But indeed we are not expected—please let us have the book and—"

"Her Royal Highness will be back in a very little while—she commanded me to tell you so—and you must wait."

Well, the soldiers were there close by—there was no use trying to resist—so we followed the servant up; but when he tried to beguile us into a drawing-room, Livy drew the line; she wouldn't go in. And she wouldn't stay up there, either. She said the princess might come in at any moment and catch us, and it would be too infernally ridiculous for anything. So we went down stairs again—to my unspeakable regret. For it was too darling a comedy to spoil. I was hoping and praying the princess would come, and catch us up there, and that those other Americans who were expected would arrive, and be taken for impostors by the portier, and shot by the sentinels—and then it would all go into the papers, and be cabled all over the world, and make an immense stir and be perfectly lovely. And by that time the princess would discover that we were not the right ones, and the Minister of War would be ordered out, and the garrison, and they would come for us, and there would be another prodigious time, and that would get cabled too, and—well, Joe, I was in a state of perfect bliss. But happily, oh, so happily, that big portier wouldn't let us out—he was sorry, but he must obey orders—we must go back up stairs and wait. Poor Livy—I couldn't help but enjoy her distress. She said we were in a fix, and how were we going to explain, if the princess should arrive before the rightful Americans came? We went up stairs again—laid off our wraps, and were conducted through one drawing room and into another, and left alone there and the door closed upon us.

Livy was in a state of mind! She said it was too theatrically ridiculous; and that I would never be able to keep my mouth shut; that I would be sure to let it out and it would get into the papers—and she tried to make me promise—"Promise what?" I said—"to be quiet about this? Indeed I won't—it's the best thing that ever happened; I'll tell it, and add to it; and I wish Joe and Howells were here to make it perfect; I can't make all the rightful blunders myself—it takes all three of us to do justice to an opportunity like this. I would just like to see Howells get down to his work and explain, and lie, and work his futile and inventionless subterfuges when that princess comes raging in here and wanting to know." But Livy could not hear fun—it was not a time to be trying to be funny—we were in a most miserable and shameful situation, and if—

Just then the door spread wide and our princess and 4 more, and 3 little princes flowed in! Our princess, and her sister the Archduchess Marie Therese (mother to the imperial Heir and to the young girl Archduchesses present, and aunt to the 3 little princes)—and we shook hands all around and sat down and had a most sociable good time for half an hour—and by and by it turned out that we were the right ones, and had been sent for by a messenger who started too late to catch us at the hotel. We were invited for 2 o'clock, but we beat that arrangement by an hour and a half.

Wasn't it a rattling good comedy situation? Seems a kind of pity we were the right ones. It would have been such nuts to see the right ones come, and get fired out, and we chatting along comfortably and nobody suspecting us for impostors.

We send lots and lots of love.

*MARK.*

*The reader who has followed these pages has seen how prone Mark Twain was to fall a victim to the lure of a patent-right—how he wasted several small fortunes on profitless contrivances, and one large one on that insatiable demon of intricacy and despair, the Paige type-setter. It seems incredible that, after that experience and its attending disaster, he should have been tempted again. But scarcely was the ink dry on the receipts from his creditors when he was once more borne into the clouds on the prospect of millions, perhaps even billions, to be made from a marvelous carpet-pattern machine, the invention of Sczezepanik, an Austrian genius. That Clemens appreciated his own tendencies is shown by the parenthetic line with which he opens his letter on the subject to Mr. Rogers. Certainly no man was ever a more perfect prototype of Colonel Sellers than the creator of that lovely, irrepressible visionary.*

To Mr. Rogers, in New York:

*March 24, '98.*

DEAR MR. ROGERS,—(I feel like Col. Sellers).

Mr. Kleinberg [agent for Sczezepanik] came according to appointment, at 8.30 last night, and brought his English-speaking Secretary. I asked questions about the auxiliary invention (which I call "No. 2 ") and got as good an idea of it as I could. It is a machine. It automatically punches the holes in the jacquard cards, and does it with mathematical accuracy. It will do for $1 what now costs $3. So it has value, but "No. 2" is the great thing (the designing invention.) It saves $9 out of $10 and the jacquard looms must have it.

Then I arrived at my new project, and said to him in substance, this:

"You are on the point of selling the No. 2 patents to Belgium, Italy, etc. I suggest that you stop those negotiations and put those people off two or three months. They are anxious now, they will not be less anxious then—just the reverse; people always want a thing that is denied them.

"So far as I know, no great world-patent has ever yet been placed in the grip of a single corporation. This is a good time to begin.

"We have to do a good deal of guess-work here, because we cannot get hold of just the statistics we want. Still, we have some good statistics—and I will use those for a test.

"You say that of the 1500 Austrian textile factories, 800 use the jacquard. Then we will guess that of the 4,000 American factories 2,000 use the jacquard and must have our No. 2.

"You say that a middle-sized Austrian factory employs from 20 to 30 designers and pays them from 800 to 3,000 odd florins a year—(a florin is 2 francs). Let us call the average wage 1500 florins ($600).

"Let us apply these figures (the low wages too) to the 2,000 American factories—with this difference, to guard against over-guessing; that instead of allowing for 20 to 30 designers to a middle-sized factory, we allow only an average of 10 to each of the 2,000 factories—a total of 20,000 designers. Wages at $600, a total of $12,000,000. Let us consider that No. 2 will reduce this expense to $2,000,000 a year. The saving is $5,000,000 per each of the $200,000,000 of capital employed in the jacquard business over there.

"Let us consider that in the countries covered by this patent, an aggregate of $1,500,000,000 of capital is employed in factories requiring No. 2.

"The saving (as above) is $75,000,000 a year. The Company holding in its grip all these patents would collar $50,000,000 of that, as its share. Possibly more.

"Competition would be at an end in the Jacquard business, on this planet. Price-cutting would end. Fluctuations in values would cease. The business would be the safest and surest in the world; commercial panics could not seriously affect it; its stock would be as choice an investment as Government bonds. When the patents died the Company would be so powerful that it could still keep the whole business in its hands. Would you like to grant me the privilege of placing the whole jacquard business of the world in the grip of a single Company? And don't you think that the business would grow-grow like a weed?"

"Ach, America—it is the country of the big! Let me get my breath—then we will talk."

So then we talked—talked till pretty late. Would Germany and England join the combination? I said the Company would know how to persuade them.

Then I asked for a Supplementary Option, to cover the world, and we parted.

I am taking all precautions to keep my name out of print in connection with this matter. And we will now keep the invention itself out of print as well as we can. Descriptions of it have been granted to the "Dry Goods Economist" (New York) and to a syndicate of American papers. I have asked Mr. Kleinberg to suppress these, and he feels pretty sure he can do it.

*With love,*

*S. L. C.*

*If this splendid enthusiasm had not cooled by the time a reply came from Mr. Rogers, it must have received a sudden chill from the letter which he inclosed—the brief and concise report from a carpet-machine expert, who said: "I do not feel that it would be of any value to us in our mills, and the number of jacquard looms in America is so limited that I am of the opinion that there is no field for a company to develop the invention here. A cursory examination of the pamphlet leads me to place no very high value upon the invention, from a practical standpoint."*

*With the receipt of this letter carpet-pattern projects would seem to have suddenly ceased to be a factor in Mark Twain's calculations. Such a letter in the early days of the type-machine would have saved him a great sum in money and years of disappointment. But perhaps he would not have heeded it then.*

*The year 1898 brought the Spanish-American War. Clemens was constitutionally against all wars, but writing to Twichell, whose son had enlisted, we gather that this one was an exception.*

To Rev. J. H. Twichell, in Hartford:

*KALTENLEUTGEBEN, NEAR VIENNA,*

*June 17, '98.*

DEAR JOE,—You are living your war-days over again in Dave, and it must be a strong pleasure, mixed with a sauce of apprehension—enough to make it just schmeck, as the Germans say. Dave will come out with two or three stars on his shoulder-straps if the war holds, and then we shall all be glad it happened.

We started with Bull Run, before. Dewey and Hobson have introduced an improvement on the game this time.

I have never enjoyed a war-even in written history—as I am enjoying this one. For this is the worthiest one that was ever fought, so far as my knowledge goes. It is a worthy thing to fight for one's freedom; it is another sight finer to fight for another man's. And I think this is the first time it has been done.

Oh, never mind Charley Warner, he would interrupt the raising of

Lazarus. He would say, the will has been probated, the property distributed, it will be a world of trouble to settle the rows—better leave well enough alone; don't ever disturb anything, where it's going to break the soft smooth flow of things and wobble our tranquillity.

Company! (Sh! it happens every day—and we came out here to be quiet.)

Love to you all.

*MARK.*

*They were spending the summer at Kaltenleutgeben, a pleasant village near Vienna, but apparently not entirely quiet. Many friends came out from Vienna, including a number of visiting Americans. Clemens, however, appears to have had considerable time for writing, as we gather from the next to Howells.*

To W. D. Howells, in America:

*KALTENLEUTGEBEN, BEI WIEN,*

*Aug. 16, '98.*

DEAR HOWELLS,—Your letter came yesterday. It then occurred to me that I might have known (per mental telegraph) that it was due; for a couple of weeks ago when the Weekly came containing that handsome reference to me I was powerfully moved to write you; and my letter went on writing itself while I was at work at my other literature during the day. But next day my other literature was still urgent—and so on and so on; so my letter didn't get put into ink at all. But I see now, that you were writing, about that time, therefore a part of my stir could have come across the Atlantic per mental telegraph. In 1876 or '75 I wrote 40,000 words of a story called "Simon Wheeler" wherein the nub was the preventing of an execution through testimony furnished by mental telegraph from the other side of the globe. I had a lot of people scattered about the globe who carried in their pockets something like the old mesmerizer-button, made of different metals, and when they wanted to call up each other and have a talk, they "pressed the button" or did something, I don't remember what, and communication was at once opened. I didn't finish the story, though I re-began it in several new ways, and spent altogether 70,000 words on it, then gave it up and threw it aside.

This much as preliminary to this remark: some day people will be able to call each other up from any part of the world and talk by mental telegraph—and not merely by impression, the impression will be articulated into words. It could be a terrible thing, but it won't be, because in the upper civilizations everything like sentimentality (I was going to say sentiment) will presently get materialized out of people along with the already fading spiritualities; and so when a man is called who doesn't wish to talk he will be like those visitors you mention: "not chosen"—and will be frankly damned and shut off.

Speaking of the ill luck of starting a piece of literary work wrong-and again and again; always aware that there is a way, if you could only think it out, which would make the thing slide effortless from the pen—the one right way, the sole form for you, the other forms being for men whose line those forms are, or who are capabler than yourself: I've had no end of experience in that (and maybe I am the only one—let us hope so.) Last summer I started 16 things wrong—3 books and 13 mag. articles—and could only make 2 little wee things, 1500 words altogether, succeed:—only that out of piles and stacks of diligently-wrought MS., the labor of 6 weeks' unremitting effort. I could make all of those things go if I would take the trouble to re-begin each one half a dozen times on a new plan. But none of them was important enough except one: the story I (in the wrong form) mapped out in Paris three or four years ago and told you about in New York under seal of confidence—no other person knows of it but Mrs. Clemens—the story to be called "Which was the Dream?"

A week ago I examined the MS—10,000 words—and saw that the plan was a totally impossible one-for me; but a new plan suggested itself, and straightway the tale began to slide from the pen with ease and confidence. I think I've struck the right one this time. I have already put 12,000 words of it on paper and Mrs. Clemens is pretty outspokenly satisfied with it-a hard critic to content. I feel sure that all of the first half of the story—and I hope three-fourths—will be comedy; but by the former plan the whole of it (except the first 3 chapters) would have been tragedy and unendurable, almost. I think I can carry the reader a long way before he suspects that I am laying a tragedy-trap. In the present form I could spin 16 books out of it with comfort and joy; but I shall deny myself and restrict it to one. (If you should see a little short story in a magazine in the autumn called "My Platonic Sweetheart" written 3 weeks ago) that is not this one. It may have been a suggester, though.

I expect all these singular privacies to interest you, and you are not to let on that they don't.

We are leaving, this afternoon, for Ischl, to use that as a base for the baggage, and then gad around ten days among the lakes and mountains to rest-up Mrs. Clemens, who is jaded with housekeeping. I hope I can get a chance to work a little in spots—I can't tell. But you do it—therefore why should you think I can't?

*[Remainder missing.]*

*The dream story was never completed. It was the same that he had worked on in London, and perhaps again in Switzerland. It would be tried at other times and in other forms, but it never seemed to accommodate itself to a central idea, so that the good writing in it eventually went to waste. The short story mentioned, "My Platonic Sweetheart," a charming, idyllic tale, was not published during Mark Twain's lifetime. Two years after his death it appeared in Harper's Magazine.*

*The assassination of the Empress of Austria at Geneva was the startling event of that summer. In a letter to Twichell Clemens presents the tragedy in a few vivid paragraphs. Later he treated it at some length in a magazine article which, very likely because of personal relations with members of the Austrian court, he withheld from print. It has since been included in a volume of essays, What Is Man, etc.*

To Rev. J. H. Twichell, in Hartford:

*KALTENLEUTGEBEN, Sep. 13, '98.*

DEAR JOE,—You are mistaken; people don't send us the magazines. No—Harper, Century and McClure do; an example I should like to recommend to other publishers. And so I thank you very much for sending me Brander's article. When you say "I like Brander Matthews; he impresses me as a man of parts and power," I back you, right up to the hub—I feel the same way—. And when you say he has earned your gratitude for cuffing me for my crimes against the Leather stockings and the Vicar, I ain't making any objection. Dern your gratitude!

His article is as sound as a nut. Brander knows literature, and loves it; he can talk about it and keep his temper; he can state his case so lucidly and so fairly and so forcibly that you have to agree with him, even when you don't agree with him; and he can discover and praise such merits as a book has, even when they are half a dozen diamonds scattered through an acre of mud. And so he has a right to be a critic.

To detail just the opposite of the above invoice is to describe me. I haven't any right to criticise books, and I don't do it except when I hate them. I often want to criticise Jane Austen, but her books madden me so that I can't conceal my frenzy from the reader; and therefore I have to stop every time I begin.

That good and unoffending lady the Empress is killed by a mad-man, and I am living in the midst of world-history again. The Queen's jubilee last year, the invasion of the Reichsrath by the police, and now this murder, which will still be talked of and described and painted a thousand years from now.

To have a personal friend of the wearer of the crown burst in at the gate in the deep dusk of the evening and say in a voice broken with tears, "My God the Empress is murdered," and fly toward her home before we can utter a question-why, it brings the giant event home to you, makes you a part of it and personally interested; it is as if your neighbor Antony should come flying and say "Caesar is butchered—the head of the world is fallen!"

Of course there is no talk but of this. The mourning is universal and genuine, the consternation is stupefying. The Austrian Empire is being draped with black. Vienna will be a spectacle to see, by next Saturday, when the funeral cortege marches. We are invited to occupy a room in the sumptuous new hotel (the "Krantz" where we are to live during the Fall and Winter) and view it, and we shall go.

Speaking of Mrs. Leiter, there is a noble dame in Vienna, about whom they retail similar slanders. She said in French—she is weak in French—that she had been spending a Sunday afternoon in a gathering of the "demimonde." Meaning the unknown land, that mercantile land, that mysterious half-world which underlies the aristocracy. But these Malaproperies are always inventions—they don't happen.

Yes, I wish we could have some talks; I'm full to the eye-lids. Had a noble good one with Parker and Dunham—land, but we were grateful for that visit!

*Yours with all our loves.*

*MARK.*

*[Inclosed with the foregoing.]*

Among the inadequate attempts to account for the assassination we must concede high rank to the German Emperor's. He justly describes it as a "deed unparalleled for ruthlessness," and then adds that it was "ordained from above."

I think this verdict will not be popular "above." A man is either a free agent or he isn't. If a man is a free agent, this prisoner is responsible for what he has done; but if a man is not a free agent, if the deed was ordained from above, there is no rational way of making this prisoner even partially responsible for it, and the German court cannot condemn him without manifestly committing a crime. Logic is logic; and by disregarding its laws even Emperors as capable and acute as William II can be beguiled into making charges which should not be ventured upon except in the shelter of plenty of lightning-rods.

*MARK.*

*The end of the year 1898 found Mark Twain once more in easy, even luxurious, circumstances. The hard work and good fortune which had enabled him to pay his debts had, in the course of another year, provided what was comparative affluence: His report to Howells is characteristic and interesting.*

To W. D. Howells, in New York:

*HOTEL KRANTZ, WIEN, L. NEVER MARKT 6*

*Dec. 30, '98.*

DEAR HOWELLS,—I begin with a date—including all the details—though I shall be interrupted presently by a South-African acquaintance who is passing through, and it may be many days before I catch another leisure moment. Note how suddenly a thing can become habit, and how indestructible the habit is, afterward! In your house in Cambridge a hundred years ago, Mrs. Howells said to me, "Here is a bunch of your letters, and the dates are of no value, because you don't put any in—the years, anyway." That remark diseased me with a habit which has cost me worlds of time and torture and ink, and millions of vain efforts and buckets of tears to break it, and here it is yet—I could easier get rid of a virtue.....

I hope it will interest you (for I have no one else who would much care to know it) that here lately the dread of leaving the children in difficult circumstances has died down and disappeared and I am now having peace from that long, long nightmare, and can sleep as well as anyone. Every little while, for these three years, now, Mrs. Clemens has come with pencil and paper and figured up the condition of things (she keeps the accounts and the bank-book) and has proven to me that the clouds were lifting, and so has hoisted my spirits temporarily and kept me going till another figuring-up was necessary. Last night she figured up for her own satisfaction, not mine, and found that we own a house and furniture in Hartford; that my English and American copyrights pay an income which represents a value of $200,000; and that we have $107,000 cash in the bank. I have been out and bought a box of 6-cent cigars; I was smoking 4 1/2 centers before.

At the house of an English friend, on Christmas Eve, we saw the Mouse-Trap played and well played. I thought the house would kill itself with laughter. By George they played with life! and it was most devastatingly funny. And it was well they did, for they put us Clemenses in the front seat, and if they played it poorly I would have assaulted them. The head young man and girl were Americans, the other parts were taken by English, Irish and Scotch girls. Then there was a nigger-minstrel show, of the genuine old sort, and I enjoyed that, too, for the nigger-show was always a passion of mine. This one was created and managed by a Quaker doctor from Philada., (23 years old) and he was the middle man. There were 9 others—5 Americans from 5 States and a Scotchman, 2 Englishmen and an Irishman—all post-graduate-medical young fellows, of course—or, it could be music; but it would be bound to be one or the other.

It's quite true—I don't read you "as much as I ought," nor anywhere near half as much as I want to; still I read you all I get a chance to. I saved up your last story to read when the numbers should be complete, but before that time arrived some other admirer of yours carried off the papers. I will watch admirers of yours when the Silver Wedding journey begins, and that will not happen again. The last chance at a bound book of yours was in London nearly two years ago—the last volume of your short things, by the Harpers. I read the whole book twice through and some of the chapters several times, and the reason that that was as far as I got with it was that I lent it to another admirer of yours and he is admiring it yet. Your admirers have ways of their own; I don't know where they get them.

Yes, our project is to go home next autumn if we find we can afford to live in New York. We've asked a friend to inquire about flats and expenses. But perhaps nothing will come of it. We do afford to live in the finest hotel in Vienna, and have 4 bedrooms, a dining-room, a drawing-room, 3 bath-rooms and 3 Vorzimmers, (and food) but we couldn't get the half of it in New York for the same money ($600 a month).

Susy hovers about us this holiday week, and the shadows fall all about us of

*"The days when we went gipsying*

*A long time ago."*

Death is so kind, so benignant, to whom he loves; but he goes by us others and will not look our way. We saw the "Master of Palmyra" last night. How Death, with the gentleness and majesty, made the human grand-folk around him seem little and trivial and silly!

With love from all of us to all of you.

*MARK.*

## XXXVIII. LETTERS, 1899, TO HOWELLS AND OTHERS. VIENNA. LONDON. A SUMMER IN SWEDEN.

The beginning of 1899 found the Clemens family still in Vienna, occupying handsome apartments at the Hotel Krantz. Their rooms, so often thronged with gay and distinguished people, were sometimes called the "Second Embassy." Clemens himself was the central figure of these assemblies. Of all the foreign visitors in the Austrian capital he was the most notable. Everywhere he was surrounded by a crowd of listeners—his sayings and opinions were widely quoted.

A project for world disarmament promulgated by the Czar of Russia would naturally interest Mark Twain, and when William T. Stead, of the Review of Reviews, cabled him for an opinion on the matter, he sent at first a brief word and on the same day followed it with more extended comment. The great war which has since devastated the world gives to this incident an added interest.

To Wm. T. Stead, in London:

No. 1.

*VIENNA, Jan. 9.*

DEAR MR. STEAD,—The Czar is ready to disarm: I am ready to disarm. Collect the others, it should not be much of a task now.

*MARK TWAIN.*

To Wm. T. Stead, in London:

No. 2.

DEAR MR. STEAD,—Peace by compulsion. That seems a better idea than the other. Peace by persuasion has a pleasant sound, but I think we should not be able to work it. We should have to tame the human race first, and history seems to show that that cannot be done. Can't we reduce the armaments little by little—on a pro rata basis—by concert of the powers? Can't we get four great powers to agree to reduce their strength 10 per cent a year and thrash the others into doing likewise? For, of course, we cannot expect all of the powers to be in their right minds at one time. It has been tried. We are not going to try to get all of them to go into the scheme peaceably, are we? In that case I must withdraw my influence; because, for business reasons, I must preserve the outward signs of sanity. Four is enough if they can be securely harnessed together. They can compel peace, and peace without compulsion would be against nature and not operative. A sliding scale of reduction of 10 per cent a year has a sort of plausible look, and I am willing to try that if three other powers will join. I feel sure that the armaments are now many times greater than necessary for the requirements of either peace or war. Take wartime for instance. Suppose circumstances made it necessary for us to fight another Waterloo, and that it would do what it did before—settle a large question and bring peace. I will guess that 400,000 men were on hand at Waterloo (I have forgotten the figures). In five hours they disabled 50,000 men. It took them that tedious, long time because the firearms delivered only two or three shots a minute. But we would do the work now as it was done at Omdurman, with shower guns, raining 600 balls a minute. Four men to a gun—is that the number? A hundred and fifty shots a minute per man. Thus a modern soldier is 149 Waterloo soldiers in one. Thus, also, we can now retain one man out of each 150 in service, disband the others, and fight our Waterloos just as effectively as we did eighty-five years ago. We should do the same beneficent job with 2,800 men now that we did with 400,000 then. The allies could take 1,400 of the men, and give Napoleon 1,400 and then whip him.

But instead what do we see? In war-time in Germany, Russia and France, taken together we find about 8 million men equipped for the field. Each man represents 149 Waterloo men, in usefulness and killing capacity. Altogether they constitute about 350 million Waterloo men, and there are not quite that many grown males of the human race now on this planet. Thus we have this insane fact—that whereas those three countries could arm 18,000 men with modern weapons and make them the equals of 3 million men of Napoleon's day, and accomplish with them all necessary war work, they waste their money and their prosperity creating forces of their populations in piling together 349,982,000 extra Waterloo equivalents which they would have no sort of use for if they would only stop drinking and sit down and cipher a little.

Perpetual peace we cannot have on any terms, I suppose; but I hope we can gradually reduce the war strength of Europe till we get it down to where it ought to be—20,000 men, properly armed. Then we can have all the peace that is worth while, and when we want a war anybody can afford it.

*VIENNA, January 9.*

P. S.—In the article I sent the figures are wrong—"350 million" ought to be 450 million; "349,982,000" ought to be 449,982,000, and the remark about the sum being a little more than the present number of males on the planet—that is wrong, of course; it represents really one and a half the existing males.

*Now and then one of Mark Twain's old comrades still reached out to him across the years. He always welcomed such letters—they came as from a lost land of romance, recalled always with tenderness. He sent light, chaffing replies, but they were never without an undercurrent of affection.*

To Major "Jack" Downing, in Middleport, Ohio:

*HOTEL KRANTZ, WEIN, I, NEUER MART 6,*

*Feb. 26, 1899.*

DEAR MAJOR,—No: it was to Bixby that I was apprenticed. He was to teach me the river for a certain specified sum. I have forgotten what it was, but I paid it. I steered a trip for Bart Bowen, of Keokuk, on the A. T. Lacy, and I was partner with Will Bowen on the A. B. Chambers (one trip), and with Sam Bowen a whole summer on a small Memphis packet.

The newspaper report you sent me is incorrect. Bixby is not 67: he is 97. I am 63 myself, and I couldn't talk plain and had just begun to walk when I apprenticed myself to Bixby who was then passing himself off for 57 and successfully too, for he always looked 60 or 70 years younger than he really was. At that time he was piloting the Mississippi on a Potomac commission granted him by George Washington who was a personal friend of his before the Revolution. He has piloted every important river in America, on that commission, he has also used it as a passport in Russia. I have never revealed these facts before. I notice, too, that you are deceiving the people concerning your age. The printed portrait which you have enclosed is not a portrait of you, but a portrait of me when I was 19. I remember very well when it was common for people to mistake Bixby for your grandson. Is it spreading, I wonder—this disposition of pilots to renew their youth by doubtful methods? Beck Jolly and Joe Bryan—they probably go to Sunday school now—but it will not deceive.

Yes, it is as you say. All of the procession but a fraction has passed. It is time for us all to fall in.

*Sincerely yours,*

*S. L. CLEMENS.*

To W. D. Howells, in New York:

*HOTEL KRANTZ, WIEN I. NEUER MARKT 6*

*April 2, '99.*

DEAR HOWELLS,—I am waiting for the April Harper, which is about due now; waiting, and strongly interested. You are old enough to be a weary man, with paling interests, but you do not show it. You do your work in the same old delicate and delicious and forceful and searching and perfect way. I don't know how you can—but I suspect. I suspect that to you there is still dignity in human life, and that Man is not a joke—a poor joke—the poorest that was ever contrived. Since I wrote my Bible, (last year)—["What Is Man."]—which Mrs. Clemens loathes, and shudders over, and will not listen to the last half nor allow me to print any part of it, Man is not to me the respect-worthy person he was before; and so I have lost my pride in him, and can't write gaily nor praisefully about him any more. And I don't intend to try. I mean to go on writing, for that is my best amusement, but I shan't print much (for I don't wish to be scalped, any more than another.)

April 5. The Harper has come. I have been in Leipzig with your party, and then went on to Karlsbad and saw Mrs. Marsh's encounter with the swine with the toothpick and the other manners—["Their Silver Wedding Journey."]—At this point Jean carried the magazine away.

Is it imagination, or—Anyway I seem to get furtive and fleeting glimpses which I take to be the weariness and condolence of age; indifference to sights and things once brisk with interest; tasteless stale stuff which used to be champagne; the boredom of travel: the secret sigh behind the public smile, the private What-in-hell-did-I-come-for!

But maybe that is your art. Maybe that is what you intend the reader to detect and think he has made a Columbus-discovery. Then it is well done, perfectly done. I wrote my last travel book—[Following the Equator.]—in hell; but I let on, the best I could, that it was an excursion through heaven. Some day I will read it, and if its lying cheerfulness fools me, then I shall believe it fooled the reader. How I did loathe that journey around the world!—except the sea-part and India.

Evening. My tail hangs low. I thought I was a financier—and I bragged to you. I am not bragging, now. The stock which I sold at such a fine profit early in January, has never ceased to advance, and is now worth $60,000 more than I sold it for. I feel just as if I had been spending $20,000 a month, and I feel reproached for this showy and unbecoming extravagance.

Last week I was going down with the family to Budapest to lecture, and to make a speech at a banquet. Just as I was leaving here I got a telegram from London asking for the speech for a New York paper. I (this is strictly private) sent it. And then I didn't make that speech, but another of a quite different character—a speech born of something which the introducer said. If that said speech got cabled and printed, you needn't let on that it was never uttered.

That was a darling night, and those Hungarians were lively people. We were there a week and had a great time. At the banquet I heard their chief orator make a most graceful and easy and beautiful and delicious speech—I never heard one that enchanted me more—although I did not understand a word of it, since it was in Hungarian. But the art of it!—it was superlative.

They are wonderful English scholars, these people; my lecture audience—all Hungarians—understood me perfectly—to judge by the effects. The English clergyman told me that in his congregation are 150 young English women who earn their living teaching their language; and that there are others besides these.

For 60 cents a week the telephone reads the morning news to you at home; gives you the stocks and markets at noon; gives you lessons in 3 foreign languages during 3 hours; gives you the afternoon telegrams; and at night the concerts and operas. Of course even the clerks and seamstresses and bootblacks and everybody else are subscribers.

(Correction. Mrs. Clemens says it is 60 cents a month.)

I am renewing my youth. I made 4 speeches at one banquet here last Saturday night. And I've been to a lot of football matches.

Jean has been in here examining the poll for the Immortals ("Literature," March 24,) in the hope, I think, that at last she should find me at the top and you in second place; and if that is her ambition she has suffered disappointment for the third time—and will never fare any better, I hope, for you are where you belong, by every right. She wanted to know who it is that does the voting, but I was not able to tell her. Nor when the election will be completed and decided.

Next Morning. I have been reading the morning paper. I do it every morning—well knowing that I shall find in it the usual depravities and basenesses and hypocrisies and cruelties that make up civilization, and cause me to put in the rest of the day pleading for the damnation of the human race. I cannot seem to get my prayers answered, yet I do not despair.

(Escaped from) 5 o'clock tea ('sh!) Oh, the American girl in Europe!

Often she is creditable, but sometimes she is just shocking. This one, a minute ago—19, fat-face, raspy voice, pert ways, the self-complacency of God; and with it all a silly laugh (embarrassed) which kept breaking out through her chatter all along, whereas there was no call for it, for she said nothing that was funny. "Spose so many 've told y' how they 'njoyed y'r chapt'r on the Germ' tongue it's bringin' coals to Newcastle Kehe! say anything 'bout it Ke-hehe! Spent m' vacation 'n Russia, 'n saw Tolstoi; he said—" It made me shudder.

April 12. Jean has been in here with a copy of Literature, complaining that I am again behind you in the election of the 10 consecrated members; and seems troubled about it and not quite able to understand it. But I have explained to her that you are right there on the ground, inside the pool-booth, keeping game—and that that makes a large difference in these things.

13th. I have been to the Knustausstellung with Mrs. Clemens. The office of art seems to be to grovel in the dirt before Emperors and this and that and the other damned breed of priests.

*Yrs ever*

*MARK.*

*Howells and Clemens were corresponding regularly again, though not with the frequency of former years. Perhaps neither of them was bubbling over with things to say; perhaps it was becoming yearly less attractive to pick up a pen and write, and then, of course, there was always the discouragement of distance. Once Howells wrote: "I know this will find you in Austria before I can well turn round, but I must make believe you are in Kennebunkport before I can begin it." And in another letter: "It ought to be as pleasant to sit down and write to you as to sit down and talk to you, but it isn't..... The only reason why I write is that I want another letter from you, and because I have a whole afternoon for the job. I have the whole of every afternoon, for I cannot work later than lunch. I am fagged by that time, and Sunday is the only day that brings unbearable leisure. I hope you will be in New York another winter; then I shall know what to do with these foretastes of eternity."*

*Clemens usually wrote at considerable length, for he had a good deal to report of his life in the Austrian capital, now drawing to a close.*

To W. D. Howells, in New York:

*May 12, 1899.*

DEAR HOWELLS,—7.15 p. m. Tea (for Mr. and Mrs. Tower, who are leaving for Russia) just over; nice people and rather creditable to the human race: Mr. and Mrs. Tower; the new Minister and his wife; the Secretary of Legation; the Naval (and Military) Attach; several English ladies; an Irish lady; a Scotch lady; a particularly nice young Austrian baron who wasn't invited but came and went supposing it was the usual thing and wondered at the unusually large gathering; two other Austrians and several Americans who were also in his fix; the old Baronin Langeman, the only Austrian invited; the rest were Americans. It made just a comfortable crowd in our parlor, with an overflow into Clara's through the folding doors. I don't enjoy teas, and am daily spared them by Mrs. Clemens, but this was a pleasant one. I had only one accident. The old Baronin Langeman is a person I have a strong fondness for, for we violently disagree on some subjects and as violently agree on others—for instance, she is temperance and I am not: she has religious beliefs and feelings and I have none; (she's a Methodist!) she is a democrat and so am I; she is woman's rights and so am I; she is laborers' rights and approves trades unions and strikes, and that is me. And so on. After she was gone an English lady whom I greatly like, began to talk sharply against her for contributing money, time, labor, and public expression of favor to a strike that is on (for an 11-hour day) in the silk factories of Bohemia—and she caught me unprepared and betrayed me into over-warm argument. I am sorry: for she didn't know anything about the subject, and I did; and one should be gentle with the ignorant, for they are the chosen of God.

(The new Minister is a good man, but out of place. The Sec. of Legation is a good man, but out of place. The Attache is a good man, but out of place. Our government for displacement beats the new White Star ship; and her possible is 17,200 tons.)

May 13, 4 p. m. A beautiful English girl and her handsome English husband came up and spent the evening, and she certainly is a bird. English parents—she was born and reared in Roumania and couldn't talk English till she was 8 or 10. She came up clothed like the sunset, and was a delight to look at. (Roumanian costume.).....

Twenty-four young people have gone out to the Semmering to-day (and to-morrow) and Mrs. Clemens and an English lady and old Leschetitzky and his wife have gone to chaperon them. They gave me a chance to go, but there are no snow mountains that I want to look at. Three hours out, three hours back, and sit up all night watching the young people dance; yelling conversationally and being yelled at, conversationally, by new acquaintances, through the deafening music, about how I like Vienna, and if it's my first visit, and how long we expect to stay, and did I see the foot-washing, and am I writing a book about Vienna, and so on. The terms seemed too severe. Snow mountains are too dear at the price....

For several years I have been intending to stop writing for print as soon as I could afford it. At last I can afford it, and have put the pot-boiler pen away. What I have been wanting is a chance to write a book without reserves—a book which should take account of no one's feelings, and no one's prejudices, opinions, beliefs, hopes, illusions, delusions; a book which should say my say, right out of my heart, in the plainest language and without a limitation of any sort. I judged that that would be an unimaginable luxury, heaven on earth.

It is under way, now, and it is a luxury! an intellectual drunk: Twice I didn't start it right; and got pretty far in, both times, before I found it out. But I am sure it is started right this time. It is in tale-form. I believe I can make it tell what I think of Man, and how he is constructed, and what a shabby poor ridiculous thing he is, and how mistaken he is in his estimate of his character and powers and qualities and his place among the animals.

So far, I think I am succeeding. I let the madam into the secret day before yesterday, and locked the doors and read to her the opening chapters. She said—

"It is perfectly horrible—and perfectly beautiful!"

"Within the due limits of modesty, that is what I think."

I hope it will take me a year or two to write it, and that it will turn out to be the right vessel to contain all the abuse I am planning to dump into it.

*Yours ever*

*MARK.*

*The story mentioned in the foregoing, in which Mark Twain was to give his opinion of man, was The Mysterious Stranger. It was not finished at the time, and its closing chapter was not found until after his death. Six years later (1916) it was published serially in Harper's Magazine, and in book form.*

*The end of May found the Clemens party in London, where they were received and entertained with all the hospitality they had known in earlier years. Clemens was too busy for letter-writing, but in the midst of things he took time to report to Howells an amusing incident of one of their entertainments.*

To W. D. Howells, in America:

*LONDON, July 3, '99*

DEAR HOWELLS,—..... I've a lot of things to write you, but it's no use—I can't get time for anything these days. I must break off and write a postscript to Canon Wilberforce before I go to bed. This afternoon he left a luncheon-party half an hour ahead of the rest, and carried off my hat (which has Mark Twain in a big hand written in it.) When the rest of us came out there was but one hat that would go on my head—it fitted exactly, too. So wore it away. It had no name in it, but the Canon was the only man who was absent. I wrote him a note at 8 p.m.; saying that for four hours I had not been able to take anything that did not belong to me, nor stretch a fact beyond the frontiers of truth, and my family were getting alarmed. Could he explain my trouble? And now at 8.30 p.m. comes a note from him to say that all the afternoon he has been exhibiting a wonder-compelling mental vivacity and grace of expression, etc., etc., and have I missed a hat? Our letters have crossed.

*Yours ever*

*MARK.*

*News came of the death of Robert Ingersoll. Clemens had been always one of his most ardent admirers, and a warm personal friend. To Ingersoll's niece he sent a word of heartfelt sympathy.*

To Miss Eva Farrell, in New York:

*30 WELLINGTON COURT, ALBERT GATE.*

DEAR MISS FARRELL,—Except my daughter's, I have not grieved for any death as I have grieved for his. His was a great and beautiful spirit, he was a man—all man from his crown to his foot soles. My reverence for him was deep and genuine; I prized his affection for me and returned it with usury.

*Sincerely Yours,*

*S. L. CLEMENS.*

*Clemens and family decided to spend the summer in Sweden, at Sauna, in order to avail themselves of osteopathic treatment as practised by Heinrick Kellgren. Kellgren's method, known as the "Swedish movements," seemed to Mark Twain a wonderful cure for all ailments, and he heralded the discovery far and wide. He wrote to friends far and near advising them to try Kellgren for anything they might happen to have. Whatever its beginning, any letter was likely to close with some mention of the new panacea.*

To Rev. J. H. Twichell, traveling in Europe:

*SANNA, Sept. 6, '99.*

DEAR JOE,—I've no business in here—I ought to be outside. I shall never see another sunset to begin with it this side of heaven. Venice? land, what a poor interest that is! This is the place to be. I have seen about 60 sunsets here; and a good 40 of them were clear and away beyond anything I had ever imagined before for dainty and exquisite and marvellous beauty and infinite change and variety. America? Italy? The tropics? They have no notion of what a sunset ought to be. And this one—this unspeakable wonder! It discounts all the rest. It brings the tears, it is so unutterably beautiful.

If I had time, I would say a word about this curative system here. The people actually do several of the great things the Christian Scientists pretend to do. You wish to advise with a physician about it? Certainly. There is no objection. He knows next to something about his own trade, but that will not embarrass him in framing a verdict about this one. I respect your superstitions—we all have them. It would be quite natural for the cautious

Chinaman to ask his native priest to instruct him as to the value of the new religious specialty which the Western missionary is trying to put on the market, before investing in it. (He would get a verdict.)

*Love to you all!*

*Always Yours*

*MARK.*

*Howells wrote that he was going on a reading-tour-dreading it, of course-and asking for any advice that Clemens felt qualified to give. Naturally, Clemens gave him the latest he had in stock, without realizing, perhaps, that he was recommending an individual practice which few would be likely to imitate. Nevertheless, what he says is interesting.*

To W. D. Howells, in America:

*SANNA, SWEDEN, Sept. 26, '99.*

DEAR HOWELLS,—Get your lecture by heart—it will pay you. I learned a trick in Vienna—by accident—which I wish I had learned years ago. I meant to read from a Tauchnitz, because I knew I hadn't well memorized the pieces; and I came on with the book and read a few sentences, then remembered that the sketch needed a few words of explanatory introduction; and so, lowering the book and now and then unconsciously using it to gesture with, I talked the introduction, and it happened to carry me into the sketch itself, and then I went on, pretending that I was merely talking extraneous matter and would come to the sketch presently. It was a beautiful success. I knew the substance of the sketch and the telling phrases of it; and so, the throwing of the rest of it into informal talk as I went along limbered it up and gave it the snap and go and freshness of an impromptu. I was to read several pieces, and I played the same game with all of them, and always the audience thought I was being reminded of outside things and throwing them in, and was going to hold up the book and begin on the sketch presently—and so I always got through the sketch before they were entirely sure that it had begun. I did the same thing in Budapest and had the same good time over again. It's a new dodge, and the best one that was ever invented. Try it. You'll never lose your audience—not even for a moment. Their attention is fixed, and never wavers. And that is not the case where one reads from book or MS., or where he stands up without a note and frankly exposes the fact, by his confident manner and smooth phrasing, that he is not improvising, but reciting from memory. And in the heat of telling a thing that is memorised in substance only, one flashes out the happiest suddenly-begotten phrases every now and then! Try it. Such a phrase has a life and sparkle about it that twice as good a one could not exhibit if prepared beforehand, and it "fetches" an audience in such an enthusing and inspiring and uplifting way that that lucky phrase breeds another one, sure.

Your September instalment—["Their Silver Wedding journey."]—was delicious—every word of it. You haven't lost any of your splendid art. Callers have arrived.

*With love*

*MARK.*

*"Yes," wrote Howells, "if I were a great histrionic artist like you I would get my poor essays by heart, and recite them, but being what I am I should do the thing so lifelessly that I had better recognise their deadness frankly and read them."*

*From Vienna Clemens had contributed to the Cosmopolitan, then owned by John Brisben Walker, his first article on Christian Science. It was a delicious bit of humor and found such enthusiastic appreciation that Walker was moved to send an additional $200 check in payment for it. This brought prompt acknowledgment.*

To John Brisben Walker, in Irvington, N. Y.:

*LONDON, Oct. 19, '99*

DEAR MR. WALKER,—By gracious but you have a talent for making a man feel proud and good! To say a compliment well is a high art—and few possess it. You know how to do it, and when you confirm its sincerity with a handsome cheque the limit is reached and compliment can no higher go. I like to work for you: when you don't approve an article you say so, recognizing that I am not a child and can stand it; and when you approve an article I don't have to dicker with you as if I raised peanuts and you kept a stand; I know I shall get every penny the article is worth.

You have given me very great pleasure, and I thank you for it.

*Sincerely Yours*

*S. L. CLEMENS.*

*On the same day he sent word to Howells of the good luck which now seemed to be coming his way. The Joan of Arc introduction was the same that today appears in his collected works under the title of Saint Joan of Arc.*

To W. D. Howells, in New York:

*LONDON, Oct. 19, '99.*

DEAR HOWELLS,—My, it's a lucky day!—of the sort when it never rains but it pours. I was to write an introduction to a nobler book—the English translation of the Official Record (unabridged) of the Trials and Rehabilitation of Joan of Arc, and make a lot of footnotes. I wrote the introduction in Sweden, and here a few days ago I tore loose from a tale I am writing, and took the MS book and went at the grind of note-making—a fearful job for a man not used to it. This morning brought a note from my excellent friend Murray, a rich Englishman who edits the translation, saying,

"Never mind the notes—we'll make the translators do them." That was comfort and joy.

The same mail brought a note from Canon Wilberforce, asking me to talk Joan of Arc in his drawing-room to the Dukes and Earls and M. P.'s—(which would fetch me out of my seclusion and into print, and I couldn't have that,) and so of course I must run down to the Abbey and explain—and lose an hour. Just then came Murray and said "Leave that to me—I'll go and do the explaining and put the thing off 3 months; you write a note and tell him I am coming."

(Which I did, later.) Wilberforce carried off my hat from a lunch party last summer, and in to-day's note he said he wouldn't steal my new hat this time. In my note I said I couldn't make the drawing-room talk, now—Murray would explain; and added a P. S.: "You mustn't think it is because I am afraid to trust my hat in your reach again, for I assure you upon honor it isn't. I should bring my old one."

I had suggested to Murray a fortnight ago, that he get some big guns to write introductory monographs for the book.

Miss X, Joan's Voices and Prophecies.

The Lord Chief Justice of England, the legal prodigies which she performed before her judges.

Lord Roberts, her military genius.

Kipling, her patriotism.

And so on. When he came this morning he said he had captured Miss X; that Lord Roberts and Kipling were going to take hold and see if they could do monographs worthy of the book. He hadn't run the others to cover yet, but was on their track. Very good news. It is a grand book, and is entitled to the best efforts of the best people. As for me, I took pains with my Introduction, and I admit that it is no slouch of a performance.

Then I came down to Chatto's, and found your all too beautiful letter, and was lifted higher than ever. Next came letters from America properly glorifying my Christian Science article in the Cosmopolitan (and one roundly abusing it,) and a letter from John Brisben Walker enclosing $200 additional pay for the article (he had already paid enough, but I didn't mention that—which wasn't right of me, for this is the second time he has done such a thing, whereas Gilder has done it only once and no one else ever.) I make no prices with Walker and Gilder—I can trust them.

And last of all came a letter from M-. How I do wish that man was in hell. Even-the briefest line from that idiot puts me in a rage.

But on the whole it has been a delightful day, and with M——in hell it would have been perfect. But that will happen, and I can wait.

Ah, if I could look into the inside of people as you do, and put it on paper, and invent things for them to do and say, and tell how they said it, I could writs a fine and readable book now, for I've got a prime subject. I've written 30,000 words of it and satisfied myself that the stuff is there; so I am going to discard that MS and begin all over again and have a good time with it.

Oh, I know how you feel! I've been in hell myself. You are there tonight. By difference in time you are at luncheon, now—and not eating it. Nothing is so lonesome as gadding around platforming. I have declined 45 lectures to-day-England and Scotland. I wanted the money, but not the torture: Good luck to you!—and repentance.

*With love to all of you*

*MARK.*

## XXXIX. LETTERS OF 1900, MAINLY TO TWICHELL. THE BOER WAR. BOXER TROUBLES. THE RETURN TO AMERICA.

The New Year found Clemens still in London, chiefly interested in osteopathy and characteristically glorifying the practice at the expense of other healing methods.

To Rev. J. H. Twichell, in Hartford:

*LONDON, Jan. 8, 1900.*

DEAR JOE,—Mental Telepathy has scored another. Mental Telegraphy will be greatly respected a century hence.

By the accident of writing my sister and describing to her the remarkable cures made by Kellgren with his hands and without drugs, I brought upon myself a quite stunning surprise; for she wrote to me that she had been taking this very treatment in Buffalo—and that it was an American invention.

Well, it does really turn out that Dr. Still, in the middle of Kansas, in a village, began to experiment in 1874, only five years after Kellgren began the same work obscurely in the village of Gotha, in Germany. Dr. Still seems to be an honest man; therefore I am persuaded that Kellgren moved him to his experiments by Mental Telegraphy across six hours of longitude, without need of a wire. By the time Still began to experiment, Kellgren had completed his development of the principles of his system and established himself in a good practice in London—1874—and was in good shape to convey his discovery to Kansas, Mental Telegraphically.

Yes, I was greatly surprised to find that my mare's nest was much in arrears: that this new science was well known in America under the name of Osteopathy. Since then, I find that in the past 3 years it has got itself legalized in 14 States in spite of the opposition of the physicians; that it has established 20 Osteopathic schools and colleges; that among its students are 75 allopathic physicians; that there is a school in Boston and another in Philadelphia, that there are about 100 students in the parent college (Dr. Still's at Kirksville, Missouri,) and that there are about 2,000 graduates practicing in America. Dear me, there are not 30 in Europe. Europe is so sunk in superstitions and prejudices that it is an almost impossible thing to get her to do anything but scoff at a new thing—unless it come from abroad; as witness the telegraph, dentistry, &c.

Presently the Osteopath will come over here from America and will soon make himself a power that must be recognized and reckoned with; and then, 25 years from now, England will begin to claim the invention and tell all about its origin, in the Cyclopedia B——-as in the case of the telegraph, applied anaesthetics and the other benefactions which she heaped her abuse upon when her inventors first offered them to her.

I cannot help feeling rather inordinately proud of America for the gay and hearty way in which she takes hold of any new thing that comes along and gives it a first rate trial. Many an ass in America, is getting a deal of benefit out of X-Science's new exploitation of an age-old healing principle—faith, combined with the patient's imagination—let it boom along! I have no objection. Let them call it by what name they choose, so long as it does helpful work among the class which is numerically vastly the largest bulk of the human race, i.e. the fools, the idiots, the pudd'nheads.

We do not guess, we know that 9 in 10 of the species are pudd'nheads. We know it by various evidences; and one of them is, that for ages the race has respected (and almost venerated) the physician's grotesque system—the emptying of miscellaneous and harmful drugs into a person's stomach to remove ailments which in many cases the drugs could not reach at all; in many cases could reach and help, but only at cost of damage to some other part of the man; and in the remainder of the cases the drug either retarded the cure, or the disease was cured by nature in spite of the nostrums. The doctor's insane system has not only been permitted to continue its follies for ages, but has been protected by the State and made a close monopoly—an infamous thing, a crime against a free-man's proper right to choose his own assassin or his own method of defending his body against disease and death.

And yet at the same time, with curious and senile inconsistency, the State has allowed the man to choose his own assassin—in one detail—the patent-medicine detail—making itself the protector of that perilous business, collecting money out of it, and appointing no committee of experts to examine the medicines and forbid them when extra dangerous. Really, when a man can prove that he is not a jackass, I think he is in the way to prove that he is no legitimate member of the race.

I have by me a list of 52 human ailments—common ones—and in this list I count 19 which the physician's art cannot cure. But there isn't one which Osteopathy or Kellgren cannot cure, if the patient comes early.

Fifteen years ago I had a deep reverence for the physician and the surgeon. But 6 months of closely watching the Kellgren business has revolutionized all that, and now I have neither reverence nor respect for the physician's trade, and scarcely any for the surgeon's,—I am convinced that of all quackeries, the physician's is the grotesquest and the silliest. And they know they are shams and humbugs. They have taken the place of those augurs who couldn't look each other in the face without laughing.

See what a powerful hold our ancient superstitions have upon us: two weeks ago, when Livy committed an incredible imprudence and by consequence was promptly stricken down with a heavy triple attack—influenza, bronchitis, and a lung affected—she recognized the gravity of the situation, and her old superstitions rose: she thought she ought to send for a doctor—Think of it—the last man in the world I should want around at such a time. Of course I did not say no—not that I was indisposed to take the responsibility, for I was not, my notion of a dangerous responsibility being quite the other way—but because it is unsafe to distress a sick person; I only said we knew no good doctor, and it could not be good policy to choose at hazard; so she allowed me to send for Kellgren. To-day she is up and around—cured. It is safe to say that persons hit in the same way at the same time are in bed yet, and booked to stay there a good while, and to be in a shackly condition and afraid of their shadows for a couple of years or more to come.

It will be seen by the foregoing that Mark Twain's interest in the

Kellgren system was still an ardent one. Indeed, for a time he gave most of his thought to it, and wrote several long appreciations, perhaps with little idea of publication, but merely to get his enthusiasm physically expressed. War, however, presently supplanted medicine—the Boer troubles in South Africa and the Boxer insurrection in China. It was a disturbing, exciting year.

To W. D. Howells, in Boston:

*WELLINGT ON COURT, KNIGHTSBRIDGE,*

*Jan. 25, 1900.*

DEAR HOWELLS,—If you got half as much as Pond prophesied, be content and praise God—it has not happened to another. But I am sorry he didn't go with you; for it is marvelous to hear him yarn. He is good company, cheery and hearty, and his mill is never idle. Your doing a lecture tour was heroic. It was the highest order of grit, and you have a right to be proud of yourself. No mount of applause or money or both could save it from being a hell to a man constituted as you are. It is that even to me, who am made of coarser stuff.

I knew the audiences would come forward and shake hands with you—that one infallible sign of sincere approval. In all my life, wherever it failed me I left the hall sick and ashamed, knowing what it meant.

Privately speaking, this is a sordid and criminal war, and in every way shameful and excuseless. Every day I write (in my head) bitter magazine articles about it, but I have to stop with that. For England must not fall; it would mean an inundation of Russian and German political degradations which would envelop the globe and steep it in a sort of Middle-Age night and slavery which would last till Christ comes again. Even wrong—and she is wrong—England must be upheld. He is an enemy of the human race who shall speak against her now. Why was the human race created? Or at least why wasn't something creditable created in place of it. God had his opportunity. He could have made a reputation. But no, He must commit this grotesque folly—a lark which must have cost him a regret or two when He came to think it over and observe effects. For a giddy and unbecoming caprice there has been nothing like it till this war. I talk the war with both sides—always waiting until the other man introduces the topic. Then I say "My head is with the Briton, but my heart and such rags of morals as I have are with the Boer—now we will talk, unembarrassed and without prejudice." And so we discuss, and have no trouble.

*Jan. 26.*

It was my intention to make some disparaging remarks about the human race; and so I kept this letter open for that purpose, and for the purpose of telling my dream, wherein the Trinity were trying to guess a conundrum, but I can do better—for I can snip out of the "Times" various samples and side-lights which bring the race down to date, and expose it as of yesterday. If you will notice, there is seldom a telegram in a paper which fails to show up one or more members and beneficiaries of our Civilization as promenading in his shirt-tail, with the rest of his regalia in the wash.

I love to see the holy ones air their smug pieties and admire them and smirk over them, and at the same moment frankly and publicly show their contempt for the pieties of the Boer—confidently expecting the approval of the country and the pulpit, and getting it.

I notice that God is on both sides in this war; thus history repeats itself. But I am the only person who has noticed this; everybody here thinks He is playing the game for this side, and for this side only.

*With great love to you all*

*MARK.*

*One cannot help wondering what Mark Twain would have thought of human nature had he lived to see the great World War, fought mainly by the Christian nations who for nearly two thousand years had been preaching peace on earth and goodwill toward men. But his opinion of the race could hardly have been worse than it was. And nothing that human beings could do would have surprised him.*

To Rev. J. H. Twichell, in Hartford:

*LONDON, Jan. 27, 1900.*

DEAR JOE,—Apparently we are not proposing to set the Filipinos free and give their islands to them; and apparently we are not proposing to hang the priests and confiscate their property. If these things are so, the war out there has no interest for me.

I have just been examining chapter LXX of "Following the Equator," to see if the Boer's old military effectiveness is holding out. It reads curiously as if it had been written about the present war.

I believe that in the next chapter my notion of the Boer was rightly conceived. He is popularly called uncivilized, I do not know why. Happiness, food, shelter, clothing, wholesale labor, modest and rational ambitions, honesty, kindliness, hospitality, love of freedom and limitless courage to fight for it, composure and fortitude in time of disaster, patience in time of hardship and privation, absence of noise and brag in time of victory, contentment with a humble and peaceful life void of insane excitements—if there is a higher and better form of civilization than this, I am not aware of it and do not know where to look for it. I suppose we have the habit of imagining that a lot of artistic, intellectual and other artificialities must be added, or it isn't complete. We and the English have these latter; but as we lack the great bulk of these others, I think the Boer civilization is the best of the two. My idea of our civilization is that it is a shabby poor thing and full of cruelties, vanities, arrogancies, meannesses, and hypocrisies. As for the word, I hate the sound of it, for it conveys a lie; and as for the thing itself, I wish it was in hell, where it belongs.

Provided we could get something better in the place of it. But that is not possible, perhaps. Poor as it is, it is better than real savagery, therefore we must stand by it, extend it, and (in public) praise it. And so we must not utter any hateful word about England in these days, nor fail to hope that she will win in this war, for her defeat and fall would be an irremediable disaster for the mangy human race.... Naturally, then, I am for England; but she is profoundly in the wrong, Joe, and no (instructed) Englishman doubts it. At least that is my belief.

Maybe I managed to make myself misunderstood, as to the Osteopathists. I wanted to know how the men impress you. As to their Art, I know fairly well about that, and should not value Hartford's opinion of it; nor a physician's; nor that of another who proposed to enlighten me out of his ignorance. Opinions based upon theory, superstition and ignorance are not very precious.

Livy and the others are off for the country for a day or two.

*Love to you all*

*MARK.*

*The next letter affords a pleasant variation. Without doubt it was written on realizing that good nature and enthusiasm had led him into indiscretion. This was always happening to him, and letters like this are not infrequent, though generally less entertaining.*

To Mr. Ann, in London:

*WELLINGTON COURT, Feb. 23, '00.*

DEAR MR. ANN,—Upon sober second thought, it won't do!—I withdraw that letter. Not because I said anything in it which is not true, for I didn't; but because when I allow my name to be used in forwarding a stock-scheme I am assuming a certain degree of responsibility as toward the investor, and I am not willing to do that. I have another objection, a purely selfish one: trading upon my name, whether the enterprise scored a success or a failure would damage me. I can't afford that; even the Archbishop of Canterbury couldn't afford it, and he has more character to spare than I have. (Ah, a happy thought! If he would sign the letter with me that would change the whole complexion of the thing, of course. I do not know him, yet I would sign any commercial scheme that he would sign. As he does not know me, it follows that he would sign anything that I would sign. This is unassailable logic—but really that is all that can be said for it.)

No, I withdraw the letter. This virgin is pure up to date, and is going to remain so.

*Ys sincerely,*

*S. L. C.*

To Rev. J. H. Twichell, in Hartford:

*WELLINGTON COURT,*

*KNIGHTSBRIDGE, Mch. 4, '00.*

DEAR JOE,—Henry Robinson's death is a sharp wound to me, and it goes very deep. I had a strong affection for him, and I think he had for me. Every Friday, three-fourths of the year for 16 years he was of the billiard-party in our house. When we come home, how shall we have billiard-nights again—with no Ned Bunce and no Henry Robinson? I believe I could not endure that. We must find another use for that room. Susy is gone, George is gone, Libby Hamersley, Ned Bunce, Henry Robinson. The friends are passing, one by one; our house, where such warm blood and such dear blood flowed so freely, is become a cemetery. But not in any repellent sense. Our dead are welcome there; their life made it beautiful, their death has hallowed it, we shall have them with us always, and there will be no parting.

It was a moving address you made over Ward Cheney—that fortunate, youth! Like Susy, he got out of life all that was worth the living, and got his great reward before he had crossed the tropic frontier of dreams and entered the Sahara of fact. The deep consciousness of Susy's good fortune is a constant comfort to me.

London is happy-hearted at last. The British victories have swept the clouds away and there are no uncheerful faces. For three months the private dinner parties (we go to no public ones) have been Lodges of Sorrow, and just a little depressing sometimes; but now they are smiley and animated again. Joe, do you know the Irish gentleman and the Irish lady, the Scotch gentleman and the Scotch lady? These are darlings, every one. Night before last it was all Irish—24. One would have to travel far to match their ease and sociability and animation and sparkle and absence of shyness and self-consciousness.

It was American in these fine qualities. This was at Mr. Lecky's. He is Irish, you know. Last night it was Irish again, at Lady Gregory's. Lord Roberts is Irish; and Sir William Butler; and Kitchener, I think; and a disproportion of the other prominent Generals are of Irish and Scotch breed-keeping up the traditions of Wellington, and Sir Colin Campbell of the Mutiny. You will have noticed that in S. A. as in the Mutiny, it is usually the Irish and the Scotch that are placed in the fore-front of the battle. An Irish friend of mine says this is because the Kelts are idealists, and enthusiasts, with age-old heroisms to emulate and keep bright before the world; but that the low-class Englishman is dull and without ideals, fighting bull-doggishly while he has a leader, but losing his head and going to pieces when his leader falls—not so with the Kelt. Sir Wm. Butler said, "the Kelt is the spear-head of the British lance."

*Love to you all.*

*MARK.*

*The Henry Robinson mentioned in the foregoing letter was Henry C. Robinson, one-time Governor of Connecticut, long a dear and intimate friend of the Clemens household. "Lecky" was W. E. H. Lecky, the Irish historian whose History of European Morals had been, for many years, one of Mark Twain's favorite books:*

*In July the Clemenses left the small apartment at 30 Wellington Court and established a summer household a little way out of London, at Dollis Hill. To-day the place has been given to the public under the name of Gladstone Park, so called for the reason that in an earlier time Gladstone had frequently visited there. It was a beautiful spot, a place of green grass and spreading oaks. In a letter in which Mrs. Clemens wrote to her sister she said: "It is simply divinely beautiful and peaceful; the great, old trees are beyond everything. I believe nowhere in the world do you find such trees as in England." Clemens wrote to Twichell: "From the house you can see little but spacious stretches of hay-fields and green turf..... Yet the massed, brick blocks of London are reachable in three minutes on a horse. By rail we can be in the heart of London, in Baker Street, in seventeen minutes—by a smart train in five."*

*Mail, however, would seem to have been less prompt.*

To the Editor of the Times, in London:

SIR,—It has often been claimed that the London postal service was swifter than that of New York, and I have always believed that the claim was justified. But a doubt has lately sprung up in my mind. I live eight miles from Printing House Square; the Times leaves that point at 4 o'clock in the morning, by mail, and reaches me at 5 in the afternoon, thus making the trip in thirteen hours.

It is my conviction that in New York we should do it in eleven.

*C.*

DOLLIS HILL, N. W.

To Rev. J. H. Twichell, in Hartford:

*DOLLIS HILL HOUSE, KILBURN, N. W.*

*LONDON, Aug. 12, '00.*

DEAR JOE,—The Sages Prof. Fiske and Brander Matthews were out here to tea a week ago and it was a breath of American air to see them. We furnished them a bright day and comfortable weather—and they used it all up, in their extravagant American way. Since then we have sat by coal fires, evenings.

We shall sail for home sometime in October, but shall winter in New York where we can have an osteopath of good repute to continue the work of putting this family in proper condition.

Livy and I dined with the Chief Justice a month ago and he was as well-conditioned as an athlete.

It is all China, now, and my sympathies are with the Chinese. They have been villainously dealt with by the sceptred thieves of Europe, and I hope they will drive all the foreigners out and keep them out for good. I only wish it; of course I don't really expect it.

Why, hang it, it occurs to me that by the time we reach New York you Twichells will be invading Europe and once more we shall miss the connection. This is thoroughly exasperating. Aren't we ever going to meet again?

*With no end of love from all of us,*

*MARK.*

P. S. Aug. 18.

DEAR JOE,—It is 7.30 a. m. I have been waking very early, lately. If it occurs once more, it will be habit; then I will submit and adopt it.

This is our day of mourning. It is four years since Susy died; it is five years and a month that I saw her alive for the last time-throwing kisses at us from the railway platform when we started West around the world.

Sometimes it is a century; sometimes it was yesterday.

*With love*

*MARK.*

*We discover in the foregoing letter that the long European residence was drawing to an end. More than nine years had passed since the closing of the Hartford house—eventful years that had seen failure, bereavement, battle with debt, and rehabilitated fortunes. All the family were anxious to get home—Mark Twain most anxious of all.*

*They closed Dollis Hill House near the end of September, and put up for a brief period at a family hotel, an amusing picture of which follows.*

To J. Y. M. MacAlister, in London:

*Sep. 1900.*

MY DEAR MACALISTER,—We do really start next Saturday. I meant to sail earlier, but waited to finish some studies of what are called Family Hotels. They are a London specialty, God has not permitted them to exist elsewhere; they are ramshackle clubs which were dwellings at the time of the Heptarchy. Dover and Albemarle Streets are filled with them. The once spacious rooms are split up into coops which afford as much discomfort as can be had anywhere out of jail for any money. All the modern inconveniences are furnished, and some that have been obsolete for a century. The prices are astonishingly high for what you get. The bedrooms are hospitals for incurable furniture. I find it so in this one. They exist upon a tradition; they represent the vanishing home-like inn of fifty years ago, and are mistaken by foreigners for it. Some quite respectable Englishmen still frequent them through inherited habit and arrested development; many Americans also, through ignorance and superstition. The rooms are as interesting as the Tower of London, but older I think. Older and dearer. The lift was a gift of William the Conqueror, some of the beds are prehistoric. They represent geological periods. Mine is the oldest. It is formed in strata of Old Red Sandstone, volcanic tufa, ignis fatuus, and bicarbonate of hornblende, superimposed upon argillaceous shale, and contains the prints of prehistoric man. It is in No. 149. Thousands of scientists come to see it. They consider it holy. They want to blast out the prints but cannot. Dynamite rebounds from it.

Finished studies and sail Saturday in Minnehaha.

*Yours ever affectionately,*

*MARK TWAIN.*

*They sailed for New York October 6th, and something more than a week later America gave them a royal welcome. The press, far and wide, sounded Mark Twain's praises once more; dinners and receptions were offered on every hand; editors and lecture agents clamored for him.*

*The family settled in the Earlington Hotel during a period of house-hunting. They hoped eventually to return to Hartford, but after a brief visit paid by Clemens alone to the old place he wrote:*

To Sylvester Baxter, in Boston:

*NEW YORK, Oct. 26, 1900.*

DEAR MR. BAXTER,—It was a great pleasure to me to renew the other days with you, and there was a pathetic pleasure in seeing Hartford and the house again; but I realize that if we ever enter the house again to live, our hearts will break. I am not sure that we shall ever be strong enough to endure that strain.

*Sincerely yours,*

*S. L. CLEMENS.*

*Mr. and Mrs. Rogers wished to have them in their neighborhood, but the houses there were not suitable, or were too expensive. Through Mr. Frank Doubleday they eventually found, at 14 West Tenth Street, a large residence handsomely furnished, and this they engaged for the winter. "We were lucky to get this big house furnished," he wrote MacAlister in London. "There was not another one in town procurable that would answer us, but this one is all right—space enough in it for several families, the rooms all old-fashioned, great size."*

*The little note that follows shows that Mark Twain had not entirely forgotten the days of Tom Sawyer and Huck Finn.*

To a Neighbor on West Tenth Street, New York:

*Nov. 30.*

DEAR MADAM,—I know I ought to respect my duty and perform it, but I am weak and faithless where boys are concerned, and I can't help secretly approving pretty bad and noisy ones, though I do object to the kind that ring door-bells. My family try to get me to stop the boys from holding conventions on the front steps, but I basely shirk out of it, because I think the boys enjoy it.

My wife has been complaining to me this evening about the boys on the front steps and under compulsion I have made some promises. But I am very forgetful, now that I am old, and my sense of duty is getting spongy.

*Very truly yours,*

*S. L. CLEMENS.*

# About Author

Samuel Langhorne Clemens (November 30, 1835 – April 21, 1910), known by his pen name Mark Twain, was an American writer, humorist, entrepreneur, publisher, and lecturer. He was lauded as the "greatest humorist this country has produced", and William Faulkner called him "the father of American literature". His novels include The Adventures of Tom Sawyer (1876) and its sequel, the Adventures of Huckleberry Finn (1884), the latter often called "The Great American Novel".

Twain was raised in Hannibal, Missouri, which later provided the setting for Tom Sawyer and Huckleberry Finn. He served an apprenticeship with a printer and then worked as a typesetter, contributing articles to the newspaper of his older brother Orion Clemens. He later became a riverboat pilot on the Mississippi River before heading west to join Orion in Nevada. He referred humorously to his lack of success at mining, turning to journalism for the Virginia City Territorial Enterprise. His humorous story, "The Celebrated Jumping Frog of Calaveras County", was published in 1865, based on a story that he heard at Angels Hotel in Angels Camp, California, where he had spent some time as a miner. The short story brought international attention and was even translated into French. His wit and satire, in prose and in speech, earned praise from critics and peers, and he was a friend to presidents, artists, industrialists, and European royalty.

Twain earned a great deal of money from his writings and lectures, but he invested in ventures that lost most of it—such as the Paige Compositor, a mechanical typesetter that failed because of its complexity and imprecision. He filed for bankruptcy in the wake of these financial setbacks, but he eventually overcame his financial troubles with the help of Henry Huttleston Rogers. He eventually paid all his creditors in full, even though his bankruptcy relieved him of having to do so.

Twain was born shortly after an appearance of Halley's Comet, and he predicted that he would "go out with it" as well; he died the day after the comet returned.

## Biography

### Early life

Samuel Langhorne Clemens was born on November 30, 1835, in Florida, Missouri, the sixth of seven children born to Jane (née Lampton; 1803–1890), a native of Kentucky, and John Marshall Clemens (1798–1847), a native of Virginia. His parents met when his father moved to Missouri, and they were married in 1823. Twain was of Cornish, English, and Scots-Irish descent. Only three of his siblings survived childhood: Orion (1825–1897), Henry (1838–1858), and Pamela (1827–1904). His sister Margaret (1830–1839) died when Twain was three, and his brother Benjamin (1832–1842) died three years later. His brother Pleasant Hannibal (1828) died at three weeks of age.

When he was four, Twain's family moved to Hannibal, Missouri, a port town on the Mississippi River that inspired the fictional town of St. Petersburg in The Adventures of Tom Sawyer and the Adventures of Huckleberry Finn. Slavery was legal in Missouri at the time, and it became a theme in these writings. His father was an attorney and judge, who died of pneumonia in 1847, when Twain was 11. The next year, Twain left school after the fifth grade to become a printer's apprentice. In 1851, he began working as a typesetter, contributing articles and humorous sketches to the Hannibal Journal, a newspaper that Orion owned. When he was 18, he left Hannibal and worked as a printer in New York City, Philadelphia, St. Louis, and Cincinnati, joining the newly formed International Typographical Union, the printers trade union. He educated himself in public libraries in the evenings, finding wider information than at a conventional school.

Twain describes his boyhood in Life on the Mississippi, stating that "there was but one permanent ambition" among his comrades: to be a steamboatman.

Pilot was the grandest position of all. The pilot, even in those days of trivial wages, had a princely salary – from a hundred and fifty to two hundred and fifty dollars a month, and no board to pay.

As Twain describes it, the pilot's prestige exceeded that of the captain. The pilot had to:

> ...get up a warm personal acquaintanceship with every old snag and one-limbed cottonwood and every obscure wood pile that ornaments the banks of this river for twelve hundred miles; and more than that, must... actually know where these things are in the dark

Steamboat pilot Horace E. Bixby took Twain on as a cub pilot to teach him the river between New Orleans and St. Louis for $500 (equivalent to $14,000 in 2018), payable out of Twain's first wages after graduating. Twain studied the Mississippi, learning its landmarks, how to navigate its currents effectively, and how to read the river and its constantly shifting channels, reefs, submerged snags, and rocks that would "tear the life out of the strongest vessel that ever floated". It was more than two years before he received his pilot's license. Piloting also gave him his pen name from "mark twain", the leadsman's cry for a measured river depth of two fathoms (12 feet), which was safe water for a steamboat.

As a young pilot, Clemens served on the steamer A. B. Chambers with Grant Marsh, who became famous for his exploits as a steamboat captain on the Missouri River. The two liked each other, and admired one another, and maintained a correspondence for many years after Clemens left the river.

While training, Samuel convinced his younger brother Henry to work with him, and even arranged a post of mud clerk for him on the steamboat Pennsylvania. On June 13, 1858, the steamboat's boiler exploded; Henry succumbed to his wounds on June 21. Twain claimed to have foreseen this death in a dream a month earlier, which inspired his interest in parapsychology; he was an early member of the Society for Psychical Research. Twain was guilt-stricken and held himself responsible for the rest of his life. He continued to work on the river and was a river pilot until the Civil War broke out in 1861, when traffic was curtailed along the Mississippi River. At the start of hostilities, he enlisted briefly in a local Confederate unit. He later wrote the sketch "The Private History of a Campaign That Failed", describing how he and his friends had been Confederate volunteers for two weeks before disbanding.

He then left for Nevada to work for his brother Orion, who was Secretary of the Nevada Territory. Twain describes the episode in his book Roughing It.

**Travels**

Orion became secretary to Nevada Territory governor James W. Nye in 1861, and Twain joined him when he moved west. The brothers traveled more than two weeks on a stagecoach across the Great Plains and the Rocky Mountains, visiting the Mormon community in Salt Lake City.

Twain's journey ended in the silver-mining town of Virginia City, Nevada, where he became a miner on the Comstock Lode. He failed as a miner and went to work at the Virginia City newspaper Territorial Enterprise, working under a friend, the writer Dan DeQuille. He first used his pen name here on February 3, 1863, when he wrote a humorous travel account entitled "Letter From Carson – re: Joe Goodman; party at Gov. Johnson's; music" and signed it "Mark Twain".

His experiences in the American West inspired Roughing It, written during 1870–71 and published in 1872. His experiences in Angels Camp (in Calaveras County, California) provided material for "The Celebrated Jumping Frog of Calaveras County" (1865).

Twain moved to San Francisco in 1864, still as a journalist, and met writers such as Bret Harte and Artemus Ward. He may have been romantically involved with the poet Ina Coolbrith.

His first success as a writer came when his humorous tall tale "The Celebrated Jumping Frog of Calaveras County" was published on November 18, 1865, in the New York weekly The Saturday Press, bringing him national attention. A year later, he traveled to the Sandwich Islands (present-day Hawaii) as a reporter for the Sacramento Union. His letters to the Union were popular and became the basis for his first lectures.

In 1867, a local newspaper funded his trip to the Mediterranean aboard the Quaker City, including a tour of Europe and the Middle East. He wrote a collection of travel letters which were later compiled as The Innocents Abroad (1869). It was on this trip that he met fellow passenger Charles Langdon, who showed him a picture of his sister Olivia. Twain later claimed to have fallen in love at first sight.

Upon returning to the United States, Twain was offered honorary membership in Yale University's secret society Scroll and Key in 1868. Its devotion to "fellowship, moral and literary self-improvement, and charity" suited him well.

**Marriage and children**

Twain and Olivia Langdon corresponded throughout 1868. She rejected his first marriage proposal, but they were married in Elmira, New York in February 1870, where he courted her and managed to overcome her father's initial reluctance. She came from a "wealthy but liberal family"; through her, he met abolitionists, "socialists, principled atheists and activists for women's rights and social equality", including Harriet Beecher Stowe (his next-door neighbor in Hartford, Connecticut), Frederick Douglass, and writer and utopian socialist William Dean Howells, who became a long-time friend. The couple lived in Buffalo, New York, from 1869 to 1871. He owned a stake in the Buffalo Express newspaper and worked as an editor and writer. While they were living in Buffalo, their son Langdon died of diphtheria at the age of 19 months. They had three daughters: Susy (1872–1896), Clara (1874–1962), and Jean (1880–1909).

Twain moved his family to Hartford, Connecticut, where he arranged the building of a home starting in 1873. In the 1870s and 1880s, the family summered at Quarry Farm in Elmira, the home of Olivia's sister, Susan Crane. In 1874, Susan had a study built apart from the main house so that Twain would have a quiet place in which to write. Also, he smoked cigars constantly, and Susan did not want him to do so in her house.

Twain wrote many of his classic novels during his 17 years in Hartford (1874–1891) and over 20 summers at Quarry Farm. They include The Adventures of Tom Sawyer (1876), The Prince and the Pauper (1881), Life on the Mississippi (1883), Adventures of Huckleberry Finn (1884), and A

Connecticut Yankee in King Arthur's Court (1889).

The couple's marriage lasted 34 years until Olivia's death in 1904. All of the Clemens family are buried in Elmira's Woodlawn Cemetery.

**Love of science and technology**

Twain was fascinated with science and scientific inquiry. He developed a close and lasting friendship with Nikola Tesla, and the two spent much time together in Tesla's laboratory.

Twain patented three inventions, including an "Improvement in Adjustable and Detachable Straps for Garments" (to replace suspenders) and a history trivia game. Most commercially successful was a self-pasting scrapbook; a dried adhesive on the pages needed only to be moistened before use. Over 25,000 were sold.

Twain was an early proponent of fingerprinting as a forensic technique, featuring it in a tall tale in Life on the Mississippi (1883) and as a central plot element in the novel Pudd'nhead Wilson (1894).

Twain's novel A Connecticut Yankee in King Arthur's Court (1889) features a time traveler from the contemporary U.S., using his knowledge of science to introduce modern technology to Arthurian England. This type of historical manipulation became a trope of speculative fiction as alternate histories.

In 1909, Thomas Edison visited Twain at his home in Redding, Connecticut and filmed him. Part of the footage was used in The Prince and the Pauper (1909), a two-reel short film. It is the only known existing film footage of Twain.

**Financial troubles**

Twain made a substantial amount of money through his writing, but he lost a great deal through investments. He invested mostly in new inventions and technology, particularly the Paige typesetting machine. It was a beautifully engineered mechanical marvel that amazed viewers when it worked, but it was prone to breakdowns. Twain spent $300,000 (equal to $9,000,000 in inflation-adjusted terms) on it between 1880 and 1894, but before it could be perfected it was rendered obsolete by the Linotype. He lost the bulk of his book profits, as well as a substantial portion of his wife's inheritance.

Twain also lost money through his publishing house, Charles L. Webster and Company, which enjoyed initial success selling the memoirs of Ulysses S. Grant but failed soon afterward, losing money on a biography of Pope Leo XIII. Fewer than 200 copies were sold.

Twain and his family closed down their expensive Hartford home in response to the dwindling income and moved to Europe in June 1891. William M. Laffan of The New York Sun and the McClure Newspaper Syndicate offered him the publication of a series of six European letters. Twain, Olivia, and their daughter Susy were all faced with health problems, and they believed that it would be of benefit to visit European baths. The family stayed mainly in France, Germany, and Italy until May 1895, with longer spells at Berlin (winter 1891/92), Florence (fall and winter 1892/93), and Paris (winters and springs 1893/94 and 1894/95). During that period, Twain returned four times to New York due to his enduring business troubles. He took "a cheap room" in September 1893 at $1.50 per day (equivalent to $42 in 2018) at The Players Club, which he had to keep until March 1894; meanwhile, he became "the Belle of New York," in the words of biographer Albert Bigelow Paine.

Twain's writings and lectures enabled him to recover financially, combined with the help of his friend, Henry Huttleston Rogers. He began a friendship with the financier in 1893, a principal of Standard Oil, that lasted the remainder of his life. Rogers first made him file for bankruptcy in April 1894, then had him transfer the copyrights on his written works to his wife to prevent creditors from gaining possession of them. Finally, Rogers took absolute charge of Twain's money until all his creditors were paid.

Twain accepted an offer from Robert Sparrow Smythe and embarked on a year-long, around the world lecture tour in July 1895 to pay off his creditors in full, although he was no longer under any legal obligation to do so. It was a long, arduous journey and he was sick much of the time, mostly from a cold and a carbuncle. The first part of the itinerary took him across northern America to British Columbia, Canada, until the second half of August. For the second part, he sailed across the Pacific Ocean. His scheduled lecture in Honolulu, Hawaii had to be canceled due to a cholera epidemic. Twain went on to Fiji, Australia, New Zealand, Sri Lanka, India, Mauritius, and South Africa. His three months in India became the centerpiece of his 712-page book Following the Equator. In the second half of July 1896, he sailed back to England, completing his circumnavigation of the world begun 14 months before.

Twain and his family spent four more years in Europe, mainly in England and Austria (October 1897 to May 1899), with longer spells in London and Vienna. Clara had wished to study the piano under Theodor Leschetizky in Vienna. However, Jean's health did not benefit from consulting with specialists in Vienna, the "City of Doctors". The family moved to London in spring 1899, following a lead by Poultney Bigelow who had a good experience being treated by Dr. Jonas Henrik Kellgren, a Swedish osteopathic practitioner in Belgravia. They were persuaded to spend the summer at Kellgren's sanatorium by the lake in the Swedish village of Sanna. Coming back in fall, they continued the treatment in London, until Twain was convinced by lengthy inquiries in America that similar osteopathic expertise was available there.

In mid-1900, he was the guest of newspaper proprietor Hugh Gilzean-Reid at Dollis Hill House, located on the north side of London. Twain wrote that he had "never seen any place that was so satisfactorily situated, with its noble trees and stretch of country, and everything that went to make life delightful, and all within a biscuit's throw of the metropolis of the world." He then returned to America in October 1900, having earned enough to pay off his debts. In winter 1900/01, he became his country's most prominent opponent of imperialism, raising the issue in his speeches, interviews, and writings. In January 1901, he began serving as vice-president of the Anti-Imperialist League of New York.

**Speaking engagements**

Twain was in great demand as a featured speaker, performing solo humorous talks similar to modern stand-up comedy. He gave paid talks to many men's clubs, including the Authors' Club, Beefsteak Club, Vagabonds, White Friars, and Monday Evening Club of Hartford.

In the late 1890s, he spoke to the Savage Club in London and was elected an honorary member. He was told that only three men had been so honored, including the Prince of Wales, and he replied: "Well, it must make the Prince feel mighty fine." He visited Melbourne and Sydney in 1895 as part of a world lecture tour. In 1897, he spoke to the Concordia Press Club in Vienna as a special guest, following the diplomat Charlemagne Tower, Jr. He delivered the speech "Die Schrecken der Deutschen Sprache" ("The Horrors of the German Language")—in German—to the great amusement of the audience. In 1901, he was invited to speak at Princeton University's Cliosophic Literary Society, where he was made an honorary member.

**Canadian visits**

In 1881, Twain was honored at a banquet in Montreal, Canada where he made reference to securing a copyright. In 1883, he paid a brief visit to Ottawa, and he visited Toronto twice in 1884 and 1885 on a reading tour with George Washington Cable, known as the "Twins of Genius" tour.

The reason for the Toronto visits was to secure Canadian and British copyrights for his upcoming book Adventures of Huckleberry Finn, to which he had alluded in his Montreal visit. The reason for the Ottawa visit had been to secure Canadian and British copyrights for Life on the Mississippi. Publishers in Toronto had printed unauthorized editions of his books at the time, before an international copyright agreement was established in 1891. These were sold in the United States as well as in Canada, depriving him of royalties. He estimated that Belford Brothers' edition of The Adventures of Tom Sawyer alone had cost him ten thousand dollars (equivalent to $280,000 in 2018). He had unsuccessfully attempted to secure the rights for The Prince and the Pauper in 1881, in conjunction with his Montreal trip. Eventually, he received legal advice to register a copyright in Canada (for both Canada and Britain) prior to publishing in the United States, which would restrain the Canadian publishers from printing a version when the American edition was published. There was a requirement that a copyright be registered to a Canadian resident; he addressed this by his short visits to the country.

**Later life and death**

... the report is greatly exaggerated.

—Twain's reaction to a report of his death

Twain lived in his later years at 14 West 10th Street in Manhattan. He passed through a period of deep depression which began in 1896 when his daughter Susy died of meningitis. Olivia's death in 1904 and Jean's on December 24, 1909, deepened his gloom. On May 20, 1909, his close friend Henry Rogers died suddenly. In 1906, Twain began his autobiography in the North American Review. In April, he heard that his friend Ina Coolbrith had lost nearly all that she owned in the 1906 San Francisco earthquake, and he volunteered a few autographed portrait photographs to be sold for her benefit. To further aid Coolbrith, George Wharton James visited Twain in New York and arranged for a new portrait session. He was resistant initially, but he eventually admitted that four of the resulting images were the finest ones ever taken of him.

Twain formed a club in 1906 for girls whom he viewed as surrogate granddaughters called the Angel Fish and Aquarium Club. The dozen or so members ranged in age from 10 to 16. He exchanged letters with his "Angel Fish" girls and invited them to concerts and the theatre and to play games. Twain wrote in 1908 that the club was his "life's chief delight". In 1907, he met Dorothy Quick (aged 11) on a transatlantic crossing, beginning "a friendship that was to last until the very day of his death".

Oxford University awarded Twain an honorary doctorate in letters in 1907.

Twain was born two weeks after Halley's Comet's closest approach in 1835; he said in 1909:

I came in with Halley's Comet in 1835. It is coming again next year, and I expect to go out with it. It will be the greatest disappointment of my life if

I don't go out with Halley's Comet. The Almighty has said, no doubt: "Now here are these two unaccountable freaks; they came in together, they must go out together".

Twain's prediction was accurate; he died of a heart attack on April 21, 1910, in Redding, Connecticut, one day after the comet's closest approach to Earth.

Upon hearing of Twain's death, President William Howard Taft said:

Mark Twain gave pleasure – real intellectual enjoyment – to millions, and his works will continue to give such pleasure to millions yet to come … His humor was American, but he was nearly as much appreciated by Englishmen and people of other countries as by his own countrymen. He has made an enduring part of American literature.

Twain's funeral was at the Brick Presbyterian Church on Fifth Avenue, New York. He is buried in his wife's family plot at Woodlawn Cemetery in Elmira, New York. The Langdon family plot is marked by a 12-foot monument (two fathoms, or "mark twain") placed there by his surviving daughter Clara. There is also a smaller headstone. He expressed a preference for cremation (for example, in Life on the Mississippi), but he acknowledged that his surviving family would have the last word.

Officials in Connecticut and New York estimated the value of Twain's estate at $471,000 ($13,000,000 today).

**Writing**

**Overview**

Twain began his career writing light, humorous verse, but he became a chronicler of the vanities, hypocrisies, and murderous acts of mankind. At mid-career, he combined rich humor, sturdy narrative, and social criticism in Huckleberry Finn. He was a master of rendering colloquial speech and helped to create and popularize a distinctive American literature built on American themes and language.

Many of his works have been suppressed at times for various reasons. The

Adventures of Huckleberry Finn has been repeatedly restricted in American high schools, not least for its frequent use of the word "nigger", which was in common usage in the pre-Civil War period in which the novel was set.

A complete bibliography of Twain's works is nearly impossible to compile because of the vast number of pieces he wrote (often in obscure newspapers) and his use of several different pen names. Additionally, a large portion of his speeches and lectures have been lost or were not recorded; thus, the compilation of Twain's works is an ongoing process. Researchers rediscovered published material as recently as 1995 and 2015.

**Early journalism and travelogues**

Twain was writing for the Virginia City newspaper the Territorial Enterprise in 1863 when he met lawyer Tom Fitch, editor of the competing newspaper Virginia Daily Union and known as the "silver-tongued orator of the Pacific". He credited Fitch with giving him his "first really profitable lesson" in writing. "When I first began to lecture, and in my earlier writings," Twain later commented, "my sole idea was to make comic capital out of everything I saw and heard." In 1866, he presented his lecture on the Sandwich Islands to a crowd in Washoe City, Nevada. Afterwards, Fitch told him:

Clemens, your lecture was magnificent. It was eloquent, moving, sincere. Never in my entire life have I listened to such a magnificent piece of descriptive narration. But you committed one unpardonable sin – the unpardonable sin. It is a sin you must never commit again. You closed a most eloquent description, by which you had keyed your audience up to a pitch of the intensest interest, with a piece of atrocious anti-climax which nullified all the really fine effect you had produced.

It was in these days that Twain became a writer of the Sagebrush School; he was known later as its most famous member. His first important work was "The Celebrated Jumping Frog of Calaveras County," published in the New York Saturday Press on November 18, 1865. After a burst of popularity, the Sacramento Union commissioned him to write letters about his travel experiences. The first journey that he took for this job was to ride the steamer Ajax on its maiden voyage to the Sandwich Islands (Hawaii).

All the while, he was writing letters to the newspaper that were meant for publishing, chronicling his experiences with humor. These letters proved to be the genesis to his work with the San Francisco Alta California newspaper, which designated him a traveling correspondent for a trip from San Francisco to New York City via the Panama isthmus.

On June 8, 1867, he set sail on the pleasure cruiser Quaker City for five months, and this trip resulted in The Innocents Abroad or The New Pilgrims' Progress. In 1872, he published his second piece of travel literature, Roughing It, as an account of his journey from Missouri to Nevada, his subsequent life in the American West, and his visit to Hawaii. The book lampoons American and Western society in the same way that Innocents critiqued the various countries of Europe and the Middle East. His next work was The Gilded Age: A Tale of Today, his first attempt at writing a novel. The book, written with his neighbor Charles Dudley Warner, is also his only collaboration.

Twain's next work drew on his experiences on the Mississippi River. Old Times on the Mississippi was a series of sketches published in the Atlantic Monthly in 1875 featuring his disillusionment with Romanticism. Old Times eventually became the starting point for Life on the Mississippi.

**Tom Sawyer and Huckleberry Finn**

Twain's next major publication was The Adventures of Tom Sawyer, which draws on his youth in Hannibal. Tom Sawyer was modeled on Twain as a child, with traces of schoolmates John Briggs and Will Bowen. The book also introduces Huckleberry Finn in a supporting role, based on Twain's boyhood friend Tom Blankenship.

The Prince and the Pauper was not as well received, despite a storyline that is common in film and literature today. The book tells the story of two boys born on the same day who are physically identical, acting as a social commentary as the prince and pauper switch places. Twain had started Adventures of Huckleberry Finn (which he consistently had problems completing) and had completed his travel book A Tramp Abroad, which describes his travels through central and southern Europe.

Twain's next major published work was the Adventures of Huckleberry Finn, which confirmed him as a noteworthy American writer. Some have called it the first Great American Novel, and the book has become required reading in many schools throughout the United States. Huckleberry Finn was an offshoot from Tom Sawyer and had a more serious tone than its predecessor. Four hundred manuscript pages were written in mid-1876, right after the publication of Tom Sawyer. The last fifth of Huckleberry Finn is subject to much controversy. Some say that Twain experienced a "failure of nerve," as critic Leo Marx puts it. Ernest Hemingway once said of Huckleberry Finn:

If you read it, you must stop where the Nigger Jim is stolen from the boys. That is the real end. The rest is just cheating.

Hemingway also wrote in the same essay:

All modern American literature comes from one book by Mark Twain called Huckleberry Finn.

Near the completion of Huckleberry Finn, Twain wrote Life on the Mississippi, which is said to have heavily influenced the novel. The travel work recounts Twain's memories and new experiences after a 22-year absence from the Mississippi River. In it, he also explains that "Mark Twain" was the call made when the boat was in safe water, indicating a depth of two fathoms (12 feet or 3.7 metres).

**Later writing**

Twain produced President Ulysses S. Grant's Memoirs through his fledgling publishing house, Charles L. Webster & Company, which he co-owned with Charles L. Webster, his nephew by marriage.

At this time he also wrote "The Private History of a Campaign That Failed" for The Century Magazine. This piece detailed his two-week stint in a Confederate militia during the Civil War. He next focused on A Connecticut Yankee in King Arthur's Court, written with the same historical fiction style as The Prince and the Pauper. A Connecticut Yankee showed the absurdities of political and social norms by setting them in the court of King Arthur. The book was started in December 1885, then shelved a few months later until the summer of 1887, and eventually finished in the spring of 1889.

His next large-scale work was Pudd'nhead Wilson, which he wrote rapidly, as he was desperately trying to stave off bankruptcy. From November 12 to December 14, 1893, Twain wrote 60,000 words for the novel. Critics[who?] have pointed to this rushed completion as the cause of the novel's rough organization and constant disruption of the plot. This novel also contains the tale of two boys born on the same day who switch positions in life, like The Prince and the Pauper. It was first published serially in Century Magazine and, when it was finally published in book form, Pudd'nhead Wilson appeared as the main title; however, the "subtitles" make the entire title read: The Tragedy of Pudd'nhead Wilson and the Comedy of The Extraordinary Twins.

Twain's next venture was a work of straight fiction that he called Personal Recollections of Joan of Arc and dedicated to his wife. He had long said[where?] that this was the work that he was most proud of, despite the criticism that he received for it. The book had been a dream of his since childhood, and he claimed that he had found a manuscript detailing the life of Joan of Arc when he was an adolescent. This was another piece that he was convinced would save his publishing company. His financial adviser Henry Huttleston Rogers quashed that idea and got Twain out of that business altogether, but the book was published nonetheless.[citation needed]

To pay the bills and keep his business projects afloat, Twain had begun to write articles and commentary furiously, with diminishing returns, but it was not enough. He filed for bankruptcy in 1894. During this time of dire financial straits, he published several literary reviews in newspapers to help make ends meet. He famously derided James Fenimore Cooper in his article detailing Cooper's "Literary Offenses". He became an extremely outspoken critic of other authors and other critics; he suggested that, before praising Cooper's work, Thomas Lounsbury, Brander Matthews, and Wilkie Collins "ought to have read some of it".

George Eliot, Jane Austen, and Robert Louis Stevenson also fell under Twain's attack during this time period, beginning around 1890 and continuing until his death. He outlines what he considers to be "quality writing" in several letters and essays, in addition to providing a source for the "tooth and claw" style of literary criticism. He places emphasis on concision, utility of word choice, and realism; he complains, for example, that Cooper's Deerslayer purports to be realistic but has several shortcomings. Ironically, several of his own works were later criticized for lack of continuity (Adventures of Huckleberry Finn) and organization (Pudd'nhead Wilson).

Twain's wife died in 1904 while the couple were staying at the Villa di Quarto in Florence. After some time had passed he published some works that his wife, his de facto editor and censor throughout her married life, had looked down upon. The Mysterious Stranger is perhaps the best known, depicting various visits of Satan to earth. This particular work was not published in Twain's lifetime. His manuscripts included three versions, written between 1897 and 1905: the so-called Hannibal, Eseldorf, and Print Shop versions. The resulting confusion led to extensive publication of a jumbled version, and only recently have the original versions become available as Twain wrote them.

Twain's last work was his autobiography, which he dictated and thought would be most entertaining if he went off on whims and tangents in non-chronological order. Some archivists and compilers have rearranged the biography into a more conventional form, thereby eliminating some of Twain's humor and the flow of the book. The first volume of the autobiography, over 736 pages, was published by the University of California in November 2010, 100 years after his death, as Twain wished. It soon became an unexpected best-seller, making Twain one of a very few authors publishing new best-selling volumes in the 19th, 20th, and 21st centuries.

### Censorship

Twain's works have been subjected to censorship efforts. According to Stuart (2013), "Leading these banning campaigns, generally, were religious organizations or individuals in positions of influence – not so much working librarians, who had been instilled with that American "library spirit" which honored intellectual freedom (within bounds of course)". In 1905, the Brooklyn Public Library banned both The Adventures of Huckleberry Finn and The Adventures of Tom Sawyer from the children's department because of their language.

### Views

Twain's views became more radical as he grew older. In a letter to friend and fellow writer William Dean Howells in 1887 he acknowledged that his views had changed and developed over his lifetime, referring to one of his favorite works:

When I finished Carlyle's French Revolution in 1871, I was a Girondin; every time I have read it since, I have read it differently – being influenced and changed, little by little, by life and environment ... and now I lay the book down once more, and recognize that I am a Sansculotte! And not a pale, characterless Sansculotte, but a Marat.

### Anti-imperialist

Before 1899, Twain was an ardent imperialist. In the late 1860s and early 1870s, he spoke out strongly in favor of American interests in the Hawaiian Islands. He said the war with Spain in 1898 was "the worthiest" war ever fought. In 1899, however, he reversed course. In the New York Herald, October 16, 1900, Twain describes his transformation and political awakening, in the context of the Philippine–American War, to anti-imperialism:

I wanted the American eagle to go screaming into the Pacific ... Why not spread its wings over the Philippines, I asked myself? ... I said to myself, Here are a people who have suffered for three centuries. We can make them as free as ourselves, give them a government and country of their own, put a miniature of the American Constitution afloat in the Pacific, start a brand new republic to take its place among the free nations of the world. It seemed to me a great task to which we had addressed ourselves.

But I have thought some more, since then, and I have read carefully the treaty of Paris [which ended the Spanish–American War], and I have seen that we do not intend to free, but to subjugate the people of the Philippines. We have gone there to conquer, not to redeem.

It should, it seems to me, be our pleasure and duty to make those people free, and let them deal with their own domestic questions in their own way. And so I am an anti-imperialist. I am opposed to having the eagle put its talons on any other land.

During the Boxer rebellion, Twain said that "the Boxer is a patriot. He loves his country better than he does the countries of other people. I wish him success."

From 1901, soon after his return from Europe, until his death in 1910, Twain was vice-president of the American Anti-Imperialist League, which opposed the annexation of the Philippines by the United States and had "tens of thousands of members". He wrote many political pamphlets for the organization. The Incident in the Philippines, posthumously published in 1924, was in response to the Moro Crater Massacre, in which six hundred Moros were killed. Many of his neglected and previously uncollected writings on anti-imperialism appeared for the first time in book form in 1992.

Twain was critical of imperialism in other countries as well. In Following the Equator, Twain expresses "hatred and condemnation of imperialism of all stripes". He was highly critical of European imperialists, such as Cecil Rhodes, who greatly expanded the British Empire, and Leopold II, King of the Belgians. King Leopold's Soliloquy is a stinging political satire about his private colony, the Congo Free State. Reports of outrageous exploitation and grotesque abuses led to widespread international protest in the early 1900s, arguably the first large-scale human rights movement. In the soliloquy, the King argues that bringing Christianity to the country outweighs a little starvation. Leopold's rubber gatherers were tortured, maimed and slaughtered until the movement forced Brussels to call a halt.

During the Philippine–American War, Twain wrote a short pacifist story titled The War Prayer, which makes the point that humanism and Christianity's preaching of love are incompatible with the conduct of war. It was submitted to Harper's Bazaar for publication, but on March 22, 1905, the magazine rejected the story as "not quite suited to a woman's magazine". Eight days later, Twain wrote to his friend Daniel Carter Beard, to whom he had read the story, "I don't think the prayer will be published in my time. None but the dead are permitted to tell the truth." Because he had an exclusive contract with Harper & Brothers, Twain could not publish The War Prayer elsewhere; it remained unpublished until 1923. It was republished as campaigning material by Vietnam War protesters.

Twain acknowledged that he had originally sympathized with the more moderate Girondins of the French Revolution and then shifted his sympathies to the more radical Sansculottes, indeed identifying himself as "a Marat" and writing that the Reign of Terror paled in comparison to the older terrors that preceded it. Twain supported the revolutionaries in Russia against the reformists, arguing that the Tsar must be got rid of by violent means, because peaceful ones would not work. He summed up his views of revolutions in the following statement:

I am said to be a revolutionist in my sympathies, by birth, by breeding and by principle. I am always on the side of the revolutionists, because there never was a revolution unless there were some oppressive and intolerable conditions against which to revolute.

**Civil rights**

Twain was an adamant supporter of the abolition of slavery and the emancipation of slaves, even going so far as to say, "Lincoln's Proclamation ... not only set the black slaves free, but set the white man free also". He argued that non-whites did not receive justice in the United States, once saying, "I have seen Chinamen abused and maltreated in all the mean, cowardly ways possible to the invention of a degraded nature ... but I never saw a Chinaman righted in a court of justice for wrongs thus done to him". He paid for at least one black person to attend Yale Law School and for another black person to attend a southern university to become a minister.

Twain's sympathetic views on race were not reflected in his early writings on American Indians. Of them, Twain wrote in 1870:

His heart is a cesspool of falsehood, of treachery, and of low and devilish instincts. With him, gratitude is an unknown emotion; and when one does him a kindness, it is safest to keep the face toward him, lest the reward be an arrow in the back. To accept of a favor from him is to assume a debt which you can never repay to his satisfaction, though you bankrupt yourself trying. The scum of the earth!

As counterpoint, Twain's essay on "The Literary Offenses of Fenimore Cooper" offers a much kinder view of Indians. "No, other Indians would have noticed these things, but Cooper's Indians never notice anything. Cooper thinks they are marvelous creatures for noticing, but he was almost always in error about his Indians. There was seldom a sane one among them." In his later travelogue Following the Equator (1897), Twain observes that in colonized lands all over the world, "savages" have always been wronged by "whites" in the most merciless ways, such as "robbery, humiliation, and slow, slow murder, through poverty and the white man's whiskey"; his conclusion is that "there are many humorous things in this world; among them the white man's notion that he is less savage than the other savages". In an expression that captures his East Indian experiences, he wrote, "So far as I am able to judge nothing has been left undone, either by man or Nature, to make India the most extraordinary country that the sun visits on his rounds. Where every prospect pleases, and only man is vile."

Twain was also a staunch supporter of women's rights and an active campaigner for women's suffrage. His "Votes for Women" speech, in which he pressed for the granting of voting rights to women, is considered one of the most famous in history.

Helen Keller benefited from Twain's support as she pursued her college education and publishing despite her disabilities and financial limitations. The two were friends for roughly 16 years.

Through Twain's efforts, the Connecticut legislature voted a pension for Prudence Crandall, since 1995 Connecticut's official heroine, for her efforts towards the education of African-American young ladies in Connecticut. Twain also offered to purchase for her use her former house in Canterbury, home of the Canterbury Female Boarding School, but she declined.

**Labor**

Twain wrote glowingly about unions in the river boating industry in Life on the Mississippi, which was read in union halls decades later. He supported the labor movement, especially one of the most important unions, the Knights of Labor. In a speech to them, he said:

Who are the oppressors? The few: the King, the capitalist, and a handful of other overseers and superintendents. Who are the oppressed? The many: the nations of the earth; the valuable personages; the workers; they that make the bread that the soft-handed and idle eat.

**Religion**

Twain was a Presbyterian. He was critical of organized religion and certain elements of Christianity through his later life. He wrote, for example, "Faith is believing what you know ain't so", and "If Christ were here now there is one thing he would not be – a Christian". With anti-Catholic sentiment rampant in 19th century America, Twain noted he was "educated to enmity toward everything that is Catholic". As an adult, he engaged in religious discussions and attended services, his theology developing as he wrestled with the deaths of loved ones and with his own mortality.

Twain generally avoided publishing his most controversial opinions on religion in his lifetime, and they are known from essays and stories that were published later. In the essay Three Statements of the Eighties in the 1880s, Twain stated that he believed in an almighty God, but not in any messages, revelations, holy scriptures such as the Bible, Providence, or retribution in the afterlife. He did state that "the goodness, the justice, and the mercy of God are manifested in His works", but also that "the universe is governed by strict and immutable laws", which determine "small matters", such as who dies in a pestilence. At other times, he wrote or spoke in ways that contradicted a strict deist view, for example, plainly professing a belief in Providence. In some later writings in the 1890s, he was less optimistic about the goodness of God, observing that "if our Maker is all-powerful for good or evil, He is not in His right mind". At other times, he conjectured sardonically that perhaps God had created the world with all its tortures for some purpose of His own, but was otherwise indifferent to humanity, which was too petty and insignificant to deserve His attention anyway.

In 1901, Twain criticized the actions of the missionary Dr. William Scott Ament (1851–1909) because Ament and other missionaries had collected indemnities from Chinese subjects in the aftermath of the Boxer Uprising of 1900. Twain's response to hearing of Ament's methods was published in the North American Review in February 1901: To the Person Sitting in Darkness, and deals with examples of imperialism in China, South Africa, and with the U.S. occupation of the Philippines. A subsequent article, "To My Missionary Critics" published in The North American Review in April 1901, unapologetically continues his attack, but with the focus shifted from Ament to his missionary superiors, the American Board of Commissioners for Foreign Missions.

After his death, Twain's family suppressed some of his work that was especially irreverent toward conventional religion, including Letters from the Earth, which was not published until his daughter Clara reversed her position in 1962 in response to Soviet propaganda about the withholding. The anti-religious The Mysterious Stranger was published in 1916. Little Bessie, a story ridiculing Christianity, was first published in the 1972 collection Mark Twain's Fables of Man.

He raised money to build a Presbyterian Church in Nevada in 1864.

Twain created a reverent portrayal of Joan of Arc, a subject over which he had obsessed for forty years, studied for a dozen years and spent two years writing about. In 1900 and again in 1908 he stated, "I like Joan of Arc best of all my books, it is the best".

Those who knew Twain well late in life recount that he dwelt on the subject of the afterlife, his daughter Clara saying: "Sometimes he believed death ended everything, but most of the time he felt sure of a life beyond."

Twain's frankest views on religion appeared in his final work Autobiography of Mark Twain, the publication of which started in November 2010, 100 years after his death. In it, he said:

There is one notable thing about our Christianity: bad, bloody, merciless, money-grabbing, and predatory as it is – in our country particularly and in all other Christian countries in a somewhat modified degree – it is still a hundred times better than the Christianity of the Bible, with its prodigious crime – the invention of Hell. Measured by our Christianity of to-day, bad as it is, hypocritical as it is, empty and hollow as it is, neither the Deity nor his Son is a Christian, nor qualified for that moderately high place. Ours is a terrible religion. The fleets of the world could swim in spacious comfort in the innocent blood it has spilled.

Twain was a Freemason. He belonged to Polar Star Lodge No. 79 A.F.&A.M., based in St. Louis. He was initiated an Entered Apprentice on May 22, 1861, passed to the degree of Fellow Craft on June 12, and raised to the degree of Master Mason on July 10.

Twain visited Salt Lake City for two days and met there members of The Church of Jesus Christ of Latter-day Saints. They also gave him a Book of Mormon. He later wrote in Roughing It about that book:

The book seems to be merely a prosy detail of imaginary history, with the Old Testament for a model; followed by a tedious plagiarism of the New Testament.

### Vivisection

Twain was opposed to the vivisection practices of his day. His objection was not on a scientific basis but rather an ethical one. He specifically cited the pain caused to the animal as his basis of his opposition:

I am not interested to know whether Vivisection produces results that are profitable to the human race or doesn't. ... The pains which it inflicts upon unconsenting animals is the basis of my enmity towards it, and it is to me sufficient justification of the enmity without looking further.

### Pen names

Twain used different pen names before deciding on "Mark Twain". He signed humorous and imaginative sketches as "Josh" until 1863. Additionally, he used the pen name "Thomas Jefferson Snodgrass" for a series of humorous letters.

He maintained that his primary pen name came from his years working on Mississippi riverboats, where two fathoms, a depth indicating water safe for the passage of boat, was a measure on the sounding line. Twain is an archaic term for "two", as in "The veil of the temple was rent in twain." The riverboatman's cry was "mark twain" or, more fully, "by the mark twain", meaning "according to the mark [on the line], [the depth is] two [fathoms]", that is, "The water is 12 feet (3.7 m) deep and it is safe to pass."

Twain said that his famous pen name was not entirely his invention. In Life on the Mississippi, he wrote:

Captain Isaiah Sellers was not of literary turn or capacity, but he used to jot down brief paragraphs of plain practical information about the river, and sign them "MARK TWAIN", and give them to the New Orleans Picayune. They related to the stage and condition of the river, and were accurate and valuable; ... At the time that the telegraph brought the news of his death, I was on the Pacific coast. I was a fresh new journalist, and needed a nom de guerre; so I confiscated the ancient mariner's discarded one, and have done my best to make it remain what it was in his hands – a sign and symbol and warrant that whatever is found in its company may be gambled on as being the petrified truth; how I have succeeded, it would not be modest in me to say.

Twain's story about his pen name has been questioned by some with the suggestion that "mark twain" refers to a running bar tab that Twain would regularly incur while drinking at John Piper's saloon in Virginia City, Nevada. Samuel Clemens himself responded to this suggestion by saying, "Mark Twain was the nom de plume of one Captain Isaiah Sellers, who used to write river news over it for the New Orleans Picayune. He died in 1869 and as he could no longer need that signature, I laid violent hands upon it without asking permission of the proprietor's remains. That is the history of the nom de plume I bear."

In his autobiography, Twain writes further of Captain Sellers' use of "Mark Twain":

I was a cub pilot on the Mississippi River then, and one day I wrote a rude and crude satire which was leveled at Captain Isaiah Sellers, the oldest steamboat pilot on the Mississippi River, and the most respected, esteemed, and revered. For many years he had occasionally written brief paragraphs concerning the river and the changes which it had undergone under his observation during fifty years, and had signed these paragraphs "Mark Twain" and published them in the St. Louis and New Orleans journals. In my satire I made rude game of his reminiscences. It was a shabby poor performance, but I didn't know it, and the pilots didn't know it. The pilots thought it was brilliant. They were jealous of Sellers, because when the gray-heads among them pleased their vanity by detailing in the hearing of the younger craftsmen marvels which they had seen in the long ago on the river, Sellers was always likely to step in at the psychological moment and snuff them out with wonders of his own which made their small marvels look pale and sick. However, I have told all about this in "Old Times on the Mississippi." The pilots handed my extravagant satire to a river reporter, and it was published in the New Orleans True Delta. That poor old Captain Sellers was deeply wounded. He had never been held up to ridicule before; he was sensitive, and he never got over the hurt which I had wantonly and stupidly inflicted upon his dignity. I was proud of my performance for a while, and considered it quite wonderful, but I have changed my opinion of it long ago. Sellers never published another paragraph nor ever used his nom de guerre again.

## Legacy and depictions

### Trademark white suit

While Twain is often depicted wearing a white suit, modern representations suggesting that he wore them throughout his life are unfounded. Evidence suggests that Twain began wearing white suits on the lecture circuit, after the death of his wife Olivia ("Livy") in 1904. However, there is also evidence showing him wearing a white suit before 1904. In 1882, he sent a photograph of himself in a white suit to 18-year-old Edward W. Bok, later publisher of the Ladies Home Journal, with a handwritten dated note. The white suit did eventually become his trademark, as illustrated in anecdotes about this eccentricity (such as the time he wore a white summer suit to a Congressional hearing during the winter). McMasters' The Mark Twain Encyclopedia states that Twain did not wear a white suit in his last three years, except at one banquet speech.

In his autobiography, Twain writes of his early experiments with wearing white out-of-season:

Next after fine colors, I like plain white. One of my sorrows, when the summer ends, is that I must put off my cheery and comfortable white clothes and enter for the winter into the depressing captivity of the shapeless and degrading black ones. It is mid-October now, and the weather is growing cold up here in the New Hampshire hills, but it will not succeed in freezing me out of these white garments, for here the neighbors are few, and it is only of crowds that I am afraid. (Source: Wikipedia)

Lightning Source UK Ltd.
Milton Keynes UK
UKHW011836200520
363522UK00001B/90

9 789353 839062